Juds Aug 2017

Enjoy the journeys,

The Nottingham Connection

Lee Arbouin

AuthorHouse™
1663 Liberty Drive
Bloomington, IN 47403
www.authorhouse.com
Phone: 1-800-839-8640

© 2012 by Lee Arbouin. All rights reserved.

Cover Design by Leeanne Arbouin

No part of this book may be reproduced, stored in a retrieval system, or transmitted by any means without the written permission of the author.

Published by AuthorHouse   10/31/2012

ISBN: 978-1-4685-8191-1 (sc)
ISBN: 978-1-4685-8192-8 (hc)
ISBN: 978-1-4685-8190-4 (e)

This book is printed on acid-free paper.

Because of the dynamic nature of the Internet, any web addresses or links contained in this book may have changed since publication and may no longer be valid. The views expressed in this work are solely those of the author and do not necessarily reflect the views of the publisher, and the publisher hereby disclaims any responsibility for them.

CONTENTS

Acknowledgements vii
Inspiration ix
Introduction xi

BOOK 1
Olga's Story 2
   Jamaica 3
   Europe 12
   Jamaica 54
Madge's Story 60
   Jamaica 61
   England 89
Eunice's Story 103
   Jamaica 104
   England 110

BOOK 2
My Story 132
   Jamaica 133
   England 182
   Jamaica 231

Glossary Of Words And Phrases 285
About the Author 287

ACKNOWLEDGEMENTS

Many, many thanks to the three brave women, Madge, Eunice and Olga, for sharing their experiences; to Louise Garvey and my cousin, Pamela Powell, for their advice on reading the manuscript; to my family and friends for their encouragement and to you the reader for making the writing of this book a worthwhile endeavour.

INSPIRATION

"Doctor bud a cunning bud, hard bud fi dead."
("Doctor bird is a cunning bird, a hard bird to die.")

My friend, Olga, and I sat in her little Eden overlooking the Caribbean Sea. I shared with her how strongly I felt about the muted voices of women from the Caribbean who were transplanted into the England of the 1960s and 1970s, their childhood and their struggles, survival and contributions as adults. She agreed that she would be a contributor to such a book on condition that I also told my story. And so we laughed this book into existence that summer's day in the year 2000.

Olga, a caterer and part-time youth worker is rarely seen without her radiant smile. Like hot air, she rises from every disaster life metes out.

Madge, a potter, gives a lot of pleasure as teacher and demonstrator of her art. Warm and gregarious, like Jamaican sunshine she lights up a room.

Eunice, a community activist and Labour Party councillor since 1989, brings a caring attitude to that role.

I asked these three local Nottingham women who come from Jamaica to share their stories with you. I, however, agonized about the length of my story. Friends finally dissuaded me from further cuts. And so our stories of quiet courage as we struggled to survive in an alien culture give examples of Life's rich tapestry.

Women world-wide, regardless of cultural differences, will relate to episodes in our lives because this is a woman's thing—**her story.**

INTRODUCTION

During the period of our childhood, 1941 to 1968, Jamaica experienced the throes of moving from being a colony to a fledgling state as an independent nation of the British Commonwealth. Former Prime Minister, Michael Manley, in his book, *Jamaica — the Struggle in the Periphery*, summed it up thus: "The Caribbean was entirely a product of the colonial process." People of African and Indian descent formed the broad base of workers and 'have-nots'. Their forebears had been transported from their native lands to Jamaica, as slaves and indentured labourers respectively, to work on the sugar plantations that helped to make Britain a great empire. Over the years Jamaica has become a melting pot for the people who came and its population a pot-pourri of ethnic groups -Africans, Asians, Middle Easterners, Europeans and a mixture of all these.

In 1944 Jamaica held its first election based on universal adult suffrage. A few years later, several governments of the English-speaking Caribbean sought ways to improve the socio-economic condition of the region and a federation was mooted. But in Jamaica, the man in the street did not see himself as Caribbean and the idea of federation was rejected. Its positive aspects were not readily embraced and what seemed most troubling was that Jamaica, the biggest island, would have to bear the heaviest financial burden in that venture. 'The Federation of the West Indies', inaugurated in 1958, unsurprisingly, collapsed. In 1962, Jamaica gained independent status, the first among the British Caribbean Islands, with the motto: "*Out of many, one people*".

Jamaica began to experience the full force of neo-colonialism. Britain had left its British structures in areas such as government, education and health-care but did not give the kind of support Jamaica needed for sustainable development. The major industries, bauxite, sugar and bananas could not provide enough jobs. The birth pangs of this new nation with a population of approximately 2 million were higher levels of unemployment and ever increasing poverty.

As unemployment grew to 20 per cent, people began to look beyond the island for opportunities. A few had always found work in Cuba, Panama, and the United States of America, but in the 1950s and 1960s, emigration to Britain increased rapidly because Britain needed labour to drive its post-war development. The Conservative government sent representatives to Jamaica and other English speaking Caribbean islands to encourage people to come and work in Britain to fill vacancies in hospitals and transport services.

Many Jamaicans saw this as a golden opportunity for a better life; they hoped that their hard-earned money would improve the lives of their families in Jamaica. Their dream was to work in Britain for five or so years and then return to their homeland.

BOOK 1

Olga's Story

JAMAICA

It was a hot, humid day in September 2001 when I returned to Olga's home. She served a delicious lunch, a popular Jamaican meal - rice and peas with baked chicken and a salad of lettuce, cucumbers, tomatoes and grated carrots. This was accompanied by a fresh fruit punch, made from papaya - known in Jamaica as pawpaw - bananas and oranges. Mine, of course, was laced with Jamaican over-proof white rum that excites the taste buds.

With lunch over, we found a cool spot in the garden under the mango tree where the sea breeze gently caressed our cheeks. I asked Olga to share her memories of her childhood in Jamaica. Without much pondering, she took me on a journey into her past. Her story begins in 1953.

Earliest Memories

"Aunt Vindie, wake up! Wake up, Aunt Vindie! Aunt Vindie!" I waited for a while and when she still did not get up I realised that it was not normal. I shook her but still getting no response, I panicked and ran to my mum's house. Shaking and out of breath, as my mum came to the door I said, "Mama, Aunt Vindie won't wake up!" My mum walked briskly back to my grandmother's house with me running after her.

"Stay out here," she said to me in a stern voice as she went in, returning almost at once to call to the neighbour. They whispered together a while and a little later one of my aunts and other people began coming into the house but I still wasn't allowed into the bedroom. Then Dr Lopez came, his stethoscope hanging round his neck. As he went into the bedroom leaving the door ajar, I peered in to see what was happening. I saw him put the stethoscope on my grandmother's body. He spoke to my mom and aunt who both looked very sad. The doctor then left. I was very curious but no-one would say a word to me. There was nothing to do but to sit quietly and wait for my mum.

At last she came out but took no notice of me. She asked someone to go to the village of Bath and tell Uncle Clarence that Aunt Vindie had died. Someone else was asked to go to the post office at Golden Grove to send a telegram to Uncle Bertie in Kingston.

The following days were filled with activities, none of which seemed to me to have anything to do with my grandmother. I did not understand the concept of death. Every night there was a lot of eating and drinking. Most of the cooking took place in the big yard at my mum's home. The women cooked curry goat and rice, green bananas, fried dumplings, fried fish, chicken stew and pork stew. The men cooked mannish water - a spicy soup made with the goat's head and entrails and vegetables. Men drank rum and beer, women drank tea or coffee and we children drank lemonade. Each evening people came with packets of rice, flour or sugar or with hands of bananas. Mr Albert brought a goat and Daddy Carty a pig. Uncle Clarence brought live chickens.

Every day blocks of ice were taken into the bedroom. When I was older and asked what the ice was used for in Aunt Vindie's bedroom when she died, I was told the ice was packed around my grandmother's body to preserve it until the day of the funeral.

People slept in the house and were always going in and out. We children played popular games like "*Go Dung 'Manuel Road*" or "*River to the Bank, Coverley*". For "*Go dung 'Manuel Road*" the older children sat in a circle of six and passed stones to and fro like the stone breakers did at the road side. The adults would stand behind us and join in the singing:

> *Go dung a 'Manuel Road, gal and boy*
> *Fi go bruck rock stone, gal and boy.*
> *Go dung a 'Manuel Road, gal and boy*
> *Fi go bruck rock stone, gal and boy.*
> *Bruck dem one by one, gal and boy,*
> *Bruck dem two by two, gal and boy,*
> *Bruck dem three by three, gal and boy,*
> *Bruck dem four by four, gal and boy,*
> *Bruck dem five by five, gal and boy.*
> *Finger mash no cry, gal and boy.*
> *'Member a play wi a play, gal and boy.*

The song continued to 'ten by ten', at which point they passed the stones faster and faster as the tempo increased. Then the counting went down again, from ten to six, and from five to one.

Here they slowed down the passing to end the game:

> *Finger mash no cry, gal and boy.*
> *'Member a play wi a play, gal and boy.*

During the game, anyone who dropped the stone had to leave the circle.

According to my mother, my grandmother's funeral took place three days after her death. I remember hearing my mum and my aunt talking about "dressing Aunt Vindie". Then the coffin arrived. I was taken into the room and lifted across the coffin three times. I heard the people saying this was to protect me from evil spirits. The coffin was put on a cart pulled by a mule and the procession followed it to the Anglican church in Golden Grove. Afterwards the procession filed into the cemetery where my grandmother was buried under a tree. In answer to my question about what they were doing to Aunt Vindie, I was told that she was dead and was not coming home again.

At nights I would miss my grandmother and worried that they had forgotten her at the cemetery. Family members were not adept at explaining difficult things to children and could not explain death in ways that I understood. They quickly got fed up with my questions and I would get: "*Pickney*, go and sit down!" or "You ask too much question. *Cho*!"

I was not yet four years old and my earliest memories are of my home in Stokes Hall, here in St Thomas. We were a big family living in my father's house: my mum and dad, my dad's mother and father, my big sister who is eight years older than me and my two younger sisters.

I have fond memories of my grandmother. She worked for the Anglican rector. I was told that she went to the Chinaman's shop in the next village of Golden Grove to shop for me every Friday after getting paid. What I remember is that she would give me one item at a time to take into the house. She would say each time, "This is for you." I would get packets of biscuits, a tin of Milo or Ovaltine and a tin of condensed milk. It was a weekly ritual. My grandma would also play with me on the bed so that I didn't have to go on the floor. If anyone said anything about this she would say, *"Lef me alone, a me first gran'pickney."* I became very precocious and loved to jump up and down on the bed. Nobody touched me or shouted at me when she was around but once when she wasn't there I got a *bitch-lick* from my mother to stop it. I learnt fast. Every week my grandmother would put down money on the table and tell me it was for me when I went to school. Our house was near to the main road and she was then living in a house in the nearby lane, where I slept with her at nights to keep her company. She loved me and I felt her loss.

My parents separated when I was five years old. Their constant quarrelling upset us children. I would stay close to my mother when a quarrel started and, if she tried to shoo me away, I would hover nearby. One afternoon an argument started. My mother told my father that a woman was *throwing words* at her and he had better warn the woman to leave her alone. My father *kissed* his teeth at her and began to blame her for the problem. My mother said the next time she would not stand for any insult. The row escalated and my father hit my mother. My mother fought back and I was so angry with my father I grabbed his leg, hitting and biting him. He pushed us off and rode away on his bike. I was still angry so I ran to the side of the house, picked up some stones and began to fling them at him. My mother, noticing what I was doing, rebuked me. I felt hurt because I had been fighting for her. I went off sulking.

Not long after that my mother left my father's home. She bought a small house in a nearby district called Chiswick and took us with her. Mr Grant's donkey cart was our removal van. It was also the ambulance, the taxi, the hearse and the wedding vehicle for the entire district -the hired vehicle for all occasions. I cannot remember all our belongings but I remember walking with my family behind the heavily laden cart and my mother carrying my youngest sister who was just over a year old. I do not remember being traumatised by the separation. We saw our dad regularly and I was happy as a young child tagging along with the older boys and girls.

One of our favourite pastimes was swinging from a rope which hung from the branch of a tree on the river bank. The point of the game was to swing across the river and swing back again. The daring boys added excitement by jumping into the river on the way back. Well, as a ten-year-old, I was not about to be outdone by any boy, so, I jumped into the river too. As luck would have it I fell into deep water and started screaming blue murder. I was dragged ashore by a big boy. I guess I wasn't remorseful enough to please him, so he slapped me a few times. I was furious and ran off.

But did this stop me? Oh no! A few weeks later, determined to have another go, I tried again, and again mistimed my drop and fell into the middle, the deepest part of the river. Terrified, I thrashed about until someone hauled me out. This time a couple of boys held me while another cut a switch from the nearby bushes and gave me a good hiding. I hollered and struggled to get free. The worst of it was that I couldn't tell my mum when I got home because I would likely get another hiding for doing something so dangerous.

My funniest memory happened when I was eleven. My mum was renowned as a "wicked cook" - in other words, the very best. That evening she came in late and tired from work and decided to rustle up a quick meal. She cooked ackee and saltfish and food. Food consisted of slices of yam, green bananas and dumplings. When she had finished I said to her, "Let's eat together, Mama." I liked the idea, the four of us children and my mum eating from the big pudding pan which, incidentally, is still in use today, battered but treasured. But my mum didn't seem too keen and replied, "*Oono* too craven . . ."

"Please!" I begged. She conceded and we sat down to eat. The meal was put in the pudding pan, a container 12 inches in diameter which was used for baking puddings. We girls began eating as fast as we could, each one trying to outdo the other. My nine-year-old sister was the greediest; instead of cutting her dumpling into pieces small enough to chew, she popped it whole into her mouth and tried to swallow it. Suddenly she started to gag. As the rest of us stopped eating and stared her eyes grew huge and bulging, small beads of sweat covered her face which now took on a reddish blush. My mum grabbed her out of her chair and rushed her outside, the rest of us following closely behind. She slapped her hard on the back of her neck and the dumpling flew out of her mouth. Now a Jamaican boiled dumpling is made of plain flour dough and that one was not soft. It did not just drop onto the ground, it flew out of my sister's mouth, dropped onto the ground and rolled down the path going blop, blop, blop. My greedy sister, no longer choking, and seeing her dumpling rolling away, roared like a lion. The sight of the rolling dumpling and my bawling sister was so funny that we all burst out laughing. I have never seen my mother laugh so much. As my sister continued to bawl, my mom said to her, "Never mind, mi darling. Next time, remember to cut up your food, you hear? And chew before you swallow."

When we were young, my mother made her living selling food to the workers on the banana and sugar plantations near our home. She would be up *well before day* preparing the food for sale. She would bake sweet potato pudding and corn pone and fry dumplings. Before going off to school we often helped her with the pans of food, carrying them on our heads to her selling spot.

Her job before this was as a domestic, cooking and cleaning for a well-to-do Jewish family. She told us of her introduction to the children on her first day. The five-year-old girl was introduced as Miss Vicky and the four-year-old boy as Master Joshua. She introduced herself as Mrs Lindsay.

"But what do we call you?" the children demanded as servants were usually addressed by their Christian names.

"Well, Miss Vicky and Master Joshua, you can call me Mrs Lindsay or Miss Ethlyn." They eventually settled for Christian names all around.

I respected my mother for her quiet demeanour and pride in being a black woman. In fact she was my role model. I hero-worshipped her and emulated her.

My father had had an easier life than she had. Like many Jamaicans he was a mixture of races. From his side of family I have inherited my oriental eyes and cheekbones. Brown-skinned, he learnt at an early age that he could get *blighs*, special treatment. For instance, without a licence he got a sugar estate truck driver's job. But, sadly, he had not been taught the importance of education.

Lee Arbouin

Schooldays

I went to kindergarten before I was three. I have been told that I was very bright and that I started elementary school at five instead of the usual seven. My first elementary school was Dalvey Elementary, but it wasn't a very nice school. I had a most unpleasant teacher. She was light-skinned and not very pretty and she didn't like the poor or dark-skinned children. On the other hand, she petted the light-skinned children and rarely told them off.

One day when we were told "no talking in class" a light-skinned boy with curly hair began to talk to me. I didn't answer him. But guess what? The teacher shouted, "Olga Thompson, come out here!"

"It wasn't me, Miss," I said, not wanting to be punished for something I had not done.

"Come on out here!" she ordered. I went up to her table at the front of the class and stood before her. She took off one of her mule slippers and hit me on the head with it. I was furious at this injustice. Although I was only seven, I grabbed the slipper from her, ripped it, threw it outside and ran home like a bat out of hell.

I told my mother what had happened and she took me back to school. We went to see the headteacher and my mum complained about the class teacher's behaviour. The headteacher summoned the class teacher who at first tried to lie by blaming me for talking in class and for being insolent. My mum wasn't satisfied and suggested the headteacher ask the class what had happened. So the headteacher sent for a child in my class and asked him what had happened. His story tallied with mine. The headteacher then asked the class teacher to explain her behaviour. Her lame excuse was, "My head was hurting me, Sir."

My mum was furious and did not want me to stay in that class. The headteacher agreed to move me into his class, a higher class, but I managed the work. Still, things did not much improve. My younger sister and I were being bullied and beaten up by some of the children. Fed up with it, my mother decided to move us to Duckensfield Elementary School in another village. Later on, my youngest sister joined us. I stayed there until I was thirteen. At first I was no happier, as some children would pick on me and call me "teacher's pet" because I was bright and the teacher, Miss Lawrence, was nice to me. Of all my teachers, Miss Lawrence was my favourite. Sometimes she would take me home with her for lunch where I enjoyed the sardines and crackers she offered. She also played the piano and when I was nearby she would say, "Sit down, Olga." I loved hearing her play.

Munchy, my classmate, was also bright and we became close friends. When the children picked on Munchy and me, I would fight them off. I had decided quite early that it was death before the dishonour of running away from any of them, but I dared not tell mum because she would punish me for fighting. School began to be fun as soon as my reputation as a fighter was established. I had some wonderful times except for one or two teachers who were colour, or class, prejudiced and favoured the lighter-skinned, more affluent children. *Hard to believe, but one of those suffering from colour prejudice was quite black!*

By the time I was ten, not only was I a daredevil but I was also unafraid of bullies older and bigger than me. These character traits nearly caused me to be seriously injured when I was eleven. In my class was a boy called Gibaski Chisholm whose family owned the local butcher's shop. He was the dunce of the class; at fifteen he had not been moved up for a couple of years and was often flogged for misbehaving. He was bigger than most of us and everyone in the class was a little afraid of him.

Well, one day the class teacher left her strap on the table at lunch time. Gibaski thought it was fun to use his penknife to deeply score the strap, then he replaced it on the table. When the teacher came back after lunch Gibaski began to act the fool so that he would be flogged. After a couple of warnings the teacher called him out to the front of the class to teach him a lesson. With each stroke of the strap, strips fell away and the teacher soon realised what had happened.

"Who did this?" she asked the class. No answer. She asked the question three times. Then she said that the whole class would be punished until the culprit was found. I did not see why I should be punished for Gibaski's stupid prank, so I told the teacher what had happened. Gibaski was sent to the headteacher and was flogged. Later, when the teacher's back was turned, Gibaski said he would teach me a lesson. I ignored the threat.

As soon as the going-home bell rang and class was dismissed, Gibaski ran out of the school yard. I started to walk home. Several children followed me and I knew something was up. One of them shouted, "Olga, Gibaski gone to get a butcher's knife to cut you up!" I pretended not to hear, but as I turned the corner, there was Gibaski laying in wait for me. He approached me with a long, sharp butcher's knife in his hand.

"You big mouth! Informer! I goin' cut you up!"

"Go on, nuh," I said arrogantly. "You think me scared of you?" The children crowded around us in anticipation. He was inches from me.

"So you think you a bad *ooman*?" I made as if to pass him and he pulled me back to face him as the crowd of children let out a barely audible "Oooh!"

"Let me go, *bwoy*," I said staring him in the face. He raised the knife. I wasn't scared. I was about to give him a good kick where it would hurt when I heard a thud. The headteacher, Mr Ford, had come up behind Gibaski and thumped him in the back. Someone had obviously told the headteacher of the threat.

"Gibaski, you've gone too far this time! Go home and don't bother coming back," ordered the headteacher in an icy tone. Gibaski walked away kicking the dirt as he went.

"Home, everybody!" the headteacher waved at the spectators. "Come with me, Olga." He took me home in his car and told my mother what had happened. She was very disturbed while I was as cool as a cucumber. Imagine! I had been driven home in the headteacher's car!

I wonder if Gibaski remembers the incident? He now runs the family's butcher business.

Nowadays the majority of children get the minibus or are driven to school, but in my time, we walked. I walked a couple of miles to school every morning and the same again after school. A group of us from Chiswick would walk together and it was great fun, talking and playing along the way. Some of us, to keep our shoes clean, would walk barefooted until we reached the standpipe near school where we would wash our feet and put on our shoes. We always had to look well-groomed for school - clean, well-pressed uniform, neat hair and shiny shoes. We were poor but never saw ourselves as poor and certainly never felt deprived!

My mother encouraged us to do well in school. To her, education was very important, she wanted us to have a better life than the hard one she had led. Her mother had died when she was only six years old. Living with various relatives she had received no schooling but had taught herself to read and write and to speak proper English. Her first marriage was disastrous and when it ended she was left on her own to bring up my older sister. Then she met my dad and had three more children, but it too turned out to be disastrous. She had the responsibility for four girls and hardly any support when she left that relationship. She found lasting happiness with Daddy, the man she married in her fifties. Sadly she died in March 2000 and he followed within days; neither wanted to live without the other. They were buried the same day, side by side.

England - The Solution

When I was thirteen my mum wanted to get me into Buxton High School in Kingston but she needed financial help which was not forthcoming from my father. Although my older sister was working by then and, fortunately, my younger sister had won a scholarship to Happy Grove High School in the neighbouring parish of Portland, my mother knew she could not find the money to send three of us to high school in Jamaica. She appealed to my father, who was living in England at the time, for help. He told her in a letter that it would be cheaper for me to live with him, as secondary education was free in England. After months of agonising, my mother made the heartbreaking decision to send me to my dad. I was devastated by the news and begged to stay but it was useless, the decision had been made.

While waiting for my passport, I went to Kingston to stay with my uncle and his wife. My uncle was a fireman and lived in Jones Town which was then a nice area. It was a horrible experience. I was treated like a domestic helper and had to do all the housework. My stay there turned out to be much longer than my mum had anticipated as my passport took not two months but several months to come through. When at last things got moving, my mum came to Kingston to make the final arrangements. My father had sent the money for the airfare and my ticket was booked with Chin Yee's Travel Service.

Near the time of my departure I felt like killing myself. I was so frightened. I was afraid of the journey and dreaded what I was going to. I didn't feel close to my father and knew no other family in England. I would be all alone in this strange country. I was depressed at the thought of leaving my mom and sisters; I felt sorry for myself and desperate.

The dreaded day arrived. My mum and younger sisters came to the airport to see me off. My mum kept saying, "Keep courage!" But that was very difficult for me to do. However, I tried for my mum's sake to put on a brave face until I waved my final goodbye and entered the plane.

My family had made sure I would be presentable when I arrived in England and met my father. My uncle's wife had made my clothes as a gift and they made me look very well dressed. With my bottle-green pinafore dress I wore a cream and green pinstripe blouse; a white pillbox hat, gloves and shoes completed my outfit. My stockings were held up by elastic, my home-made garters, and even before I sat in the plane the stockings were wrinkled and slowly sliding down.

I left on a BOAC (British Overseas Airways Corporation) flight on the 12th of April, 1965. It was my mother's birthday so I can never forget it. When the plane took off I was very frightened. We landed in Florida where we had to change planes. My little brown grip had my clothes as well as a few coconut cakes and sweets called tamarind balls, a piece of yam and a couple of mangoes. The black customs officer in Florida said, "Mangoes? No, no!" And that was the last I saw of my East Indian mangoes. I was well vexed.

The second part of the journey seemed to take forever.
I had left my home, my family and friends for the unknown.

EUROPE

Olga's English Education

I arrived at Manchester Airport anxious, not knowing what to expect. It was a pleasant April day, not hot but not cold either. I was relieved and pleased to see my father. He was with another man whom he introduced as his friend, Gilbert. I recognised my father at once, he was exactly as I remembered him. He, on the other hand, was surprised at how much I had grown. I was five-foot six and skinny, and weighed seven and a half stones. I thought I looked okay but over the next few weeks whenever my father introduced me to his friends they would comment that I was meagre.

"She tall, eh, but she mawger," was how one woman put it.

At the airport my father handed me an ugly grey and black coat. It was actually an adult's coat, dead old-fashioned. I had no choice but to put it on because I did need it. Gilbert led the way to a car and got in the driver's seat, while my father seated me in the back and got in next to Gilbert. My father talked non-stop, asking about people back home; I answered mostly in monosyllables. I didn't want to talk because I wasn't interested in what he was asking but he must have thought I was shy so he kept on talking. The truth of the matter was that the row upon row of red brick buildings with chimneys that we passed from time to time in the built-up areas puzzled me.

"Pa, why do they have so many prisons and bakeries?" I asked at last, unable to contain myself any longer.

"They're not prisons and bakeries. They are houses and you're going to live in one."

My heart skipped a beat; I saw no front yard. I also noticed that people were dressed in dull colours, mainly grey and black and were hunched over, walking fast. They looked miserable and their homes and other buildings looked drab. I was used to people in Jamaica wearing bright colours and sauntering along. I could not help it; there in the back seat of that car I began to cry silently. I desperately wanted to go back home.

When we reached Nottingham, Gilbert dropped us off outside my new home and drove away. My father opened the front door and walked in. I followed and stood inside the passage. He then opened another door and beckoned me to come in. As I entered I saw a woman sitting in front of a coal fire.

"Miss Evelyn, this is Vernie . . ."

That was my introduction to my stepmother who barely acknowledged me. There was no warmth in her voice as she looked up briefly and said, "So this is the Vernie I hear about. Come in and sit down." She pointed to a chair and I sat down tentatively. My father set down my grip by an armchair which he sat in. After what seemed an eternity, Miss Evelyn asked, "How things in Jamaica?"

"Alright, Mam."

"It a rain when you leave there?"

"No, Mam."

"The flight did alright?"

"Yes, Mam."

"You hungry?"

"No, Mam." I was so nervous I did not feel hungry, all I could feel was an awful tightness in my throat.

"Put your grip round there so." She pointed to a curtained-off area in a bedroom. I put the suitcase where she indicated. She got up, beckoned to me and I followed her into the bathroom. It was dirty but she said nothing about that, pointing instead to a thing on the wall and remarking, "You have to put a penny in it to get hot water. Let you' father show you."

We returned to the room with the coal fire. My father shouted to someone called Jean and a girl about my age appeared with a younger girl in tow. I later learnt that Jean was my fourteen year-old step-sister and that Sonia was my stepmother's nine year-old granddaughter. Jean said, "Hello," and smiled. She and Sonia made me feel a little better. They seemed friendly enough as they showed me around the flat that my new family rented - the ground floor of 17A Gedling Grove in a house owned by a Mr Singh. They occupied two bedrooms and a living/dining room, and shared the kitchen and bathroom with the other occupants of the house. Jean and Sonia shared the smaller bedroom; I was to share the bedroom of my father and stepmother, in a space separated by a curtain, just big enough to hold my single bed.

When my father suggested that I should have a bath and get ready for bed, Jean gave me a cloth to clean the bath. When I had finished she put a *Willy penny*, the big, old one, into the meter slot and turned on the geyser. I jumped at the sudden hissing sound and Jean collapsed with laughter. I had a bath and dried myself with my wash rag, too timid to ask for a towel when none had been offered. I then went back into the living room where my father and Miss Evelyn were watching television.

"See, I buy a television for you to look at." My father said to me sticking out his chest with pride. I made no response. I could tell he expected me to be grateful but my mind was consumed with another matter to do with my survival over the next few years, my stepmother. I was sure she did not like me. A few minutes later, to my surprise, my father said he was off to the pub and I was left all alone with Miss Evelyn. After what seemed an eternity of silence, she said, "When you ready you can go to bed." I went at once. That night I cried for my mother. I felt as if someone had cut out half of my heart and I was bleeding to death. I cried myself to sleep.

The next morning I woke up to my new life. My father and stepmother had left for work and Jean and Sonia were at home because it was the Easter holiday. After breakfast Jean said, "Let's go to the Arboretum. It's a nice park; you'll like it." It sounded interesting and I was pleasantly surprised when we got there. The Arboretum was beautiful with lots of flowers and flowering shrubs. The grassy areas were nicely mown lawns and the tree-lined walkways seemed to go on and on. We strolled around then sat on the grass for a rest. Jean asked me a lot of questions about myself and my family in Jamaica. As we sat on the grass I heard a rustling of leaves coming from a nearby tree.

"See a mongoose there!" I grabbed Jean's hand and pointed excitedly.

"That's a squirrel," she laughed. On closer observation I saw it was not a mongoose although it did have a bushy tail. The squirrel was very tame and did not run away like a mongoose would have done.

"So, it don't eat chicken then?"

"No. They eat nuts. Isn't it lovely?" Jean made cooing noises to attract the squirrel but it sniffed, turned and dashed away between the trees.

It was then that I noticed a couple nearby, sitting on the grass kissing. I had never seen people kiss like that in public. "Look! Look!" I pointed covering my mouth in amazement.

"Oh, take no notice; they do it all the time," Jean educated me. But it was difficult not to nudge her and point my head in the direction of any couple I saw 'making a spectacle of themselves', as we would say in Jamaica.

I enjoyed the park so much I did not want to go home. When we got back they invited me to their room to watch television. They continued to ask a lot of questions about Jamaica and, finding my jokes funny, rolled about on their beds laughing. We quickly developed a good rapport and were friends by the time the grown-ups returned home. After dinner my father said he planned to take the day off to have me enrolled at the local secondary modern school where I would start at the beginning of the next term.

On my first day of school I took the number 58 bus to Cottesmore Secondary Modern School which was off Derby Road. I knew the bus route as my father and I had been before and by my second week at school I had worked out a way to get there walking in order to save my bus fares. I was very nervous and apprehensive as I entered the school gates. I had still not got used to seeing so many white people. I did not know what it was going to be like in an English school. Were the children going to be friendly? Were the teachers going to be as strict as the teachers in Jamaica? These and other thoughts about school ran riot in my head.

I went to the school office, called Reception, and was taken to my form room. It was a prefab and not part of the main building. After Registration there was Assembly. The class walked in double file, led by the teacher, to the hall in the main building. The hall was also used as the gym and the equipment, all new to me, was stored against the walls for those classes. The children sat cross-legged on the floor, and the new pupils were placed near the front. Looking around to orientate myself to my surroundings, my eyes lighted on this black girl sitting near to me. There were not many black children in the school and I must have stared a little longer at her. "What big lips that gal got," I said to myself and looked at her a second time. Her eyes caught mine and I clearly heard her say, "A wha ya gal a look in a mi mawnin so fa?" That was fighting talk and I wanted to show her that I was not afraid of her. I *cut my eye* at her and very slowly looked away.

It turned out that she was the other new girl in my form. At break-time that morning Gloria accosted me. "Gal, wha you did a look 'pon me so fa?" Her manner suggested that she thought she could frighten me, but I stood my ground, looked her up and down inch by inch to make her aware that I wasn't even going to bother to answer her. "You t'ink say me a joke?" And not waiting for an answer she repeated, "Gal, you t'ink say me a joke? Me will t'ump you down, you know?"

"Gal, you ever feel jackass kick yet?" I retorted and slowly walked off to the sound of tittering from the gawkers standing by. Gloria got the message and for the rest of our school life never spoke to me. She did, however, get into a lot of arguments with other girls knowing that her older sister would back her up if there was a fight.

I knew from the way she behaved that she was self-conscious about her thick lips. Years later, her daughter and one of my daughters became good friends. One day I saw her in town with her granddaughter and greeted her, "Hi Gloria. How you doing?" She was taken aback for a few seconds before she answered. As far as I was concerned it made no sense keeping up this malice as we were then in our late forties. And besides, her big lips had by then become trendy. *I recently read that American white women are paying upwards of three thousand U.S. dollars to have silicone implants done in order to have lips like Gloria's!*

Carlene, one of the other black girls in the form, and I hit it off from day one, we became friends and have remained so over the years. Later in that first week I met Veronica who was older than me but with such a warm personality that I was automatically drawn to her. The Veronica of our schooldays was fun to be with and a good athlete. Sadly, she became an alcoholic, the result of a broken heart. She had fallen in love with a man and together they had five beautiful children but when he died a wife appeared out of nowhere to collect his body. Veronica was traumatised to learn that he had a wife and that his parents knew, while she had been kept in the dark. When she turned to drink I tried to help her but to no avail. When I lived in Belgium she refused my invitation to come over; much later I asked my sister to find her a job in Germany but again Veronica would not take up the offer. She looked haggard the last time I saw her, yet an inner beauty still shone through.

School was not a pleasant experience for me. On my first day the form tutor asked me a lot of questions about what I had done in Jamaica, and told me what I would be doing and gave me a timetable. Over that week I was introduced to a syllabus for each subject, subjects being taught in different rooms, 'break-time' instead of 'recess' and racism as a reality. In my form of forty-one girls five were black and we black girls had to be tough to survive the racism of both teachers and children. It is hard to believe but without any provocation we were verbally abused on a regular basis in the classroom, the cloakroom and on the playground. Common taunts such as *"Nigger"*, *"Golliwog"* and *"Black bastard, go back to your jungle"* were hurled at us. Complaining to the teachers was a complete waste of time as the perpetrators were rarely punished and nothing constructive was done to stop the abuse. So, most of the time when we were attacked we simply resorted to giving as good as we got; we knew there was no justice for us. But we were victims twice over because when we fought back we were the ones punished for breaking school rules!

A few black girls, in an attempt to avoid conflict with the teachers, hung out with only white girls and took all the abuse thrown at them. I am sure some of them wanted desperately to be white so they could have a normal school life. *Sad, isn't it?*

I got into lots of scrapes because I was not going to tolerate the constant bullying. In one unforgettable incident I actually stood up to the headmistress. An older white girl not only pushed her face up to mine and spat out, "Nigger! Black bastard! Bitch!" but shoved me against the wall. I punched her good and proper. As blood spurted from her mouth, a crowd gathered. Soon she moved towards me as if to fight back but she must have seen blood in my eye as I warned, "Come near me and I'll rip you to pieces!" She walked away with her friends. The next thing I knew was that my form teacher came up to me with the girl who had attacked me.

"You little savage! Look what you've done!" she shouted angrily.

She must have expected me to look sorry but I just stared through her, my eyes like icicles.

"We'll go and see the Head, now!" she ordered.

She marched beside me to the headmistress' office, knocked and went in. A few minutes later the office door opened and she beckoned me in. The headmistress did not ask me what had happened; she simply came from behind her desk and began to tell me off for my "disgraceful behaviour". At the end of her speech she informed me that I would be caned. There was no way I was going to accept this injustice. I folded my arms.

"Hold out your hand," she demanded.

"She called me a black bastard," I said in my defence. My arms stayed folded.

"We do not hit people here. You assaulted a girl."

"So it's right for her to call me names?" My arms stayed folded.

She lost her temper and exploded, "This is not how we do things here. I will not tolerate this kind of behaviour. You can take a letter to your father and come back with him to see me." She turned away and the form tutor having ushered me out, I was left to wait outside the office for the letter.

Before handing the letter to my father that evening, I related the incident. From his expression I could tell that he was not pleased with how the school had dealt with the matter. The next afternoon we went to see the headmistress after school. My father listened to the headmistress' complaint that I had assaulted a fellow pupil, had been defiant and disobedient to teachers and her remark that she would not allow me to stay in school unless I changed my attitude. My father agreed with her that I was wrong to hit the girl, but asked what action was being taken to stop me from being attacked in the future. He said that he thought we had both done something wrong and that both should be punished in the same way. I was surprised to find that the headmistress conceded that we were both wrong and the agreement was that we should apologise to each other and should both be caned for breaking the rules. I was far from pleased with this but took my punishment, realising that I had won a victory. The white girls now knew that I was not to be messed with.

Of all the teachers I had, I respected only a couple. The Geography teacher was my favourite. He was fair and he was the only one who praised my work when it was good, encouraging me to achieve. I started school in May and end of year exams were in June. Carlene, one of the black girls, came over-all first in the form. I was first in English, Geography and Religious Education. Imagine my amazement when at Prize-giving I received only one prize for English and the English girls who had come second in Geography and in R.E. were given prizes! I knew that the school's policy was to give a prize for first place in a subject. To me it seemed that the school was telling me that it could not let a black person have three first prizes.

The Geography teacher, seeing my disappointment, said to the Geography class at our next lesson, "If anyone deserves a prize for excellent work it is Olga and I'm going to give her a prize." He presented me with a book, saying, "I hope you'll continue to work hard. You'll go far." That man redeemed white people in my eyes. He also raised my confidence when it was taking a beating from the other teachers.

Racism in the system was clear in the sets we were placed in for our last two years of schooling. Not one black girl was put in a G.C.E.(General Certificate of Education) group. That said to us that no black girl was intelligent enough to take even one G.C.E. subject. The brighter black girls were offered commercial subjects. What made it blatant racism was the fact that white girls who had performed less well in their class work and the annual examinations by which our ability was assessed, were nonetheless placed in G.C.E. groups. It seemed to me then that the education system at Cottesmore set out deliberately and blatantly to ensure that black people became second-class citizens. *The education so many of us received in Nottingham at that time failed us.* When as young people we met and shared our experiences of school, the same pattern of racism would emerge. Very few of us managed to escape those racist teachers' expectations. Dr Neville Ballin is one of the exceptions; he succeeded, despite being told that he was incapable of doing G.C.E. On leaving Cottesmore he went to People's College of Further Education where he obtained the qualifications to get a place at Edinburgh University, one of the best in the United Kingdom - proof of racism at work.

Racism in school affected not only my education but also my mental health. I'm sure it affected the other black girls in the same way. Our frustration led us inevitably to display hostile behaviour. It was not normal to live under such continuous stress and my personality changed. I was not the same person I had been in Jamaica, believing in God and loving my neighbours. How could I love people who hated me and made my life a living hell? Our only coping mechanism was to appear vicious and untouchable.

I tried hard at school for a while then lost interest. What was the point of giving your best, only to be put down by teachers? I will never forget an American teacher who taught us American history. Her introduction to the topic had been so interesting that I went off to the library and did a lot of reading on it. Imagine how I felt when, with my hand in the air, aching to be acknowledged, I was ignored over and over again! The final straw was when the woman said, "Olga, put down your hand!" She made no attempt to hide her irritation. I was being excluded. Devastated, I shut off.

Then there were the two lesbian teachers who terrorised the black girls. One taught Physical Education, the other one taught Home Economics. In PE the white girls were coaxed to do well with, "Come on, you can do it!" or "Have another try". But all we ever heard from them was abuse or accusation. "What do you think you're doing?" was the favourite question of one. If looks could kill, many of our teachers would be dead.

There was no love lost between the black girls and the only Asian teacher at the school. She was married to a doctor and carried on as if she were white, sucking up to the white teachers and putting us down at every opportunity. When we played rounders, our shouts of "Run! Run! Run!" to our team mates were louder than the white girls. In an exasperated tone, and no doubt to hurt us, she would shout back at us, "Stop that racket, you're not in the bush!" We yelled louder because we saw what she was doing and it hurt even more coming from her, someone whose countrymen were also suffering from the very insults we got from whites. Another of her comments was, "I can't stand you Jamaican girls!" She did not earn our respect and we treated her as she treated us. There were stock insults we hurled at her. "Move from there, you 'tink like, 'tink like curry and garlic," referring to the strong curry and garlic smell on many Asians at that time. Another insult was taken from Jamaican culture in which some believe that it takes two Indians to be as strong as any one person of African origin. When one of the black girls chanted, "*Two fi one! Two fi one!*" and the Asian teacher looked around, raucous laughter erupted from the rest of us.

Overt racism was painful but another form of racism practised by a few teachers was equally so, for it was harder to hit back. Some teachers pretended to be nice when all the time they were being patronising and telling you in the sweetest of voices that you were not as good as white people. The French teacher comes to mind. I was keen to learn French and studied really hard but noticed that I was being held back. When I asked pertinent questions that needed her help, she fobbed me off with condescending remarks such as, "That's too difficult. You'll only confuse your little head," said in the sweetest of voices and accompanied with what was intended to appear a friendly pat. I was deeply scarred by these insults to my intelligence.

It was not a happy situation and, by December, I was fed up with my first year at Cottesmore. I wanted to leave. I thought my father could have been more supportive but he took no interest in my education. He fed and clothed me and expected me to go to school and learn enough to get an office job. He showed no interest in what I wanted to do and offered no encouragement. My father listened to my complaints then told me it would be the same wherever I went and advised me to "Grin and bear it". This was what the majority of black parents said to their children because they too faced racism at work. When they met we heard them sharing the insults they suffered at work and learnt that those who defended themselves against the racists often got the sack. Our parents could not risk losing their jobs because they had families here, and often in Jamaica too, to support and they needed the money.

As the time for leaving school drew near, I decided to make my own decisions about my future and not seek help from home or school. I wanted to be an air hostess. I was not going to be fobbed off and patted on the head nor be told I could not be what I wanted to be. I wrote to British Airways telling them I was a sixteen-year-old Jamaican who wanted to be an air hostess and asked them to send me details of the qualifications I needed. They wrote back giving the qualifications, but adding that I was too young and that they only recruited British nationals. Disappointed but not defeated, I determined to continue to learn French, convinced that one day I would get a job using French.

I was not going to give up on my dream.

Life And Loves

I left school and joined the labour force, not in an office but in a lingerie factory on Alfreton Road. I was glad to see the back of school. I would now be earning, which meant I would soon be independent. The work in the lingerie factory was far from interesting and I realised at once that machining was not for me. The work was boring but the people were friendly, kind and helpful. There was no name-calling and the working atmosphere was pleasant. Florrie, a busty, motherly white woman, took me under her wing.

"Come, me duck, I'll show you how to use this machine," she said when the supervisor introduced me as the new girl for Florrie to train. I had one week's training in overlocking. I was also taught how to keep the machine clean.

The only other black teenager working in that area of the factory was a girl who lived near me. We struck up a friendship and walked together to and from work. I guess she saw me as a poor thing because for a while I did not have many nice clothes. I was thankful when my father did not take my first wage packet which I handed to him after the second week at work. I had to work a week in hand before receiving a week's wage, this was the norm. I used most of the money to buy some new clothes. Gradually, I built up my wardrobe and began to dress stylishly. My girlfriend advised me to not dress up for work but to save my nice clothes for going out. Although I had nowhere to go but to work, I heeded her advice and went back to wearing my dull skirts but with nice tops. The women were very complimentary about my figure and looks but I did not pay much attention to this. Then one day the penny dropped.

It was a Monday morning and I called for my friend as usual.

"Hurry up or we're going to be late!" I shouted through her bedroom door after waiting for a long time.

"Go on if you can't wait!" she replied sharply.

"No need to bite my head off. I'll see you at work."

She knew exactly how I would respond. I left her. Imagine my surprise when she walked in, dressed to kill. Everyone went "Oooh!" and some of the women told her how nice she looked. She looked very pleased with herself. At break I asked if she was going out after work, thinking that must be the reason she was so dressed up. When her answer was no, I couldn't help saying, "But you told me not to dress up for work."

"Leave me alone! Is my clothes and I can wear them if I want to." She spoke as if she was spoiling for an argument. It dawned on me then that she was jealous of me. She never spoke to me from that day in 1967 until 1982 when we met one day along Canning Circus.

"Hello, Olga," she said, stopping me in my tracks.

"Hello," I replied tentatively, wondering what she was up to.

"I'm a Christian now. Let's put childish things behind us . . ." She carried on for a while trying to convince me to give my heart to Christ and come to church. I listened politely, told her I would think about it, and said goodbye.

I had not forgotten my dream to learn French and find a job using it. On leaving school, I enrolled at Clarendon College of Further Education to attend evening classes to do the G.C.E. 'O' Level in French and English. The English teacher reminded me of those in school, he pretended to be open to questions but saw them as a challenge to his authority. At first I fell for his pretence. "Sir, I think that's incorrect," I said when he made a grammatical error. I had not been rude but that man in a superior voice told me he was the teacher. I pointed out that I had spoken because he had told us that if we felt something was not correct, we should say so. He cut me dead with a hard stare and continued the lesson. When I went home I checked in my textbook and found that I was indeed correct. I showed this to a few of the other students and when there was a lull in the next lesson I went up to his table and showed him the point I was trying to make. He reddened and gave a dismissive "Mmm". *I learnt that day a lesson I would pass on to my children: teachers are not always correct but many will not own up to making mistakes.*

When I was seventeen I met Aston at the home of some friends of my father. He asked my father if he could take me out. My father thought he was a nice young man and did not mind us going out together. Before I knew what had hit me, I was pregnant. My stepmother and I had never got on and when she suspected that I was pregnant, she started to *throw words* at me. When I knew for sure that I was more than two months pregnant, I gave up evening classes and confided in the woman upstairs, begging her not to tell my father. I was waiting for the right time when my stepmother was out of the way to tell him. What did that snitch do? She told my father and stepmother.

"What me tell oono? Them whore gal what breed, serve them right!"

My stepmother waited for my father to be out of the way to gloat. What offended me was that Miss Evelyn had five children with different fathers and that one of her daughters was a known prostitute. How dare she point a finger at me?

I was not the only one finding the woman obnoxious. My father was finding her more and more intolerable and we both moved out when I was four months pregnant. My father and Aston had found accommodation in an Indian man's house; my father rented the ground floor flat and Aston rented the two-roomed flat on the second floor for us. Aston was very generous and for a couple of months things were perfect; most of all, I was happy to be away from my stepmother. It did not take long, however, to discover that Aston had a very bad temper. He exploded whenever I disagreed with him. We were soon having rows and he became physically abusive. His violence worried me. During my pregnancy he hit me several times. He would go off like a rocket, hit out not caring that he hurt me and afterwards say he was sorry. When our son was born Aston was over the moon and wanted us to get married straightaway but I had doubts about our relationship and kept delaying.

My father's attitude to Aston's behaviour surprised and worried me. It was pure male chauvinism; as a woman I was at fault for provoking the man.

"Pa, look what Aston do." I showed my father the bruises on my arms.

"How Aston manage do that?" he asked, surprised.

I explained to him how Aston and I were talking and because I had disagreed with him he had become violent.

"You see you? You too feisty and full of mouth!"

I could not believe my father was siding with Aston against me, seeing Aston as a good man, a good provider and annoyed with me for not setting a wedding date.

I began to feel a coldness towards Aston and the relationship deteriorated. Our arguments were no longer done in private and he would curse me in front of my friends. One day my friend, Dixie, came to visit me. An argument developed in the kitchen between Aston and me and, in a rage, he slapped me so hard that I reeled across the kitchen floor, my ear ringing. I saw red. My eye fell on my father's machete in the corner and I grabbed it. My intention was to chop off the hand that had hit me once too often. Aston saw me with the machete and headed for the door. Dixie held on to me and, as she tried to get the machete from me, it scratched her leg. It was her cry of pain that brought me to my senses.

I listened as Aston, his father and my father sat around planning our wedding. Aston saw the minister and my father ordered the wedding cakes. I refused to join in. My plan was to save enough money for me and my child to get away to London. But one night in bed Aston was rabbiting on so much about the wedding that I snapped.

"I'm not marrying you!" I blurted out.

Aston grew furious as I refused to change my mind. He exploded and slapped me. That was it. I decided then and there not to take any more abuse and fought back. The landlord hammered on the door shouting, "What's going on? I call police!" Aston left the house and to avoid seeing him when he returned I went down to my father's flat with my baby. The landlord waylaid my father and I heard, "You do something 'bout that man. He hit, hit your daughter."

The landlord must have shamed my father into seeing Aston for what he really was because when Aston came around the following day to apologise my father told him he had to stop hitting me. Aston erupted and began to curse my father for interfering. Taken aback, my father turned to me and asked me what I wanted to do. Before I could speak Aston said, "It's my flat. I'm not leaving. Olga can go."

"Go where?" my father was annoyed. "Where you want her to go? She has the baby. Or you forget?"

"Okay. I'm leaving but don't think I'm coming back."

A little later I saw him leave the house with his suitcase and get into his car. My father left shortly after. He returned within the hour; he was livid. He told me what had happened when Aston left the house. Aston, still in a rage, had driven his car at my father as he stood outside talking to a neighbour. My father had gone with his machete to the police station and told them to warn Aston to leave us alone or he would chop him up. Silently I praised my father for taking a stand at last.

A couple of days went by and Aston came back, asking forgiveness, as usual. We were not in a forgiving mood but we were polite. He kept coming around and eventually I agreed to go with him for a night out. We went to Havana Club, the black-owned night club in Derby, which was the place to go on a Saturday night. We were there for about an hour when Aston said, "Soon come". Half an hour later I went to the toilet and returning to the dance hall, saw him chatting with two girls. Someone asked me for a dance and as soon as we began to dance Aston appeared.

"Is who you come here with?" he accosted me. I ignored him. "Ready," he commanded and before I could respond, he grabbed me by the arm and dragged me out of the club. As we reached the car park he started accusing me of flirting and began whacking me.

"Jesus, look how the man a do the woman!" I heard a passing man say. Incensed, I slipped off a shoe and started beating him on the head with it. A friend of his came up, parted us and put me in his car to take me home. As I sat in the car Aston came to the door.

"I'm sorry. I don't know what got into me. Please . . ."

I shut him out; I didn't want to hear anything he had to say.

He turned up at the flat that Monday evening when he had calmed down and thought I had calmed down too. He came in and put down a pound note on the table.

"What's that for?"

"To buy baby food."

"That's okay, as long as you realise we are through." It took him some time to get the message but in the end he had no choice but to accept it.

There I was alone with a three-month-old baby but glad to be rid of Aston.

Managing was not easy but at least I had peace of mind. I felt I had no choice but to cope. It was really hard going. The only social life I had was visiting friends. And that was how I met Justus. We each had friends who lived in the same house. His friend and mine began to go out together and Justus and I saw more and more of each other. He was an engineering student in his final year and was very ambitious. As time went by, I grew to respect him and we started a serious relationship one evening when he took me out to dinner.

When he graduated as an engineer he began to work with Raleigh, earning a good salary. He showered me with expensive presents of jewellery and clothes and, before long, he proposed. I dithered, unsure what to do, and before giving him an answer, wrote to my mother in Jamaica for advice. I told her about Justus' good points, that he was twelve years older than I was and that he wanted us to get married and go to live in Nigeria where he was from. Her advice surprised me. She told me I should only marry him if he was prepared to live in England and warned me not to marry him and go to Africa. Her fear was based on the experiences of several Jamaican women who had married African men and gone to Africa, only to find themselves trapped there, unable to visit their families in England and Jamaica. Her fears made me anxious.

Justus suggested that he should rent a house and we should move in together. I agreed. My son was not yet a year old but I trusted Justus as an honourable person and felt confident that he would take care of us as he had promised. I went to work leaving my son with a white childminder. I was not happy doing this but it was what we black women felt we had to do in order to support ourselves and our children. The childminder was a nice person but Michael was always dirty when I went to pick him up after work and the house never smelt as if it had been properly cleaned. When I found myself pregnant again, I gave up my job.

My life with Justus was one of running our home and looking after our children because in the space of three years there were three. He was a good provider but was also very domineering, wanting always to be totally in control of us. He did the shopping and took over the financial management of the house from the beginning. When I stopped working he gave me money for my personal use but still wanted to control how I spent it.

Once, I saw a lovely dress and bought it from the spending money that he gave me. That evening I put it on to show him and although I looked stunning in it he was not pleased that I had bought something without first seeking his approval. He said he didn't like it and I had to take it back and exchange it for one that he liked although I thought his choice was not as nice. At times like that I was made to feel as if I were a child and incapable of making my own decisions. This domineering streak was the part of his personality that I did not like but I tried to avoid confrontation, concentrating all my energies on taking care of my family.

From time to time I suggested to Justus that I would love him to meet my mother. This was because I wanted my mother to see him and then give me her opinion of him before I would agree on a wedding date. Justus' response was always the same; it was not feasible for him to go to Jamaica. Then one day, out of the blue, he told me he was going back to Africa and asked me, "Have you decided what you're going to do?"

"No," I responded tentatively.

"Why?" He was obviously irritated.

"My mother says it's better for us to get married and stay in England. I think she's right. Don't you?"

He didn't speak for some time, then he said he had to go home to see his family and he wanted them to see his son. He suggested taking Kevin with him to Nigeria for a holiday. I knew how important boys were in the Yoruba culture and I could hear warning bells ringing in my head. I was quite worried and thought, "What if the family there decided to keep our son?" I convinced Justus that Kevin would cry for me and it was best not to take him. He asked if he could take one of the two girls, Tina was still a young baby and Charmaine was almost a year old. We agreed that he could take Charmaine.

Little did I know when I said goodbye to my eleven- month-old daughter and her father, that I would not see her again for sixteen years!

I was so sure that Justus and Charmaine would return that I did not worry, even when they should have returned and he wrote instead asking me to "come with the children". I wrote back that we had agreed he was only taking a holiday and I hoped he would be back soon so we could discuss and decide our future. I received no reply to that letter and to several others that I wrote appealing to him to bring back my daughter. I began to panic. I rang the Nigerian ambassador who knew Justus quite well and asked him if he knew Justus' whereabouts. He said he had not heard from Justus. I asked the ambassador to contact me if he got any useful information as I was worried sick. A few weeks later I received twenty pounds from Justus through the embassy. I also learnt that Justus was working for Shell International. I wrote to him in care of their Nigerian office but heard nothing.

By now numb with fear and in total shock, I kept saying to myself, "This can't be happening to us." But as the weeks went by I came to accept the reality of my situation. I took my children to a childminder and went to work in a clothes factory. It was so hard working full-time and looking after three children, all under five and one still a baby. I gritted my teeth and got on with it, but by the end of each week I was worn out. I gave up the privately rented house and moved into a cheaper Council flat. My flat was in the recently built City Council complex in Old Basford, near the railway crossing. There were high-rise flats joined by maisonettes along the concourse. I had a maisonette on the Alice Walk concourse. There were a few black people in the complex; some had been re-housed from houses being demolished in Hyson Green and The Meadows, others, like me, were new Council tenants. This island complex in the midst of older properties was away from the communities where we could find childminders. It was very difficult taking three small children on the bus to the childminder in the early morning and getting to work for an eight-hour shift at Jersey Kapwood, the lingerie factory. My life was a grind. I was always tired at the end of the day and thankfully crawled into bed as soon as I put the children to bed.

One day I met a young woman along the concourse who mentioned to me that in my situation I could claim 'welfare' and stay home to take care of my children. I didn't know about welfare benefits and she kindly offered to take me to the Social Security Office to make enquiries. The experience was humiliating, some of the questions they asked were embarrassing but the financial help given paid the rent and with careful management, I was able to keep myself and my children.

One year after Justus had left I was still trying to contact him when a letter arrived from a woman claiming to be Justus' wife. Instead of harassing Justus for money, I should agree to send the children to Nigeria where they would be properly cared for and receive a good education she harangued. I was angry. Justus had abandoned his children and me, had not supported us for a year and this woman was making out that I was harassing him! I wrote her a nasty letter telling her she should be ashamed of herself and should get her husband to support his children instead of attacking me. I thought of going to Nigeria to have it out with Justus and get my daughter but after talking with his friends I had to admit this was not feasible. I did not have any money and would be at a great disadvantage in Nigeria, knowing no-one there.

It was at this point that his friends told me that Justus had taken to Nigeria not only Charmaine but also a son he had in London, a boy the same age as our son Kevin. I was stunned. There was nothing left for me to do but to close this episode of my life. The one thing I could not forget was that my daughter was growing up not knowing her mother and her family in England and in Jamaica. I cried for her, all the time hoping that somehow I would see her again.

The emptiness I felt never left until I found her.

My life took another turn in February 1971. A friend came to visit me and, looking out of the window, saw Reg, an acquaintance of ours. She told him to come up and the three of us had a pleasant evening. It turned out that Reg came from my parish in Jamaica, was working in an engineering factory and, when not at work, did photography as well as painting and decorating. After this meeting he got into the habit of dropping by whenever he was in Old Basford. He was good with the children; they liked him and enjoyed his visits. It was good to see them all romping on the floor.

Our relationship gradually became closer but I did not want to rush into things. Reg convinced me that what he felt for me was "real". We had a good rapport, we were friends as well as lovers and I believed that at last I had found my soul-mate. Reg and I shared a love of adventure and we would take the family caravanning to different places on weekends. We visited places in Scotland and Wales as well as in England.

Eventually, Reg moved in with me and this enabled me to work evenings for an agency as a waitress or barmaid, bringing in a little more money so that we could pool our resources and plan for the future.

One of Reg's endearing qualities was his kindness to people outside the home. This was all well and good but often jobs in our house did not get done. Once I got so frustrated with the flat not being redecorated that I painted one wall in the living room bright yellow and blue. It was a sight but it made the point better than reasoning with Reg. He was aghast when he saw it and the decorating finally got done.

It was eight years since I'd left Jamaica and I longed to see my mother. I still missed her. I knew it was impossible for her to find the airfare to visit us or for me to earn the money to take the children to visit her in Jamaica. I racked my brain for a way forward and finally I realised that there was a way; if I saved my tips from work I could eventually afford to buy her a ticket. This gave me hope, something to work towards and I began to save my tips in a jam jar until one day I found that I had achieved my goal.

It was wonderful to see my mother again. My youngest sister, who my father had sent for a few years after my arrival, was as overjoyed as I was to see our mother. My children were pleased to know their grandmother and they had lots of fun together.

If asked at the time who my role model was, I would have said at once, not Angela Davis or any such famous person, but my mother, Mrs Ethlyn Jones. We argued a lot because we were both strong-willed women but a mutual respect was always there. We had an easy relationship and shared the same sense of humour. Anyone listening would think I was being rude but Mama and I always cracked up with laughter in the end. For instance, she would say, "Gal, you feisty, you know!" To which I would reply, "Me take after the lady that born me."

Mama was wise and I respected her wisdom even though sometimes it was hard to take her advice because it was not what I wanted to hear. She liked Reg as a person but had reservations about him as a husband for me. When I spoke to her about our marriage plans she warned, "Don't put too much store by Reg, you know. I think he's not serious." Of course I chose to ignore her warning. I was pregnant with Gaynor and although I was worried about having another child it was what Reg wanted.

In the midst of our happiness at having our mother with us tragedy struck. My father fell ill and deteriorated rapidly. Sadly, he died three weeks after my mother left for home. It was a traumatic time for me - saying goodbye to my mother, losing my father and being pregnant as well. I don't know how I did it but I continued to work until a few weeks before the birth.

Reg had a holiday in Jamaica and came back very excited with the idea of going back to Jamaica to live. His brother-in-law had told him that there were opportunities to be had there. It was my dream to return home so he did not have to try hard to convince me. We set ourselves two years to save enough for the move. When Gaynor was a year old, Reg changed our plans. He decided that it would be better for him to go ahead of the family to prepare for us and that it was necessary for him to get a new car to take home. Our wedding was put on the back burner because, like most Jamaicans, we wanted a big reception for our friends and that would be costly. In view of this, I thought it best to buy things as we went along in preparation for the wedding. I began buying drinks for our wedding reception but I noticed that when we had visitors Reg would use the drinks from our reception store. When I complained about this, he would promise to replenish the store but never did. I should have twigged that all was not right but I was too foolishly trusting.

That was not the only warning sign that I ignored. Reg was having trouble getting the Bill of Sale which he needed to ship the car to Jamaica. I rang the car firm only to be told that he had not kept up with the repayments. I tackled him about it and, to get things sorted out, gave him, from my own savings, one hundred pounds for the repayments and one hundred pounds for the shipping. He looked sheepish but took the money.

Over the months I had been buying things for our future home in Jamaica but a friend who was like a clairvoyant warned me not to send them with the car. At first I was not convinced and defended him. "But he's going to take them to my mom's."

"Well it's up to you, but I'm telling you, you won't have anything when you finally get there."

I chewed over what she had said and a part of me grudgingly believed her as she had been right about the time of my father's death and other things. When the shippers came I told them to take the car and nothing else.

The day he was leaving I saw the bank book that held our joint savings. Reg had kept back ten pounds weekly from the housekeeping for our Jamaican fund yet the account was empty. I was dumbstruck. "Reg!" I shouted and when he appeared I held out the book, "What's happened to all the money?"

"You know how it go, Thompson. Spending. You couldn't send me home empty-handed."

I reminded him about the car and also about the clothes I'd bought for him: a suit, two pairs of trousers, twelve shirts, underwear, socks, even handkerchiefs. He tried to make a joke of the situation but I was deeply hurt. Later, I learnt that he had also been given lots of presents from friends about which he had said not a word to me.

I received a postcard from him while he was on his stopover in New York. That was in September and nothing arrived for a couple of months so I wrote to him in Jamaica. His reply was one long moan; he had not found a job and was depressed. I had wised up by then and saw Reg for what he was: a waste of time. I had had it with him.

Childminding was again a problem and with my mind set on going home, I decided to check out the 'repatriation' scheme. At the time 'race' was a big issue in England. Enoch Powell, a West Midland Conservative Member of Parliament, was whipping up prejudice against black immigrants with his "rivers of blood" speeches and promoting repatriation as the solution to get rid of us. I contacted my Member of Parliament about repatriation and shortly after a man from the Department of Social Security came to see me with some forms. He explained that I had to sign a form accepting the three hundred pounds repatriation money as a loan, not a gift. The money was to pay the boat fare for my family, twenty pounds was for transportation from the docks to my mother's home and fifty pounds to help us resettle in Jamaica. I would be allowed only ninety pounds in weight for clothes and all household goods. My passport would be stamped

'Repatriated' and I would not be allowed back in Britain; this did not apply to my children as they were British subjects. On my arrival in Jamaica I would have to surrender my passport to the Jamaican Government until the three hundred pounds had been repaid.

I was amazed at what was on offer. I asked him how on earth clothes, bed-linen and pots and pans for a family could fit into their ninety-pound baggage allowance. He was unaccommodating. I then pointed out that I was getting eight pounds weekly for Family Allowance and three hundred pounds represented only nine months of Family Allowance. I asked him what incentive he thought that was for me to leave. He could barely conceal his annoyance. When I told him I had expected an offer of about two thousand pounds as a reasonable sum to give me a fresh start in Jamaica he was openly upset and rudely complained about the number of calls he had made and all that he had done to help me. I snapped. I thought of how my forebears in Jamaica had worked as slaves to help build Britain and that had continued with cheap labour after slavery and now that Enoch Powell and his ilk wanted to get rid of us, they were insulting us, pretending to help when all they were offering was a totally unrealistic loan.

"Mister, you're being rude, get out of my house." I opened the door.

"I'll see that you never get another penny . . ."

I slammed the door, shutting out his threats. The scheme was an insult and I decided on a plan of action. I finished work at the end of that week and on the following Monday morning went to register as unemployed. I stayed unemployed for several months and was able to take care of my children full-time.

But I was not happy with this state of affairs and became very depressed. At one stage I felt suicidal when I thought of the mess I had made of my life. One night after putting the children to bed I felt so hopeless, I could see no way forward. In a moment of madness, I emptied a half bottle of aspirins into the palm of my hand, walked to the cabinet and picked up the bottle of whiskey; I wondered what it would feel like to take the aspirins and whiskey. Would life be over quickly? What was there to lose, anyway? Then suddenly my beautiful children flashed before me; in my image they had knotted and uncombed hair because they were living with white people and they bore the sad faces of children bereft of a mother's love. The horror of what my action would do to them jolted me back to my senses. I knew then that, whatever the cost to me, I had to carry on for their sakes. The next day I rang the agency I had worked for and asked them to put me back on their books for a couple nights a week.

I nearly died when the guy at the agency asked if I was interested in topless waitressing. "Jesus Christ, are you mad?" I shrieked at him. He went on to tell me that it was all the fashion and paid very well. I cheekily bargained with him saying I could look better than topless if he gave me the job. I bought a pair of black boots, made myself a bra top and a mini skirt and presented myself for his opinion. He agreed that I looked ravishing and I began working at functions around the country. I was very self-conscious at first but steeled myself to see it as just a job. It was quite safe in that the customers were not allowed to touch the waitresses. It was hard work travelling wherever the function was being held and one had to be on one's feet from 7.00 to 10.00 p.m., but three nights brought me forty-five pounds after paying the driver and ten per cent to the agency. My tips added to this made it well worthwhile.

It was about then that I had a letter from Reg. He wanted to know if it was true that I was working as a topless waitress. If it was, he said, I could consider our relationship at an end. Imagine, no support for his child for the months he had been away and then having the cheek to write me that kind of letter. "What a laugh!" I thought as I ripped it to bits.

One night I was waitressing for a roundtable function for a group of doctors when there was a near riot. The 'go-go' dancer had not turned up and desperate, the organisers asked if any of us could dance. I had done African dancing with a black community project when I was a teenager and I enjoyed dancing, so I volunteered. I was introduced as "a beautiful dancer from the West Indies who will tit-illate you". I was having butterflies as I went on stage in a lurex costume, but concentrated on the music and danced my butt off. When I went back to waitressing, one of the doctors told me my dancing was great and gave me a whacking five-pound tip. That night with tips I made thirty-six pounds!

One of the waitresses I had met had been offered a month's contract dancing on the continent but she needed someone to look after her child and because I knew how hard it was for us as Jamaican single mothers, I agreed to help. She brought two packets of cornflakes when she dropped off her child and when she returned she paid me a measly five pounds. I had also made two costumes for her and charged her only three pounds. She paid me for one and still owes me for the other. No wonder she now owns two big houses, one in Florida, U.S.A. and one in Jamaica! She was a first class user and very selfish. I asked for her help in getting a dancing job on the continent as I heard that they were well paid. She tried to put me off by telling me that I was too fat and not what the clubs were looking for. I knew I was not fat and was prettier than she was, so I decided to approach my agency for help.

My agent advised me to get some nice costumes and he would find me something. A few weeks later he handed me a return plane ticket to Brussels, the cost to be repaid on my return to England. With very little time to prepare and to find someone to keep all of my four children, I had no choice but to separate them for the few weeks I expected to be away. My father's partner took the two boys, Tina went to my girlfriend from schooldays and Gaynor, my youngest, was left with another friend, a white girl with a black partner.

I was met at the airport by a Belgian agent who asked me to sign a contract before putting me on the train to Ghent for an audition. The contract stated that I had to pay him ten per cent of my earnings and if I broke my contract I would have to reimburse my employer for expenses incurred on my behalf. When I turned up at the famous *Maxim's* there were other girls waiting. I was twenty-four, shit-scared and didn't speak French. It felt surreal. I sat there thinking, "This isn't happening. They'll tell me at the end that I'm not needed." Then I was called.

I was accepted on trial and met the owner and the other performers at my first rehearsal. It was a melange of fire-eaters, 'go-go' dancers and cabaret artistes. On the night of my debut I told myself that I would give of my best and even if the customers slung shit at me I would continue. At the end of the show the boss came up to me clapping, "You're in, girl!" This was music to my ears. I was given a month's contract and a studio flat. My agent promised to find me another job if this contract was not extended. I worked for two months and earned two thousand pounds to take home. I was not happy away from my children and had to keep focussed because it was my only means to provide for my children. At the same time, however, I had no intention of allowing anyone to exploit me. I had noticed that in Brussels at the time Jamaicans were a novelty and seen as exploitable targets because we came from a poor country.

I made friends with the three other black girls in the troupe, one was from Gabon and the other two were Jamaicans living in England. One of the Jamaicans was not nice, she was *a user with a capital U*, never paying her way. We girls developed a camaraderie, cooked together and went out together to restaurants and cinemas. Sometimes we went dancing and people in the clubs would watch us fascinated by our movements. We had lots of free time as working hours consisted of rehearsal and being in the club from 8:00 to 10:00 p.m., six nights a week.

There were three Arab belly dancers in our troupe but we kept away from them because they were devious and sometimes spiteful. Once they painted and cut up the costumes of one of the troupe; the poor girl could hardly stop crying. It was some time before the culprits were found out.

Before leaving England, I had written to my mother begging her to look after my children so that I could work and in return I would buy her a home and support her. I saw this as the best choice for me as a single mother wanting to support my family and give them a good education. Her response was that she had already brought up her family and the answer was no. I was, therefore, taken completely by surprise when I returned from Belgium and found a letter from her telling me that she and her husband had discussed the matter again and they were willing to take care of my children. Overjoyed, I sent a reply giving the date of my arrival with the children. The telegram took ten days to reach Jamaica, arriving the very day that we landed! My poor mother was in a panic trying to get a van to collect us from the airport.

I stayed two months to help the children to get used to their new home. They were then six, five, three and nearly two years old. They were not too happy about staying but I knew it was the best thing for all of us. Reg saw me one day travelling to town in a car and found himself at my mum's house. I heard her surprised remark, "*Ku here*, look who's coming!" Reg was very embarrassed as I had made sure that he got the message that we were managing fine without him and that I really was not interested in any of his excuses for the way he had treated us. I think he was amazed that I had been able to bring the children home.

I arrived back in England in October 1974, undecided whether to pursue working in Belgium where language was a barrier or to stay in England. In the meantime I worked full-time for the agency and the decision was made for me in December when my mother wrote to say she had found a house in St. Thomas which was a bit of paradise. She suggested that she would find a half of the deposit if I could find the rest. I wanted a home for my mother and my children but hadn't enough for my share of the deposit. I knew that I could earn much more on the continent than in England and that with Belgium as a base I could afford the mortgage. I borrowed the deposit money from an English friend who owned a small hotel in Nottingham. I got my agent in England to put me in contact with the agent in Belgium and relocated there. I accepted that I would just have to learn French and Flemish if I was not to be exploited.

The house was bought in the names of my sister, Hazel, my stepfather and me. My mother sold a piece of land that she owned for her share of the deposit. Her husband became a co-owner purely for security reasons and he drew up his will at the same time giving his share of the property to Hazel and me. The house was a one-bedroom holiday cottage owned by Hazel's boyfriend, Glanville. We paid nine thousand pounds and spent another three thousand making it into a home with three bedrooms, a lounge, a dining room, kitchen, front veranda, car port and the walk-in closet converted into a small additional bedroom.

Nearly three years later, on my visit to Jamaica, my mother complained that although Hazel's and Glanville's relationship had broken up he would walk into the house ". . . as though he own the place". One day he came and, true to form, walked up on to the veranda. I met him at the dining room door.

"Oh, you've done wonders with this place," he said inspecting the freshly painted house.

"What are you doing?" I asked.

"I'm just looking around."

"This is our house. You don't just walk in, you ask permission."

"I can look around if I want to."

"Get the hell out of here and don't come back!" I said firmly, adding a few choice Jamaican words to drive home my point.

"Mrs Jones, you want to teach your daughter some manners!" he shouted as he made a quick retreat through the gate.

All was revealed a few days later when my mother went as usual to pay the mortgage to the lawyer on Duke Street. The secretary, who was also the lawyer's sister, informed my mother that Glanville had been in to find out how we were doing with the repayments. During this conversation my mother found out that the arrangement made by Glanville had not been for a twenty-year mortgage as she had been led to believe but for three years, at which time he would repossess if we defaulted. We were saved by that woman. I had to hare back to Europe, borrow some money and, with what I had saved, I was able to pay off for the house in the given time. From that experience I learnt never to trust anyone in a business deal but to check everything myself.

I love our house. We have been approached many times by people wanting to buy it. One day as I was relaxing on the veranda, a posh chauffeur-driven car drew up at the gate and a gentleman was ushered out. I wondered what he wanted and was quite surprised when, after pleasantries, he asked if I would be prepared to sell the house for a good price.

"We're not selling. Sorry."

"I was interested in this property three years ago as a holiday home, but things cropped up. I'll make you a deal. I'll buy you a house in Kingston or wherever you choose. I'm serious. Please consider the offer."

Dad had overheard the conversation and was annoyed at the persistence of the man. He cleared his throat to let us know he was there and said in a dismissive manner to the man, "If it means so much to you, imagine how much it means to us! It's not for sale." The man got the message. In the newspaper the following Sunday there was a photograph of the man who turned out to be a government minister.

Belgian Sojourn

I went to Belgium in March 1975, the beginning of yet another episode in my life. I had continuous contracts to work a month at a time in Belgium, Luxembourg, Switzerland and Italy for the next eight months. It was horrendous. I lived out of a suitcase and had to be careful because the people I was working with were not trustworthy.

Members of the various troupes came from different countries and it was commonplace to be robbed. One girl had saved her three months' earnings only to have it stolen. She was disconsolate. A man was going crazy as he had a family and was left penniless after being robbed. The police investigated the robberies but had no success for some time because, as it turned out, it was a member of the troupe who had stolen the victim's key and returned it after her accomplice had done the robbery. I protected myself by keeping very little money.

There was also a lot of petty jealousy. One Algerian girl complained to the boss that I was gossiping about her with another Jamaican girl in Jamaican patois. It turned out that she saw me looking at her and overheard the word 'jealous' and interpreted that as saying she was jealous of me. I began learning French and Italian, gradually becoming fluent in both; I also picked up some Flemish.

There was a nightmarish situation in Ostend that toughened me and made me very wary of employers. The troupe I was with had agreed to be paid at the end of a month's work but when we went to collect our wages we were told by the manager that the boss had not yet turned up. He had left earlier that evening telling us that he would see us later. We waited and waited, then someone phoned his house but there was no answer. At 6:00 next morning we were still anxiously waiting. Finally, some-one suggested that we should go to the boss' house to find out what was going on. There was no response to our knocking. Eventually, a neighbour came out and informed us that the boss and his wife had moved earlier that morning. They had done a runner. Devastated we were obliged to pool our resources in order to manage until the next payday. That was the last time I agreed to a contract paying me monthly; from then I asked to be paid weekly.

I was earning money but was very lonely away from my family. I missed the children and there was no phone at their house, so for regular contact I had to speak with my sister, Hazel, ringing her at the office. At the end of the eight months I was dying to see my children and flew home to Jamaica for a well-earned break.

Shortly after returning to Belgium I became depressed and was iffing and butting about continuing. What kept me going was the responsibility for the mortgage and the children. It was often a lonely life without family; people I felt I could trust were few and not always near when I needed a listening ear. I met a Jamaican troupe of six girls who had previously worked at the Sheraton Hotel in Kingston but we didn't hit it off. Two people who have remained lifelong friends are Maizie, a Jamaican from London who was living in Switzerland and Pet, also a Jamaican from England who was running an upmarket nightclub with her Belgian partner. Maizie is gentle and caring and it was a comfort whenever she was around. Now, as a practising Christian, she fundraises for African children in need. Other people who have stayed in touch are those from the Jamaican Diplomatic Corps then based in Belgium. As there were so few Jamaicans resident in Belgium we got to know each other and Pet and I were invited to many functions. We were also helpful in providing a touch of home for visiting diplomats.

Work was regular. I enjoyed sightseeing in the countries where I worked but, after a while, became travel-weary. Luxembourg was a nice, small country; the contracts there paid well and living was cheap but the place was not interesting. Italy was my favourite. I loved the countryside, mountains and lakes. It reminded me of Jamaica. France was fascinating and I went quite often. I was introduced to the Camargue area by a French singer. I loved its wild expanse and the horses that recalled the Wild West. Sightseeing in Paris was always fun: the quaintness of the Pigalle, the Left Bank, the cafés. I, however, did find the French rather arrogant and uncooperative in their dealings with black people.

I lived in Switzerland for eight months and met some crazy people who led interesting lives and filled my days with laughter so that I no longer felt lonely. I visited Swiss valleys and mountains. I liked Basle. Zurich I found ugly but Geneva reminded me of Paris, very chic and opulent. Lake Geneva was magical for me and Lucerne was very clean and historical but it did not take my breath away as I had been told it should. Some of the benefits we had working in the clubs were the opportunity to meet interesting people and to be wined and dined in some of the famous spots of Europe. Some of the girls also met and married well-heeled men. One of my friends from Jamaica married a Norwegian tycoon who named his yacht after her!

For me as a black person, living on the continent was no better than living in Britain. Some Belgians seemed to think of black women only as easy sex objects and, once more, I learnt very quickly to be on my guard. One night I was walking to the underground after seeing a film when I noticed a man following me, stopping whenever I stopped to look in a shop window. I crossed the street and quickened my step. I have always believed in women protecting themselves against male predators and at the time I kept a big nappy pin in my bag or pocket. Sure by now that I was being followed and that my pursuer was up to no good, I held the pin open in my pocket. My suspicion was well-founded for when he thought no-one was watching, he rushed at me exposing himself and grabbed my breast. I raked his offending hand with the pin and ran. I heard him scream but he was nowhere in sight when I reached the end of the street and hailed a passing taxi. I was angry and said aloud, "The dirty swine!" When I told the taxi driver what had happened he suggested I report it to the police but I told him that as a black woman, I expected nothing would be done and, anyway, I had already had my revenge.

Another nasty incident happened when I was on tour in Athens. I decided to leave a party in the centre of town early one evening and walk the quarter-mile to Place de America where we were staying. Two young Greeks approached me and one asked if I was American. I said I was not and ignored them. The men continued to walk in step with me and as we were passing a burnt-out building, one grabbed my arm and his partner went around to my other side. I had no idea what they were saying to each other but I was suddenly conscious of the possibility of rape or robbery. I screamed and dug the tweezers I was holding into the arm of the one who had grabbed me. He hit me on the side of my head and ran off. I hurried home to safety.

It was during this period that I met Nino and we have remained friends although we parted as lovers. He said he fell in love with me at first sight; I fell in love with him gradually. I was in a nightclub with some girlfriends when Nino sent a message with the waiter asking me if I would like a drink. As I spoke neither French nor Italian at that time, the waiter became our translator. Nino was going to Africa for two weeks and asked me to meet him on his return. I was not sure about this and said I would phone him. After agonising about it, I contacted him and our romance began. *La Méditerrané,* a restaurant in the middle of Brussels, became our favourite place. Nino owned a car sales and repair garage specialising in vintage cars and he travelled a lot. He took me to many beautiful places in Holland, Spain, Portugal, France and Italy.

Nino is Italian and what I most remember about him are his beautiful brown eyes and endearing smile. I knew he loved me. He treated me like a princess and showered me with gifts. He was spontaneous and full of fun. We would go for a walk and suddenly he would whisk me off for a romantic evening. It was one of the happier times of my life.

When he introduced me to his mother I knew instinctively that she did not like me. I think she was racist, she found it difficult to even call me by name. She referred to me as "Okay", so Nino would get a message that Okay had called.

When Nino asked me to marry him I was not ready for the big commitment. There was still a lot of hurt in me and I did not want to go down that road again, taking a chance on love, as the song goes. He was devastated by my response but nothing he said could make me change my mind. I was happy with things as they were while he wanted more. To show me that he was serious he rented an apartment for me in Rue Florence in a nice part of Brussels. We then went to Jamaica and my family fell in love with him too; he fitted easily into our Jamaican lifestyle. But I still refused to marry him. Something inside me just would not let go of the fear of another relationship turning sour.

Then he dropped a bombshell. He said he was ready to settle down and have a family; he wanted me to have his child. I had no intention of having any more children and told him so. He would fantasise about how our child would look and went so far as to offer to put in my bank account seven hundred and sixty thousand Belgian francs to meet all my expenses while I was pregnant. I refused to budge and told him, as kindly as I could, that he would have to find someone else to have his child. He grew sad and I could see how hurt he was, but my mind was made up; so we began to drift apart. Then I found out that he was seeing another woman in Switzerland. I was shocked and it was now my turn to be hurt, although things were not so good between us. I moved out of the apartment and went to live in the countryside.

I found out a couple of years later when I was married to Paul that Nino had tried to find me. He wrote letters to me in care of my agent begging me to get in touch so that we could marry and settle down. My agent read them and tore them up. My agent's secretary spilled the beans when they fell out. Today, Nino has a daughter and lives in Switzerland but a special bond remains between us. He rings me often and he never forgets my birthday. He sends me birthday gifts and sometimes surprise gifts. I have not seen him for some time now and know he is not in the best of health. He has wangled a promise out of me that when I am in Europe I will see him before he dies. He tells me that when he is depressed he thinks of me and still chuckles over some of my jokes that made him laugh so long ago.

After my break up with Nino, still hurting from his betrayal, I took a contract to work in Greece and spent a longer time there, toying with the idea of settling there. However, Paul whom I had met in Belgium when I moved from Brussels to the countryside, kept phoning, trying to persuade me to return to Belgium and marry him. He was a non-commissioned officer in the Belgian Army. We were buddies sharing a flat before I left for Greece. I thought about his offer of marriage. He was a nice person and a safe choice as a husband but, don't ask me why, I did not feel the same way about him as I had about Nino. I loved Nino. With Paul it was a kind of companionship which, for some reason, felt safer. For some inexplicable reason I suddenly thought that marriage would provide the stability I felt I needed and would also give me some security as a Belgian resident. A big plus in Paul's favour also was that I liked his mother, who was a lovely woman.

Six weeks after I returned to Belgium, we were married. We had one hundred guests, mainly my friends and acquaintances. Paul's guests were his mother, his brother and his wife, his bank manager, a girlfriend and a male friend from his camp. Our marriage lasted two years. I soon realised that he was not in love with me. He saw me as a means to what he really wanted, which was to live in Jamaica and to build a hotel on a piece of land that he knew I had bought. *Just my luck!*

For some time while I was married to Paul I had been thinking of giving up dancing and having a café or a restaurant. I worked out that the outlay and upkeep for a restaurant was more than that for a café and I didn't want to borrow too much money. As soon as Paul and I separated, I began to look around for such a café. I found one in an ideal location opposite a football stadium. The bank's borrowing rate was high but, lucky for me, I was able to borrow from a business friend at a much lower rate. I intended to sell alcohol, and snacks such as toasted sandwiches, salads and light lunches. I also wanted to have gaming machines. When I applied for a licence from the Commissioner of Police for that area I was turned down. He refused to tell me why and was very dismissive. Roger, my Belgian lawyer friend, who was helping me with the paperwork, saw racism in this and advised me to use the Commissioner in Brussels who was less racist. Once the licence was obtained, Pet and my Flemish friend, Geoff, helped me with the setting up.

The opening night at 'Café Brasil' was a resounding success. Many of our customers had come out of curiosity, among them several other café owners. No doubt they wanted to see what this black woman was up to. We worked our butts off to get everything ready; the spread of sandwiches, spare ribs and snacks on the house looked lavish in their layout. I was ever so nervous but somehow managed the pumps at speed on that busy night. I made quite a profit and felt elated. "Nothing can stop me now!" I thought.

Keeping the place open was far from an easy job for a foreigner and a black woman at that. I was sorely tested but my enemies had no idea who they were tangling with and I came out fighting every time. Erwin, one of the local café owners decided that he would run me out of town. One evening he came into the café and ordered four rounds of drinks without offering to pay. Having served the last round, I asked him to settle his bill.

"Just put down the drink. Don't ask me for money." I took the drinks off the counter and he became abusive. I asked him to leave and his response was to pick up a stool and throw it at me. I ducked and it shattered a mirror behind me. He picked up a second stool and again threw it at me. Horrified, some customers began to run out, others stared aghast at what was happening. The brewery manager from whom I had rented the café went up to him and said, "Erwin, what do you think you're doing?" Erwin grabbed the man and started to strangle him. I ran to the back and got my sharp, long knife, threw a chair at Erwin and, as he doubled over in shock, I stabbed him in the arm.

One of the men with him ran off while the other cowered in a corner. By now they were the only persons left in the café. Sizing up the situation, I ran to the door, locked it and started screaming like a banshee. I was so angry I fully intended to cut Erwin to bits. As he came towards me I blocked him with a chair and started slashing at him with my knife. He ran to the door and, finding it locked, smashed the glass window and scrambled out. Seeing his friend cowering in the corner I ran over and put the knife to his throat. "You bastard!" I hissed. I was so mad that I was beyond considering the consequences.

"Please don't cut my face!" he squealed like a chicken. I moved the knife to his heart and the playboy cried, "You can stick it in my heart but not in my face!" His plea was so farcical. As I looked at the wimp, I felt like laughing at his vanity but by now I was calm and with enough venom in my voice to let him know I was deadly serious, I threatened him and let him go.

Half-an-hour later, Erwin and his friends came back and smashed my place to smithereens.

The brewery manager had called the police but they did not come. I was told by another café owner that the police would not come out after 1.00a.m. and I was also advised that when they interviewed me, I should not own up to drawing blood as that was a very serious offence in Belgium. Erwin complained to the police next day and I was duly questioned. I pointed to the broken window and said that Erwin must have cut himself jumping through it. The police were scared of Erwin and were quite menacing, warning me that they would be back. I had to act and act fast to protect myself. I sent a message to Erwin that I was going to Brussels to see my mafia friends and he had better watch his back because if he came anywhere near my café again, he, his friends and his café wouldn't be around. The threat worked. A year later, a friend of a girlfriend of mine asked, "Olga, do you know Erwin?"

When I said yes, he told me that he had asked Erwin to meet him at Café Brasil and Erwin had asked, "Is that black woman still there?" When he heard that I was, he said, "No way." I never set eyes on him again.

Another incident that left a nasty taste in my mouth involved another racist Belgian. He came in with a friend who was a regular and said, "Good evening," in Flemish as he ordered drinks. I answered him in English. He ordered more drinks and, sitting there in front of me, began to make derogatory comments about black women. He boasted that in Africa he could have several black women for only one hundred dollars and that we were all stupid and, moreover, we stank. People nearby were uncomfortable and looked at him in amazement. His friend kept saying to him, "Come on, stop it. Don't keep insulting the woman."

"She doesn't understand anyway. They are stupid I tell you. Imagine living in a Flemish area and she can't even speak Flemish!" The insults went on for a while. I wanted to hear what he had to say so I bided my time before giving him a piece of my mind. He ordered a third round of drinks.

"No," I said in English, "I want you to leave now." Of course since he didn't speak English, he ordered again in Flemish.

"So black women stink, eh?" I spoke in Flemish. I cursed him good and proper and, opening the door, shouted, "Now get out of my café!" to the cheers of the other customers.

"You told me she didn't speak Flemish," he stuttered, turning shamefaced and angry to his friend as they left.

"I didn't. I said she spoke English."

As a black person, I had to deal with harassment by the racist Belgian police nearly every day until I took a stand. They would wait until the café was busy then come in to check that all the customers had the correct identification cards. This frightened those who did not like to have a run-in with the police, and who were scared of being harassed. I began to lose customers when it became known that the café was getting regular police checks. Some customers thought that there must be a link with drugs for this to be happening. Fortunately for me, I was tipped off by a relative of the police informant. Can you believe that this informant was a local café owner with whom I was quite friendly? She visited my café regularly and we met socially over dinner. She had informed the police that the reason my café was so popular was that I drugged the beer. Of course this was impossible because the beer came in sealed, pressurised vats but the stupid police believed her.

Armed with this piece of information, I made ready for the next police visit. Two of them came in, officious as usual, but before they could approach a customer, I tackled them. "If you check one ID tonight, I will complain to your Commissioner. I will tell him you are harassing me for a bribe." I said loudly. They stopped in their tracks, stared at me and left. That did the trick.

However, the harassment only shifted from the café to the street. I was an easy target, being the only black person living in Lebbeke. When I first moved there, people would stand and stare at me as if I were an animal in a zoo. It was horrible! Then when the police started to harass me it became almost intolerable but I had to get on with living. I was not going to let the buggers feel they were winning.

Yet amidst all the harassment there were some light moments. There were some really nice Belgians. Two were regular customers whom I had nicknamed "Lucky Luke" and "Crazy Luke". We had many good laughs and they were very helpful to me. When I couldn't manage the changing of the pumps they did it. In return, I would cook something special for them and for Crazy Luke's wife. On one of my birthdays, I closed early and the Lukes and I decided to go to 'The Barn', a nightclub with straw on the floor and beams, but then I changed my mind, wanting to go somewhere different. I settled on an upmarket club to which both Lukes kept telling me we would not be admitted. They bet me one hundred francs that we couldn't do it and I surprised them by betting them one thousand francs that we would. I told them to follow my lead. We strolled up to the door and, in a perfect American accent, I said to the bouncers, "Good evening," to which they politely replied: "Good evening, Madam." I then waved in the direction of the Lukes, "These are my bodyguards." The guys joined in the escapade and when we were let in, they sat stiffly near me, keeping an eye on other patrons while I enjoyed my night out. "Now you can bugger off, I no longer need your service as my bodyguards," I laughingly dismissed them when they took me home. But they had the last laugh; they unceremoniously dumped me in the wheelie bin and left.

My mother's update on the children was becoming a growing concern. She was feeling physically overburdened and thought I should have them back in Europe. They were all now in high school and when I checked out the Belgian education system, I found that the children would need to learn French and Flemish before they could benefit from mainstream education. Private tuition would be extremely expensive. The two older ones would also be too old for a state school, which would mean paying privately for them to complete secondary education. The whole thing was a nightmare; if I wanted to stay in Belgium my only other option was to board them with a family or families in England as I did not want to interrupt their academic progress. I missed the children and did not want to board them in England so I decided it would be better for us all to move back to England. I was not sure I could find work that would bring in as much as I was then earning; as the sole breadwinner, this was a real worry. But once I'd made the decision I began planning the move.

After twelve years in Belgium I left.

Back In England

January 1985, and here I was again back in England. It was a big upheaval selling the contents of the café and shipping my household goods to Nottingham. With no home in England, I stayed with my friend, Edna, for three months and applied for a Council property. As soon as I got a maisonette, I sent for the boys who joined me that August. Seventeen-year-old Michael went to Bilborough College to do his G.C.E. and Kevin, at sixteen, entered a Youth Training Scheme to learn carpentry. Early the following year Tina, who was fourteen and twelve-year-old Gaynor joined us and they went to my old school in our area. It was no longer Cottesmore Secondary Modern School but renamed Sandfield. Had it changed? Not much. Its reputation as a racist school persisted.

The Nottingham Connection

I now had all my children with me except Charmaine, whom I still could not locate in Africa. There was always a painful emptiness when I thought about her - and that was every day. My family was just not complete without her.

Adjusting to our new relationship proved none too easy for me and the children. I was no longer the fun-to-be-with person who, when visiting in Jamaica, got restrictions lifted. I was also under a lot of stress as a single mother trying to settle them back into England and also having to find a job. Michael and Tina were easy to manage but Kevin and Gaynor were rebellious.

I got a job at Marcus Garvey, the African/Caribbean centre, working in the daycentre facility as an assistant to the elderly. When a better paying job in the kitchen at Hyson Green Boys' Club came up, I applied for it. One of the interviewers said I was overqualified for the job of a canteen worker. I thought, why on earth did they think I'd applied for it? Looking directly at him I simply said, "I have applied for this job because I need to work and I know I can do it." My honesty paid off and I was given the job.

As I became familiar with the young people using the facility I began to take an interest in what was happening at the club. The youth workers, seeing this, asked if I would like to do a couple of sessions with the youngsters. So began my career in youth work. Twice a week I worked from 7:00 a.m. to 3:00 p.m. in the kitchen and then from 7:00 to 10:00 p.m. with the youngsters. After two years I was given an extra youth work session.

At this time the canteen was about to close and I was approached to run it on a self-employed basis. Knowing that I could make it a profitable business, I accepted. I put a lot of thought and energy into it and it paid off. My lunches were so popular that, in no time at all, people came from all over town to eat there; on average ninety a day.

As often happens, there's always someone who tries to make another's life difficult. I did not get on with a senior youth worker who was no good at management and, under whose watch, food was often taken away without being recorded. I realised I had to do something about this and tightened up the management of stock. The worker in question was angry, feeling that I had put his nose out of joint and so he decided to get me out of the canteen. He complained to the Management Committee and to the Director of Youth Services that I was obstructive. The Management Committee gave me an ultimatum; I was to choose between the canteen and my youth work sessions.

I thought, "Right, if you want me to choose that's not a problem for me. We'll see what happens to the canteen when I leave." I was peeved that the daily rent at the end of my first year of running the canteen had gone up from fifteen pounds to twenty, on top of which I had to pay fifty pounds a week to each of the two staff members. The youth work session was not very well paid, only twenty-one pounds per session but I enjoyed the work, so I gave up the canteen.

A delegation of black and white youth workers tried to convince me not to give up the canteen because the youth club was buzzing since I had taken it over. One of them said, "Olga, you're doing a disservice to the community." My response was, "It's the community that's doing a disservice to me." I was angry as I knew that the canteen would more than likely have to close. A short time after, it did.

While still at the canteen, Sylvie, an acquaintance from my teenage years when we were learning African dance, came in for lunch. "Olga," she said, "that meal was wonderful. Do you do private catering?"

"Not really," I replied, "just for the occasional function and usually only for someone I know."

"County Council is putting on a training day at the Meadows Community Centre. Why don't you put in a tender for the catering?"

"What's my chance of getting it?"

"Good, but remember you have to cater for vegetarians."

This was a golden opportunity not to be missed. Sylvie was most helpful, filling me in about price range and types of menu for such an event. After a lot of research on vegetarian meals, I put in my tender. I got the job and didn't I do a superb selection of vegetarian food! This included lasagne with calalloo, calalloo rundown - that is calalloo cooked in coconut milk - escovitch fish, Jamaican ackee and salt fish, Jamaican rice and peas, onion bhajis and samosas. So many people came and thanked me for a wonderful meal that it quite made my day.

With that first good impression, setting up my own business proved easier than I had expected. It was very hard work, partly because I was loath to give up my youth work sessions which I enjoyed and which I knew provided a useful service to the community. Many days I ate on the run and some nights, too tired to climb the stairs, I fell asleep on the settee. I tried always to give excellent service and sometimes found clients were willing to pay more than I had intended to ask. One such instance was in 1994 when I was asked by the local Task Force to put on a buffet for fifty dignitaries including a government minister and twenty youngsters. I found out that what I had intended to ask was two-thirds the figure they had budgeted for, so I increased my quotation but ensured they had a sumptuous lunch and were well satisfied with my service. The Nottingham Evening Post carried an article on my catering business and I was interviewed on B.B.C. Radio Nottingham about my international cuisine. The business took off and, as it expanded, I decided to go into partnership with a friend. We provided an excellent service at a reasonable cost. Our clientele increased. I remember vividly our biggest wedding when we catered for three hundred and twenty-five people. By this time I was making the cakes too!

While in Belgium I had become competent in making cakes but not in decorating them. My daughter, Tina, proved very helpful in decorating the cakes for children's parties, simple decorations that she had learnt from my mother who was an expert. When I saw an advert for a twelve-week cake decorating course to be held at ACNA, the local African Caribbean Centre in the St Anns area, I promptly enrolled. It was an excellent beginner's course. The instructor encouraged me to go on to the advanced level at Arnold and Carlton College as she said I had a flair for decorating and a willingness to experiment. It took me four years part-time to complete this course which I thoroughly enjoyed. In the first year I won first prize for my Christmas cake decorated with the Three Wise Men bringing gifts. After this big boost, I never looked back.

I began to develop the art of making cakes of interesting shapes. I soon became expert at it and developed my portfolio so that this side of the business took off in a big way. Minnie Mouse and Mickey Mouse were the children's favourites. Another popular one was the Jamaican Independence Day cake decorated with the flag, the ackee, our national fruit, and the hummingbird, our national bird. Couples getting married loved my design of a bride and groom with bridesmaids and groomsmen coming out of a church. One of my wedding cakes was shown on the BBC's Panorama programme. It was for an English/Caribbean wedding, and I designed it with a white bride and a black groom. Always aware of the less fortunate, each year I would donate a cake to the Save the Children Fund to be raffled. The cake was a yellow teddy with a polka dot eye patch. My favourite design to date is the replica of an African couple I once saw. In the design they are wearing white robes with gold trimmings and golden slippers; he wears a skullcap and she a magnificent head wrap and gold earrings.

"Olga, are you racist?" Mrs Leigh, my cake decorating instructor, once asked me as she admired one of my cakes.

"Why?" I asked, quite taken aback.

"You only put black people in your decorations."

"Mrs. Leigh, are you racist?"

"Me? No. You know my husband is black."

"Well, if you're not, why are your cakes only decorated with white people?" We had a good laugh.

I continued with the catering as well as my youth work until one month before I left England to return to Jamaica. I actually did ten years of youth work during which time I attended several courses to give myself the necessary skills. In the early years I went on an Arts and Craft course and later a Counselling course run by the local council. After six years with the service I was doing four sessions a week. I did a Leader-in-Charge course as well as one on Conflict Resolution. The hardest part of my job as a youth worker was working with people who were clock watchers and those who had very little imagination. Often I had to do extra hours because some workers had not done their allocated tasks according to what had been agreed for our summer programme. I was often thrown out of the building by the caretaker at 11.00p.m.

I guess I was not your average youth worker. I did not always follow rules that I knew left children bored and restless or disruptive. For instance, when they did not bring their deposit to use the equipment I would take from them things I knew they would be anxious to retrieve, a watch or an expensive cap, until they brought the money. It did not make sense to me to follow the rule that stopped them participating, for this would leave them idling and provide opportunities for them to do something silly.

We had about forty youngsters on each programme. I loved working with them, black and white, the well-behaved and the difficult. I found it very rewarding when they got a lot of pleasure from doing something positive. Our summer programme included African dancing and drumming which the youngsters loved. We also took part in the Nottingham Carnival each year. I was coordinator for our carnival float. We were ecstatic the first year we entered and won the first prize. Ann Kimuyu and I designed the costumes and the children worked with us to make them. Our float was a colourful sea scene of mermaids, King Neptune, fishes and seaweed.

Since leaving, I miss the youngsters a lot. It was a joy working with them and seeing them getting some fun out of life, as many of them were, like my daughters, living a nightmare in their schools.

It may be difficult to believe, but throughout my daughters' time in school they faced similar problems of racism to those that I had faced twenty years earlier. Gaynor was a difficult child but school only made her more rebellious and anti-authority. Tina, on the other hand, was a hardworking and conscientious student but this made no difference as she was held back and not given the chance to achieve like the white children in her year group. I had to make my presence felt in Sandfield Comprehensive School or my girls would have given up trying altogether. A few examples highlight the struggle we had.

Gaynor was suspended just before the end of year exams which decided the subjects she could take and at what level. When I contacted the school the form teacher claimed he was too busy to see me and the headmaster was unavailable. I, therefore, took things into my own hands and investigated the incident leading to the suspension. I spoke to the girls who had been present and then walked one mile to an Asian boy's home to verify their story. What he told me he had witnessed tallied with the girls' report. I then went up to the school and entered Gaynor's form room at registration. The form teacher tried to brush me off, asking me to make an appointment, but I would not budge.

"You are too busy to see me but I am not leaving until my daughter is reinstated. Why haven't you suspended the other girls involved? And why is school taking action for an incident that happened off the school premises?" I raised my voice so the children could hear.

"It did happen on school premises." He was uncomfortable and became defensive.

"You are a liar!" I eyeballed him.

"Are you calling me a liar?"

"Yes. And I want the children to hear because I have checked what happened and know you are lying. Why are you punishing my child so that she misses her exams?"

He was so embarrassed to have the children watching all this that he asked me to come with him to the headmaster's office. At the time the school had a black Section X1 teacher to help the school and parents resolve concerns; I asked for her to be present. A white Section X1 teacher came instead. I knew the form teacher was going to try to browbeat me and was seeking help to do so, and I flatly refused to have that teacher. An Asian teacher replaced her and we began to discuss the matter. I had found out that two afternoons before an Asian girl and a white girl had attacked Gaynor in the park hitting her with an electric flex. The next afternoon Gaynor found the flex and belted them back with it. The Asian teacher agreed with me that Gaynor's suspension should not interfere with her exams and in the end Gaynor was permitted to return to school the next day.

Tina's experience at the school was also fraught with trouble. Once she complained to me that the Home Economics teacher had not given her a text book when books were handed out. There were not enough books to begin with but when the teacher brought in additional ones, Tina was again left out while a white child who had mislaid hers, was given a second copy. I sent a message asking for an appointment and when I expressed my concern the teacher's response was, "Well, you know Tina can be difficult at times."

"What's that got to do with it?" I couldn't believe what I was hearing. She went on to tell me that Tina had come in halfway through the syllabus and had finished ahead of the class and she didn't know what to do with Tina because she was "restive".

This same woman one year later did not want to put Tina in for the exam on the grounds that she was not ready! I told her then that I had worked hard and wasn't expecting a hand-out and I would pay for the exam. My daughter got an 'A' grade in the subject, no thanks to her teacher who did not want to enter her for it. My daughter who had to fight against being put down by teachers, now has a B.A. from Aston University and a M.A. from the University of Nottingham. The sad thing is that her story is the norm for the majority of black children who eventually get to university — they get there despite the racism in the school system.

Some teachers were insensitive but, thank God, big enough to accept when they made mistakes. The Asian teacher who called Gaynor a cow fits into this category. Gaynor was caught throwing a paper missile in class and, when rebuked, had been rude. The teacher told her that he had heard about her bad reputation and called her a cow. Knowing how the school operated a system to frustrate parents who had a complaint against a member of the staff, I decided that I was not going to be fobbed off by the school secretary, so I went up to see the teacher without an appointment. I stood just inside the classroom and asked to speak with him. He explained what had happened and agreed with me that what he had said was quite out of order. I pointed out that his apology should be made in front of the class as that was how he had humiliated Gaynor. He called Gaynor to the front of the class and apologised. With a big grin Gaynor went back to her seat. Her grin disappeared when I said, "Gaynor, you will now come up and apologise to your teacher for misbehaving in his class."

"But Mom . . ."

"No buts. Now, please!" She knew I meant it and she did the right thing. I did not for one moment condone Gaynor's bad behaviour and was prepared to work with the school but that school still had a high percentage of racist staff members who were not fit to be teachers, especially in a school with a fair number of black children. As one listens to black children, in particular boys, talk about their school life one learns that they come in for a rough time with teachers some of whom, through sheer ignorance, are afraid of black people. This is not so much the case for Asian children whom most teachers consider less noisy and less lippy.

Black people have suffered, and are still suffering, some terrible racial abuse but do you hear about it in the media? Hardly ever. One horrific racial incident that two of my daughters and I experienced happened when we were on holiday in Germany in 1986. Travelling from Berlin to Brussels by train, we went into a first class compartment because the train was quite full. I asked for my tickets to be upgraded, as is the custom, and the conductor gave me a receipt which showed less than the amount of money he had taken, intending, no doubt, to pocket the difference. When I pointed it out, he became abusive and grabbed back the receipt calling me "a black swine" in German. I responded in German that he was "a thieving white bastard". When the train stopped at the next station he and two railway policemen came into the carriage and ordered us off the train. I was told by one of the policemen that I had verbally assaulted the conductor. They refused to hear my complaint and began to manhandle us. We were subjected to more racial abuse as we were dragged off the train. I did not go willingly and struggled with them. On the platform one of the policemen handcuffed me while the other telephoned for the state police. I whacked him hard with the handcuffs and he backed off. When the police arrived we were taken to jail and my daughters and I were put in a room to await a magistrate. The charge against me was verbal and physical assault of the railway staff.

After being in that room for eight hours without anyone seeing us, I began to yell and we banged on the door making a horrendous noise until someone came. I was taken before a magistrate who heard both sides of the story. I showed him my bruises and asked if it was right for my two frightened children to be subjected to racial abuse and then to be locked in a cell for so long. I could tell that the magistrate was not convinced of the truth of the statements of the railway policemen who wanted me fined. In the end the magistrate ordered our release, the return of our passports and transport to take us back to the railway station. I was relieved but quite distraught and having decided not to continue with the planned trip, we returned to England.

My generation and my father's generation of African-Caribbean people living in England belonged to a close-knit community who depended on each other for comfort when there was trouble or a death in the family. When we were going to or coming from the Caribbean, people gave us gifts to take to their families; we saw this as a part of our community duty to help each other. So, when I was approached by someone the community considered an 'upright citizen' to bring back a parcel from Jamaica I thought nothing of it until he offered me ten thousand pounds. The penny dropped. "Je-sus!" I nearly jumped out of my skin. "A what sort a parcel that?" I could not believe it when he admitted it was illegal drugs that I would be given in Jamaica. I was offended and cheekily said to him, "What happen to your wife? Let her carry it, she's travelling too."

"She too nervous, man. Them would stop her and she'd be found out."

"So what about me being caught?"

"That's not likely. But if the worst comes to the worst, we'd look after your family."

"I've looked after myself since I was fourteen years old. I don't need you or anybody else to take care of me or my family." I was incensed at the cheek of the man thinking I could be bribed. Did he really think I was so greedy or stupid? He must have been desperate because he persisted.

"You live in a Council house . . ."

"So?" I interrupted.

"I tell you what, we could make the deal twenty-five thousand . . ."

"I live in a Council house, but I have a house in Jamaica. I don't need your money. So tell you what, find another mug!"

I cannot find words to express the joy I felt when I was finally reunited with my daughter who had been taken to Africa by her father when she was only eleven months old. My hopes had been raised with a phone call from her father when she would have been twelve. Justus was in Holland and asked me to meet him at the Holiday Inn in Antwerp to discuss our children. I was married at the time and living in Belgium. During the four hours of travel to meet Justus I devised all sorts of arguments to get him to return my daughter to me. When I arrived it was obvious that he had no such intention. He said that he had brought her to see me on an earlier occasion but I was in Jamaica. He also said that he was arranging for me to get one thousand pounds for the other children but it would not be ready until the next day. To this day I cannot believe what he suggested next. That man had the cheek to ask me to spend the night with him! What an insult. I felt so incensed I just started to curse him, warning him that when I returned the next day I would not be prepared to be messed about. He got the message. The next day I got the money, was promised regular support and assured that I would hear from him about Charmaine's return. That was the last I heard from Justus. The financial support never materialised, but somehow that did not surprise me. However, the pain of not having Charmaine with me became even more acute when my other children rejoined me in England.

A few years later, in 1988, a Sierra Leonian I knew asked me if I could give a holiday job to a young woman. I took Dora on for three days a week in the canteen and she quickly settled into the job. She was likeable and I enjoyed her company. One day I was feeling very low and told her about my daughter whom I had not seen for seventeen years. I mentioned that the last news I had had was that her stepmother, who was a radio journalist, had left Justus and gone to Sierra Leone; I said I was not sure what had happened to my daughter and her half-brother also from England. Dora's eyes lit up with excitement when I mentioned their surname and told me she knew of such a woman with two children.

"Olga, I know this family but the girl's name is not Charmaine. It is Henrietta. We went to the same girls' school!"

"Can't be, then," I said, "my daughter's name is Charmaine." Yet even as I spoke, a little flutter of hope stirred in my heart. Dora promised to find out more from a friend of Henrietta who was in London. Hope surged within my breast. True to her promise, Dora located Henrietta's friend and Dora and I went to London that weekend to check out the identity of Dora's Henrietta.

Dora telephoned Henrietta's friend who became deliberately unhelpful once it was apparent that Henrietta was indeed my Charmaine. I took the phone from Dora and appealed to the young lady asking her to just give me Henrietta's address. There was a pause and then I heard my daughter's voice - *a voice I did not know*. My heart was beating so hard I had to take deep breaths. I don't know how it came out but I told her I loved her and had been searching for her for seventeen years and had never given up hope of finding her. Her responses were very wary and I had to plead with her to meet me that weekend. She tentatively agreed to ring me to let me know her decision. I could not think straight for the rest of that Saturday and did not sleep a wink that night. I prayed as I'd never prayed before that she would agree to see me.

Henrietta telephoned the Sunday morning and came to see me. When I saw my beautiful daughter, tall and graceful like her sister, Tina, I hugged her to me and my heart's crying for the years we had lost was staunched. She, however, remained very distant, almost cold.

I was nervous and scared that she would not believe me as we talked and she filled in some of the gaps of her life without me. Until she was thirteen she had not been aware that Joyeaux, Justus' wife, was not her mother. She had found out when she had an argument with a woman in the yard who had told her, "Your mother didn't want you." When she had confronted Joyeaux about it, she had said the woman was talking rubbish. However, she discovered the truth later. Joyeaux after they had had another row, had snapped in anger and had screamed at her, "Your mother is Jamaican and abandoned you like she abandoned her other six children on the street!" Deeply wounded, Henrietta had hidden the hurt she felt. Nothing else was ever said on the subject but she had never felt the same again. She began to feel she did not belong. At sixteen she had been sent to England and had lived in London for two years. The first family she had lived with had treated her like a skivvy and had taken away her passport. She had left them and was then finding it financially difficult to manage while studying. When she arrived in England, one of the first things she had done was to go to Somerset House to find out about her mother. She found a Charmaine with her date of birth and her father's name, but no Henrietta. This puzzled her for a while and then she realised that her name must have been changed when she was in Nigeria.

I told her how she had been taken from me and the pain that was always there because I could not get her back. I filled my daughter in about the family she had never met and how much she looked like her sister, Tina. She did not show much enthusiasm about her family here in England except that she wanted to meet Tina. I did not want to let her out of my sight again but had to accept that it would probably take some time for her to accept me as her mother. My emotions were in turmoil. Before we said goodbye, I gave her some money and told her I would help her financially. As I hugged her again, I promised I would always stay in touch with her. I was overjoyed but also apprehensive. I could not bear to lose my daughter again.

But broken fences do not mend easily and reconciliation has taken years. Sometimes in those early days, I felt such pain when I realised that my daughter did not see me as her mother. For instance, when she was planning her wedding she mentioned to Tina that her mother would be paying for her white and gold wedding. Tina innocently asked, "You've checked with Mom then?" The response was, "Not her, my mother in Sierra Leone." Another sad moment for me was that I did not see my daughter get married. She was by then living in U.S.A. and got married there.

I am so proud of her, with all the trauma in her life she was able to obtain a Bachelor degree from Bristol University, win a scholarship to the London School of Economics where she obtained her Master's and is now the proud mother of two children. The mother/daughter bond has strengthened over the years and Henrietta is again part of the family.

My family has had its ups and downs. Gaynor has caused me much pain over the years. As a teenager counselling did not help, partly because she would not attend the sessions regularly. Friends who have tried to help her to be more responsible have also failed. In the past my blood pressure rocketed as a direct result of the stress she caused me. I ended up in the hospital and had my wake-up call. Today, I have accepted that only Gaynor can sort out herself. She can be so charming and funny it is difficult to remain angry with her. I just keep praying that she will settle down which she seems to be doing. Kevin left home at seventeen. He wanted to be his own man, doing as he pleased. Michael now works as a prison officer. Tina is married with two children and works in the local Land Registry. We keep in contact and accept each other for what we are, warts and all.

In 1997 returning by train from London, I made a decision to agree to a divorce. In Belgium I had been deeply hurt to discover that Paul was having an affair with one of my Belgian girlfriends. I had asked him for an amicable divorce before leaving Belgium but he wanted me to disclose all my assets, claiming that under Belgian law he was entitled to half of whatever I possessed. Later, when he wanted to marry his girlfriend, he began divorce proceedings but I refused to play ball because he was trying to sully my reputation. I returned the divorce papers to him. On the envelope in which the papers had come to Nottingham I wrote him this message: "Kiss my black arse". Things were left hanging after that until one evening in 1997. On the train coming from London I was reflecting on my life. I realised that it was time to have closure on that chapter of my life with Paul. I still had no intention of agreeing to give him anything that I had worked for, but I wanted my life to be truly free of him. I decided then and there that the following day I would contact my lawyer friend in Belgium to start the ball rolling.

I walked into my house and checked my phone messages. One was an urgent message asking me to ring a friend in London who had important news for me from Belgium. When I rang she told me that Paul had been pruning an apple tree when he fell out of the tree, broke his neck and died. A few days later, his lover who was in hospital also died of cancer. Unbelievable! I rang my Belgian lawyer for advice. Later that week he advised me to go to Belgium to see Paul's lawyer. It transpired that Paul's daughter had tried to get all his assets by claiming that no-one knew where I was. She was quite put out when I turned up. She tried very hard to stop me from inheriting anything but in the end she was thwarted by the law. I felt it was only right for her to have a share of whatever her father had left and so I shared it with her. I was quite happy with the army widow's pension I would receive as long as I did not remarry.

I firmly believed then that God had smiled on me and answered my prayer to get back to Jamaica to look after my parents. Christmas of 1996, I had visited my parents and was concerned at how frail they both were. I had said to my mother that I was going to try to get back to Jamaica as soon as possible to take care of them. When she did not argue that was a sure sign to me that she was not feeling well enough to cope. At the time, I had no idea how I would accomplish this; the money I earned was from my catering business and if I left Nottingham that source would dry up. "What to do?" was the question I asked myself over and over. At night I prayed for a path forward. Suddenly, here it was, in a way I could never have dreamt of. With the pension I was to receive I could go home and look after my parents and, with careful handling of my finances, I would manage. What joy I felt as the pieces fell into place and I saw that I had all I needed for the future!

Back in England I began planning my return to Jamaica, winding up my business affairs and resigning as a youth worker at the Boys' Club.

That December, after thirty-two years of my life as an immigrant in Europe, I left England to return home.

JAMAICA

Returned Resident

After so many years living abroad, I was glad to be home to look after Mama and Daddy and, although I had only two years with them, they were years I will always treasure. I watched them eat the meals I prepared; I combed my mother's hair; we shared jokes and participated in the Sabbath eve's family service on Fridays. Just being there for them in their hour of need when they could no longer help themselves was a joy to me. But it was not always easy caring for them.

Daddy was easier than Mama, he never complained although I could see how much pain he was in. He would close his eyes and his ebony face would take on an ashy shade. He was suffering from prostate cancer and there was nothing the doctors could do to help him except to give him painkillers that worked only some of the time. Mama fussed a lot. Sometimes she drove me to distraction and I wanted to scream because nothing I did for her was good enough. In the beginning she was able to do things around the house and take care of her personal hygiene but her health deteriorated rapidly as the fluid increased around her heart and, as she became more and more dependent, her personality changed to one of almost non-stop complaining. Many afternoons I ended up in the gazebo for a moment's reprieve. I would wake up an hour or so later having fallen asleep from exhaustion, soothed by the sound of the sea. It was also a financially draining period. The doctor's visits cost an arm and a leg because my parents had no health insurance to help with such expenses. My health too was suffering; my blood pressure sky-rocketed and I had to watch that my diabetes did not get out of control. So I took my tablets and laughed away my fears. What else was there to do?

I don't know what I would have done without our two faithful helpers, Miss Romey and Miss Lucille. They were in my parents' age group and had come to work with them when my children were in Jamaica. Both lived in the neighbourhood and stayed in touch with my parents even after the children came to me in England. They came back to work for us when my parents began to lose their mobility and my sister and I needed help to take care of them. When my parents were totally incapacitated in the last six months of their lives, these two old ladies helped with spoon-feeding, bed baths, turning them over to avoid bedsores and the toileting which became our routine. All this they did without ever a moan.

My garden was my refuge during the difficult days. When I weeded or tended my flowers I grew relaxed and it was as though a load had been lifted from my shoulders. I also found peace sitting in the gazebo at the end of the garden, perched on the cliff overlooking the sea. I thanked God that I had built the gazebo as a quiet nook and refuge from the day-to-day activities. When I decided to tile the floor myself the men working on it were quite amused. The laugh was on them! I bought bags of broken tiles from the wholesalers, did my 'crazy paving' and was very proud of the end product.

In March 2000 I had to go to England to sort out some business. While there I planned to buy things for my parents, and the thought never entered my head that I would not see them again. When I received the phone call from my sister, I shouted to my daughter, "Tina! Tina!" As she hurried into the room, she knew even before I spoke. My desolate look said it all. I felt indescribably sad that I was not there at the end. It had come so suddenly that I was not mentally prepared. I felt that my place was with my sister, Hazel, who was now faced with all the funeral arrangements.

I knew that Daddy was not going to last too long, he had always said he did not want to live when his wife died. "Poor Daddy," I thought, "he will just pine away." Even so, I did not expect how soon he, too, would be gone. Within days of the phone call about Mama, I had another telling me that Daddy had followed her. He had been granted his wish or, as the talk in the district went, he had willed himself to die and be with her in death as in life. Hazel told me that he had refused to eat after Mama died. When she tried to coax him, he would smile and say, "I'm alright. I'm fed by the angels." *Bless him!* He was a quietly caring man who had made my mother very happy. They were buried together, side by side.

We didn't have the usual '*nine night*'. I don't believe in it anyway, and I wanted only peace and quiet. I wanted to remember the happy times spent with Mama and Daddy and talk about them with my family. Hazel felt the same. By the time we had the funeral I had come to accept that their deaths were for the best; that it was a release from their suffering. I like to think that their love was so strong that not even death could separate them!

Many months after they died it was as if they were still around. I would walk onto the veranda and see them sitting facing each other, she on the veranda and he in the car port that we had converted to a second veranda. I remember how they used to *run joke* with each other when they were not feeling too ill. One thing my friends and I still remember when we talk about him is that it did not matter how much Daddy enjoyed a meal cooked by anyone he would always praise his wife's cooking as he paid the compliment. "This is nearly as nice as my wife's cooking," was one we heard all the time. It was a joke among our family, as well as with friends, and we would often say it for him when we knew he was going to say it. He would simply laugh and tell us it was good that we knew. It was so nice to hear how their first thought was for each other's welfare. The way they were is how I would like to be with someone as I grow old. The house felt empty without them for a long time and Hazel and I still miss them terribly.

The pace of my life has changed beyond recognition. I am healthier and happier than I have ever been as an adult. I am up by 6:00 in the morning and, before having children in the house, I would potter about in my garden until the sun got hot and it was time to go in for breakfast about 9:00. I have learnt so much about gardening in the last three years, about such things as colour coordination and textures in designing beds, as well as the care of plants. I love to sit in the gazebo and admire my garden and then turn from it to breathe in the beauty of the sea below. I consider myself fortunate to be surrounded by such beauty. When people visit, they rave about my little Eden atop the cliff with views of beautiful sunrises and sunsets. However, I live a very simple life.

I sew cushions and curtains, paint the house inside and out and help Miss Romey and Miss Lucille with the cleaning. They are my extended family and I care for them as such. We don't really need their services to wash and clean but we appreciate the fact that it gives them dignity to work for their wages which allow them enough to live well. I make sure to cook them a good meal when they are with me. Miss Romey is a *dress puss*, and sometimes I have to tell her that the money I give her is for necessities, not clothes. Miss Lucille is a darling. I know I can depend on her to be there whether or not I have money to give her.

Some 'returned residents', as we are dubbed, find it difficult to adjust to a society that has changed and is certainly very different from that of England and North America where we have spent most of our adult years. My re-entry was painless; it did not take me long to settle in. Visiting regularly over the years, I had made it my business to know the people in the district and to be polite and helpful, so they do not see me as an outsider but as one of them.

As soon as I felt settled I wanted to be involved with helping young people and when I heard about the local Botany Bay Hill Football Club I got involved. I fundraised in Jamaica and when I went to England I managed to get Leicester City Football Club to donate kits for fifteen players and two goalkeepers. The club did well for a while and then problems developed among management members as to how to manage. After a couple of years hanging in there to keep things going for the youngsters, I realised that much would not be achieved because of the disorganised ways of the management committee and that I could not influence change as I sought to. I bowed out gracefully.

After my parents died I suddenly had a lot of time on my hands. Not wanting to sit living an idle life, I looked around for a voluntary group to join. I am now a member of the Yallahs Returned Residents' Association and when I was the Activities Coordinator I was kept busy helping with the organising of events to raise funds for various charities in Jamaica. We have a lot of fun together and, as most of us share a common history as immigrants in England, we often recall some of the hardships we faced which, looking back, seem almost unbelievable compared to the present world of our children who have job choices and who can now have homes in places where we could not even go into the pub for a drink.

I joined the local branch of the National Council for Senior Citizens as a volunteer. It is a far more active group than the Returned Residents' Association. I like it very much because its members are local people from all walks of life and I think it's good to be a part of the wider community, not just a member of the returned residents' group. The Senior Citizens are active in many areas: art and craft, culinary skills, horticulture including floral arrangement and vegetable gardening. Our group has several volunteers who devote time to leading sessions in their areas of expertise. I teach cake decorating and, because of the interest it generated in the media, now run a class for those who want to do it professionally. I am forever being advised to charge a fee for my services but I won't until I am really broke. How's that?

I have continued to fundraise for Jamaica National Children's Home (JNCH) since being introduced to its work in 1996. My sister, Hazel, was also persuaded to work for JNCH. Hazel and I gave the staff and children a treat at Christmas in 2000. We prepared the Christmas breakfast and dinner using funds I had raised in the course of that year from donations given by friends in England and those who visited me here. We had three entertainers for the after-dinner concert and had to do all the transporting. But a great time was had by all and it was a *'wicked'* concert, as the kids would say. When it was all over, I was fit to drop but the effort was well worth while. I shall continue to do something like that every year.

Hazel, while she was the supervisor, would tell me what was needed in the Home. Between us we gave what we could and fundraised by begging food from the big shops in Morant Bay and from anyone that we thought could help.

Before Hazel went to JNCH we fell in love with one of the nine-year-old girls there and wanted to adopt her, or foster her if adoption was not possible. We were dissuaded from this course of action because the girl's family did not indicate it as an option, but we were encouraged to be mentors, and we take her for weekends and holidays and offer whatever support we can towards her upbringing. We have watched her grow into a lovely, bright young lady who won a place at Campion, a prestigious Kingston high school. We are hoping she will continue to do well.

There is another teenager who stays a lot with us because she and her parents live in such a poor condition, with barely a roof over their heads in one room and sometimes having to go hungry. The mother works when she can get jobs. The father is severely disabled as a result of an accident he had whilst driving a truck. It is quite impossible for him to find work now and there is little help from the government. I do what I can, providing weekly groceries for them and helping the girl with things for school. She now practically lives with us at the week-ends.

One little girl of six claimed my home as hers in 2001 when my sister went abroad to live and I was alone in the house. This child is very bright and a pleasure to have around. She's like a dainty flower. Her father, an AIDS victim, had died. Her mother, also an AIDS victim, wanted me to foster her child when she died. The situation was so sad as the mother went downhill fast and her two children, my little friend and her older brother, suffered from the stigma. The adverts to stop the stigma attached to this illness have very little effect on the children and parents in this area. I helped as much as I could with food and clothing as well as seeing to it that the mother got her treatment. I also made a statement to the community by having the children in my home.

Well, the mother died and the grandmother said she could not take care of them. The Children's Services knowing of my involvement asked me to foster the little girl. It was done formally through the court. I will never forget that day as long as I live. Everything went smoothly with the little girl. She told the judge she wanted to live with 'Aunty Olga'. She came and sat next to me, her head resting on me. Then it was her brother's turn to be placed in a boys' home. He refused to go with the children's officer, ran to me, threw his arms around my neck and would not let go. He kept crying out, "I want to go with Aunty Olga. I want to go with Aunty Olga . . ." I didn't know what to do. I whispered to him that he could come and see us every week. He still wouldn't let go. Then he started pleading, "Please Aunty Olga! Please! Please! . . ." I begged him to stop and told him we would sort something out. He let go of me then. I held his hand to reassure him as we faced the judge. The poor child was shivering in agony. I guess the judge, the officers and I were all flummoxed. The judge cleared her throat and looking at me pleaded, "Aunty Olga, I know it's asking a lot but could you please take him too?" I nearly fell over. I explained why I couldn't do it. I already had two sisters of ten and eleven living temporarily with me, only temporary was more like permanent as their mother was in England and their father said they couldn't live with him because he didn't have the space and the grandmother having returned from her Canadian holiday said she couldn't have them back because they gave too much trouble. The sisters were indeed hard work. I also pointed out that I was diabetic and a single woman. The judge was very persuasive but what made me give in was the look of desperation on that young boy's face.

It has not been all a bed of roses but I love these two children and we are a very happy family. They had to have months of weekly visits to the psychologist. The boy was very wild at first because he was used to running about the village. He had been a law onto himself. Oh boy, it was hard! Then the two sisters hated what they saw as intruders taking over. At one stage I think I was nearing a nervous breakdown with those sisters. I had to deal with lies, promiscuity, truancy and bullying of the younger children. On top of trying to give them a good home I had to be constantly battling with their father to take more responsibility for his children. I continued with this temporary/permanent arrangement for over a year but in the end I had to ask their father to take them as my health was suffering. It was like I could breathe freely when they left.

Sometimes my home is full to overflowing with kids, especially during the holidays. While Hazel was at JNCH, we were bombarded with teenage girls from JNCH wanting to spend time with us. I think the girls liked coming because they saw me as a little crazy and different in the way I treated them. I know it was because I laughed so much and was not as serious-faced as the adults who looked after them. They helped with the cooking and other chores but we also did enjoyable things such as going to the beach or going on day trips. They enjoyed eating, eating, eating. In mango season they picked mangoes from our trees non-stop. Sometimes I had to say, "*Beg oono*, leave one on the tree for me." Nowadays, the visitors are those I meet at the children's school and at church as well as some of the locals. This house is like a magnet. When friends ask me how I cope, they find it difficult to accept what I tell them, but it's the truth - "It's not a chore but a pleasure."

I have found peace at last. There are obviously things that I miss, a companion for one. However, I feel very fortunate that I can live in Jamaica and with careful management of my finances I can visit my family and friends in England at least once every two years, although since being here I have made that every year. In fact I see them very regularly during the year as they too visit me here. I think my home is to them 'the get-away' where they come to relax. And isn't that wonderful!

Madge's Story

JAMAICA

Madge Remembers . . . .

Madge lives in the middle of Sutton-in-Ashfield, a busy little town in North Nottinghamshire. When I arrived she was at her potter's wheel. The aroma of Jamaican baked chicken wafted from the kitchen into the potting area, a converted outhouse.

Her latest find, "Classic Irish Airs", by the Irish singer Reg Keating, floated on the air. The warmth of Madge's greeting enveloped me; she always exuded the warmth of the Caribbean. Within minutes I was totally relaxed in her back garden.

On that glorious early summer's day it was difficult to believe that we were not in the heart of the English countryside. The garden was a profusion of colours; flowering plants and shrubs bordered the garden paths; birds darted about in the trees or hovered by the bird bath. It is often difficult to get Madge to sit still for long, but I finally prevailed on her to relax and travel back to her childhood.

Early Days

I was born in 1941 in a little village called Sweetland in the parish of Manchester. I don't think it's even on the map of Jamaica. Everybody knew everybody and everybody knew everybody's business too. It was a close-knit community where people worked the land for a living and church on Sunday was a part of everyone's life, especially for us children.

The nearest village to Sweetland is Pratville, a mile away. Pratville is on the map as it is quite a big village, more like a small country town. There's a post office, a police station and a school for the children to attend. It also has a big tank where people from the surrounding villages go to fetch water when there is a bad drought. Back then nearly every home in Sweetland had its own tank.

We were a happy family and, although I was aware that we were by no means rich, I never felt poor. Our house had four rooms, three bedrooms and a hall where visitors sat and special meals were eaten. Our kitchen was a separate structure as was our pit toilet which was a little way from the house. In our yard were lots of fruit trees, mostly oranges and tangerines.

I was a 'love child'. My mother met my father when she lived in Kingston with her older sister, Mrs Baugh. When she became pregnant she had to go back to 'country', as we called anywhere out of town at that time. My stepfather married her while she was pregnant because she was the love of his life. In time I had a younger sister and brother.

I loved my stepfather very much and he was very good to me. The first nine years of my life were the best. I was carefree and happy, going to school and church and playing with other children who lived nearby. We loved playing 'hide and seek' and 'house' which we called *dutty pot* because we fashioned our play utensils from dirt, in Jamaican parlance, *dutty*. The boys made carts, some simple, others quite sophisticated. A simple one would be just a flat piece of board with four wheels and a long shaft attached to its base. It was manoeuvred by pulling the shaft. Older boys built the more sophisticated models that they would sit on to speed downhill.

I was a tomboy. I loved climbing fruit trees to pick oranges, tangerines, grapefruits, star apples, jackfruit, raspberries, guavas, sweet sops, mangoes, hogsberry - whatever was in season. The hogsberry tree was a big tree on the common. A hogsberry, called hog-plum in some places, is about the size of a grape with a seed almost as big as the whole fruit. When ripe, it is yellowish brown and sweet. We children, on our way to school, would pick hogsberries and stuff a handful in our mouths, spitting out the seeds as we went.

My earliest memory is of my fifth birthday. I was given a goat kid which I grew to love very much. I would get up early in the morning like the adults to *tie her out*. This meant tethering her to a tree, usually a little distance from the house, where she would graze. After school I would stop and lead her home to tie her up in the yard for the night. She was my pride and joy. Sometimes I would pretend she was a patient. "I am Nurse Spencer," I would say in my most grown-up voice, "now what's the matter with you?"

I am laughing because these early memories are so sweet—the innocence of childhood.

I remember helping my mom and dad in the field from I was knee high. They rented a piece of land from the big landowner of Sweetland village and grew food crops for the family and also to sell to the shops in nearby districts and to higglers, who would load the produce on a market truck on a Friday morning and go to a big town - Mandeville, our parish capital, or May Pen in Clarendon; some even went to Kingston, over eighty miles away, to sell the produce. The main crops we grew were yam, sweet potato, cocoa and cassava. We also reared animals and would sell our goats, pigs, chickens and the young of our only cow to the butcher when they were grown.

The Nottingham Connection

My stepfather, seeing how keen I was to help, gave me a small square of land for myself when I was only seven. I was in heaven. I grew calalloo, gungo peas, sweet potato and coco yam. I weeded and watered my garden and watched things grow. I nurtured my little plot.

That's probably where I got my love for gardening; wherever I am I can't help but plant things. Since moving here just over a year ago, I have cleared the jungle that was my garden and just look at it now! I've reaped vegetables from it already. Isn't that wonderful?

I remember going to the beach, not to swim but to buy fish. Mama would wake up *before day* and I would go with her to meet the other women in the village who were going to Farquhar. The six or so women would walk together, balancing pans on their heads and chattering as we walked along a dirt track, this was the short cut connecting the mountain village where we lived to the beach. We usually left at about six, at daybreak, to get to the beach before the fishermen pulled into the bay with their catch at about eight o'clock. Some women bought loads of fish to sell in the other districts but Mama only bought for our family. As we didn't have a fridge she used to go to Farquhar Bay twice a week, on Wednesday and Saturday. The four-mile journey back to our village was far less exciting. It was an uphill trudge and seemed longer in the heat of the sun.

There was a wide choice of fish. Mama bought goat fish, jack fish in the right season when it was not poisonous, parrot fish which were either blue or green, or pinkish-red and fat; then there were whiting, trunk fish and sprat. The trunk fish had a delicate flesh under a hard casing and I loved to break the shell after it was boiled and eat the soft flesh. Mama used the whiting for fish tea, a sort of clear soup, because the fish was thin with not much flesh. The parrots Mama fried until they were crisp, to which she added onions also lightly fried, then pepper and lastly vinegar. We were able to keep these for a couple of days after cooking because they were by now preserved. As the seasoning soaked into them, they became tastier. We ate them with hard-dough bread. I can still taste it. Mmmm!

Looking back, my childhood lifestyle seems so simple. I had no toys except those my friends and I made ourselves. The rag doll was my favourite. At home our only book was the bible. When I went to school the books we read from were given out in class and collected at the end of lessons. But imagine the joy of just having a book to read! That was one of the reasons I loved going to school; it gave me the opportunity to read books. I ached for books to read. The nearest library was in the parish town of Mandeville, a couple hours away by bus and rarely visited by Sweetland villagers.

I went to Pratville Elementary School, starting off in 'A' class when I was seven, moving to 'B' class the next year and to 'First Class' when I was nine. My school was like a fat capital T. It was open plan. The six lower classes formed the stem. The two sides of the stem were partially divided by a central wall and each was again subdivided by huge blackboards creating the classrooms. The lower school had a different entrance from the two upper classes. 'Fifth Class', 'Sixth Class' and the head teacher's room formed the top of the T. A class was on either side of the head teacher's platform where he sat at his desk and observed what was happening. Behind his platform was his little office.

I can see the classrooms in my mind's eye — the blackboard, teacher's table and chair at the front of the room and, facing these, rows of children's desks in which we kept our exercise books. The desks were joined in twos and we children sat on long benches, each bench seating six.

Each desk had a lid with an inkwell and a groove next to it for a pen. The inkwell contained ink mixed by the teacher using blue ink powder and water. The pen was a stick tapered at the top and fatter where the nib was fastened to it. We dipped the pen into the ink for doing joined up writing in our exercise books. As we did not get to use pens until we were in 'First Class', I would dream of going up into 'First Class' to use a pen. In 'A' and 'B' classes we used slates which we would wipe clean as we finished each task. I looked after my slate carefully because if it broke my parents had to buy me a new one. My name was written at the top of the frame so that I would not lose it.

Classes had thirty-five to forty children each. Children who didn't pass the year's test couldn't move up, so some were two years older than the average age in a class.

The teachers were very strict; when they said "no talking" they meant "no talking". Each had a strap and used it. Parents trusted teachers and respected their judgement so if you got a hiding, or as we called it a *beating*, in class, it would be stupid to go home and tell your parents about it, because you were then likely to get another hiding for being disobedient or not paying attention and not learning in class. Parents really saw education as important and supported the school in whatever the teachers were doing.

Unhappy Years

The happy years of my childhood ended when I was nine.

One day I was playing with my friends in my yard when I noticed a man staring at us. He had one foot on our retaining wall which was about three feet above our yard.

"Come here, Marron," he called out.

"No, sah."

"Come here, man!" He waved.

"No, sah," I said shyly because I didn't know who he was.

One of our neighbours, seeing what was happening, shouted across to my mother, "Miss Ida, Marron father come." My mother who was at the back of the house quickly went inside and when she came back out again she had on clean clothes and her hair was tidy. She went to the gate and talked to the man. After a little while he turned to me again and, putting out his hand, called in a coaxing voice, "Here, look what I have for you. Come nuh, man!"

Seeing that my mother was talking to him, I edged towards him and took what he handed to me. I could not believe my luck. It was a ten shilling note! But I was confused. The man said he was my father. The only father I had known up to then was "Dada" whom I had always lived with and loved very much. I looked at the ten shilling note. It was a lot of money in those days and when the man told me it was all for me I felt good that I had something that I did not have to share. I expected Mama to explain things to me when the stranger left and so I got on with the important matter of the moment, treating myself. I ran off to the shop and bought a beef patty and a drink, just for me.

When I returned the man had gone. Mama was waiting for me by the gate. She sat me down beside her on her bed and holding both my hands in hers told me that Dada was my stepfather and that my real father had been in Panama until recently. It was quite painful at first to hear that my stepfather was not my real dad, and I only heard bits of what she was saying because things were whirling around in my head. I kept thinking that I had two dads. By the time Mama stopped talking I figured that having two dads might not be such a bad thing after all; I would still live with Dada and my other father would bring me gifts.

When my father came again I was still scared of him. This time he brought me some material to make a frock. He said he had got it in Mandeville. I felt very proud to be special, receiving all that attention. My father went and got me some ice cream while Mama and I talked about the material.

Two weeks later he came again. He must have asked Mama when she would be in and came when he knew she would not be there. After school we were looked after by Aunt Charlotte, my stepfather's sister. Aunt Charlotte and my father chatted for a while. He gave her a box and said there was another which he had to take off the bus on its return journey. He asked Aunt Charlotte and me to come with him to wait for the bus.

The bus stop was a short distance from our house. When the bus arrived, he got on at the back entrance, then called me to come and help him with the box. Walking up to the front of the bus he beckoned me to follow him. As soon as I was next to him, he waved to the driver and said, "Drive, driver!" As the bus moved off, I could see Aunt Charlotte getting smaller and smaller. I was terrified. I began to bawl.

I understood then that I was being taken away from home. I was angry that Aunt Charlotte and I had been tricked. I wanted my Mama and Dada. My father tried to console me as he found seats for us. He told me that I was his daughter and he loved me and wanted me to live with him, but this did not make me feel better. I did not know him and his trickery made me afraid of him.

I did not know it then but I would not see my mother again for nine long years!

The bus journey was long and I cried myself to sleep. I was awakened by my father who told me we had arrived in St. Elizabeth where he lived. We got off the bus and went to the house where he was staying. It was only for a short while, he said, because his proper home was in town. I can't remember much about being in St. Elizabeth except that it was for two weeks. I didn't go to school, just stayed around the yard when my father left for work until he returned. I can vaguely remember the lady whose house it was and that she had a big boy. I cried a lot over those two weeks because I missed Mama and Dada.

I have a bad memory of my stay in St. Elizabeth because I nearly got raped. One late afternoon this big boy who lived in the house and I went to the woods nearby to collect brushwood for fire. The next thing I knew he pushed me down onto the ground and was trying to get on top of me. I realised something wasn't right when he tried to draw down my panty, so I fought him off, scratching and biting him when he tried to cover my mouth so that I would not scream. I got away and ran back to the house, too scared to tell anyone what had happened. I couldn't anyway because my father was angry with me for being out late. Darkness was falling and he said I had no right to be out of the yard. He gave me a beating.

So traumatised was I by the happening, that when my father said we were going to town I asked no questions. We got on the Kingston bus and the next thing I knew we were in a tenement yard. My stepmother hated me on sight. She never hit me but if looks could kill, I'd be dead. I think she knew that if she physically ill-treated me my father would beat her. My father, his wife, my six month-old brother and I lived in one room. My bed was an ironing board standing on two chairs.

Can you imagine, I existed in this family for eighteen months!

Seven families lived in that house at 61 High Holborn Street in downtown Kingston. The house had an upstairs and downstairs. Attached to it were a kitchen, three shower rooms and two toilets. There was a tiny yard with a clothes line. The guava tree next door had branches hanging over from which we picked guavas. The one good memory was that it was next door to Coney Island with all the amusement of a fair ground and I had a lot of freedom to go there because my stepmother didn't give a damn about me.

I was back in school and loving it. Franklyn Town Elementary School was a haven away from home. I remember one teacher, Mr Blake, who encouraged me to do well and praised me when I did. He was strict but very kind. Once when I finished my sums before the rest of the class, he let me have extra recess time.

"Madge, you've done very well. You can go out but don't disturb the class." This made me feel so happy, it made my day.

A few months after moving to Kingston I caught measles and had a high fever. One day my stepmother had to go out and she insisted that I stay outside. She locked up the room leaving me shivering on the steps. I caught a cold and became very ill. As I recovered I became aware that I wasn't hearing well in one ear. I thought this was part of my illness and I would get back my hearing when I was fully better. Only much later did I realise that I had become slightly deaf. As an adult I mentioned my hearing problem to a doctor and discovered that the mucus from my measles had affected the nervous function of my ear.

I cannot express how unhappy I was at that time. I finally found enough courage and money to write my mother a letter begging her to come and get me. It wasn't a long letter because I didn't want to upset her too much. Years later when I returned to Sweetland, a neighbour told me how badly my mother had been affected by the way my father had taken me away. She said my mother was heard bawling for her *pickney, her big daughta*. Mama told them she didn't know where I could be. She told them how industrious I was at making beds and cleaning the house and even showed them a mattress that I had stuffed with grass just before my abduction.

Mama was overjoyed to hear from me. She immediately wrote to her sister, Mrs Baugh, for help. Grown-ups didn't discuss things with children in those days, so all I knew was that my aunt took me to live with her. I can't remember her visiting but my father and stepmother sent me to visit her a few times before I went to live with her.

I was transported to a different world for the next eight years. My aunt and her husband lived in Vineyard Town in a lovely home. My aunt felt she was in high society because her husband was a master potter and a well-respected figure in Jamaica. She spoke posh English and was full of 'airs and graces'. She worked as a floor walker in one of the big stores near the city centre; today I think her job would be that of a supervisor.

To my aunt, I was merely cheap labour. I can't forget how she got rid of her maid. One day I heard her say, "Grace, I shan't be needing you anymore as my niece is here now and she'll be helping me." I worked like a slave in that house. I worked so hard hoping she might say, "Thank you, Madge," or "That floor is nice, Madge," or "That's a nice meal you've cooked, Madge," or "Thank you for going to the market".

Fifty years later, I'm still crying! Oh God, I worked so hard.

I remember my aunt had one of the bedrooms re-floored and, not knowing that the man was coming back to polish it, I sanded and polished it while she was at work that Saturday. She never even said, "Thank you". I can't remember being loved by her; she never put her arms around me, hugged me or touched me. All those years of not seeing my Mama and Dada and living with my aunt, I felt starved of love.

Probably that's the reason I gave so much love to my children when they were at home. I can't help crying. I can't! There's still a lot of pain here in my heart.

For most of the eight years I lived with her I had no friends. When I first moved to my aunt's there was a girl next door who went to the same school as I did and we would walk home together. Rita and I would laugh and talk about what we were going to do when we grew up. My aunt didn't like Rita and a few months later said, "I don't want you to talk to that girl anymore. Is that clear?" I must have looked crushed because she added, "She is not nice". Rita would sometimes come to the fence, look over and shout my name. All I could do was look out the window. I could not go out to play. I was too ashamed to tell her what my aunt had said and had to find all kinds of excuses when we met at school. She eventually got fed-up and didn't bother seeking my friendship anymore.

From time to time there were other young family members staying at my aunt's; she would talk and laugh with them. I couldn't understand why she was nice to them and not to me. If I tried to ask her questions or begin a conversation she would rebuff me with, "You and I are not companions," and send me off to do some chore or other. The first six months with my aunt was a learning experience for me. I tried to please her in every way. I modelled my speech on hers. I answered the phone the way she had taught me to. "Hello, Baugh's residence, how can I help you?" Or, "There is no-one at home at present. May I take a message?" But it seemed the more I tried, the more useless I felt. I became flustered at times. I began to stammer, not wanting to incur my aunt's wrath, yet not quite sure what to say. My stammering grew worse and worse. I stammered even when I was not flustered. I was a bag of nerves for all those years I lived with my aunt.

Lord, have mercy on her soul! I wonder if she ever realised what she was doing to me. She's gone now and I'll never know.

As a child I was so innocent. I thought she must have spies. This fear began when I was twelve and I got a bad beating from her for smoking. She had allowed me to go with someone from school to the Kingston College Fair. We were naughty; I bought two cigarettes and we had a smoke behind a booth where I thought no-one would see us. Yet, somehow, my aunt learnt about it and I paid dearly for the lark. It wasn't worth it at all!

My uncle was quite different from my aunt. He was kind to me although he never said much. My memory of him is of seeing him in the mornings at the table reading the newspaper until I served him his porridge. My aunt on the other hand, thought more of her dog than she did of me. At the time, Mrs Edna Manley, wife of the famous Norman Manley, Prime Minister of Jamaica, was also the well-respected first lady of the arts in Jamaica. She gave my aunt a little dog which became, of course, her prized possession. It was fussed over and petted, not allowed outside on its own. But it was not toilet trained, did its business all over the house and I had to clean up after it. One day I asked, "Auntie, can't the dog go out for a little while? He's messing up the kitchen." The woman looked at me and said, "What do you think you're here for?"

Can you believe it?

I couldn't believe it. I went into my bedroom, fell on my knees and prayed, "Lord, is there nothing I'll be able to do besides cleaning up after this dog?"

Looking back I'm not sure whether she was cruel or simply ignorant of the damage she was doing. For instance, when I was fifteen I asked her if I could take extra lessons to do my first year local examination. I had felt really good when my teacher told me I should study for the examination. If I passed my 'First Year', 'Second Year' and 'Third Year' local examinations, I would be able to train as a nurse. That was my dream. The lessons after school were one pound for a month. But what a blow it was when she laughed in my face. "You? You can't be a nurse with that stammer! By the time you've explained to the doctor what's wrong, the poor patient will be dead!" I felt totally demoralised. But I was not ready to give up and asked myself, "Is there anything else I can do?" A week later I recovered enough to go back to her and asked if I could do hairdressing. She said, "No. I think dressmaking is best for you. You will be able to make your own clothes then."

I didn't want to do dressmaking but I had no choice. I left school and left my childhood behind me.

Reluctantly, I became an apprentice dressmaker to Mrs Baker, an excellent dressmaker who did not need a pattern to cut a dress to perfection. Being able to cut a dress without a pattern or design your own style were the signs of a good dressmaker in Jamaica.

Mrs Baker took me on a three-year apprenticeship. When I joined her establishment she had two rooms upstairs with seven foot-pedal Singer machines. There were four young students and two adults. The two adults were sisters and were Mrs Baker's assistants. I was shy and at first worried that I would never master dressmaking skills. Mrs Baker, who was very strict, increased my fear. However, I liked my fellow students and soon began to enjoy being there. When I arrived each morning at nine o'clock I had to set up the machines, threading them, filling the bobbins and setting out pins and needles for the day's work to begin.

In my first year, I was given the tasks of hemming, overlocking and ironing seams after they were pinned. Later in the year I was taught how to do gathers and darts. Mrs Baker would have us watch her carefully as she fitted her customers. I can remember once a lady wanted a sailor collar on a dress; Mrs Baker thought a roundish sailor collar would look different and be stylish, so she cut a paper pattern of the collar and fitted it onto the dress for the lady to see how it looked. The lady was very pleased with the effect. At such times Mrs Baker would say to us, "I hope you're watching carefully." We got so used to this that we would mime it when we knew she wasn't watching or she was out of earshot. By my second year I had lost some of my shyness and was learning more and mastering some of the different aspects of dressmaking.

I was also growing up. At seventeen I wanted to look like a young lady. I began to dress well. I bobbed the front of my hair and used what had been cut off to fashion a French roll to wear at the back. At that age young girls are blossoming into womanhood and although I was still painfully shy with strangers, I too was blooming. Looking good made me feel good about myself.

My friend, Yvonne, whom I admired, was jolly. At lunch time, we often stood by one of the windows and watched the world go by. Yvonne would shout hello to people she knew and I would mimic her and say hello too. One day I saw a handsome man pass by. Yvonne greeted him and he waved to us as he passed. He fascinated me. I asked her who he was. I wanted her to tell me all about him. She said he was an acquaintance, about twenty-four years old, who worked as a buyer for one of the downtown stores. I thought him a dream, although he was much older than me. Yvonne realised that I liked him and, unknown to me, told him so. The next thing I knew was that he sent a message through her asking me to meet him after work.

"Paul say he likes you," Yvonne teased one lunch time.

"Me?"

"Yes, man. Him see you at the window, say he'll wait for you this evening after work."

"I can't."

"Well, he's going to be waiting."

"All right. We'll go together then, you and me." She agreed.

I was gobsmacked that this gorgeous man should want to meet me, little Madge! That afternoon after work he was going to be waiting for me. I was very excited, but at the last moment I got cold feet and common sense kicked in. I was terrified of being seen with a man. Auntie had warned me about boys when I started my period. I could still hear her words ringing in my ears, "Man is danger! They'll get you into serious trouble. I'm warning you!" She had gone on to tell me not to talk to boys without other people around because they would "inveigle" me into bad trouble. The talk frightened me and I heeded her warning. Remembering how she had found out that time I had smoked a cigarette, I was sure she would soon discover anything I did. I knew in my heart that I would get a beating if she ever heard that I was seen with Paul. Fear won over fascination and as Paul waited at the front of our building, I asked Yvonne to go ahead.

"Why?"

"I'll catch you up, man. I need to go to toilet." As soon as she went through the front door, I crept out through the back and hurried to my bus stop. Next day Yvonne was annoyed with me but understood when I told her about my aunt.

About a week later as I approached my bus stop I was electrified. I stopped dead in my tracks. I rubbed my eyes in disbelief. I panicked. Paul was there staring at me. He had obviously been waiting for me. I made up my mind to ignore him and walked to the bus stop refusing to answer any of his questions. When my bus arrived I got on, weak at the knees. I thanked God that he did not come on the bus and follow me home.

The very next evening there he was again. This time he followed me onto the bus but I still refused to talk to him. When I got off, so did he. My belly turned over. "Please Lord, don't let him walk next to me," I prayed. But that was exactly what he did. The warning going round and round in my head was, "Take foot and run!" And that's what I did. I ran all the way to my gate, too scared even to look back to see if he saw where I lived. When he finally caught up with me, I was inside and he was on the road. "This can't go on Madge," he called. "I want you to be my girl. I'm coming to see your Auntie." I realised then that Yvonne had told him that I lived with my aunt. My heart was pounding so hard I had to put my hand to my chest in an effort to calm myself. I thanked God he didn't come through the gate and into the yard.

A few days later the same thing happened again. This time he sauntered past the gate. My knees turned to jelly and I was so confused I could not open the door quick enough. I was mixed up in my thoughts. A part of me was frightened of my aunt, the other part of me felt very special that this man was so attracted to me that he would not take no for an answer.

For six months Paul followed me around trying to get me to talk to him. Then one Sunday everything changed. I was totally taken aback when my aunt called out, "Madge! Madgie!" Her voice was sweetness itself.

"Yes, Auntie," I replied as I opened my bedroom door.

"Madge darling, there's someone here to see you." I could not believe it was my aunt as she added conspiratorially, "Around the front!"

"Who could it be?" I wondered as I went out onto the veranda. I nearly had heart failure when I saw Paul, the man of my dreams. This tall, dark and handsome man with beautiful, laughing eyes was standing there. I pinched myself to be sure I wasn't dreaming. Then he spoke. He said he had come to ask me out and would be asking my aunt's permission. In a state of shock I ran back into the house and bumped into my aunt who had been standing behind the door. "It's not me he wants to speak to. It's you!" I blurted out. A few minutes later my aunt opened my bedroom door and called, "Madgie!" In that unusually sweet voice, she told me she had given Paul permission to visit, and that we could sit out on the veranda. She said he had asked to take me out ". . . but I feel it's not quite right at present," she ended. I couldn't believe my ears. I could not believe my luck! Auntie was allowing this man, my dream man, to see me!

I completed my apprenticeship and left Mrs Baker's establishment. I found a job in a shirt factory. It was my first job and it felt good to be earning instead of being dependent on my family. The work was not exciting but the atmosphere was friendly. Groups of workers, mainly women, worked on a production line making shirts. The leader handed out to each of us a box with the work we were expected to complete each day and which she would examine, handing back any garment that she found unsuitable. This would have to be redone to her satisfaction.

After a brilliant start, things began to change for the worse. For no apparent reason that I could work out, the leader began to hand me back work. I really couldn't see anything wrong with my stitching. At first I was too timid to say anything so I would undo the stitching on each shirt and redo it. She continued to hand me back stuff until I began to feel harassed. Puzzled, I asked some of the other workers to examine the returned shirts. They, too, could find nothing wrong with my work.

Then the penny dropped when someone said, "You no see say de gal jealous. Watch you back!" A young man that the work leader fancied had been showing an interest in me and this had incensed her. It was true that he came over to me regularly, asking me to do one thing or another and hanging about waiting for the job to be done. He would strike up a conversation while he waited. He was pleasant but I was not interested in him and did not realise that he was 'chatting me up'. *I was so green, I tell you!* Not wanting to be harassed or, worse, lose my job, I decided to keep my head down and not attract the wrath of the work leader. So, the next time that he came over, I made out that I was very busy and discouraged any conversation. After a few weeks he cooled off and the harassment stopped.

I did not notice any men around because I was very happy with my personal life now that Paul was a regular visitor. We sat on the veranda, knowing that Auntie was listening behind the lounge door, but I didn't care; I was with Paul and that was what mattered. He was allowed to walk me home from church. We were very circumspect and did not even hold hands. My cousin, Iris, who had come to live with Auntie and was attending college, was always with us. She was Auntie's trusted favourite and was left in charge of the house on Saturdays when Auntie had to work. Of course Iris was all sweetness and light around Auntie and did as she pleased behind Auntie's back.

Iris had met a friend of Paul who shared his apartment. On Saturdays Paul would phone to check if he could visit. If no-one was home except Iris and me, he would come around and Iris would leave us to go and see the friend at the apartment. Time alone with Paul was very special. Iris and I would sometimes both go and visit our boyfriends at their apartment. We took the bus there, spent a couple of hours with them and returned home ahead of Auntie. I was passionately in love with Paul. God! That feeling of first love can never be repeated. When he called me "Madgie" it was like music to my ears. To be loved was a good feeling. Even today when someone says "Madgie" a little blood leaves my heart for a second and I have a flashback seeing Paul with his twinkling eyes and gorgeous smile.

I was young and naive too. One day I was not feeling well and I couldn't understand why my period was so late, nearly a month late. The nauseous feeling continued for a while but I did not mention it to my aunt because it did not seem serious enough and the spells did not last long. I did mention it to Paul one Saturday and he suggested that I see a doctor. I said it was not that bad but he insisted, giving me the money and making an appointment.

After the doctor examined me, he said, "You've been naughty. You're going to have a baby." I thought he must be joking.

"No," I told him. "I'm not having a baby. My aunt says that the time to have a baby is when I'm twenty-four." I could not grasp the situation. I had only had sex three times and could not believe I was pregnant. But the doctor's face said it all. In a daze, I told Paul what had happened and he could see how alarmed I was. He put his arms around me and told me not to worry. "Come with me next week to see a friend. He'll sort it out and you'll be all right again." He explained that his friend was a pharmacist and would help me. I was horrified at what he was suggesting.

"I want to have my baby!" I howled. "I may never have another!" I thought Paul quite horrible to suggest that I get rid of our baby.

Looking back, I often wonder what made me say those words. I look at my child, my beautiful daughter, and thank God that, in the midst of my confusion, I did make the right decision.

Paul tried to comfort me. He joked off his suggestion, telling me that he was only testing me to see what sort of person I was. He went on to offer the alternative; he would find a place for us to move in together. I was now almost three months pregnant. I had to tell my mother. I could not face my aunt with the news.

"No," I said to Paul's suggestion, "I'm going home to my mother." I knew in my heart that she was my only refuge.

Bertie, one of my brothers, came to town a couple of weeks later bringing ground produce for Auntie. Desperately wanting to talk to someone I could trust, and thinking that he would understand, I confided in him, begging him not to tell Auntie but to tell Mama as soon as he got home. He told Auntie. When he left Auntie turned on me. It was a Saturday and she was home early; she hurled abuse at me. Her face looked like *rain about to fall*. As she left the house she looked at me as if I were dirt and told me not to be there when she got back. I had just enough money for my bus-fare home. Iris offered no support.

When I arrived at my mother's home just after 6 p.m., she took me in her arms and we wept together. "No mind, me *daughta*, no mind," she kept repeating to comfort me. I felt lost. I felt so small. My aunt had made me feel like rubbish. She had already been to see Mama, catching an earlier bus. Mama said that my aunt strode into the house and angrily pointing out that I was "no good". She said she did not want me in her house a day longer because I was a disgrace.

As luck would have it, I also missed my chance to go to England. My family, like many other Jamaican families, helped each other. My aunt had lent the fare to one relative to go to England and he was repaying the loan. That money, once repaid, would have been my fare. Instead what happened was that my brother, who had broken my confidence, was given the money as his fare to England. Next in line was my cousin, Iris. She did not get pregnant because, as she told me later, she always made sure that her boyfriend used a condom. Why didn't she advise me knowing what could, and did, happen to me? When my period was a few days overdue and I told her all she had said to me was, "Wait until next month".

Sometimes I wonder about family loyalty.

I was back in Sweetland and feeling very bad at having let down my mother. It was a relief when Paul visited because for a brief while I did not feel so alone. We walked to the next district of Asia and walked back. He told me that he went to see my aunt who cursed him out. He wrote asking her for my address but she did not respond. He had to waylay Iris who was staying on Auntie's best side and being careful not to be seen out with anyone. She gave him my address but also informed Auntie about it. When Auntie heard that Paul had visited she sent us his letter to her.

I found out from my mother that this was history repeating itself, for I had been a love child. When my mother was sent to Kingston to live with her sister, Auntie, it was to stop her from seeing the man she loved, but whom her family thought not good enough for her. They thought that living in Kingston would give her the chance to better herself. What happened was not what they had planned. Lonely in the big city she met and fell in love with another man. She found out she was pregnant only after he had left for Panama in an attempt to better himself. Auntie threw her out. That man was my father. He wrote my mother at Auntie's address but Auntie never passed the letters on to my mother. My mother had to return to her family in Sweetland and she married the man her family had tried to keep her away from.

Our village was small then and still is. No pregnancy went unnoticed. Gossip was rife. It upset mama so much that she attempted to shut up the gossips by *throwing words*. When she saw one of the newsmongers passing she would position herself on the veranda and loudly exclaim to no-one in particular, "Lord, now is one thing I'm glad for, the man my daughter pregnant for standing by her" or some such pointed statement. This stopped the gossiping for a while.

Paul on his last visit had promised to stand by me and I believed him. When he did not come again I became concerned and so did my mother. Each week I went to the post office expecting a letter, only to return home disappointed. I could not believe Paul was not writing or visiting me. I was five months pregnant and very worried. I wrote to Iris who replied a few weeks later and dropped a bombshell. Paul had migrated to Canada. I could not believe it! He had deserted me after all he had said. I grew up fast, realising that I was going to be the only parent my child would have.

It always surprises me how women in Jamaica manage when their men let them down. Most of them become mother and father and do a good job of it too. Six months pregnant, left by Paul to survive the best I could, I decided to focus on my baby. My mother talked to me about the care the baby would need. I had helped with my younger brother and sisters and began to feel more positive that I could look after my own child. I tried to put Paul out of my mind and began to prepare for the birth. I ate well, except for avocado pears which made me sick. I slept well. I helped as much as I could around the home, trying to pay my way as best I could. I tried to be happy to ensure that I would have a happy baby. The general belief in Jamaica was that if a pregnant woman is sad and miserable, the baby will also turn out an unhappy, fretful child.

The day my daughter was born is memorable. I was alone in the house, having been left to sleep. I was awakened by terrible pains in my tummy. It was still morning so I got up and made myself a cup of *bush* tea to ease the pain; in Jamaica then, and even now, different herbal teas are used for everyday ailments. Feeling a little better after drinking the tea, I made my bed and cleaned the house using bundles of Spanish needles to rub their sap on the floors and a coconut brush to shine the floors until they looked highly polished. The pain continued on and off and I tried to ignore it, but gradually it got worse all around my tummy until I became quite frightened. I ran to my mother who was about half a mile away working in the field. Several people tried to stop me running. One older woman actually grabbed me and stopped me briefly.

"*Pickney*, how you so big an' a run so, eh?"

"I'm going to my mother, Ma'am," I said and rushed off. She must have thought I was odd because as I looked back I saw her standing where I had left her, shaking her head in disbelief. When I got to Mama, she calmed me down with a drink of water. The pain had stopped but as we talked it came back with a vengeance. My mother took my hand and we went home.

"What is it, Mama?" I asked.

"Chile, it look as if you baby going come today." She shouted to a neighbour to fetch Nurse Williams for us. I had a bath, put on a clean nightie and clean underwear and although Mama said I should rest, when the pain came again and again, I walked up and down, up and down.

The midwife came and examined me. The pains were big ones now and so bad that I grabbed the bed head and screamed, oblivious to everything but the pain. A week before, while I was cooking, the steam from the pot had burnt my arm and new skin was now growing over the burn; the area was still very tender to the touch, but when the pains came I must have wriggled so much that I tore the new skin off without feeling a thing.

At about twelve-thirty the nurse teased, "You can't have your baby with your panty on." I hadn't even enough strength to smile. During a lull in the pain, I heard the children going back to school. My baby was born at 1:00 in the afternoon that Tuesday, a week before Christmas day. As soon as I heard her cry, I said to the midwife, "Give me my baby, please! Give me my baby!"

I held the little girl in my arms until she fell asleep. Looking at her I said to myself, "I've done this thing, this wonderful thing." I felt an unbelievable sense of achievement.

I knew life would not be easy for us but I also knew I would do anything for my baby. I nursed her for two years. During that time I stayed with my mother, stepfather, brother and sisters who gave me unconditional love and support. When Charmaine was two, I discussed my situation with my mother and we agreed that I would have to leave my daughter with her while I found work outside the village, as there was no work opportunities there.

My mother came home one day and told me she had heard of a job in Mandeville, about fifteen miles away. A woman who visited our district had told her that a Seventh Day Adventist minister wanted a live-in housekeeper. My mother trusted the woman whom she considered a good Christian. A job with a minister seemed, literally, a godsend. I went for the interview the lady had arranged, got the job and moved to Mandeville. But I felt such heartache at leaving my baby behind although I knew Mama would look after her well and that it was only by working that I could support her. But leaving her behind was one of the hardest things I have ever done. The minister's home was quite pleasantly situated. He had a wife and two boys. I was expected to do everything. I learnt how to be a creative cook. Soup was a regular meal, made with lots of meat bones. The wage was not great and I hoped eventually to find something better that would allow me to have my daughter with me.

One day as I was cleaning the master bedroom, I saw a letter among the things I was about to throw out. I picked it up and it was as if something in my head said, "Read it!" It was from the lady who had got me the interview. Her advice to the minister has stuck with me. I read it over and over again. ". . . I would suggest that you pay Madge monthly as that way, you will get two to three days extra out of her . . ." *The bitch!* I hid the letter in my pocket, packed my bags and left. I had been six months on that job, working my fingers to the bone for peanuts because I had to support my child. I was angry and wasn't prepared to work there anymore.

Mama was surprised to see me. I explained what had happened and showed her the letter. Mama and Aunt Vie decided to tackle the woman the next time she came to our village. When she did turn up, she claimed to have been very upset that I had let her down by suddenly leaving the job. I took out the letter and handed it to her. She didn't even bother to try to make an excuse, she just left and never returned to the village for years after that.

So there I was, back at home again. I did the housework and enjoyed being with my daughter. We did not have a sewing machine so I made her dresses, all by hand. She looked really cute in her little gingham sun-top dresses. Her facial features were her father's and sometimes, as I looked at her I would think about Paul and wonder how he could desert his beautiful child. I stayed at home for six months before I heard of another job in Montego Bay. The position was for a nursemaid. I applied and was so pleased to get the job and to be able to support my daughter again.

It was a family with two children. The father worked at the airport. The mother was a nice woman who taught me how to cook chicken paella. The father I did not like at all. Soon after taking up the job I noticed that, like a snake, he watched my behind every time I bent over or stretched up while doing something. I grew more and more uncomfortable whenever he was around and his wife was out. He would find some reason to brush against me or touch me. As time went by I became more and more concerned at his behaviour. It was a difficult situation and although I desperately wanted to support my daughter and myself, I was not prepared to risk being abused. It was a well-known fact then that many men abused their helpers and nursemaids, women who were in no position to seek redress. The wisest thing to do was to leave the job and after summoning up enough courage, that's what I did.

Not long after arriving in Montego Bay I had met my father's mother and his two sisters who lived there. I spent most Sundays, my days off, with them. When I left the job I moved in with them, intending to find another as quickly as possible. But going to live with them turned out to be another big mistake. I just couldn't find a job. I was worried and it showed. One of my aunts would cheer me up by inviting me to come out with her. What that meant was that we went to a bar and had a drink. But after one drink my aunt would disappear for a while. I was puzzled by her disappearing act but thought it was not my place to question her. At first I didn't realise what she was doing when she started up a conversation with a young man who lived upstairs the bar and then wheedled him into buying me drinks. This pattern continued for a while and then she began to cajole me to be nice to the man. I was depressed at not finding a job and enjoyed his attention for the couple hours I was in the bar. But it did not take him long before he began pressuring me into having sex. I considered the whole situation and was not happy with it. I was not in love with him and didn't want such a relationship.

An older man who was around sometimes sussed the situation and cornered me one evening as I sat in the bar waiting for my aunt.

"Where is your aunt?"

"I don't know."

"What're you doing here?"

I stared at him. That was a stupid question. Then a light penetrated the darkness of my own stupidity. My aunt always had money when she returned. Where did she get it? My thoughts veered between her having an affair with a married man and being a prostitute. Jesus!

"Yes," the man said as if he had read my thoughts. "Take care, *daughta*." I nodded, feeling very uncomfortable. "Where you come from?"

"Near Pratville, sir."

"Look here, write your parents to send for you. Dis life is not for you." He got up, went to the bar, paid for a cream soda for me and waved good bye, giving me a thumbs-up sign.

The next time my aunt asked me to go out with her I pretended to have a headache. I was waiting anxiously for my mother's response to my letter telling her that I wanted to come home because the situation in Mo'Bay was not good. I begged her to write a letter telling me that she really needed me to come and help out. I kissed the letter when it came. I showed it to my grandmother. She called my aunts to her and told them I had to go home because there was trouble there and I was needed urgently. On the bus home I gave a sigh of relief.

God had sent that old man there to save me. I dread to think what would have happened if I had stayed with those people.

What was my aunt playing at, exposing me like that? I was annoyed at myself for being so naive and begged God to make me more aware of dangers, especially from those wearing trousers and with a sweet tongue. I was getting nowhere in life. "Why can't I find a decent job?" I moaned. As the bus came closer to home I felt more and more depressed. The only joy awaiting me was my daughter's smiles and hugs.

Discovering My Talent

The days that followed were dark ones. I did not want to be a burden to Mama, but as one day followed another, no job came my way. As the saying goes, light comes after the darkest hour. And so it did for me. Out of the blue I had a letter from Auntie's husband. It was so touching I cried. He asked me to come and see him as he had a proposition for me which he was sure I would want to take up. My first thought was that he had found me a job with one of his many contacts. He was becoming quite well known as the Jamaican master potter.

When I arrived at my aunt's home in Kingston, I was no longer afraid of her, but still I was thankful that she was at work, it being a weekday. Mr Baugh sat me down and, after pleasantries about my little girl and my family in *country*, he outlined his proposition. "Madge, come and stay with us for a while." I was convinced he could not have discussed this with my aunt. I could not believe my ears and my expression must have conveyed my amazement. He patted my knee. "Just for a while until you find somewhere to live." I waited to hear about the job but instead I heard, "Come with me to the college to enrol in an art course with pottery as your main subject. I know you're wondering why you. I'll tell you. I've watched you. Of all the nieces and nephews that have lived here, you are the only one who has worked hard without a grumble. You have scrubbed floors, shopped, picked breadfruit and ackees, and cooked. You deserve a break." I was gobsmacked. Me, at the College of Arts and Crafts? We talked and he agreed with me that it was probably not a good idea to come back to live at my aunt's but that he would help by paying my tuition, paying for a room and giving me a little money to meet my needs. He said that he would make enquiries to see if someone in any of the courses would like a room-mate.

I was so excited I walked on air to the bus stop. All the way back to country people must have thought I had gone mad, I was smiling and laughing happily as I went over what Mr Baugh had proposed.

I am forever grateful for this break and that kind act of Mr Baugh, although he exacted a price for it.

In a few days my life changed totally. I got a room in a shared house and enrolled at the college. The course sounded exciting and I couldn't wait to start. The only sad note was that I again had to leave my daughter behind in the country with Mama.

Classes were from 9:00 in the morning to 2:00 in the afternoon. We did a general course that included sculpting, drawing, lithography and printing, after which I had pottery with Mr Baugh. I had never thought of pottery as something I wanted to do, nursing was my love; but once I felt the clay under my fingers and saw the end product in the pottery room, I was totally hooked. I wanted to succeed at being a first class potter. I became a dedicated student; I would spend half an hour before each teaching session preparing the clay and hours on my own practising to create pots. Mr Baugh was an excellent mentor.

After three months I began to earn from my pots. Mr Baugh had a few moulds of fat piggy banks. He taught me how to make and fire them. I made six or seven a week as well as ashtrays and vases, which Mr Baugh sold through the craft market outlet.

In those first few months, Mr Baugh insisted that I visit their home on Sundays and stay for lunch. The visits were weird and uncomfortable but I didn't have enough money to allow me to decline his offer. My aunt would ignore me throughout my visit, speaking to me only when it was absolutely necessary. Needless to say I tried to arrive just before dinner and leave as soon as it was polite to do so. Mr Baugh made sure that I had enough to eat. It was a relief when I began to earn enough to pay back Mr Baugh in instalments for my tuition and still have enough to keep myself.

I spent three years at the Jamaica School of Arts and Crafts. In my first year I experimented, using my fingers to do indentations as patterns. I used to think, "I wonder if Mr Baugh will be pleased with this?" He was the boss and I had tremendous respect for his skill. I remember the first fluted jug I made. I threw this very nice jug and decided to press the edge so that it was fluted. Mr Baugh was angry with me. "You mustn't do that! You're not experienced enough," he said patronisingly.

Ha! I can't help smiling. As soon as I turned my back what did he do? He began to do fluted jugs, of course!

One day as I hurried into the pottery room I noticed that everyone had on clean aprons and the room was exceptionally tidy. But I didn't bother to enquire about it; I got to my wheel and set to work at once. I heard laughter and there was a sudden change in the way the students talked, in hushed tones. I looked up and saw several strangers in the room, one of whom came over and enthused about my pot. "Oh, I say, that's wonderful!" I smiled and thanked him. Cameras flashed and Mr Baugh hurried over. It was then that I learnt that the admirer of my pot was a senior government minister touring the college. We chatted about pottery and somehow I stole the limelight, quite unintentionally.

The following week my photos were in the *Jamaica Gleaner*, the number one newspaper. The article was the talk of the week and me, little country girl Madge, was seen as the aspiring female potter. That October Mr Baugh surprised me with an invitation to enter some of my pieces in his fourth annual exhibition of students' work. He said he wanted a small table with my exhibits. Wishing to give myself enough time to do my very best, I asked when he would need them. "I've got them already," he said laughing. I was quite taken aback. "Come," he said and led the way into his private room. "All these are yours," he said pointing to a shelf. Surprised, I had to turn each piece upside down to check that it was mine. There was no doubt; my signature was on them all. Mr Baugh explained, "While you were potting, I saved your best pieces."

At the opening of the exhibition, the director of the college, Mr Lewis, looked at my pieces. "Madge, are these your pots?"

"Yes, sir" I muttered shyly.

"Did you make them on your own?"

"Yes, sir," I repeated, nodding.

"Well, I won't buy one this time, but if next year you produce exhibits like these, I'll be buying. I can't believe you, a first year student, could have done this after only ten months with us." He seemed genuinely amazed at my achievement. As he moved on I, for my part, was secretly pleased with myself. Mr Lewis seemed to be thinking I might have had help and I decided then and there that I would meet his challenge. My self-esteem rose by notches and I immediately thought of my aunt. I whispered to myself, "I'll prove to you, Auntie. I'll make you eat your words! I am not rubbish!"

For the next twelve months I worked unbelievably hard. I loved experimenting with designs and when I created a piece that I found exceptionally pleasing I would wonder, "Did I really make this!" Creating a pot was a little like giving birth, an *exquisite* experience.

At the end of that year, Mr Baugh arranged for me to have my own pottery exhibition at the Institute of Jamaica, a hundred and fifty pieces of my work were on display. The exhibition was officially opened by Mr Lewis. He congratulated me and, making good his promise of the previous year, he bought several pieces including a lovely teapot. I was twenty-two then, thoroughly enjoying my work and really thrilled with the comments people made. The media made much of the fact that I was the first woman to take up pottery as a profession; I was on radio and television and in the newspapers. They said I was setting a trend and indeed I was, for the media coverage led to the college being inundated with enquiries about the course. I was pleased. To me Mr Baugh was a wonderful mentor and teacher and had a lot to impart to me and to others. As my mentor he encouraged me and I went on to win the Jamaica Festival prize for pottery.

In my final year I had another exhibition at the library on Tom Redcam Road which, again, was well attended. Mrs Edna Manley, doyenne of the Jamaican art scene, attended the exhibition and said she was impressed with the quality of my work. She was very encouraging and told me I had a great talent. Thrilled to bits, I again silently promised myself to become a first class potter.

This emerging interest in pottery lifted it from obscurity. Up to then it had not been taken seriously as a profession. In fact, one of my brothers, on hearing what I was training for, laughed and declared that the only time he would get his hands dirty with clay would be if he fell down. The last laugh was certainly on him!

During my second year I became Mr Baugh's unpaid assistant, washing and preparing clay, packing the kiln and generally helping as he directed. I enjoyed this role and saw it as giving something back for all his kindness. Lady Luck also smiled on me and I was very fortunate in securing part-time work with one of the prestigious high schools in Kingston. The Art teacher at Jamaica College, Douglas Warner, having seen my work, visited me at the Arts College and invited me to work in his department part-time. The college agreed to release me each week for a day and a half. This job brought in much needed funds. At last, I was earning a living from my work!

I met John, while I was exhibiting at the library on Tom Redcam Road. It was the final year of my diploma. Having gone to the library to return books, he had visited my exhibition and bought a pot. As I was not there, he enquired where he might find me and, hearing that I taught part-time at Jamaica College where he also taught English, he asked for the pot he had bought to be delivered to the Jamaica College staff room at the close of the exhibition. One afternoon, at the end of a teaching session this man came into the Art room.

"Hello," he said.

"Hello."

"I'm the person who bought one of your pots and asked to have it left in the staff room here. I've come to thank you for bringing it." I told him it had been no trouble at all. He then went on to ask if he could come and watch me at work some time. I was still using the facilities at the Arts College and we agreed he would visit one day after school.

He came and was fascinated and asked lots of questions. As we were leaving the Art room he asked, "Would you like to go for a drink?" I accepted his friendly gesture. At the time he rode a motorbike and this was a first for me, having my hair whipped by the wind as we zipped our way through the town. It turned out to be a pleasant evening for both of us and we began seeing each other regularly, although I was also seeing other friends socially. John was very easy to talk to. He was usually described as tall, handsome and quite dashing. He was from England and, after Oxford, had come to Jamaica on a two-year contract with CAST, the College of Arts, Science and Technology.

I told him about my daughter and my ambition. I was not interested at the time in having a boyfriend I just wanted to earn enough to bring my daughter to Kingston and to provide for our life together. At the time Charmaine was spending one weekend in every month with me in Kingston. She was a curious and intelligent child and wanted to know everything about her father. It was obvious she wanted him to be like Mama's husband, good, kind and caring. It hurt me to see how vulnerable she was. When she asked me about her father, I would tell her that he was abroad and would soon come to see her. I thought, "Poor child, I can't tell her the whole truth she will be too hurt."

The first time Charmaine met John the strangest thing happened. John came to visit and Charmaine just ran up to him and said, "Are you my dad?" It was so sad, my heart stopped for a moment. But John was very good; he smiled at her and said, "We'll see." Relief flooded me. John and I laughed and the moment passed.

Without my being aware of it, John and I had gradually grown closer. I was at first very cagey when he suggested that our relationship be put on a more serious footing. I was still hurting from my first love affair and from being deserted when pregnant. I had also noticed that he seemed jealous of the friends I went out with. I realised I was growing quite fond of him. So, after six months, John and I became an item. We joined his friends for socials and my personal life became as fulfilling as my working life. What was lovely to me was that he respected me, he was considerate and not pushy, giving me the space I needed to feel comfortable in our relationship.

It was a good time for me. I was selling lots of pots through word of mouth and to people who, having seen my pieces in the homes of their friends, wanted to acquire one or two of their own. John and I were happy together. Jamaica is a funny old place. John introduced me as his girlfriend to his *brown* friends at the university and I became acceptable in their society. No longer was I seen as "the little black girl doing pottery". They would visit me and offer me lifts whenever they met me around town. In the 1960s, Jamaican brown-skinned people held top jobs in every walk of life and many looked down on their black-skinned fellows. Thank God that has changed.

One of these so-called friends overstepped the mark and tried to rape me. He gave me a lift home and the next thing I knew he was trying to force himself on me. I was so angry I bit the bugger. He let go of me and I ordered him out of my place. I was so embarrassed I could not tell John; but I learnt to keep my distance from all those men.

Two couples from that period have remained friends of ours over the years: one, an Englishman and a Jamaican woman who now live in Yorkshire; the other, both English, work in Mozambique, but we see them whenever they come to England.

My American Experience

In 1965 I had the most horrible experience of racism in USA, which made me respect John all the more.

On the ship coming to Jamaica he had met a couple and they had struck up a friendship. The following year he visited them in Miami. In 1965, he was going to see them again during his summer holiday and invited me to go with him. We stayed in a caravan parked in their yard. For two weeks we worked in a box factory and made enough money to cover our fares and have some left for spending. To celebrate the beginning of our holiday with work behind us and money in our pockets, one Friday evening John and I decided to go into the nearest town for a meal. We were in San Antonio and it was quite a long distance into town, so we took a taxi. As we went along we noticed that the driver kept looking at us in his mirror; obviously he was not used to seeing mixed couples.

When he left us at the diner, we entered and sat down. John went up to the counter and ordered two coffees and two meals. The woman serving poured one cup of coffee which John brought to me. When he returned to the counter she said, "Sorry, we've stopped serving."

"But it's twenty-four hour service," John pointed out.

"Well, we have," she said tight-lipped.

"May I see the manager?" John said firmly. She called the manager who came out and stood behind her. He was a big red-neck with hostile eyes. John very politely and calmly addressed him. "I just asked for two meals and was told that you have stopped serving. Your sign says this place is open for service twenty-four hours . . ."

"We have stopped serving."

"But it says twenty-four hours."

The manager stared at me and then at John and sneered. "Well, by law we have to serve the nigger but we don't have to serve you if we don't like you." Then raising his voice, he added, "And we don't like you!"

"Don't drink that coffee," John called to me across the room. "I ordered two and will pay for two when I get the other one."

The manager glowered at John. "You'll pay or I'll break your neck!" he said menacingly.

John realised that these people were racists and, seeing the phone, went towards it to call for help. Just then a white policeman came in, his two guns hanging from his waist and a baton in his hand. He asked no questions; he just gestured at John and me and opened the door. As soon as we were outside and before John could utter a word the policeman ordered, "Get in!"

"Get in where?" John was determined not to be bullied.

"Just get in!" he said, raising his baton threateningly. We both instinctively knew he would use it and so got in the police car. As we were being driven to the police station John's attempts to speak to him were met with a wall of silence.

At the police station we were ordered out of the car, taken through the reception area and put into two separate cells. I have never been so petrified in my life. All the horrors I had heard of happening to black people flashed before me. "God help us!" I prayed, "Please get us out of this hell." I could hear John banging his cell door and yelling, "I want to speak to someone!" This went on for about two hours. Then I heard the police asking him for his ID. Of course we didn't have our passports with us. John kept insisting that he wanted to make a phone call. The policeman went off again and returning, asked John where he was staying. John gave the names and address of our friends. The name must have rung a bell because the officer went off saying he would phone for confirmation.

He came back quite quickly this time. John and I were let out of our cells with a smile and an apology that the formalities had taken so long. He said the police had been summoned to the diner because there was a couple causing a disturbance. Charles, our friend, was obviously a prominent citizen for, not only were we let out of the cells, but we were driven home, quite a distance away. When we got there, the police officer apologised again as he opened the car door for us. John was livid over the whole incident. When Charles opened the door he asked, "What on earth happened?" John and I told him of our ordeal and an official complaint was lodged. Before we left we heard that the diner had been closed down. The whole episode was very painful then and still is. I can never forget the hatred in the manager's eyes and the coldness in the waitress'.

On our next trip to a diner Charles came with us. As the men went up to order, I noticed a woman with a child at the next table and began to talk to the child. Realising that I was the only black person in that place, I felt a bit uncomfortable and asked if we could leave as soon as we had eaten. We later heard that the place was burnt down that very night. Remembering our horrible experience at the first diner, I wondered if it might be a case of arson instigated by racial hatred. They had, after all, served a black person.

Poor John suffered a further experience of white-American racial prejudice. He had accompanied Charles to his local bar and was being introduced by him to a group of acquaintances as his English friend on holiday. As is customary, each person, on introducing himself, shook hands with John, but one man had the audacity to say to John, "Are you the man that's walking around with that nigger? I don't want to shake your hand." John told me later that there was deathly silence. He was appalled at the depth of white racism he was meeting at first hand.

I hated staying in San Antonio. They were days of nightmarish proportions. In all that time I saw only one black person, an old, uncared-for woman with worn slippers and dirty clothes. I said, "Hello." She stopped, surprised that someone had spoken to her. She responded but I could not understand what she said in her deep southern accent, so I just smiled and said goodbye.

One morning Charles and his wife found a rabbit shot dead on their doorstep. It was a warning to them. Later that week when John and I went to the local supermarket I had another scare. John had one basket and I had another, and so engrossed were we in what we were doing, talking as we shopped, that we did not notice anything amiss. As we began to take up our purchases, we heard the door open and slam shut. This still did not arouse our suspicions but as John opened the door for me to leave the supermarket, a pick-up screeched to a stop outside the door. I looked up and my blood turned to water. Two shotguns were being pointed at us by two men with angry, snarling faces. John said firmly, "Madge, just walk." I was in front of him. "Walk slowly," he said calmly. I did. But to this day I don't know how I managed it.

I was happy to return to my own country. Jamaica might be poor but our life was not fraught with dangerous surprises for black people as it was in the USA.

England It Is

One day out of the blue John asked, "Should we get a house together?"

"Yes," I responded. We knew we were going to be together and it made better sense to rent a house than for each of us to continue to have separate accommodation. It was naturally the next step in our relationship.

We house-hunted and came up with a dream of a place nestled by a rock where two rivers meet in Gordon Town. We called it *Riversmeet Pottery*. It was basic but cosy. It was a five-sided house with enough space to build a kiln. I made many trips to the cement factory to collect discarded bricks to build my kiln. When it was completed, I was delighted to have my own pottery. John and I had a wonderful time there and Charmaine spent every weekend with us.

In my work I continued to experiment with design and colour. It was my 'bird' phase. The birds were depicted in many poses. Norman Rae, then the art critic for the *Gleaner* newspaper and also a playwright/producer, fell in love with my work, gave me glowing reviews and bought several of my pieces to grace his home. I am most grateful to him for raising my profile in the media.

John proposed to me in early 1967. I sent a telegram to my mother to tell her John and I were engaged. He suggested that, as his contract was due to finish that summer, we should go to England to get married and settle there. He invited his parents over to Jamaica to meet me and my family. It was summer when they arrived; I went with John to the airport to meet them. Both came across as quite nice people who mixed well with the locals in Gordon Town and were very friendly towards me. We took them to Sweetland to meet Charmaine, Dada and Mama, who positively beamed with maternal happiness for me. Like many Jamaican parents she saw marriage to John and the prospect of living in England as a golden opportunity to better myself.

But John's mother had quite a different idea. One day she took me shopping and afterwards we had lunch. After general chit-chat she said, "Madge dear, I hear you have relatives in the USA."

"Yes," I replied.

"Wouldn't you like to go and spend six months there? I hear it's wonderful."

"I never thought of it."

"But dear," she said conspiratorially, "it would give you time to see how you really feel about Johnny. And no need to worry about money, my little treat." I saw through her game and decided to play along.

"Oh, that's an idea! I could do that." She grinned, pleased with my response.

When we got home she wasted no time. "Johnny, Madge has decided to go to America for six months, to see her relatives . . ."

"Mother," John shot back at once, "if Madge wants to go to America to her relatives, I'll go with her. If she wants to stay in Jamaica, I'll stay here and if she wants to go to England, we'll go together. So don't try to separate us."

Knowing her son, she gave up the game there and then but we never got on from then until the day she died. She became another Auntie. I could never do anything to please her; she always found fault. Sad really. She and her husband returned to England knowing that John and I would follow shortly.

I did not know what to expect when I came to England. To me it was an adventure. One thing I knew was that I would not leave without my daughter. I made this quite clear to John. As Jamaicans say, *he could not have the cow without the calf*. Thankfully this didn't pose a problem, John accepted Charmaine, he saw her as a lovely child and a promising student.

My last exhibition in Jamaica, again at the Tom Redcam Road library, was officially opened by Mrs Edna Manley. This was a great honour. In my reply to her opening speech I ended with ". . . As you know, this is my final exhibition in Jamaica, but I will be back."

We had less than two months to pack pots, glazes and other things to do with my work, as well as to entertain our many friends and acquaintances dropping in to say goodbye. We had our last farewell drink at the bar in Gordon Town square that September.

Twenty years later when I revisited this bar with some friends, the owners of the bar had not changed. I was happy to see Pearl and her husband again. The landlord did not immediately recognise me, I guess I had aged twenty years! After our party's drinks arrived I said to him, "You remember me?" He looked at me blankly for a while.

"Cho, man," I teased, "Me and John lived up the little corner house at Riversmeet."

His whole demeanour changed and he broke into a beaming smile as he threw his hands in the air, "*Lawd-a-massie*! Miss Madge! Is you?"

ENGLAND

New Home

John, Charmaine and I landed at Southampton on a cold October day in 1967 and travelled on by train to Ascot in Berkshire where his parents lived. We were met by John's parents, his sister and his friends. It was quite a homecoming for him. His parents lived in a comfortable home with lovely countryside on their doorstep.

For me it was a whole new world. Everything was strange, but strangest of all was not seeing black people around. John suggested, and I agreed, that Charmaine should go to live with his sister in Cornwall and attend school there until we found a home. The family thought it would be good for Charmaine to be with another child, the sister's son.

I did not then realise the trauma I was creating for my child and only learnt of her unhappiness many years later.

She was only eight years old, in a new environment, a different culture and without the people she knew, me and John. We stayed in Ascot for three months during which time I did not work because I could not find a job and I could not do any potting; I felt like a fish out of water. John had applied for teaching posts and he was to begin in January at Elliot Durham Comprehensive School in Nottingham.

John and I got married that December; it was a small family affair. I was so happy to have my daughter and could see how much she wanted to be with me that I decided then and there that she would stay with us. It was good having some of my family there too, my father who had emigrated to England, his wife, my brother, Bertram, and his wife from Nottingham and my cousin, Austin, from London. I enjoyed my wedding although my stepmother could not resist the opportunity to put me down. With a smile she pushed the knife in and twisted it, "What a way you lucky to find such a man. I wonder what he sees in you."

We moved to Nottingham and soon found a house on Portland Road, a big, old house with space for me to pot. We put a kiln in the cellar and had a potter's studio upstairs and a bigger kiln outside. I was in heaven making pots again. My daughter went to the Elms Primary School, a multiracial school where she soon made friends. One teacher was very kind to her as a relatively new immigrant child. Looking back, I see that I did not then realise how many changes she had had to make in her first year in England.

John enquired about a job for me in the Art department of his school and I was offered work for two days a week. I liked going there and the black children were very pleased to have a black person teaching them. I was very conscious of my stuttering as I was in this new environment and did not want to stutter while teaching. I tried hard to control it by following the advice I had been given in Jamaica. Mr McFarlane, who stuttered too, had told me that it was caused by fear.

"Look into the mirror and talk to yourself. You can control the stutter by speaking slowly until you get rid of it," he said.

It was not always easy advice to follow and I continued to be embarrassed by this weakness, especially in front of the children.

As John began to meet people, he started to arrange for me to take my pottery to people's homes, where I talked about the pieces and sold quite a few pots. It was at one such party that I met Rachel Gilliatt who was to become my first English friend. I also began meeting Caribbean people and felt less isolated. John met John Wray, one of the few black teachers in Nottingham who then introduced us to other Caribbean people. I was asked to read some of Miss Lou's poems at a Jamaican concert where all the other performers were children. There were folk songs, folk dances and poetry. The concert was a great success as were the others that followed. I enjoyed meeting people and was especially pleased that there was a Jamaican community in Nottingham where I could feel more settled. Nottingham was at last beginning to feel like home.

John approached the Nottingham Playhouse to put on an exhibition of my work. The management was very receptive and I had a favourable response from the public as well as from the Nottingham Evening Post. My pots reflected the colours of the Caribbean, bright and cheerful. On display in the foyer was a selection of goblets, tea sets, coffee sets, as well as vases and pots to adorn the home. The Playhouse, after opening night, kept the exhibition up for a month. I was the first black woman to have such an exhibition and, following this success, for the next seven years I mounted an annual exhibition there.

At home our life was pleasant and I was happy. John and I decided that it would be wonderful to set up a pottery workshop where people could come and learn the art. One day he came home very excited; he had seen an old doctor's home up for sale and thought it was just what we wanted. It was in a little village in Derbyshire about fifteen miles from Nottingham. We went to view the place. It looked massive to me but it certainly had possibilities. It would be ideal for the pottery workshop that we both wanted to start. The stables could house a kiln and the loft above could be converted into an exhibition room cum shop and still there would be room for a flat where pottery guests could stay! We were both excited and wanted to move in straight away. We put an offer in and it was accepted.

I was pleased to leave where we were living. I did not want my daughter to grow up there because the area was beginning to deteriorate. It had once been a fashionable part of town, secluded with big houses, but because it was off the busy main road its seclusion provided shelter for the prostitutes. I was actually accosted outside my gate, an experience which left me very concerned. That day, we had forgotten to buy an item while we were out, so John dropped me off near our gate and went back to the shop. As I got to the gate a car pulled alongside.

"Hello," said a man's voice from the car.

"Hello," I responded, preoccupied with what I was going to prepare for dinner.

"Are you doing business?"

"Pardon?" I turned to face him. I had no idea what he was talking about.

"Are you still doing business? I saw you come out of that car."

"You cheeky bastard!" I screamed at him. "That was my husband."

He went bright red and sped off. It was late afternoon, the time the kerb crawlers came out.

We moved to Riddings in 1972. As I've said the house was big; it had eight bedrooms and two bathrooms upstairs, and downstairs there were two living rooms, a music room, three small rooms and a big kitchen. One of the three small rooms I used as a storeroom for my pots, in another we placed the freezer and stored odds and ends and the third became my sewing room. When Charmaine was in her teens we gave her the sewing room for her own sitting room. There were the stables and a sizeable lawn, as well as a large plot with fruit trees and space for vegetables to grow. I am a countrywoman at heart and, with a big back garden, I was in heaven. I began to spend my free time, when I wasn't potting or doing housework, in the garden. I planted potatoes, beans, sweet corn, strawberries and raspberries. I tried cabbage but the soil was unsuitable. It was such a pleasure eating what we reaped from my vegetable garden. There were apple trees and I planted a cherry tree, which gave us such a harvest each year that we shared fruit with family and friends.

By this time I was doing quite a few demonstrations for women's institutes and groups around Derbyshire and Nottinghamshire and making a good living from my pottery. John, after our move, left Elliot Durham School in Nottingham for a post at Tupton Comprehensive, nearer to home. Charmaine settled into the local comprehensive. John and I had our dream and were working towards our goal to open our pottery workshop.

John applied to the local authority for a grant to convert the stables into a house with three bedrooms, dining/lounge and kitchen in one half and a pottery room for the kiln with a gallery above it in the other. This project took us four years to realise and we both felt great satisfaction when it was completed. 'Riddings Pottery' was fully operational! We were ecstatic when our first weekend guests arrived. They had daily pottery lessons and I also provided breakfast and an evening meal as part of the package.

Things were going well for us and we felt very settled in Riddings. It had become home for me. We had friends locally. I attended the local Anglican Church and felt a part of that fellowship. I got on well with my neighbours. I loved the countryside on our doorstep that provided me with walks. John and I thought that the time was now right to have a couple of children. After trying a while without success, we decided to seek professional advice. The verdict was shattering. I learnt that I had a blocked Fallopian tube and also fibroids that could become cancerous. The specialist said there was a slim chance that I might get pregnant but suggested that the wiser option was for me to have a hysterectomy and that we should think of adoption as an alternative. I was disappointed and grew depressed at the thought of not having anymore children. I often looked at Charmaine and was so, so glad to have my beautiful daughter. Eventually, the reality of the situation kicked in and I accepted that I could love a child that was adopted and try to be the best mother. Anyway, I rationalised, the child would have a better deal than Charmaine as she could be seen as my practice run!

John and I discussed the issue of adoption and we decided to find out more about adopting a child. I was thirty-four and accepted that time was running out so even if I put off the operation and continued trying it might all be in vain. As a practising Anglican, I talked to my vicar about our problem and our decision to adopt. He put us in touch with the Church of England Adoption Society and we were soon interviewed by a Mrs Crankhorn to confirm our suitability as prospective adoptive parents. When we were accepted we asked, of course, for a mixed-race child. Six months later, Mrs Crankhorn telephoned to say that there was a strong possibility a mixed-race boy would be up for adoption but that the papers had not yet been signed. The baby's mother was English and his father was from the Caribbean. We were happy that soon we would have a son and could hardly wait to hear that everything was in place. At last it was time for us to meet the baby. He was in Ipswich and John took the day off school so that we should not have to wait until the weekend to see the child we were sure we would want. On the drive to Ipswich we could barely control our excitement. We were just like expectant parents awaiting the arrival of their baby. The journey seemed so long, the wait was excruciating. When we saw the little baby in the cot my heart leapt with joy. He was beautiful! I said a silent prayer of thanks and promised

God and the baby that I would be as good to him as if I had given birth to him. He was then ten weeks old.

We took him home and Charmaine was delighted to have a brother. For sixteen years she had been an only child and I see now how lonely she must have been. We agreed that I should choose the baby's first name and John his second. But John changed his mind, he said the baby did not need a middle name. So I named our son Michael after our Jamaican Prime Minister, Michael Manley. John was an attentive father and I a doting mother. When Michael was still a baby I would sleep with him in another room so as not to disturb John who had to work the next day. As soon as he was a toddler Michael followed John around; John became his hero. He even walked like his dad and people who did not know that he was adopted would often comment how much Michael resembled his father!

My home life began to change then in more than one way. Potting took second place as I nurtured my baby. Then all too soon Charmaine was going off to university, and it hit me that Michael would suffer the same lonely childhood that Charmaine had. I talked about my fears with John and we agreed to adopt another child. We contacted Mrs Crankhorn again, expressing our wish to adopt another child. This time we did not have to wait long; she soon rang to say that she had a boy, both of whose parents were Jamaicans. This time around we knew the routine but I still had butterflies in my tummy on the way to meet this new child. We hoped Michael would love his brother and not feel jealous. We were pleased that the two boys would have each other. We were so excited that time flew by and before we knew it we were being ushered in to meet the baby. He was the cutest little boy with fat cheeks. We took him home when he was six weeks old and Michael was delighted with his baby brother. We called him Haydn. Our family was now complete or so we thought.

Not long after this Mrs Crankhorn contacted us, she wanted to visit. When she came we realised it was not just to see the boys. After saying how lovely they were she showed us pictures of a lovely two-year-old mixed race boy whom she wanted us to foster. She said we were the ideal family and begged us to think about it. John fell in love with the boy in the photos and later when we met him we were both captivated by his warm smile. We agreed to foster Lennie.

Lennie's father was black and his mother white; his mother's family kept in touch with him and did not want him to be adopted. When Lennie came home with us John went overboard, buying him tracksuits and other items of clothing, the kinds of things he had never bought for our two boys. I soon began to notice that Michael was getting jealous that John was paying him less attention and pampering Lennie. It was as if John was obsessed with Lennie and totally oblivious as to how the other two boys were feeling. When John heard that Lennie's maternal grandmother wanted to take him out of the country to go and live in Greece, he decided that this would be bad for the boy as the grandmother did not have a stable home. He even toyed with the idea of making Lennie a ward of the court and said as much to Lennie's uncle. The next thing we knew was that the uncle came one evening and took him away. But some things happen for the best and I think that, had Lennie stayed, he would have disrupted our family. All the same, he was such a loveable child that I hoped with all my heart that things worked out well for him, wherever he went.

I think John found it very difficult to accept that Lennie had gone. For a long while he was angry with Lennie's family seeing them as incapable of giving the child what he could have had with us. I noticed that John continued to be less attentive to our sons. I loved reading them their bedtime stories but when it was John's turn, he would be back down so quickly, I had to ask him if he had really read to them. It was I who took them to the library and into Nottingham to the black barber and to shop for clothes. It began to feel as if I were a single mother. Things did not improve as they grew older. John half-heartedly helped them with their schoolwork. I was amazed that as a teacher he did not see the importance of giving his children as much help as he could. Michael's hobby was bike riding; he was very good at it and became a local cross-country champion representing his school. Haydn did not follow in his brother's footsteps; instead he took up roller skating and represented England in the under-14 group. He was really thrilled when he went to France with the team. They also both enjoyed going to the local youth club. Sadly, their father did not give them the kind of moral support I thought they deserved and I always felt I had to compensate for that.

I continued to earn a living from my pots and when the boys were at school I increased my output. One year John suggested that we go up to the Edinburgh Festival. It was my one and only visit to the Fringe Festival and I enjoyed it tremendously. It came about because a colleague of John had written a play that had had such good reviews that he was asked to put it on at the Fringe. John also had a friend in Edinburgh who invited us up and we stayed with him for a few days. We took lots of pots and it turned out to be a profitable trip. This was the beginning of John's annual trip to the festival to sell pots, but the children and I were never again invited to join him.

Looking back at that period I realise I was growing as a person. My confidence was increasing and I saw how important being mobile was for my job. I asked John to give me driving lessons but, as they say, it is not wise for a husband to teach his wife. We had rows during every lesson. It was not a good idea. I enrolled with a driving school and passed my test in 1980. The day I passed my test was also my choir practice evening at Heanor Parish Church. When I asked John to take me as he usually did, he said, "No. You can drive yourself." I felt confident getting into the car but as I drove further and further away from home, panic began to rise. Just before reaching my destination I drove into a police checkpoint and froze. I could not continue and the officer came over to ask what was happening.

"Are you alright?" he enquired.

"Officer, to be honest with you I've just passed my test, nine hours ago."

"Not to worry, love; just take your time." He gave me a reassuring smile that calmed me and, with my fright over, I drove off.

Not long after this John's mother died and he gave me her old Renault. I was now able to get to places where, before, I had had to depend on someone to ferry me there and back. The feeling of freedom was wonderful!

A part of my growing as a person was that I began to take more of an interest in what was happening to me. For instance I did not have any money of my own as John took care of all the money I earned from pottery sales. *Can you believe that I did not even know how much I earned from my pots and how much money we had as a family? I was so green, I trusted John with my life.*

As I became aware of my situation, part of me objected to being treated like a dependent child instead of an adult. The desire to improve my education also grew as I began reading and met people when I had demonstrations. So I enrolled at the nearest college to do English Language and English Literature. I thought that having a husband who was an English graduate and a teacher would be a boon. Wrong! John refused to help me, giving the poor excuse that if he did, it would be unfair to the other students in my class! This was the same person who gave private tuition to students from local schools. I was beginning to see his selfishness but I persevered with my studies and finally passed my GCE 'O'levels.

I did not stop there. Derbyshire Education Authority for whom I did some work offered to pay for my tuition and my travel expenses to Ilkeston College of Further Education to do the two-year 0730 Teaching Certificate, which would qualify me to teach my craft in schools and be paid at a higher rate than I was getting. I grabbed this opportunity and got my certificate. John was very pleased and organised a celebratory lunch for my family and friends. It was a lovely thought and an enjoyable afternoon and I was proud of my achievement and the advantages it made possible.

Then came a bombshell, completely knocking me for six! John informed me that he had given notice to quit teaching. There had been no prior discussion. We had two children of eight and five and, according to him, only two thousand pounds in the bank. I thought he had gone mad. He was convinced that we could make a living from the pottery and seemed to have it all worked out. He was going to manage the sales; he had also developed an interest in potting and wanted to learn about the craft so that he could talk about it with confidence.

Life at home changed. Now we were together twenty- four seven. It was a nightmare with him under my feet day in, day out, watching what I did; at the same time I had to produce enough pots to make enough money to supply our family's needs. It did not take him long to realise that we needed a steady income and he got himself a part-time teaching post. I buried my frustrations by working harder and added to the family's regular income by taking on a part-time job at Cressey Fields Day Centre for the disabled in nearby Alfreton.

My workday was very long; I was often up until 1.00a.m, tired, edgy and often tearful. Sometimes as I hunched over the wheel my chest hurt and I had to breathe in slowly until the pain eased. One night as I sat at the wheel, the pain was so severe I thought I was having a heart attack. I hugged my chest as the spasms racked my body. Terrified, I gasped for breath and could feel the tears running down my face from the sheer straining of my chest as I tried to breathe. When the pains subsided I slowly got up, clutching my aching chest, and went into the kitchen to fix myself a hot drink. I sat at the kitchen table thinking, "My God, that was awful. I don't want to go through that again." As I thought about what had happened I realised that I was dog-tired; I was not having enough sleep and my body was telling me to slow down.

The following morning I shared my experience with John and told him I was going to ease up on the work. He said nothing then, but not long after he asked me to teach him how to pot so that he could help. The only thing I could not teach him was how to be creative but I taught him everything else. He was a good student and soon people could not tell his pots from mine, as he copied my work to a tee. Then he began to change. He bought his own wheel and kiln and began to sell his pots alongside mine. Not long after this I found that he was pricing his items higher than mine and had begun to sell himself as the potter. Soon he was talking to me as if he was the authority on pottery and I his student!

Now registered as an artist, I was getting demonstration jobs all over the country. I was visiting libraries around Derbyshire and getting to know the schools in this county quite well. Then out of the blue a teacher asked me if I did storytelling. When I said that I did not he suggested that I should think about doing that as well because he had observed the way I worked with children and I was a natural storyteller. So began my second career. Requests for Caribbean storytelling took off as I was recommended by word of mouth. Now, I was visiting schools all over the country combining my craft with storytelling. I told Caribbean stories in libraries and primary schools. Dressed up in my national costume, I would get the audience to participate in the dramatization of the story. Children love the Anancy stories and the ghost ones too. I always include music in my repertoire. I introduce the children to the music of the Caribbean region, especially the calypso that very few of them have ever heard and they love it. In schools with black children an outside person who is black coming in to their school makes them brim with pride. For my part, I have a sense of doing something positive for them.

I was pleasantly surprised to have a call from Central Television in 1987. The Director of a library I had visited had contacted them and they wanted to do a documentary on my work for their community programme, *'Here and Now'*. The crew came and followed me around as I worked. When the programme 'Top of the Pots' was aired, it was twenty minutes long and showed me preparing clay, making and firing pots. The exposure brought in many requests from people who had seen it and this boosted my income. In the 1990s there was another surge of interest when I was shown working with children with disabilities on *'Lifeline'*, a BBC programme.

In 1993 the Commonwealth Institute invited me to participate in an exhibition by Commonwealth artists. I was thrilled. I had just finished working with a group of school children who had created some interesting tiles and my only request was that these be included with my exhibits. It was the beginning of my sculpture phase in which I cut pieces of pottery and joined them together to make interesting designs. Other pieces included in the exhibition were from my 'bird' phase and my 'mottled-effect' phase. The 'bird' phase depicted the Jamaican doctor bird in different poses. The 'mottled-effect' phase is reminiscent of an African pottery style; I used white and brown manganese to suggest the blowing of gentle breezes and with cobalt blue, black and grey I created the effect of waterfalls.

I remember two things from that exhibition. One was the Queen visiting the exhibition and apologising to me because she had forgotten her spectacles and could not see the pieces of work clearly. Then there was the BBC incident. They were on the floor above me and someone dropped a mike that landed among my pots. The person who came to collect it apologised profusely and promised to send me tickets for a BBC show later that month. I'm still waiting!

I was very honoured to be invited to be 'Potter in Residence' at Barnett Teacher's Centre in London. This has given me another opportunity to be a role model to some black youngsters. Seeing me there and in schools may encourage some of them to take up pottery as a profession.

Lee Arbouin

Broken Dream

Once I began to grow as a person, tension developed in our marriage. It was like a slowly growing cancer. John and I continued to maintain a stable home environment for the children and for a while, life continued with its ups and downs, but without any major disasters. However, as the years went by, I became more and more unhappy and not even potting could assuage what I was feeling. I was frustrated with my husband's attitude towards me. I felt some guilt that because of my fibroids and the hell I had to endure because of it, I was often bad-tempered at home. I decided to have the hysterectomy to stop the terrible suffering. It was the right thing to do and as my health improved, I began to feel a lot better. My recovery was quick and I soon returned to work, a much happier person.

Before Haydn left secondary school I had become suspicious of my husband's intentions towards me. Some interesting facts had come to light and I had begun to see his controlling nature. He watched my every move, wanting to know what I was doing and where I was going. If a friend phoned he wanted to know what he or she wanted me for. On the other hand he was a free agent, not asking my opinion but expecting me to agree to everything he said. One day I received a phone call that got me thinking about the money I made but never saw. The woman on the line, having confirmed that I was Madge Rivers, said she noticed that I never made any withdrawals from the joint account and that amounts for cheques paid to my account were being transferred to another one that was not in my name. That was how I discovered that John had opened his own account and been transferring some of my hard-earned money to it. I took action immediately and opened an account of my own for the income from my pottery and storytelling. Whenever he sold my pots I still did not see the money and when I asked about it I would not get an answer!

My contribution to the house was over and above what John was putting into it. I bought carpets for the stairs and sitting rooms because he refused to make the house comfortable. I had the kitchen refurbished too, done by my brother at cost price. One row we had ended with my being violently pushed onto the door because I refused to answer his question. I banged the ear that had already been damaged when I was a child and sprained my shoulder. When I went for my usual hearing test the doctor noticed the deterioration and asked about it. John must have felt guilty because he went and bought me a hearing aid, which did not help as it sent me off balance, so I did not use it for long. The shoulder still plays up sometimes with a biting sensation, especially when the weather is damp.

By the late 1990s, the children were leading their own lives. Charmaine, after getting her degree in journalism, lived and worked in Sheffield for a while. Then she went to Birmingham University to pursue a law degree. She obtained her LL.B. and remained in the West Midlands. Michael and Haydn became local disc jockeys. Then Michael began to spend six months working as a disc-jockey in Greece and the other six months in England working at a local garage. It should have been the time for John and me to enjoy our lives together, but instead our relationship was far from fulfilling. I wanted a husband who was attentive; what I had was a husband consumed with making money. Over the years he had bought a couple of houses that were rented; we also had a lodger at home and John worked long hours making and selling pots. We seemed to be just co-existing in the same space.

'Perhaps our relationship needs a fillip,' I thought. So, one night, frustrated at the situation, I decided to be provocative hoping to clear the air and bring back some romance into our life.

"Have you a girlfriend?" I asked tongue in cheek.

"Yes," came the response. Thinking he must be teasing too, I repeated the question and got the same answer. This time I could not mistake his stony tone. And in those few seconds my world was shattered. I knew we had problems and that most marriages were often not perfect, but this I had not anticipated.

"How long has it being going on?" I, finally, managed to ask.

"Three years."

I could tell he was glad it was in the open.

"How could you do this to me?" I asked numbed. He did not answer. Then I felt compelled to say out loud what my heart felt, "I guess you don't love me. But did you ever love me?" I got another shock that night. This man that had courted me, asked me to marry him, asked me to leave my country to come to England with him told me that he had never loved me, he liked me a lot but that was it.

That night he moved into another bedroom. All I could think was how I had been used. For thirty-five years I had worked my butt off, had taught this man my craft and all I got in return was a slap in the face. I too could have had an affair; I had not succumbed to temptation but had remained faithful. I wondered how I had not seen the signs of his adultery.

Thoughts swirled in my head as I tried to understand how this breakdown in trust had come about. He loved my cooking and always praised it. He got annoyed with me for leaving the housework undone when I got caught up in a creative potting mode. I hated his meanness, even going out for a meal was a rarity for us. But did such things make our marriage so unbearable that he had to cheat on me? The more I thought about it, the angrier I became, until my head began to swim and I felt nauseous. Finally I fell asleep.

The next morning I woke up a bitter woman. I went to work at Cressey Fields with a headache and a heavy heart. I tried to put things out of my mind and concentrate on the work I was doing but this proved impossible. Later that day my boss noticed that I was not my usual cheerful self and, suspecting something was very wrong, she offered a listening ear. Quite unable to contain myself any longer, I broke down and told her everything. She was very comforting and gave me the name of a solicitor in Nottingham to contact for legal advice. After weeks of agonising, I finally made an appointment with the solicitor who advised me of my rights and left me to think things through. He said he would begin divorce proceedings if and when I asked him to. That was in 1997.

Our home became a battle ground and John began to make my life a misery. He refused to give me any of the money I had earned and for which he had the bank book. He asked me for rent which I refused to pay. He said that he was getting a divorce and the unpaid rent would be deducted from my share of the settlement. I was going through hell and my only life-line was my potting. Friends were supportive but only I could make decisions about my future and I felt paralysed and unable to act. When I found out that this mistress John had been seeing for three years had been to the house on several occasions when I was away, I realised what a cad he was. I kept asking myself if I had not broached the subject when would he have told me about the affair.

After a year of feeling like a broken pot, I decided to get things over and done with. I changed solicitors and began divorce proceedings. John was trying to buy me out of the house but was being unfair, having it priced far lower than its market value. He tried to get me to go back to Jamaica, telling me that the settlement would take care of my relocation and I could get married again! He tried to get my friends to do his dirty work for him, asking them to encourage me to return to Jamaica as there was no future in England for me. His callousness hurt but I stood firm, demanding a fair settlement.

In 1999 while the solicitors were still negotiating a settlement, John suggested that we have a go-between to help us sort things out so that we could both get on with our lives. He suggested our friend, the builder, and I felt okay with that. I thought this friend was someone I could trust and I did not for one moment think that he and John had a different agenda. I was tired and wanted the whole business over. And they knew this. They drew up a letter offering me sixty-eight thousand pounds immediately so that I could put it towards a home. The go-between told me that this was not the final settlement and he thought it was in my interest to take the money and find a house. Living in the same house as John was very unpleasant and this seemed like good advice. I signed. The go-between then began to help me to find a house. In 2000 when the divorce was granted I was shocked to learn that I had no more money coming as the document I had signed had said I accepted the settlement. The amount I had been given was the total sum of that settlement. I had been cheated out of thirty-two thousand pounds! My solicitor had agreed with John's solicitor that my share of the house was to be one hundred thousand pounds. I had expected one hundred thousand pounds. Signing that document was my downfall.

But God has a way of working things out and I prayed for help in finding a home. The go-between, unknowingly, did me a big favour. As we looked at houses I fell in love with my present home. It was in a state of disrepair and he did not want me to buy it because he wanted it himself. It is a gem in the heart of the town with a huge back garden and outhouses. It is nearly three hundred years old and is a listed building of historical importance. It was as if the house itself wanted me to buy it. I had seen it advertised in the local Property Guide and each time I looked at the advert, it seemed to be saying to me, "Madge, come and see me!" I finally succumbed and saw the potential in its overgrown garden and outhouses. I knew in my bones that I would be happy living there and that this was the house I wanted. I bought it for a reasonable sum that was within my budget and moved in as soon as I could.

A few weeks after I moved in I had workmen put in a new kitchen floor. As they removed the old flooring one of them fell and had to grab hold of the side of a hole that had opened up. As his fright turned into amazement, we saw that the hole was a well! I am now the proud owner of a thirty-foot well in my kitchen. I got the workmen to build a stone wall around it and cover it with a glass top. Decorated with hanging plants, it has become a centre piece in my kitchen. Friends and neighbours cannot believe their eyes when they see my beautiful well. I measure the level after each heavy rainfall and have seen it rise and fall over the years.

I am slowly recovering from my broken marriage. It still hurts when I think of the years I invested in that marriage, but I am as excited as a school girl with my house and my new life. There was so much to do, refurbishing the house and making something of the garden. But I am gradually getting there. In summer and early autumn my garden is awash with colour. I have lots of apples, plums, pears and cherries and I use these to make preserves and desserts. I cleared the vegetable patches in the first year and have been doing some serious planting. A year after I moved in, I began to reap other crops such as potatoes, broad beans, French beans, cabbage, Brussels sprouts, cauliflower, beetroot and turnips. My garden gives me so much pleasure; I just love spending time in it.

My potting and storytelling bring me an income and I have my garden for relaxation. I have also found a new hobby, amateur dramatics. I have appeared at the Nottingham Playhouse as an extra in *Macbeth* and as Judith in *Cold Comfort*

Farm. My stuttering has almost disappeared and I continue to work at controlling it. I feel so good when I do well. It's my way of saying, "See? I can do it!"

There is a new man in my life. I met him while holidaying in Ireland with a couple of my girlfriends. He runs his family's riding school and is a farmer. He makes me happy and we are taking it one day at a time. I don't know what tomorrow will bring but I'm not going to waste any energy worrying about it. I can't see me going back to Jamaica to live although I love my country. England is my home now and I am loving every minute of my life, knowing that I can face whatever the future brings.

Mi is a Jamaican ooman an nuttin no frighten we.

Eunice's Story

JAMAICA

Eunice Remembers . . . .

It was a freezing January morning in 2002 when I visited Eunice in her suburban home in Sherwood, Nottingham. Her husband, a fellow City Councillor, left for a meeting and we settled ourselves in her cosy living room sipping herbal tea as she brought to life her Jamaican childhood. We were so engrossed that time flew by.

She began to share the story of her life as she prepared a quick Italian lunch, one she had learnt as part of her course on cuisine from around the world. She raided her husband's wine rack for a bottle of wine to accompany lunch. But after an enjoyable lunch she had to dash off to a Council meeting.

Life In Warsop

I was born on 25th April, 1954 in the very small village of Warsop, near Troy, in the northern Jamaican parish of Trelawny. This is where my family is from and from my earliest childhood I felt great pride in belonging to the Warsop community. My childhood memories are of the happy days spent there in the bosom of my extended family.

Space and freedom come to mind. Our house was on a hill on our family land. It had five bedrooms. It was a big house for our big family - my father, mother, two sisters, two brothers and me. My father's mother and father lived close by in a house with four bedrooms. My father and grandfather were builders and were able to provide comfortable homes for their families although I was not then aware of this. To me they were family houses without boundaries and we spent as much time in one as in the other. We children roamed around our land with not a care in the world. I loved my grandparents almost as much as I love my parents. My grandmother was dark-skinned with a big bosom and a comfortable lap for us little ones to sit on. My grandfather was light-skinned and always busy around the home. My father's grandmother also lived with his parents. She was not as nice to be with as was my grandmother Alice. Unfortunately, I did not know my mother's parents because they had died when my mother was a teenager. My mother married my dad when she was only sixteen years old and he was twenty-three. My dad told me that he had had to get permission from my mother's older brother, the only close family member that she had.

Our family was well respected and I learnt very early that I should not do anything wrong outside the home because it would be reported to my family. Everyone in the district knew which family we belonged to and we had to tell grown-ups "good morning" or "good afternoon" when we passed them on the road. If we didn't, it would be seen as being rude and we would be told off there and then and would later get another telling off from our parents when they were informed of our lack of respect. People cared about each other and I felt very safe in my little world, the only world I knew.

My family worked hard. They cultivated the land which was very fruitful and produced citrus fruit, beans, peas, yam, a lot of sugar cane and ginger. We sold our oranges and grapefruits for export. When the cane was ready for reaping people came to help to cut it and it was sold to the sugar company who processed it to make sugar and rum. My grandfather hired women in the district to come to our home to peel the ginger when that was reaped. The peeled ginger was bagged and sold to higglers who, in turn, sold their produce in one of the country markets. I can remember heaps of yams during the yam harvest; we grew different varieties - yellow yam, white yam and Negro yam. Our ackee and mango trees were laden with fruit in season. We did not have to buy food for our family because we farmed the land and our family members were industrious.

Our parents and grandparents were country people who believed in making use of their land and also believed in teaching us to be responsible. For this reason, each one of us as children had a plot of land to cultivate. I loved growing yams. First I dug the yam holes about a foot deep, in rows, then I planted in each hole a piece of yam with an 'eye' the beginning of new growth, just like that on a potato. As each yam vine began to grow I put a stick in the ground, twined the vine around it and watched it grow. When the yam was ripe I dug it out of the earth. The bigger the yam, the prouder I felt. It was a good feeling growing things that could be eaten.

In our country area we did not have an abattoir and when animals were ready to be slaughtered, we did it in the yard. The goat or pig was tethered and a rough table set up. I would hear the bleating of the goat or the squealing of the pig as it tried to get away; I am convinced the animal knew its end was near. Its throat was slit and the carcass cleaned and quartered and finally cut up into smaller portions. People who lived between Warsop and the nearby village of Troy came to buy the meat. Usually there would be a big wood fire in the yard and my mother or grandmother made a soup. The soup would have meat from the animal killed and vegetables grown on our land. I can remember people coming and going, many of whom would enjoy a bowl of soup. It was quite a social occasion.

In 1961 my mother had another baby, a girl. We adored our little sister and treated her like a dolly. My mother and grandmother would tell us, "Be careful with her. She's a baby, not a dolly." We girls were really pleased to have another sister in the family.

My father left for England just after the birth and my mother was very sad. We were all sad. As my father hugged each of his children, he told us that we would be joining him soon and should, till then, be good children to our mother. We knew how much he loved us and when he left we often talked about him, wondering what he was doing and hoping that he was alright. He was a good father and we missed him.

Looking back I am amazed at how focussed my father must have been to achieve what he did in such a short time in England. He must have worked very hard because after only a year in England he sent for my mother and we were left with our grandparents. Belonging as we did to an extended family with ever-present grandparents, we did not feel uprooted. We missed our parents but our lives continued much the same as before.

I did not see my parents again until 1968! I remember the letters they sent, always with money to look after us. As I grew older, I had to take the postal orders to the nearest post office in Troy, to be exchanged for money. I felt very grown-up to be given such a responsibility. When the post mistress handed over the money, I would count it carefully and put it in my bag which I tightly clutched all the way home and handed it over to my grandparents. Sometimes I was accompanied on these trips by one of my sisters. It was a long walk there and back but we were country children and used to walking the mile-and-a-half each way to and from school.

Our nearest market was in Christiana, across the parish border in Manchester. My grandparents sometimes went there to sell their food crops and I would accompany them. We used the country bus to get us there in the early morning to catch the first shoppers. The market was always bustling. Cultivators from the surrounding districts brought their produce here and the stalls were colourful with fruit and vegetables. Some weeks our produce sold quickly, but when business was slow and the evening was drawing near, we would reduce the prices so as not to have to go home again with the produce. And so my grandparents, like many Jamaican small farmers at that time, managed to make a reasonable living from their farming.

Our grandparents showered us with love and cared for us just as well as our parents would have done. When I hear some of the horror stories of children left with relatives in Jamaica, I realise now how fortunate we were to come from a close-knit family who worked together and who saw family as most important. I knew that my parents were working hard to get all their children to join them but that this would take time as there were six of us. So, in the meantime I tried to be helpful in the house and also helped to look after my brothers and sisters. I was my grandmother's little helper. In 1967 my parents sent for my two brothers and we four girls followed a year later. We all looked forward to seeing our parents and to finally being together again.

School and Church

I attended an elementary school in Troy. We travelled three miles there and back on each school day. Our grandparents made sure that we did not miss school because, to them, education was most important and the only way for their grandchildren to "better themselves". School was also fun. The teachers were strict and we couldn't mess about in class. I did not get into any scrapes, unlike some of the boys who were caught misbehaving when the teacher's back was turned. I was fascinated by the clever way my teachers had of spinning around from writing on the blackboard just in time to catch someone throwing a paper missile or making faces. That child would be in for a good telling off or 'the strap'. Everyone I knew dreaded 'the strap'; four or more strokes of it left you with burning palms for an hour or so.

One of the lessons I liked in school was Craft. In these sessions we made straw goods such as hats, bags and slippers from dried coconut fronds. We learnt a lot about Britain, especially British history and English literature. In fact, we knew more about England than about Jamaica because our school system was so very British.

My favourite teacher was Miss Spence, a most dedicated teacher who made learning a pleasure. I can see her in my mind's eye: tiny, light-skinned with a little waist and a protruding bottom, like a cartoon figure. She was small but she tolerated no nonsense in her class. We were there to learn and that was what she expected us to do. We would not dare be noisy in her class. We were taught to treat all our teachers with the utmost respect and, if we didn't, we would be punished at school and again at home when our parents found out.

In my last year at school my class teacher was Canadian. This was quite a novelty. A white teacher who spoke funny, was how we saw her. She was the first white teacher we had in the school in my time there and her Canadian accent was alien to our Jamaican ear. Some of the children tried to speak like her and that made the rest of us laugh. We had all seen the odd white person passing through our village and in Falmouth, our nearest town, but we had no close contact with them. Our Canadian teacher gradually became a part of our community and after a while we forgot that she was white and just saw her as a teacher.

Alana and Christine were my best friends. We played children's games such as hide and seek, dolly house and school, then as we got older we progressed to hopscotch and skipping. I missed them a lot when I left Troy but being with my parents, my brothers and sisters was what I wanted most.

My school was linked to the Anglican Church that my family attended. Both my mum and grandma thought I was going to be a nun because I was always helping people, running errands for the elderly and loved going to church. I was confirmed when I was eight years old. In preparation for confirmation, our group had special lessons after school and we would study from the Confirmation Book. The headteacher, Mr Peart, tested us and when we were ready we were confirmed by Father Sanguinetti. He was white, and with my Canadian teacher were the only white people with whom I had any contact in Jamaica.

The day of our confirmation was quite an occasion for the church and our families. I was so excited! I could hardly sleep the night before and woke up very early that morning, got dressed and waited impatiently for everyone in my family to be ready so that we could leave for church. I can still see it now. The church was packed as our families came out dressed in their Sunday best to see us confirmed. Candles glowed and the smell of frankincense filled the air in this high Anglican Church. In our confirmation group there were more girls than boys. We girls wore white dresses, white gloves and white shoes, while the boys were dressed smartly in white shirts, black trousers, black ties or bow-ties and black shoes. We were each given a candle to hold and, as we queued up for our first communion, I had a wonderful feeling of being blessed!

To me, my Jamaican childhood was quite normal and happy but I was pleased when our parents sent for us. We were going to be together again and that was something to look forward to. I remember the day I left as if it was yesterday. My hat was from Jamaica but my parents had sent me a peach dress, white gloves and white stiletto-heeled shoes in which I could hardly walk. There I was, a thirteen-year-old who had never worn high heels before, teetering from the house to the car and trying to look sophisticated. My uncle drove us to the airport in Kingston. Grandma and Granddad came with us.

Would you believe it, that very morning before leaving home I started my period! I was in a panic, worried about doing the right thing on the plane journey which I knew was going to be very long. Poor Grandma, she patted me and told me not to worry and that she would make sure everything would be alright. She sat down and wrote a note to the air hostess telling her my situation and asking her to take care of my hygiene. She gave me the note and told me to give it to the air hostess as soon as I got on the plane.

The journey to Kingston was long, nearly four hours of travelling mainly along narrow country roads until we reached the big city. Grandma had packed food for the journey and we ate bun and cheese followed later by corned beef sandwiches washed down with home-made lemonade. It was a tearful goodbye. We loved our grandparents and were not sure how long it would be before we saw them again.

When we boarded the BOAC plane we were all nervous. I felt in charge as I knew that my grandparents and parents expected me to be responsible for my sisters, the youngest was only seven years old and had been put on my passport. She was really scared. The air hostesses were okay except for one who was a little rough with my youngest sister when she wouldn't eat her meal. I became upset and said to the air hostess, "She's very young, you know!" In those days it was quite bold of me to speak like that to an adult but I felt I had to do it to protect my sister. I wished the journey over as quickly as possible while putting on a brave face for my sisters.

We slept for most of the flight, more than likely in an effort to quell our fears.

ENGLAND

Together Again

A sense of relief washed over me as the plane landed at Manchester Airport. My three sisters and I couldn't wait to see our parents. We had not seen our dad for seven years and our mom for six. As we came out of Customs we saw them waiting and unable to contain our excitement we ran to meet them. My mother was so overcome with joy that she could not stop crying. She was surprised at how much we had grown and remarked that I was now a proper young lady. My father finally shepherded us to his car, an Austin Cambridge.

On the way home I noticed smoke coming out of several buildings and said to him, "Dad, you've got a lot of factories here." He laughed and so did my mom.

"No luv, they are houses," he told me. I had never seen a house with smoke coming out of a chimney and this was really strange. Over the next three months I found lots of things strange as I learnt to adjust to our new way of life.

After what seemed ages, we finally arrived at our new home in Lenton, a fairly nice area of Nottingham. As owners our parents had made their home quite comfortable and I soon realised how lucky we were to have our own home, unlike many children I had met who were from Jamaica and lived with their parents in rooms or flats owned by Asian landlords. Most Caribbean people did not then own homes nor were they fortunate enough to get a council house; they lived in tenement houses in the poorer areas of town such as Hyson Green, Radford and St Anns.

My two brothers were pleased to see us but our youngest sister, born in England, was a little distant. When we met for the first time she was just five and considered us outsiders, I think. I was hurt by her strange coolness towards us but I tried not to show it. She clung to our parents when we were around and acted as if she would be happier not to have us, my four sisters and me, around. Interestingly, she got on well with the boys but all the time we lived together till the day I left home, her attitude to me remained the same. In fact it was only after she had her first child that some closeness began to develop! There was a subtle divide between her and us, the girls who had come up from Jamaica. Now looking back, I guess the four of us had a common history and a shared knowledge of things Jamaican. Our accent and the way we expressed ourselves were different from her Nottingham accent and the way she spoke English. Being 'black British', with only a British life experience, made her quite different from us as we grew up. But at the time, I was unable to see this and was baffled at how she seemed to want to exclude us while she monopolised our mother's attention.

My parents were very hard-working and, through thrift, had bought their house in 1965 so that when we children joined them we should be comfortable. My mother, like many black women, worked at John Player and Sons, the big tobacco factory in Nottingham. Jobs at Players were much sought after because the wages were better than in the other factories that employed black people. My dad worked in the building trade for big companies like Wimpey and always had work.

Except for the change in our environment, our upbringing was a continuation of what it had been in Jamaica. We went to school and church and helped with the household chores. Our parents instilled in us their belief in firm Christian discipline, love and family loyalty. As children we cared for each other and looked out for each other and, in the eyes of others, we were a close-knit family.

When my brothers, sisters and I became adults, we just accepted that our parents would grow old together and it was a shock to the family when, after a lifetime together, they split up. I remained friends with both of them but my brothers and sisters were bitter at the way our father had treated our mother. But I could not ignore my dad, knowing how much he loved us. I think my mom understands.

I was fortunate to attend Margaret Glen-Bott Secondary School in Wollaton, one of the better schools in a nice residential area of the city. I was expected to work hard and to achieve, whereas the rest of my family who went to Cottesmore felt that they were not encouraged academically but were pushed into sports. My school had approximately six hundred and fifty pupils only a few of whom were black. Many of the teachers were limited in their understanding of the black children and equated their Caribbean accent and different speech pattern with lack of intelligence. For instance, several of us were placed in lower streams; I was put in 4G and then later moved up to 4Z, the 'O' Level group. There was only one other black pupil in my form, a boy. My form teacher, Miss Broughton, was of the old school, strict, but a very committed teacher and fair. Limited in her knowledge about us, she tried to understand where I was coming from. I was shocked that, whereas in my little Jamaican country school we learnt about England, my new school taught nothing about the Caribbean! Again, unlike the experience of many of the Jamaican children I met outside of school, I got on well with my classmates. I was diligent and I think most of the teachers liked me. I was also active in sports, becoming a member of the cross-country team and the hockey team.

Nothing exceptional or traumatic happened to me in the two years I spent at Glen-Bott. The school had a high standard of discipline and everyone was expected to follow the school rules. I thought the teachers meted out punishment fairly and I never felt victimised there. For example, I got into trouble once and was sent home for not wearing my purse belt. I accepted that this was simply what had to happen; a white child would have received the same punishment.

I remember once retaliating at being provoked and not being punished for it, something alien to the experiences of my other siblings at Cottesmore. During a History lesson, I had a run-in with Linda, a school bully. She purposely knocked my fountain pen off my desk and ink splattered everywhere. I knew she was spoiling for a quarrel so I quietly cleaned up the mess then told her she owed me an apology. Laughing loudly, she refused to apologise. In my anger, I pinched her really hard and she let out a yell that attracted the teacher's attention. Linda insisted that I had attacked her. Mr. Wood looked at her sharply and said firmly, "You must have provoked Eunice. Now let's hear what really happened." When I recall this I realise how different my school experience was and how lucky I was to be in a good school with teachers who did not behave to me in any racist way at all. They did not know much about black people and, at first, some did misjudge my Jamaican way of expressing things as incorrect but when I proved myself to be as competent as anyone else, they immediately moved me up into the correct stream for my ability.

At my careers interview, I expressed an interest in nursing because, sad to say, it was the only profession in which I saw black women. I was encouraged to join the British Red Cross to get some experience. I enjoyed being in the British Red Cross and the First Aid training I received. I also decided to do some voluntary work in one of the hospitals in order to gain more experience in the field as I was not yet old enough to apply for nurse training. This turned out to be an eye-opener and I soon realised that nursing was not for me after all. It was then that I switched my career choice to office work.

I left school with a couple of 'O' Levels and went on to Basford Hall to do a one-year secretarial course with 'O' Level English Language and British Constitution as two additional subjects. At college we were treated as young adults. In this very different learning environment, I thoroughly enjoyed the atmosphere. My only regret was that, not having had a long time at school, I did not get as much as I should have from the education offered. Further Education College was a god-send for people like me to complete secondary education courses and gain vocational qualifications for work.

Starting Out

On leaving college, I went to work at S & U Company as a junior clerk. It was a credit company and I was the only black member of staff. The atmosphere in the office was friendly and there was always someone there to help me if I got into difficulty. After a year, I moved to a better position at Cavendish Woodhouse, a large furniture store, where I worked for nine years in the legal section dealing with bad debts. During this time I attended courses at Clarendon College, upgrading my office skills to include dictaphone typing and bookkeeping. Being a conscientious worker, I was promoted on merit to a senior post where I got on well with colleagues and was happy with the way my career was progressing.

I met Karl when I was eighteen. I was running to work so as not to be late when his car pulled alongside, "Excuse me, do you want a lift?"
"Pardon?" I was taken by surprise and most certainly would not think of getting into a stranger's car.
"I'm offering you a lift since you seem to be in a hurry."
"No thank you." I continued on my way at a more graceful speed, aware now that I was being watched. Not long after this he again offered me a lift and this time I had a good look at him; he seemed harmless enough and I accepted.

He introduced himself and told me that he was a Nigerian law student whose government grant had stopped because of the Biafran war raging in his country. He was then working at Jersey Kapwood, a local clothing factory. This was the beginning of our courtship. Karl was eight years older than I was and a very interesting person to be with. Six months after our first meeting we went to Cornwall on holiday together. A couple of months later I discovered that I was pregnant.

With this unexpected turn that my life had suddenly taken, I felt I could no longer remain at home so I moved into my own flat. We did not live together as that would have been frowned upon by the church and I respected the Christian values with which my parents had brought me up. My father was very protective towards me and when he and Karl were discussing the situation, I heard the implicit warning in his words: "I hope you are going to take care of my daughter."

"I'll take care of her," was Karl's response.

He sounded sincere but my mother was still hesitant. She had the stereotypical image of Karl as a Nigerian who did not respect the Jamaican woman as he would his own country-woman, however, she tried to be happy for me because I was happy. I loved Karl and thought that he loved me too. I felt we would have a wonderful life together and that together we could overcome any hurdles we encountered.

My baby, René, was born in 1973. I continued to work, leaving him at the day nursery. Karl and I had some wonderful years together. He was my mentor and never undermined me but encouraged me to explore avenues for self-improvement. He was fun to be with when he was in a good mood. We both liked travelling and we explored many places of interest in England.

At first I did not notice certain habits of his, being in love and quite blinded to his faults it took a while for them to manifest themselves. I think my growing as a person finally made me more aware and I began to see evidence of Karl's selfishness. For instance, in 1982 I moved into a house in Bulwell that needed a lot of renovation to make it comfortable, but Karl would not lift a finger to help me with it. People in our community do not usually tell you outright what they are thinking but I got the message about Karl. One day my father with sadness in his voice said to me, "Pickney chile, tree growing in your face?"

"Why?" I got no reply. But I knew something wasn't right. My father just shook his head as the message hit home. He was telling me that I was neither ugly nor desperate and should not put up with being treated by Karl as if I could not find someone else. I cried that night when I realised that Karl and I were not as before. Two weeks later, an old family friend came by and in our conversation he teased, "I told the missus that if I was a little younger I would run off with you." Bless him! His remark was intended as a confidence booster.

By 1983 I faced up to the situation that it was time to call it a day with this relationship which, for a long time, had not felt right. I realised that I was only fooling myself if I hoped for something positive to develop. It had taken me eleven years to accept that I had bought into a relationship that was going nowhere towards the future I had envisaged. I saw Karl for what he was - an attractive man with a charming personality that women were drawn to, but not a man wanting to settle for the family life I wanted. By then I had also found out that he was seeing someone else. That was the last straw. When I look back, I hold no bitterness towards him; he was a good influence in my life and, above all, he gave me my wonderful son.

When my relationship with Karl ended, my life was at a turning point in more ways than one. In 1981 I had left Cavendish Woodhouse for what I thought was a better post with Walker, Walton & Hanson Estate Agents. I would later find that it was a bad move. As personal assistant to the manager, my hours were long and unsuitable for a mother with a primary school child whose father did not live with them. My boss, however, was a lovely man. When I moved into the house in Bulwell and he discovered that I did not have enough money to immediately carpet the stairs, he gave me three hundred pounds to purchase the carpet - a most generous gift. With such a thoughtful boss I felt really bad when

I had to leave. I explained as sensitively as I could to Mr Hanson that I loved my job but had to spend more time with my child.

I then went to work for the City Council in the Youth Training Agency based at North Sherwood Street. By 1983 I had joined NALGO (National Association of Local Government Officers) and was a member of the Black Steering Group within it. At NALGO meetings I met two lesbians who were vocal members of the Equal Opportunities Consultative Group. They were instrumental in changing the direction of my working life and in my commitment to become politically active.

Political Life

My awareness of the black struggle began when I was a teenager and joined the BPFM (Black People's Freedom Movement). These meetings raised my awareness of the struggle most black people faced in their daily lives here in Britain. I realised that I had been very fortunate, not only at school but also in my work experience. I learnt about the endemic evil of racism in Britain, U.S.A. and South Africa from members who shared their experiences with us. At our meetings we also had national and international black speakers who focussed our minds on moving forward by organising and strategising to achieve economic and social objectives. I was convinced that education was important if we were to fulfil our potential and be a positive influence in our children's lives and I intended to apply this to my life. It was a pity that we could not get more black people to attend these meetings and join us in our struggle to increase awareness of who we are and what we can achieve within our communities.

In 1981 when my son was eight, because of my keen interest in education, I became a school governor for Mellors Primary School. I felt then, and still do, that the early years represent the starting point of our children's education and that this stage needs government support to ensure that children, especially those living in situations of disadvantage, get quality service from the education system. As a school governor I did not see myself as representing only black parents, but all parents, for, as far as I was concerned, good parents, black and white, want for their children an education in a safe and stimulating environment. I am still a school governor.

Soon after moving to Bulwell in 1982 I was approached by Mr. McIntosh, a local Labour Party activist, and one of his friends to join the Labour Party. They were recruiting in the area and impressed me with what they said the

Labour Party could offer all people living in Britain, regardless of their ethnicity. I promised to think about attending the next branch meeting. When I turned up at the meeting, not one other black person was in sight! I thought, "How will our views be represented if we do not become involved?"

In 1983 after giving it a lot of thought, I decided to join the Labour Party and have been a member since then. With its socialist philosophy it seems to me to offer the people of this country the quality of life needed in a caring society. As a member of NALGO and of the local Black Steering Group within it, I was also becoming more politicised. I began to understand the importance of people having their views represented. I was made acutely aware that black people were under-represented in government at both national and local levels and also in organisations that impacted on our lives. It was sometimes frustrating to see the people who represented us in the union paying mere lip service to issues of great importance to ethnic minorities.

The Black Steering Group within NALGO had to fight to get NALGO to accept the proposal for black representation at the national level. I attended the NALGO meeting in Leeds at which the proposal was to be discussed. The Nottingham black local government officers representing the Steering Group were Harry Joshua, Alf Kabie, Simon Ude and me. We were determined to win on this important issue. We were articulate and convincing in our argument and won the day! To me this was an achievement. Being at the centre where decisions were made ensured that our perspective on issues was taken on board and we were not just given lip service.

Seeking to be a 'change agent' within the Labour Party, I joined the Equal Opportunities Consultative Group. In 1985, I was nominated the Party's Nottingham North representative to the meeting of the General Committee held in Skegness. I was very nervous but, buttressed by the support of the other three branch members, I presented the resolution that the branch had passed and talked to it in the time allotted. The resolution was carried and I felt elated. This was the first time I had spoken publicly in such a political arena and relief washed over me as I sat down. This meeting also afforded me the opportunity to meet a wide cross-section of union activists and Members of Parliament. It provided a learning experience.

My political knowledge and confidence grew as I attended meetings and conferences across the country. I was impressed by certain speakers. A couple of Labour Party members come to mind. Margaret Hodge impressed me when I attended a conference in Coventry for councillors and officers looking at urban regeneration and perspectives on social policies. The pace of her delivery was one that all could follow; her speech was not full of jargon, her voice was clear and she used body language and eye contact cleverly to hold the attention of her audience. John Smith was another excellent speaker; he came across as calm, sincere and believing totally in what he was proposing. Another was Josephine Kawali, a Director of Social Services; when I heard her speak, I got the blueprint for successful innovation: "You have to plan. You have to act. You have to strategise."

In 1988 I went back to Jamaica for a holiday and also learnt a valuable lesson from my aunt who was then Head of English at one of the high schools in Port Antonio in the parish of Portland. Her commitment in her service to humanity was very impressive. The hours she devoted to her work within the community equalled those for which she was paid as a teacher! I felt a push towards service to my community. How? I was not sure.

Not long after my return to England, however, the way forward did manifest itself. I was approached by three Asian and two Caribbean local activists to put my name forward for selection as a candidate for the upcoming council election. The local Labour Party was trying to implement its Equal Opportunities policy and was keen to consider women and black people as candidates - something that had not happened so far. I sought my sixteen-year-old son's advice as I knew that, if chosen, I would have less time to spend with him. He was wonderful in his response, "Mom, do it for *you*." He convinced me that I could do it but I was still having cold feet about what would certainly be uncharted territory for me. Although black people in Nottingham tended to vote for the Labour Party, only a few were party members and even fewer were active. If elected, I would be the first black woman councillor in Nottingham. It was a huge challenge.

I sought advice from Harry Joshua who had by then become a friend and mentor. I had met Joshua in the building where we both worked and for a while we only briefly greeted each other. Mine would be a breezy, "Good morning!" to which he would respond in a somewhat more reserved manner. It was some time before we got past this and began to share ideas. I became aware of his excellent intellect and his commitment to serving the black community behind the scenes. He told me I would make a good councillor and that he would be there for me. True to his promise he has been my mentor over the years. *With him, and later with my husband, Alan, I have no inhibitions expressing my weaknesses and fears. I know they will help me through whatever I have to face.*

Feeling more confident with Joshua's support, I agreed to have my name put forward to the selection committees of three wards: Lenton and Park, Bilborough and Clifton North. As a prospective candidate, I was asked to prepare a brief Candidate's Statement for each committee, outlining what I would bring to make a difference to the ward. I was then asked to attend an interview. I had to give a five-minute presentation based on my statement, followed by a ten-minute question and answer session. In my presentation I had to identify the key issues for the area and give my response to each. Then there was the wait for their decision. I really wanted to represent Lenton and Park ward as it was the area I knew well. After the interviews I was neither disappointed nor surprised when I was not chosen by the other two selection committees. It was common knowledge who those selection committees wanted to represent them. However, I saw the experience as useful in preparing me for the ward I very much wanted to represent.

I had a close affinity with Lenton because it was where I had grown up. The ward was also considered a safe seat for Labour - although in politics nothing is safe. It was also rumoured that the committee was in search of someone to replace the incumbent councillor. Before attending the interview with the selection committee of Lenton and Park ward, I prepared myself to deal with all the issues I thought might come up.

The day of the interview finally arrived and the committee had my Candidate's Statement. In it I told them that I had a good understanding of local needs in the ward because I had lived in Lenton from 1968 to 1975, had continued to be active in the community and wanted to represent the needs of local people. The key issue I identified was that of employment. The ward was a mixed constituency - Park was affluent while the rest of the ward had a high percentage of unemployment- therefore, jobs and training were the priorities I would want to address. I thought I had done quite well with the presentation but the questions were gruelling. Waiting for the decision seemed to take an eternity. Summoned back into the interview room, I was given the decision by the presiding officer. I was the new Labour Party candidate for Lenton and Park ward in the next local government election. My strongest challenge had come from a local female school teacher, Sandie Maitland. I later learnt how very close had been the choice between us. My friends and supporters were as elated as I was. We now had to meet the next challenge, getting me elected.

The election campaign began as soon as I was selected in 1988 and continued until the day of the election in May, 1989. My campaign manager was in charge of getting me known to the people in the ward. I sent the following election address to the people asking them to vote for me:

> *My name is Eunice Campbell. I am 35 years old and the mother of a 16-year-old son. I have for some years been active both as a Trade Unionist and a member of the Labour Party. In addition, I am a member of the governing bodies of Southwark Junior and Infant Schools.*

As your candidate, I will - first and foremost - seek to represent your views, your concerns and your wishes. We are living in times of great change in local government, times in which standards in education, health, social services, care for the elderly and even local democracy are being devalued and eroded by a long line of government legislations - not least of which is the Poll Tax. We will all be affected. At no time has the need been more urgent for ordinary people to express their views and participate in local affairs. At no time has the straightforward representation of your views been more crucial.

I attended branch meetings as an observer. I visited schools to meet parents. I attended workshops and seminars where I addressed the people. Most challenging of all, but also most enlightening, was the door-to-door canvassing. I was learning such a lot more about the ward and daily growing in the confidence that, as a councillor, I would serve well the people I represented.

On election night, all the candidates for Lenton and Park ward attended the counting of the votes at Harvey Road in Bilborough. When I arrived there all the polling boxes had been delivered. In the company of a few friends and party supporters, I was nonetheless very, very nervous but tried not to show it. Each ward was allocated a table with the appropriate officers. There were seven other candidates who stood for the Lenton and Park ward. With my agents and activist friends I waited anxiously for the result which came at 11p.m. It was announced that I had 2,800 votes, a majority of over 1,000. *I was the new Labour Party councillor!* I cried in the excitement of the moment. I thanked my election agent, campaign supporters and the people who had voted for me and, after the congratulations and formalities, I went to ACNA (African-Caribbean National Artistic Centre) to celebrate with my friends and community activists. Later, I learnt that I was one of sixteen women elected to the Council of eighty-four members.

I was also the only Caribbean woman, not just in Nottinghamshire but in the whole of the East Midlands region, to be elected in that year's local election.

In the newly-elected council of 1989, the only other councillor from the Caribbean community was George Powe, an ex-Air Force serviceman, teacher and local activist. After the election balloting, I was sworn in with the other newly-elected members. I was very nervous, even a little apprehensive, not quite sure what was expected of me as a newly elected member.

My first council meeting was that of the full council in the Chamber. There I was with eighty-three other members. To start the meeting, all our names were called out and we were welcomed by the leader of the Council. Prayers were said by the Chairman's chaplain and we went through the order of business on the agenda. The presiding chairs of committees answered questions from the floor. I listened keenly to the debates and learnt the names of all the chairs for the various committees. I noted that the Chief Executive addressed a member by his/her full title. It was an exciting day for me but also one of great trepidation as I began to fully understand the enormity of the task I had undertaken.

As a new member, I knew that I had to learn the ropes, and fast, in order to make my voice heard. In my role as councillor, I intended to work for all the people in my ward by keeping abreast of what was happening and making myself available to them through regular surgeries for consultation and assistance at the branch office and also through personal contact. This I have always done and will continue to do. I take into consideration the views of the people in my ward and have used their local knowledge as a vehicle to ensure the provision of the services they need.

My re-election in 1993 indicated that the people I was serving had confidence in me. This spurred me on to work towards the realisation of the promises we, the Council, make to the people of Nottingham.

Following the Conservative Government's new legislative framework for local authorities in the 1980s, Nottingham City became a unitary authority and ceased to be a part of the County Council. The change-over period begun in 1996 and was completed in 1998. Councillors within the city boundary were City and County Councillors simultaneously during this period. In the by-election of 1996, I was the candidate for Byron ward, a new ward that included two council estates and two owner-occupier estates with a social mix. I had a brilliant team of party workers who knew the area well and this gave me a lot of confidence. There was a great deal of ground to cover as we canvassed and some nights my feet were so sore and my whole being so weary, that I could barely make it to bed when I got home.

I introduced myself to the voters in the 'Byron Ward By-Election Special' under the slogan, *"A Fair Deal for Nottingham"*:

Dear Voter,

> *My name is Eunice Campbell, Labour candidate for the local by-election for Byron Ward. I have been an active member of the Labour Party since 1983, and serve as a local school and college governor, and as a member of a local Housing Association.*
>
> *I have been helping to set up a Tenants' Action Group as well as being active in local government since 1988. I have initiated an* **"Early Start Scheme"** *to support lone parents and long-term unemployed people through jobs and training.*

> *My aim is to represent your views and concerns in the Bestwood, Rise Park and Top Valley areas, continuing to pay particular attention to work for the safety of local residents. It is my intention to work with the local community through initiatives such as BESTCO in the area of fighting crime and anti-social behaviour.*
>
> *As your local Labour Councillor, I will hold regular monthly surgeries which will give you the opportunity to raise any concerns you may have.*

As I canvassed, I met all sorts but I have never been racially abused; however, like my colleagues, I have faced hostility and have had doors slammed in my face and been told to "F . . . off!" The team's hard work and the Labour Party's history of good governance at the local level paid off. I was elected and joined Alan Clark and Carol Stapleton as the Labour Councillors for Byron Ward.

In May 2003 I was re-elected to the new boundary ward of Bulwell Forest, a ward made up of three areas of the old Byron ward and one of Bulwell and Highbury Vale. I am very accessible to the people of my ward. There are three regular surgeries held in the constituency where I deal with issues ranging from dog-fouling of the streets to problems in housing and education. There is a free phone to the Council Office and the secretaries take messages to which I respond. We produce a monthly branch report for the branch meeting, organise and attend public meetings to address current issues and do site visits to projects as well as to get first-hand information on concerns raised.

All councillors as members of the Council must serve on various committees. One of the first committees on which I served and for which I was Vice-Chair was Trading Standards & Equal Opportunities and within the County Council I was active in promoting equal opportunities. This work was often undermined by officers and Council members. The Council at that time was like many institutions in Britain where women and ethnic minorities were under-represented across the board. With a group of officers, we set up the 'Equal Opportunities Mentoring Scheme' aimed at encouraging women into lower and middle management when it was apparent that a glass ceiling was in operation. The County Council funded the workshops and, when the City Council gained unitary authority status and I became a Nottingham City Councillor, the scheme was transferred to the city.

In 1996, as well as being Councillor for Byron Ward, I became Chair of the Nottingham City Labour Group after six months as Vice-Chair. I had to make it clear, as I chaired the first meeting, that I expected cooperation, and I took a no-nonsense approach in order to control the meeting. I began, "Some of us are quite capable and some are mediocre, but we are all learning. I expect to be shown respect because I will give respect." The response was immediate silence and from then on it was down to the business at hand. I got straight to the point in discussion with my colleagues and some of them might not like me or my style but what was important was that we treated each other with respect. That is my style and it works for me.

Committed as I was to early childhood education, I was instrumental in the setting up of the 'Early Start Scheme' in two inner city primary schools, Lenton and Mellors. I can remember when we sent our first development plan to the Department of Education how anxiously we awaited their response. We felt we were on the way when our plan was accepted. The scheme has been a success, thanks to the hard work of all those involved in its inception. It provided full-time childcare for the 'under-eights' from 7:00 a.m. to 6.00p.m, in order to assist lone parents to return to employment or education/training. The places were heavily subsidised and, therefore, affordable to everyone. The project, a Central Government initiative, was funded by them and the Economic Development Fund.

The project has expanded and is now under the auspices of the Education Early Years/Childcare Sub-Committee which I chaired for two years and of which I am now a lead member. This committee deals with all the city's educational provisions for children three to fourteen years old. Our aim is for 'early years to be wrapped around care' by providing nursery places for all children, before and after school care, lunches and lunch-time supervision for children of parents working or training and support for childminders. This we see as achievable by coordinating all the services in operation to ensure a high quality of provision through the collaboration of local government, private and voluntary sectors. We achieved the targets set by Central Government for the first and second years and have been rewarded with an increase in our funding from them. Among the improvements in the delivery this has made possible, is one that we are very proud of - every four-year-old in Nottingham City now has access to a nursery place!

Another committee on which I served as a member and chaired between 1999 and 2001 is the City Council's Personal & Customer Services. This committee had a strategic role to play in the implementation of human resource policies and procedures with respect to employment, recruitment, training and equality. In July 2003, under the new political structure, I was elected to the Cabinet as a Portfolio Holder for Personnel, Equalities and Access. I am one of only two women in the Cabinet. The executive portfolio is responsible for the strategic direction of the Council and includes working with other key members. As a portfolio holder I am accountable to my Labour Party colleagues in the Council and must give regular reports to the full Council as well as answer questions on the area covered by my portfolio. This is challenging work, as the Council addresses issues concerning the delivery of quality service to constituencies and staff. It has also given me the clarity I needed to develop my political aspirations.

There are two areas in which I have a keen interest and to which I contribute, while not being a member of the committees with responsibility for them. They are the Council's Economic Regeneration Strategy and the educational achievement of black children who for years have been underachieving. I work closely with community groups so that their views are reflected in the city's Economic Regeneration Strategy. I also maintain links with schools and voluntary groups that provide support for underachieving black children and closely monitor the performance of the city's schools. When Nottingham City became responsible for its schools, we came at the bottom in the league table for schools' academic performance nationwide. The Council, recognising the need for urgent attention, put measures in place to improve the performance of pupils. Hopefully, things will continue to improve.

My wider community involvement over the years includes board membership of several local organisations. I served on the management committee of the Citizens' Advice Bureau and First Enterprise Business Agency. The latter was set up to support ethnic minorities in business ventures by providing training and business start-up loans.

Our Council promotes its city abroad and develops economic and social links with countries all over the world. We are known as the 'Robin Hood County' and this folk hero draws many tourists to our city. Our Council receives many invitations to visit other countries and I have been very fortunate to have visited several countries as part of the City Council delegation.

My first overseas visit was to attend a conference on migrant workers held in Holland in 1991. Through an interpreter, I talked about the political system in Britain and how we were dealing with our migrant workers. The participants were able to share useful information and give different perspectives on the topic. For the duration of the conference I stayed with a family who provided me with an insight into life in Holland. The man was Dutch married to a Caribbean woman from Aruba; they had two daughters, both training to be doctors. I enjoyed our social interaction immensely and found the trip a useful learning experience.

In 1993 I went to Czechoslovakia for a week when our city was being twinned with Kolin. I was able to see at first hand what things were like under communist rule. With the exception of Prague, which was untouched and remains an architecturally beautiful city, there were signs of the destruction of many buildings and we were told by the natives that many historical artefacts had been taken by the Russians. On the industrial front we noted that their factories lacked basic units and that they were far behind us in their industries. In a gesture of friendship, our city offered Kolin City a fire engine.

By English standard the people were poor but our hosts were very kind. I was the only black person present over the week and was made as welcome as a princess. At the end of the visit I was presented with a tourist guide-book with beautiful photographs of Kolin and its historical treasures. I will always hold it dear.

In 1999 I visited Helsinki with two other city councillors to look at a range of networks as part of the 'join up European bid' for an intranet system. Helsinki is part of the European network for business and information development and the trip was most informative.

It has been most pleasing to have had over the years two sheriffs and a Lord Mayor who came here as immigrants from Jamaica and who have made a valuable contribution to our city. After my two decades in local government I look forward to continuing for another term. By then I think I will have given as much as I have to give. After that I would like to work as a volunteer overseas for a Christian organisation for three months each year and for the rest of the year spend more time with my husband.

Serving The Black Community

How have I served the African-Caribbean community over the years? Opportunities to serve come in many different ways. As a councillor I am always aware of how our policies and structures impact on black people and I serve the black community in the course of my everyday activities. Serving on the 'Race Equality Advisory Committee' and as a governor of two local schools attended by many black children are two other examples of my wider community participation. To the policies and work carried out in these areas I bring a black perspective.

I have served on the management committee of the Tuntum Housing Association for several years and seen it develop into a very successful housing association. From its creation, it has aimed foremost at meeting the housing needs of the black community who felt that its members were often very low on the City Council's waiting list and when they did get houses, it was more often than not in the more run-down areas of the city. Tuntum houses are refurbished to a high standard and maintained at that level. Tuntum, therefore, has an excellent reputation among housing associations nation-wide.

The most challenging job, and the most rewarding, during my involvement with it was the 'Women's Training & Employment Programme' set up in 1993 in the heart of the black community at ACNA, the African-Caribbean centre in the St. Anns area of the city. It also turned out to be the most painful job experience that I have had. The aim of the project was to train women in an environment where they were comfortable and could focus on succeeding. On offer were GCSE in Mathematics and English, courses in Business Administration and Management, Computing and Information Technology and Sound Engineering. These courses were taught by tutors from Arnold & Carlton and, in addition, external black trainers were employed for seminars around black issues.

When I started as the manager of the project in 1993, it had a budget of twenty-one thousand pounds; when I left four years later, it had seven hundred and fifty thousand pounds in its coffers! I worked very hard seeking funds and assistance from funding agencies, a local college, one of the local universities and businesses in the region. I also networked with other groups to benefit from their expertise. East Midland Electricity sent their Head of Business to assist us with our five-year development plan and gave us five thousand pounds. Dr. Odefa, a Nigerian consultant to British Gas, gave us a lot of help, over and above that expected of him.

A year after WINA (West Indian National Association) started the Nursery Project at ACNA with funds from City Challenge and the City Council, their management committee stepped down. With the project facing financial crisis, WINA and the City Council asked me to take over the management of the Nursery and I became the coordinator in 1994. One of the first things I did was to raise funds to employ an administrative officer. I learnt how to negotiate contracts and used this to full advantage to make the Nursery project a viable business while providing the community with a much needed service. I met with Arnold & Carlton College, offered them twenty-five nursery places for the sum of sixty thousand pounds and was overjoyed when they agreed. This and other funds flowing in made it possible to double the number of nursery places, moving them from thirty to sixty!

In 1996, Dr. Odefa and others were amazed at how much I had accomplished single-handedly. "I think you may be heading for burn-out," he warned. One of the professors at Nottingham Trent University also commented on the weight of my workload saying, "Eunice, I can see your inner strength but I think you've given enough to your community." But on no account did I want this project to fail and I intended to ensure that its affairs were transparent, because I considered accountability to be extremely important, especially when ratepayers' money was involved, so I continued with my heavy workload.

Unfortunately, the conflict that had raged within the organisation before I became coordinator continued and it made my life hell. To top it all, I was having problems getting paid. Someone, amazed at what was happening, asked the Management Committee, "How could Eunice take the project to this level of success and you don't want to pay her a fair salary?" In the end the City Council had to intervene on my behalf. Can you imagine how that felt? What I had to accept finally was that not all of us in that organisation were working for the good of the community; some lacked vision. It was the old story of jealousy and the destruction it eventually brings. When I thought of this I remembered an African saying: 'The dog that buries his bone under the sand safe from predators is an educator, but the dog that leaves the bone above the sand is not'.

By the beginning of 1997, the stress of working in the project and of maintaining my other responsibilities as a councillor was having a debilitating effect on my health. I developed diabetes. My son was away at university and my poor mother was worried about me. One day she said to me, "Eunice, I can't help you, nor can anyone else. You need to get down on your knees and pray for guidance."

Not long after, as I was travelling home along Hucknall Road, I had to pull over. I felt absolutely exhausted physically and drained emotionally. I prayed silently, "Lord, make me an instrument of peace. I need your guidance." And like a flash the answer came, "Go and give in your notice." I felt a weight being lifted as peace descended. I went home. The decision was made.

I had an appointment at the doctor's and he immediately signed me off work. I had not realised how poorly I was. With friends and loved ones rallying around, I felt blessed and cared for. One day, as I sat in my lounge facing the back garden and listening to Radio 4, a nun's words lifted my spirits. She compared some people to empty ships sailing through life and said that one of the ways in which we can see God is by looking at the flowers and the trees. I raised my head and, looking out at my garden with the crocuses and spring flowers, I saw the beauty God created. How lucky I was to have this house and ready-made garden to provide me with comforts to come home to after a trying day. The young female doctor who had sold it to me had reduced the asking price by nine hundred pounds and had given me the carpets because I just could not afford them! "Because you are such a nice person," she had said. I was pleasantly surprised by her generosity.

It saddens me still when I think of this project which folded a year after I left. It had such potential and so much of my blood, sweat and tears had gone into it.

The other project in which I was heavily involved was **BUILD**, a mentoring programme that we adopted from the United States of America where it had had a successful track record among black youngsters. The need for such a programme came out of several years of research on the exclusion of black pupils from school, done by Ukaidi, another black organisation. The research highlighted the high percentage of black youngsters in local secondary schools who, as victims of exclusion, were unemployable because they had been unable to access opportunities. The black community knew it had to do something to help these youngsters back into education and to keep in school those identified as being at high risk. I worked with the Director of the Association of Caribbean Families and Friends (ACFF) to spearhead this project by which successful people in the community provided mentoring to disaffected young people. The programme has been very successful and the number of children it helps has increased over the years.

Home Life

As I became involved in community projects and took on the gruelling job of a councillor, I was unable to find the time to further my own education and to improve my management skills. In 1993 I refused to put this off any longer and made space in my busy schedule to obtain the Certificate in Administration/Business. Having completed this part-time in 1995, I went on to do a B.Sc. in Social Policy through the Open University and also gained a Certificate in Adult Teaching that enables me to work in the area in which I am really interested.

For several years after my broken relationship in 1983, with no-one else in my life, I concentrated fully on the activities in which I was involved. Things gradually changed after I met Alan. We both became councillors at roughly the same time and saw each other as colleagues for a while. Alan is very knowledgeable and capable and became my agent when I was running for Byron Ward. I felt comfortable with him and our friendship grew into love. Alan is from Lancashire and, after obtaining his M.Sc. at Cambridge University, he came to Nottingham University to do the one-year teaching certificate. On completing this he decided to make Nottingham his home and became involved in local politics. He, too, leads a very active life as a lecturer at a college in Loughborough and a councillor. We also both share a passion for travelling.

Both our families are pleased that we found each other. My mother is especially happy that I am no longer on my own. She began worrying when my son left for university. Then when he chose not to return to Nottingham after graduating but to work in London as a biochemist, she worried even more that I was too often alone. It's wonderful when my son comes home but since our marriage it has been mostly Alan and me.

But life is full of surprises. Alan thought that he would marry a black or Asian woman. I, on the other hand, thought I would marry a black man who would share the black consciousness developed in me over the years through the Black

People's Freedom Movement. And yet here we are, happy together and sharing a common commitment as Christians working as councillors in our community.

My Dad died in 1999. I miss not having him around as we had a very special relationship and he was always there for me. Yet he never breathed a word to me about how seriously ill he was and it was only when we were rushing him to hospital just before he died that he told us that he had been diagnosed with prostate cancer in 1993! For a while I found it very hard to accept that he had kept his secret for so many years. One reason may have been that, given the strained relationship he had with the family, he had not wanted to worry us with it.

The breakdown in his relationship with my brothers and sisters had come about through their disappointment after he left our mother. They were divorced in the 1970s and he then married an English woman. Later that relationship broke up as well. My heart went out to him because he was not happy in his old age. I also feel saddened for my mother that their marriage had ended in divorce after they had worked and achieved so much together. But life goes on and I wish my mother, who has never remarried, would find someone to be happy with.

When I look around Nottingham I see far too many black women, like my mother, growing old alone, unable to get past the grief of having been let down by their men. I have learnt that one should forgive because once you let the bitterness go, you can begin to live again.

My Passions

I do not have time for hobbies but I love cooking and when I have the time I experiment with cuisine from different countries. Alan and I travel at every opportunity we get and I have wonderful memories of some places we have visited. I loved Sark, beautiful, mysterious and mountainous. The Jersey Flower Show that I visited was an experience of pure delight. I have fond memories of Italy. We spent our honeymoon in Venice. It was a wonderful holiday, like a dream come true. I have also enjoyed visits to Rome and Pompeii. The greatness of the Roman Empire comes alive when you visit Rome. Such splendour! One of the pleasures of travelling around Europe is in visiting museums and learning about other cultures. There is so much to see and learn. I look forward to doing a lot more of this when Alan and I retire.

A couple of places in Spain and Tunisia are our relaxation spots, warm and pretty, not quite the beauty of the Caribbean but close enough to get away for short breaks. We had a wonderful time in Bali and spoilt ourselves taking a helicopter tour of the island. Cuba gave us lots of surprises. The hotel was very modern and comfortable; Havana had many sites to visit and it made our day when we were able to tour farms and churches and meet people in their homes. To my surprise, we were also offered black-market Cuban cigars! It just goes to show that some people will always buck the system to make money.

I was thrilled to be a member of the delegation of councillors invited by the Chinese government to visit China in 2001. We had a guided tour lasting twelve days and our hosts ensured that we saw the beauty of China and savoured some of its history. On that trip we visited altogether nine states including Hong Kong. Among the highlights for me was walking along the Great Wall just outside Beijing, seeing the terracotta warriors – an army of eight thousand men – and visiting Guillin with its mystical mountains and caves that look like faces. I felt an affinity with the dark-skinned Chinese farm workers; they reminded me of farmers and farming in Jamaica.

For Alan and me, travelling provides us quality time together, when we leave behind the rushing about of our busy lives and find time to relax. We have agreed that there are still one-hundred-and-eleven countries that we want to visit. That leaves us a lot of travelling still to do!

Having spent most of my life in England, I feel very much a part of this society. I have invested a great deal in it and will continue to do so as a citizen. But I will always love Jamaica; it is a part of me. It was there that I learnt the importance of community involvement and developed the sense of duty that I brought with me to England.

Nottingham is now my home and Jamaica my roots.

BOOK 2

My Story

JAMAICA

I Remember . . . .

The Early Years

Memories of childhood in Jamaica are snapshots, clear and bright in an otherwise hazy kaleidoscope spanning the period 1947, when I was four, to 1959. With few exceptions, the memories are not chronological but more like swathes of events.

The feeling evoked is that, as the first child of my parents, I was pampered by my family. My father was ebony black, 184cm. tall and handsome. He was soft-spoken, and hunched his shoulders when he laughed, a sound which was like water squirting through a narrow channel. He was easy-going and not much of a disciplinarian. My father left the disciplining of his children to my mother. I remember him flogging me only once, when I was thirteen.

My mother at 170cm. tall and elegant, had skin like soft brown sugar and big, light-brown eyes. As a young mother she wore her hair scooped off her round face and pinned in a bun or sometimes a plait twirled at the back of her head. She was the action woman, always on the move; she had a short temper and brooked no disobedience.

One of my earliest memories is of my father coming home after what seemed to have been ages away. He had been to USA for six months. I was fascinated by his shoes. I was only knee high and had an excellent view of his legs and shoes. The shoes were black and white with lots of little holes at the front. They were fancy and I hadn't noticed anyone else with such a pair.

On his return I followed him around in awe. I watched him as he cleaned his teeth and begged him for some of the fizzy drink he had afterwards. He would spoon this white stuff from the tin and pour water on it, stirring as he poured. The water would fizz and bubble up to the top of the glass. I enjoyed drinking it and liked the feel of the bubbles tickling my nose. What I did not know was that it was Andrew's Liver Salts taken to ease constipation!

Our home was in the village square of Daybart in Milk River, Clarendon. Milk River is famous for its spa, its mineral level being one of the highest in the world. As a child I knew nothing of the spa but did know that sugar cane was important. We lived across from the cane-workers' barracks that dominated the square. The barracks provided rooms for the cane-workers who came in droves during the harvest season. As far as the eye could see on that side of the road was a sea of green cane-fields; on closer inspection they were broken up by narrow canals for irrigation. To the right of our shop and home was the Tiveys' shop and next to that the school premises including the headteacher's home. A canal ran on our side of the road over which a little bridge led to each property. Down the lane running off the main road by the side of the school was Miss Ella's farm where we went everyday for our milk. My grand-uncle, Uncle Levi, and his wife, Aunt Beck, lived next door to Miss Ella's farm. In the square was the beautiful stone-built Anglican church at the corner where the lane joined the main road. It faced the barracks. The left side of the churchyard was fenced off from the lane and on the right side a fence separated it from woodlands. Beyond the church there was a long bend in the road which led to the other village, Preddie. Quite a little way to the left of our shop, our neighbours lived in the old vicarage. Beyond the old vicarage and all the way to the end of our district were woodlands facing cane fields for about two miles into the next village of Springfield.

My father was a fish merchant. He bought fish from the fishermen at Farquhar Bay, about four miles from our home, and sold it to restaurants and shops in our parish capital of May Pen and in the adjoining districts. My mother ran the shop and supervised our home.

Our first house was a couple hundred yards from the shop, up a path passing a pond on the edge of which stood an overhanging hog-plum tree. Across from our small house was my paternal grandfather's house. Both houses had two bedrooms and shared the kitchen which was a very big room of wattle and daub that stood under a huge acacia tree. The pit toilet was some distance from my grandfather's house and attached to it were two smaller roofless rooms which were used as bathrooms, one for each household. In ours were a big aluminium bath pan and a bucket with a bowl for scooping water. Our flannels, which we called washrags, hung on nails protruding from one wall. On the wall facing the door was a shelf on which stood a soap dish with Palmolive soap which we called 'sweet soap' to differentiate it from 'washing soap' used for clothes. On the earthen floor was a broad piece of board forming a platform where we stood whilst bathing. The bathroom and surrounding area were kept dry by the fierce sun of the tropics. To complete the boundary of our yard was the bakery. The oven looked to me like a big white-washed mound, dark and cavernous inside. Next to this was a long, low one-room building where baked goods were stored.

In the early morning the aroma of baked goods wafted into our house to make my mouth water in anticipation. My grandfather and his brother, Uncle Levi, ran the bakery. Sometimes, early in the morning, I wandered into the room next to the oven where shelves were stacked with long-handled trays laden with hard-dough bread, nine-inch- long buns, small round buns and bulla cakes. We children loved the small, round, flattened sweet rolls and lovingly called them 'bullas'. If I close my eyes I can still smell and taste the hot bread smothered in melting butter - absolutely unforgettable!

Before I went off to school in the mornings, there would be people going up and down the path to get their baked goods; bicycles would have their panniers filled with goods for the neighbouring shops. In the afternoon, Grandfather and Uncle Levi would whip off their white floury aprons and lock up shop for the day. At that time the long, wooden table in the bakery room was laden with covered trays that held the dough, prepared for the next morning's baking.

Where we lived in Clarendon, homes were not supplied with running water. Fortunately for our district there was a well on the school premises. I loved walking with our helper to the well to collect water. I loved to look at the profusion of morning glory that ran riot along the fence near the well. They were spectacular flowers with their trumpets of white tinged with purple. I would touch them with reverence. By the time I was seven I had lost interest in this jaunt but the picture of the morning glory border remains.

Memory of my 'shadow game' evokes a smile. As I walked along the lane in the morning to fetch milk from Miss Ella's and again from school to home at noon as well as at going-home time, my shadow was a mystery to me. It changed in size, but how it followed me! I loved to see it move as I jumped, leapt to one side, nodded my head and danced. This game ended when the teacher explained the phenomenon.

Our family was close-knit. Of the relatives who visited us regularly, my maternal grandmother was my favourite. All of her grandchildren called her Gangan following her first grandchild, Arnold, who was attempting to say 'grandma'. Gangan was unusually tall, five foot nine, and quite graceful. Her facial features reflected her African/European ancestry. Her hair was naturally crimped and refused to stay plaited. It was silky and I loved to brush and plait it, knowing that it would soon come undone and do its own thing. When I visited her in Manchester I was told by her peers that she had been such a beautiful girl that she had earned the name, Miss Doll. As a woman she became Sister Doll, shortened to Sa Doll. She loved being well-dressed and I remember the swishing of her underskirt as she sashayed on high heels along the village marl road to church.

Was my grandmother, a well-respected lady in her district, daring and unconventional in smoking openly? Gangan grew her own tobacco and smoked a pipe. A neighbour, Con Titi, was her smoking companion. He and his wife often came to the gate and chatted for a while with Gangan but it was Con Titi who lingered on. He would enter the yard and sit on the edge of the barbecue - an oblong, cemented area, approximately 12x9 feet, with a border standing about a foot high. Gangan would take her seat on the top front doorstep facing him. They would share their tobacco and have a smoke while they talked about the crops and the weather and traded news between the puff-puff of their pipes. When he left she would continue to sit a while longer. This ritual always took place at the end of the working day as the dark of night descended and twilight lasted for only a brief time. I think it was her meditation time.

Gangan also performed a strange ritual every Saturday at sunrise. On Friday afternoon she included white rum in the grocery shopping. The next morning she poured a libation to our ancestors. She would face the rising sun, standing on the top outside step leading from her bedroom, and sprinkle some of the rum on the ground intoning, "For my good spirits. Thank you for keeping us safe and sound." Then, using a sherry glass, she drank a little of the rum with water. She gave me a taste as I was inquisitive and would be there watching her. When I asked what she was doing she explained it away as a family custom. My mother did not follow this custom and never touched alcohol. I, on the other hand, liked the idea of my ancestors protecting us and adopted the ritual. *Years later I realised that it was an African custom transported across the Atlantic to Jamaica although my grandmother seemed unaware of the connection.*

My grandmother's first husband died when their youngest child was three months old. Like his parents before him, he was buried in the family cemetery a little way from the family house. Gangan was left on her own with seven children. Much later she married Mr Graham. He was pleasant enough but a shadowy figure as he worked in a sugar factory in Clarendon and was often away from home. Gangan, being a devout Christian, attended church and prayer meetings regularly and fasted every Monday for spiritual growth. Prayers were said first thing each morning giving God thanks for keeping her family safe through the night and asking for guidance for the day. Evening prayers thanked God for his loving kindness and many blessings, then asked for help to resolve problems and for a peaceful night for all the family, near and far. Whatever troubled her she laid at the feet of *Massa* (Master) Jesus. Her faith was unwavering.

My paternal grandmother I found mysterious. Her visits were less frequent and she did not play with me. She also smoked a pipe; holding in her mouth not the stem but the bowl filled with burning tobacco! She made sucking sounds and after a few sucks would blow the smoke through her nose. In wonderment,

The Nottingham Connection

I would ask her if her mouth was not burning. She shook her head, her small eyes, set wide in her nut-brown round face, twinkling. She spoke very little. Even when my mother took us to visit her at her home in Harmons, Manchester, she remained a distant figure. I never felt close to her but loved seeing my Aunt Beryl and Uncle Albert.

I loved my paternal grandfather who looked an older version of my father, perhaps a tad more handsome. Whereas my father was reserved, Grandfather was gregarious. In the late afternoons he would sit outside near his front door and smoke his cigar. Sometimes he would send my younger brother, Alvin, or me to buy his cigars from our shop. Grandfather had white teeth that flashed brilliantly in his black face as he laughed heartily at some joke or other. He regularly boasted that he had never lost a tooth.

I did not experience a feeling of great loss the day my grandfather died. What I felt between his death and the funeral was the sense of awe created by death among the living. I was skipping in the school yard when a teacher came and told me I had to hurry home because my grandfather was very ill. I ran all the way. There were several people in Grandfather's house - my father and mother, Uncle Levi and Aunt Beck, other family members and friends. Everyone wore a tight look as if suppressing pain. Someone took me into Grandfather's bedroom where I was met with groans coming from the bed. With every breath my poor Grandfather took, he groaned in agony, baring his teeth before letting go his breath. I felt sorry for him because he seemed to be hurting so much. His six-foot three frame took up most of the bed, and extending upwards like a mound in the middle of the bed was his very hugely swollen tummy. Curiosity got the better of me and, quick as a flash, I touched the mound; it was rock hard. I was about to quickly withdraw my hand when Grandfather grabbed it; he squeezed it and tried to smile. That was his goodbye.

Later that day I again went to Grandfather's house as part of the family procession to say our formal farewell to him. My mother held my hand as we trooped past his bedside each person lingering a little with, "So long, Mas' Hugh" or "You're at peace now" and so it went on. He looked just as if he were sleeping.

Grandfather was buried a few days later, laid to rest in a secluded spot under a tree near the *penguin* hedge, close clumps of cacti with sharp needles on long thick stems that grow to about four feet. The crowd at the graveside was not very big. My mother did not attend because it was only a day after my sister's birth and, in those days, mothers had to stay indoors for fourteen days after giving birth. My father and Uncle Levi helped to carry the coffin. I looked down the hole at the coffin, frightened at that gaping hole, and drew closer to my father. As I looked up at him for reassurance I heard a female voice close by whisper, "God be with you, Mas' Hugh". My father's face was like a piece of black granite. Then I saw a tear hover at the rim of each eye before slowly trickling down his cheeks. I took his hand and held it tightly. It was the only time I ever saw my father cry.

Christmas and Boxing Day were very special for us. Our home was a hive of activities. Like many Jamaican families then and now, my father had relatives living in the USA who, each year, sent us a Christmas barrel. We enjoyed a veritable feast at breakfast and dinner. The smell of fried ham, absent throughout the rest of the year, wafted in the air. We, children, also received very special toys. One year my brother, Alvin, was given a motorbike with rider that, when wound up, would race all over the floor. Alvin, Lillian and I spent many happy hours playing with it. My own favourite toy was the doll I got when I was four. My other dolls were only rag dolls, while this one had eyes that opened when upright and closed when lying down. Her hair was black and I also had a comb and brush set to keep it tidy. Her mouth was like a rosebud and I could pretend to feed her. But wonder of wonders, she cried! In the middle of her back was a square that, when lifted, revealed a box. This was the magic box that made Dolly cry whenever I hit her or bent her over. What fun I had dressing her, feeding her, teaching her the ABC! I took my doll everywhere I went except to school and church, because my mother would not let me. By the time I was six, poor Dolly had only one functioning eye and half of her head was bald.

In our rural community, church played an important part. From the age of three I attended Sunday school, as did my siblings. Older children looked after younger ones in the Sunday school classes. The Sunday school teacher told us bible stories and we sang children's hymns. When my parents attended church we children had to sit through the long, boring service with them. My mother gave us sweets to keep us quiet but when the supply was exhausted and we fidgeted too much or began to slide down the pew towards the floor she gave us 'the eye'. When this no longer worked, she pinched us. We knew we could not cry out so we snuffled, then kept still for a while.

For years I had a recurring nightmare of God's coming, thanks to the preachers' sermons on hell and damnation. The dream was vivid. There was a white God, just like the picture of Jesus hanging in the church, dressed in flowing, white robes, with his golden hair streaming as he rode his chariot that was aflame. Encircling him was a bright, blinding light. White angels with outstretched wings and in white dresses floated around. There were, of course, no black angels. The heavenly party's approach was thunderous. As they descended into Daybart Square I fell to the ground, covering my head and screaming. I always woke from this nightmare terrified and drenched in sweat. I would immediately make a pledge to be very good so that I should not go to hell.

Home

My mother met my father in 1941 at Preddie during war time. Love blossomed. When she married my father she moved to Daybart to his family home but, sadly, never felt a part of the community. She said that some of the young women were jealous that my father had married her and not one of them, so she was seen as a *'come long'*.

Seeing a business opportunity she borrowed money from her older brother, Uncle Tom, to set up a cookhouse. My father's younger brother, Albert, and my mother's youngest brother, Jim, cut wattle from the common land and my mother transported the bundles back to the yard where the three of them built a wattle and daub cookhouse. Its walls were washed with white lime and it had a thatched roof of coconut fronds. A platform about three feet high for two fires and shelves to hold utensils and food items were built. My mother cooked lunch and dinner for the cane-field workers.

My mother was very astute and as the cookhouse became profitable she expanded, building a small grocery shop. During crop season, Jim or Albert, whichever was not working, helped in the shop and served lunch while my mother took lunches to the cane field near Springfield, a neighbouring village. She would load the food into two boxes which she attached to the front and back of her bicycle. In the boxes she stacked lemonade, home-made ginger beer, bread and fish, bun and cheese, fried dumplings, salt-fish fritters and cigarettes. She did this Monday to Friday while Miss Lianna looked after me and later my brother who was born in 1946. By the time I was four she had given up her cane field runs. Albert and Jim had by then found full-time jobs and were no longer around and my mother said she missed their company and their helpfulness. A year later, in 1948, my sister Lillian was born.

Building the new shop was an exciting time. My parents' friend, a supervisor on the sugar estate, lent them a cement mixer. The day it was delivered, towed by a tractor, the locals gathered around to see what was happening. Uncle Albert and Uncle Jim were on holiday and helped to mix the cement which they heaped into wooden moulds which were then turned out and left in the sun to dry. The blocks were then ready to use. My father stood around admiring the work in progress but did very little, while my mother joined in and helped to stack the blocks. The builder was the craftsman but my uncles and my mother did a lot of the donkey work. During the day our helper brought jugs of lemonade and snacks for the workers and sometimes I gave her a hand with this. The day the shop was finished and the sign, **'Midway Enterprise'**, was painted across the front, there was a lot of backslapping. The day ended with beer and rum-drinking by the men.

In 1996 my mother, Lillian, Lillian's daughter, one of my daughters and I visited Daybart. The shop seemed much smaller. The square was as quiet as it was four decades before during a school holiday in the out-of-crop season. The church still stood grandly on its knoll but the old school building had been replaced by a spanking new edifice with several classrooms.

Our shop was not just a place for buying groceries and eating food, it was also a meeting place for the villagers and a rest stop for people passing through the district. Women came in, made their purchases and left. Men, on the other hand, struck up a conversation and smoked to while away the time. Sometimes they played dominoes. The end of a game was heralded by dominoes being loudly slapped on the table, with an ear-splitting bang for the very last tile. A game of dominoes tended to draw an audience. Invariably, advice was given to the losers as to what they should have done as the game was analysed. The quieter men played draughts, but even those games drew a crowd of know-alls.

My mother laughed and talked in a friendly manner with her customers. When she was not busy serving or supervising meals for sale, she would sit at her sewing machine in the shop. She sewed all our clothes and also did beautiful embroidery work. Everyone in the shop became quiet when it was time for the evening news on the Mullard radio. It was the size of two big car batteries and held pride of place on the shelf. After the news, long-drawn-out discussions ensued. To a foreigner, it would appear that a fight was about to take place!

I liked being in our shop and from an early age was given the opportunity to serve customers, take money and give change. Amongst the stacked shelves were small tins of Canadian sardines and small cans of Nestle's condensed milk that I particularly liked. The bread-case on the counter was an oblong glass cabinet. In it were loaves of hard-dough bread, small and large buns, bulla cakes and sponge cakes sold in slices. The bread-case was to ensure a high level of hygiene and to keep out flies. My mother was very particular about cleaning it each day. She impressed on our helper and me that negligence in this could lead to a health inspector dumping its contents if insects, especially flies, were found in it. The big tin of processed New Zealand cheese, once opened, was cut into wedges and kept moist by being covered with the lining paper in the tin and over that a muslin square. On the counter near the scales were jars of sweets; paradise plums, small almond-shaped with one side yellow and the other red, were my favourite, while Lillian and Alvin liked mint balls with their red and white stripes. My mother made beef patties everyday except Sundays when the shop was closed. The patties were kept hot on a shelf in a tin oven in which charcoal embers burned at the bottom.

Under the counter were crocus bags of dark-brown and light-brown sugar, flour came in white coarse cotton sacks. Jamaicans are adept at recycling even before that word came into popular use. One example of this was my mother's re-use of flour bags. She would slit the sides of the empty flour bags, soap them and spread them out to bleach in the sun on a sheet of zinc. As they began to '*quail*' or dry out, she would soak them again and continue this process until they were white. They were then washed and finally 'blue' from a two-inch square tablet of blueing agent was added to the rinse water. The end result was sparkling white materials. My mother then used the recycled material to make tablecloths and nighties which she embroidered. *I have kept one of these nighties as a precious souvenir.*

In one corner of the shop stood a keg of mackerel in brine and, on top of it, a box of salt fish. The history of salt fish is fascinating. In the early years of colonization the British slave-masters provided their slaves with salted codfish as part of their staple diet. The African slaves created many dishes with the flaked codfish, so now we have ackee (the national fruit) and salt fish as part of our national dish; cabbage and salt fish; calalloo and salt fish; flaked salt fish in seasoned rice; and just plain, cooked up salt fish with *escallions* (chives) or onions, tomatoes and pepper.

As well as groceries, the shop served what we now call brunch from about eleven in the morning until three in the afternoon and dinner from about 5:00 to 6:00 when darkness descended. The two tables with eight chairs and two bar stools for diners took up a lot of space in the shop. When not used by diners, these were usually occupied by men who loitered after a day's work to play dominoes or draughts.

On Saturdays my father made ice cream and a very thick, ice-cold milkshake we called *frisco*. The ice cream and *frisco* were made in an ice-cream bucket which was like a very big thermos with a handle for churning. The liquid was churned in the inner cylinder and the space between this and the outer bucket was packed with ice. The ice cream was served in cones and the *frisco* in the customer's mug. The customers were mainly children having a treat as they passed through our district.

During these early days of my childhood in the late 1940s and early 1950s, we did not have a refrigerator. The ice truck from May Pen delivered blocks of ice which we stored in our big icebox where we kept sodas and soft drinks. We chipped ice with the ice pick for serving home-made ginger beer and also for selling to people whose homes did not have iceboxes. On Fridays, Saturdays and holidays we also served *snowball*. The ice was shaved with an ice shear that collected the shaved ice in its compartment, it was then knocked against the block of ice to make its contents really compact before opening it to retrieve the shaved ice which was then topped with red or yellow home-made syrup, as the customer desired. The whole process took only a few minutes. *Snowball* was sometimes put into a customer's mug but, more often, children enjoyed sucking the *snowball* held in their hands. *Nowadays, snowball is served in plastic bags!*

By the time I was eleven, my mother had such trust in me that she would send me to Old Harbour, which was over thirty miles by bus, to purchase goods from our wholesalers. I was given a list and the money - quite a substantial amount at the time - to pay for the goods. After purchasing the goods I waited for the bus or our friend's truck from Kingston to take the goods and me home. I enjoyed these trips to and from Old Harbour when I either read a book or spent the time daydreaming.

We had a few helpers whom I vaguely remember but the one who became part of our lives was Marie. In those days they were known as servants or maids. Marie went weekly to the river to do the washing and I sometimes accompanied her when school was on holiday. She put the dirty clothes in a tin tub the size of a baby's bath, covered the clothes with a small white enamel basin and at the side of the tub put the scrubbing board, a bag of blue and a bar of brown soap which was about four inches long, three inches wide and three inches thick. Marie carried the bathtub on her head where it rested on a *cotter*, a yard of material coiled tightly into a cushion. She was young and graceful and walked with hips swinging and arms moving in unison with her legs for over a mile holding that load on her head! Monday was the popular washday when women, young and old, converged on the Rio Minho's bank. Each staked out her plot. Some built fires over which to boil the white clothes. The fire was made within a circle of three stones, on this was placed a five-gallon kerosene tin of water to which the clothes were added after a first wash. Others preferred to soap the white clothes and spread them on big stones to bleach in the sun.

I was not the only child around. Some girls who accompanied their mothers helped with the washing while the boys gathered driftwood and dry branches for the fires and fetched water. When the chores were finished the fun began for us while the women gossiped. Many of the boys swam and messed about in the water. The rest of us went hunting for *janga*, the crayfish that lived under stones in the river. We boiled them and made a feast, our pay-off for accompanying grown-ups to the river.

In the rainy season, crabs were plentiful. Children chased them with sticks and if we caught them the grown-ups allowed us to boil them in a kerosene tin over an outside fire. Crab hunting was a popular pastime for teenage boys. They hunted at nights when the crabs moved about a lot and were easy to catch. Will, our odd job man, loved hunting crabs and would bring back a crocus bag filled with them. The crocus bag seemed to have a life of its own as the crabs tried in vain to escape. I did not like watching Will tossing the crabs into the boiling water; somehow it seemed cruel and yet when they were cooked I enjoyed eating them as much as anyone else did. I ate mine 'Will-style'. He would crack the body shell with a stone and then use his teeth to crack the legs and squeeze out the flesh. Eating crabs under the guinep tree near the shop was like having a picnic.

My father regularly brought home lobsters and trunk fish which we cooked in the same way. The trunk fish casement fissured when hit with a stone and the flesh was of a fine texture. I was amazed to find later that lobster was very expensive and not an everyday fare in England!

One of my mother's special treats was sweet potato pudding, heavy and moist and delicious. The baking was a feat of ingenuity then practised in rural Jamaica. A *coal pot* was used as being more sophisticated than the open wood fire. A *coal pot* is like a bell-shaped iron container turned upside down. Where the *coal pot* narrows at the base, a gridiron allows charcoal to be burnt in the upper chamber and as ash falls to the floor, it is cleared out through a square opening. The diameter of the top is approximately twelve inches while that of the base below the gridiron is about six inches. I would watch my mother as she baked. She grated the sweet potato and mixed into it flour, sugar, butter and coconut milk to a cake consistency, adding spices last. She then filled the coal pot with charcoal and when the coal glowed and gave off a yellow light tinged with blue, she put some of the live coal on a piece of zinc a little bigger than the top of the *coal pot*. She then placed the baking tin with the pudding mixture on another piece of zinc over the coals in the *coal pot* and finally covered the baking tin with the zinc topped with live coal. From time to time she checked the pudding to be sure it was not burning and fanned the coal to give enough heat for baking. I never offered to help to grate the potatoes or the hard flesh of the coconut because when I was asked to perform the task, I always got my knuckles scraped bloody by the grater. But I did love to lick the leftover mixture in the bowl which I had to share with any child who happened to be around. In typical Jamaican parlance, this baking process was referred to as *'hell a top, hell a bottom, hallelujah in the middle'*.

Weekends were special to me until I was about ten, as it was when we spent most time together as a family. At dinner time, my father left a piece of dumpling or some rice with a little meat or fish on his plate and would feed a mouthful to each of his children. I always felt that his food tasted much, much more delicious than my own.

My mother and Marie served each child's meal on one plate but my father's meal was served in separate dishes. To these was added a saucer with pieces of yellow and green Scotch bonnet peppers to spice up my father's meat or fish. I did ask my mother the reason for this differentiation and was told that this was how a man had to be treated as the head of the family. I wanted my meal served as they served my father's because it looked attractive. My mother was not amused by my demands and ignored them. I also questioned the reason my father got the choice pieces of chicken. Guests, of course, were always served first and given freedom to choose and this I accepted, but I found it difficult to accept my mother's usual response that special treatment was a man's right.

In my childhood I saw all the men in my extended family receiving special treatment from the women and have always had a strong objection to this differential treatment.

My second brother, Bonnie, was born in 1951. It was a school day and when I came back for lunch my mother was hanging out clothes and singing. I liked the song and asked her to teach me the words. It was a Scottish air:

> *You'll take the high road and I'll take the low*
> *And I'll be in Scotland before you*
> *For me and my true love will never meet again*
> *On the bonny, bonny, banks of Loch Lomond.*

It was so romantic the dreamer in me wanted to visit Loch Lomond, thinking it must be a beautiful place for someone to describe it as 'bonny'. I had also learnt a new word.

That afternoon when I returned from school I heard a baby crying in my parents' bedroom. I dashed into the room and there was my brother. He had blue eyes and I thought he was bonny, so we called him 'Bonnie' although his given name is Karl. While still a baby, his eyes changed to smoky grey-green.

I did not forget the promise I made myself that day and so, many years later, on my first visit to Scotland, Loch Lomond was on my list of 'must-see' sites. It turned out to be a truly magical place, incredibly beautiful in the setting sun. I stood on the shore and gazed across its blue water to the hills rising in the distant. As I drank in its loveliness, I swear I heard my mother's voice singing that song.

I have many happy memories of holidays spent with Gangan. My parents would tell Will to watch out for the bus which passed Hermitage, about half a mile from Gangan's home. One of my parents would give instructions to the driver before waving goodbye to me. My Uncle Jim or my cousin, Arnold, would be waiting at Hermitage cross-roads in one of the two shops that faced each other on the square. One was owned by old Mr Biggs and the other by his nephew, Arthur Biggs. Old Mr Biggs' shop was quiet on Saturdays, whereas Arthur's was full of life because it had a bar. From Hermitage we had to walk to Gangan's house which was very small but surrounded by a lot of land where my cousins and I roamed in the holidays.

The early morning in Frankfield was magical because the surroundings were greener than Daybart, The fruit trees encircled the yard and the front garden was ablaze with colourful shrubs and flowers. The plants were bejewelled with early morning dew as sunlight poured from a clear blue sky. At Christmas time Gangan donned her woollen coat and leather boots before going to see to the animals, as the temperature was quite cool up in the mountains of Manchester. Later in the morning, as it grew warmer, she would change into summer clothes. At nights we used blankets which were not needed in Daybart or Kingston.

My cousins and I climbed the fruit trees to pick fruit. If we were peckish we would go to the guava trees or the mango trees or the naseberry trees or the orange trees but never to the grapefruit trees. Grapefruit was too sharp for our sweet tooth. I loved to push my face among the leaves and breathe in the aroma of the pimento branches laden with seeds. These were left on the barbecue waiting for the truck on its collection rounds of small farms.

Sometimes I used to help Gangan to pick the red berries off the coffee bushes growing on the slope that ran behind her kitchen and down to the cistern where rain-water was collected. The coffee berries were left to dry on the barbecue and we had to keep turning them as they changed from red to dark brown. After drying, they would be ready for parching. The air filled with the smell of the roasting beans that I much preferred to the taste of the brewed coffee. Gangan tended to store her roasted coffee beans and pound just enough at a time for a week's use. I enjoyed pounding the coffee beans. I would put a heap of beans in the three-foot high mortar with its twelve-inch cavity and, standing over it, pound the coffee beans into coarse powder with the pestle. Gangan prepared her coffee almost as we percolate it today. She spooned the coffee into a little muslin bag, pulling the drawstring to close it and placed it into a pot of boiling water on the fire for a few minutes, then she would remove the pot and leave the coffee to brew. Gangan always had hers black and sweet. Our family custom was that children did not drink coffee, we drank *bush tea* such as peppermint and on Sundays and special days we had *chocolate tea*.

Our cousin, Joe, my mother's nephew, also spent some holidays with Gangan. He was seen as a 'townie', not as rough as the 'country' children. He was not *au fait*, as they were, with shooting birds and running through undergrowth. Gangan's neighbour's son and Arnold, taught me how to *shinny* up trees, use a slingshot and recognise the different birds they shot. I did not like when the shot birds fell fluttering to the ground and I had to watch them twitch in their death throes, but I did enjoy the smoky taste of the birds we ate around the open fire. My companions showed me secret nooks where we would gorge ourselves on fruit and then sleep off the heaviness.

Even today, Joe and I sometimes reminisce about our escapades half a century ago.

Milk River School

In my mind's eye I see myself wearing a red, finely pleated pinafore over white blouse sitting in my pre-school class under the poinciana tree with its beautiful, tiny flowers that fell like red snowdrops to carpet the ground. The tree stood in front of the garden gate of the school cottage, facing the road. We sat on the grass with our slates on our laps copying from the blackboard. There was only one chair, our teacher's. *I wonder what happened when it rained?*

Our teacher was the mother-in-law of the headteacher of the elementary school and lived with the family in the school-house. She had a kind, round face, white-streaked hair and a warm, grandmotherly bosom. I remember chanting the alphabet, counting and singing nursery rhymes. When I began learning to read, our books were about a farm. Mr Joe, the farmer, had on his farm Mother Hen, Percy the cockerel, and Master Willy, the pig. Wanting to make my home similar to the one in the book, I christened one of our cockerels Percy, a hen became Mother Hen and a piglet was Master Willy. Sadly, Master Willy was sold but the other two were around for a while.

Elementary school was compulsory for children from seven to fifteen years old. My school, two doors from our shop, had about three hundred pupils. It was an oblong school room with a front door on the long side facing the road and a small door on each of its short sides. The room was divided into eight areas with blackboards back to back creating partitions. The headteacher who taught 'Sixth Class' had his table and chair on a platform which, being moveable, was used as the stage for concerts and other special events. Sometimes classes were held in the open air under the trees. Games and physical exercise classes were held in the school yard. Our school day was regulated by a hand bell rung by the headteacher at 9.00a.m, 12.00 noon, 1.00p.m., 4.00p.m.and at the beginning and end of morning and afternoon *recesses*.

My two best friends were my cousin, Ely Lawson, who lived about three miles away in Rest, and Patricia Smith who lived in the next village, Preddie. Patricia was the first person I thought beautiful. The famous 'Mona Lisa' portrait is not half as beautiful. I wanted to touch her face whenever I saw her each morning. She was my black rose. Her skin was charcoal black and velvety; her eyes sparkled in her face; her long, woolly hair fell in two or more plaits at the back of her head. She was always cheerful and easygoing. When I could ride a bike I was sometimes allowed to go to her home to play, which for me was a special treat.

It was great when Ely came home with me at lunch time because we would get something we really liked for lunch such as a beef patty and a soda. I did not need to take a packed lunch or have a school lunch, as I lived close by. Some children who lived in the surrounding villages carried their lunches in *shut pans* of aluminium or white enamel. These had two or three small containers held securely one on top of the other by a wire frame. Men working in the fields would have a set of three whereas children tended to have a set of two. One container held rice or *food* such as dumplings, yam and bananas; the other held *meat kind*, that is, beef or fish stew, salt fish and calalloo or salt fish and cabbage. In the *shut pan*, the meal kept warm until it was lunchtime at noon.

We were encouraged to drink milk to be healthy. The headteacher had a system whereby families paid weekly for their children to have a half-pint of milk at morning recess. We had to line up outside the headteacher's kitchen and wait for the maid to begin serving into our mugs warm milk from a big aluminium pot on the wood-burning cooking range. I always held my nose as I drank my milk. *I hated it then and still do. The smell of warm milk made me heave.* As soon as I downed that mug of milk, I would pop a sweet into my mouth.

Soon after starting school I became a regular visitor to my headteacher's home because Bertie, their son, and I became playmates. The Reids were not friends of my family, rather acquaintances, who bought their groceries from our shop. In fact I cannot remember my mother having any friends in all the years we lived in Daybart; her whole life was concentrated on her family and the shop. The Reids took a keen interest in my education and my parents trusted them implicitly. This was not unusual in the Jamaica of my childhood, where teachers played an important role in mentoring many of their pupils.

Mrs Reid not only taught one of the classes for younger pupils but also played the piano. I used to sit and listen as classical music filled the air, transporting me to other realms of my own creation, but some pieces of Beethoven were hard on my ear, and these I blocked out of my consciousness.

One of the things that puzzled me in my headteacher's house was the amount of space they had and that Mr and Mrs Reid had separate bedrooms. To my child's eye they were lovely rooms whose dark mahogany furniture and shiny floors you did not want to make a mess of. The headteacher's bedroom had a recess that he used as a study. It had bookshelves stacked with books, a small table with two drawers and a chair. I never went into his room but peeked at it from the connecting door of Mrs Reid's bedroom.

From the word go, I enjoyed school. Learning was a wonderful experience. Milk River School, with the exception of one horrible incident, has only happy memories for me. Whatever I learnt, I wanted to teach my brothers and sisters too. But Alvin was not interested and did not find learning as enjoyable as I did.

I remember getting very upset when he refused to pay attention or cried that he could not do something I had explained to him. My retort to his *belly-aching* was always, "I can't is a sluggard too lazy to try!" My children tell me this adage was my favourite saying when they were at home. Today it is a family joke used to embarrass me.

I found mathematics hard to understand at times. Perhaps the logical connection which would make things clear was missing because we were taught by rote. I developed a fear of it because I often failed to understand the logic. Although we were taught rules to solve problems, some basic concepts eluded me. Years later 'New Maths' was elucidating. At last I could see how rules were arrived at. What a revelation! A young child using square blocks to measure areas can understand the rule: *length x breadth = area*. I believe in this heuristic method of teaching and learning. The finding out is so exciting for children.

I loved the music of words and books became an important part of my life from an early age. I was fortunate to have access to the headteacher's home library. I spent many happy hours tucked away in a corner of their drawing room reading to my heart's content. I lived long spells in other worlds created by the abridged versions of classics such as *A Christmas Carol, The Water Babies, David Copperfield, Lorna Doone, Mill on the Floss, Silas Marner* and *Alice in Wonderland*. I also was a subscriber, through the school, to *Children's Own*, a national weekly with news, views and stories.

For me the highlight of each school year was the school concert in which children chosen from every class participated. Rehearsals took place after school for about eight weeks and, as the time for the concert drew near, excitement mounted. An appreciative audience of parents, family and friends came out to support the event and encourage the performers with their shouts and applause. The running commentary, directives and appreciative noises I heard from the adults at our school concerts, still persist today in Jamaica and wherever some Jamaicans are as they watch a film or play.

Perhaps my most memorable concert was the one that took place when I was eleven. I had to perform a Louise Bennett poem, 'Miss Liza', which satirized those pretentious Jamaicans who insisted on putting on 'airs and graces' because they had travelled abroad. Miss Liza came back to Jamaica speaking Spanish and pretending she did not understand patois until someone tried to rob her at which point she broke into the strongest and purest Jamaican patois.

The delivery was punctuated with applause and laughter as the audience identified with the sentiments expressed. Miss Lou, Jamaicans' endearing name for Louise Bennett, knew her people well. The audience applauded my performance for what seemed like ages. That night I also played the 'white girl' in the song '*All Day Long*'. It told the story of three girls who had different lifestyles based solely on their colour, yet shared a common desire to be married. It was a social commentary on the island's endemic colour problem demonstrated in how black people had to 'make do' with what they could get, whereas white people had the best of everything and brown people managed well enough:

> *A me the white gal sleep on divan bed*
> *A me the brown gal do the same.*
> *A me the black gal sleep on box and board*
> *But me sleeping all the same.*
> *(chorus)All day long, all night long,*
> *I'm simply dreaming,*
> *Dreaming of a honeymoon.*

My mother made me a dress with a hobble skirt to accentuate my character as being quite stylish. I sashayed across the stage in my borrowed high heels, fashionable hat and paper fan. The audience loved it.

That year I also represented the school at the Schools' Festival held in Denbigh. My item was an English poem. Louise Bennett who was one of the judges congratulated me on my delivery. Afterwards she took the time to speak to me. Of course, my vanity was greatly massaged.

The positive impact of all this was that I worked at using my voice for maximum effect. I did not have elocution lessons but in English classes we were taught how to speak with clarity and use cadence, pause, emphasis, repetition, etcetera for full effect. Those few minutes with Louise Bennett galvanised my desire to excel with confidence. In later years I would often be asked to deliver speeches and act as a rapporteur at conferences because of this skill.

In the 1980s when Miss Lou and her husband were house guests of friends of mine, I could not help but tell her of the impact she had had on me.

I think that my desire to be a teacher sprang from the valuable role of teachers in the community. They were the sole providers of extra-curricular activities. In the 4H Club, girls were taught such skills as making preserves, baking and needlework and boys husbandry, in particular looking after a few animals for a livelihood. Our teachers also ran the Guides, Scouts and Brownies. Our Brownies pack met at the door of the church vestry and we played games and were taught skills and special songs; it was fascinating to learn that these songs were sung by Brownies in different countries within the British Empire. One activity I especially enjoyed was tracking with its treasure/reward. I also enjoyed learning to tie different types of knots.

My life was carefree.

Lee Arbouin

Lessons For Life

It was our busiest time in the shop. The sugar cane was being harvested. I was often left to *mind* the shop so that my mother could have a short break. I would shout, "Mama!" when a customer came in.

The barracks across the road from our shop at that time was a hive of activity. Men from all parts of Jamaica who came in search of work in the cane fields lived there. Women from the surrounding districts were employed to work alongside the men, planting and weeding the cane fields.

One late afternoon as I sat behind the counter minding the shop, a young man came and stood on the veranda of the shop which we called the *piaza,* a corruption of piazza. His skin was white, almost translucent, all the exposed parts of his body were covered in freckles and his woolly hair was yellow-blonde. I was fascinated. He did not move on as passers-by did after having a rest but continued to lean against the veranda wall. When my mother returned, I drew her attention to him. She whispered to me that he was a *dundus*. As an eight year-old I had never heard of albinos. In her usual way she struck up a conversation with him. He told her that he had been walking from before sunup and that, realising it was then too late to find work, he was hoping someone in the barracks would put him up for the night. As he spoke I looked more closely at him. His voice told of his exhaustion and he licked his parched, cracked lips as he spoke. I felt compassion, my first memory of this feeling. At that very moment Marie called, "Lee, come for your dinner!" I realised that the man was more in need of food than I was. I took up my meal from the table.

"Where you think you going, Miss?" Marie scolded. She ate with us as she was responsible for the children. I ignored her and walked briskly from our new house next door to the shop and gave the plate to the man. I pointed to the table and chair in the shop indicating that he should sit there. My mother was surprised but did not interfere. As he sat, I fetched him a glass of water. He thanked me, saying that he had not eaten a thing all day. I left him to enjoy his meal.

"Well, I never!" issued from an exasperated Marie who had followed me into the shop.

"It's alright, Marie," my mother said to calm her.

I picked up the book I was reading and went into my parents' bedroom to get away. The only reason I can give for my action was the obvious level of that man's distress.

Cherry was my first encounter with someone suffering from mental illness. The experience left me more bewildered than fearful. Miss Crawford, a friend of my parents, owned the biggest shop cum bar in the area and lived above it. Back then, very few men owned cars and she was the only woman who did. It was a

Zephyr. I remember the name because when I saw her big, shiny car, I looked up the name and learnt that it was a Greek word for a 'gentle breeze'.

Miss Crawford informally adopted Cherry whose parents had died tragically when she was a little girl. People said she went mad following her parents' death. Cherry's father had been the headteacher at Milk River School. She was a couple of years older than I was but smaller and frail-looking with a bony, coffee-brown, oval face and tendrils of soft, curly hair fringing her forehead and clinging to it as if it was slightly damp. She did not attend church or school and seemed to stay upstairs except when taken out in the car by Miss Crawford.

When I went to Rest Post Office to collect our mail, I would stop at Preddie village on my return journey to say hello to Miss Crawford. Invariably, she suggested that I go up and see Cherry. Walking ahead of me up the stairs, she would open Cherry's bedroom door and coo, "You've got a visitor". She then left us together and I would sit on the bed next to Cherry. Her behaviour was strange. Sometimes she looked at me blankly. Sometimes as I gabbled on about school or about my family, she cocked her head, bird-like, as if listening and twiddled her thumbs. Twiddle, twiddle, twiddle. At this stage I wanted to grab hold of her hands to stop her twiddling which completely unnerved me. At other times she was in her walking mood and paced up and down her room, giggling every now and then to herself. She rarely spoke and I can't remember anything she said. The really sad times were when she sat on her bed and cried, mewing. At those times I held her hand or put my arm around her and quietly cried too. When I tried to comfort her with words, there was no response. It was as if I was not there. After such a visit, which lasted no more than half an hour, I would retrace my steps down to the shop, bid goodbye and ride home with a lump of sadness in my heart.

At school when I told my friends about my visits, they thought I was stupid to go into the same room with 'that mad *pickney*'. They were convinced that one day Cherry would attack me. Poor Cherry, she was as timid as a mouse. I often wondered what was happening inside her head.

I have always abhorred lies and liars; I can't even bluff. My children laugh at me because they say I am hopeless. Looking back I realise that this originated in an incident that happened when I was eight I became painfully aware of how damaging lies can be. When I started formal school at seven, I spent only a short time in 'A Class' before being transferred to 'B Class' and was in first class when I was eight. *Skipping* was an acceptable norm then. One day after lunch, my teacher could not find her fountain pen. She asked if anyone had seen it and the class chorused, "No, Miss". Looking very sad, she remarked that it was very special. When school was dismissed I was walking home with friends when I heard, "Lee Lawson!" shouted in anger. Turning I saw my teacher striding towards me; she grabbed my arm saying, "Come with me!" and marched me back into school. She was furious. She said I had let her down and that she could not believe I had stolen her pen. For my part, I could not believe what I was hearing and began to cry, "I didn't, Miss, I didn't!" Ignoring my denial, she ordered me to turn out my pockets. When nothing was found she threatened to send for my parents if I did not tell her where I had hidden the pen. I was in a panic because I knew my mother would believe the adult, not me, and that I would get a hiding to teach me not to steal.

"Please Miss, I didn't steal it!" I begged. But my plea was in vain. My teacher went to the door and sent one of the children still hanging around with a note to our shop. By then I was crying, angry at being totally unable to defend myself.

As my mother entered the schoolroom my heart stopped. The teacher told her that a boy in the class had seen me touching the pen at lunchtime. My mother asked me where the pen was. I admitted that I had been in the classroom and had passed the table to go to my desk for my reading book but had not touched any pen. She told the teacher she would get her pen back and, grabbing my arm, dragged me home. I could hear the sniggering of the children hanging about outside the school gate. A few of the more daring ones ran ahead making monkey faces and grunting, relishing my disgrace. I died a thousand deaths.

At home my mother gave me a hiding with a leather belt. With each stroke she berated me for stealing and railed at me for disgracing the family. I was sent to bed until I decided to tell her where the pen was. Later that evening the incident was relayed to my father. Standing by my bedside, he gave me a good ticking off.

"You're a good girl. I can't believe you stole a pen. Why you steal somebody's pen, eh?" Not waiting for a response he hissed his teeth in disgust and walked away. I went to sleep angry with my parents, my teacher and the boy who had lied about me.

The next morning I dreaded going to school; I felt miserable and lost. Even Marie was on their side, suggesting that I gave up the pen and ask forgiveness. As I was leaving for school, heavy-hearted and frightened, I saw my teacher approaching our shop. I hid and waited. She went into the shop and a few minutes later my mother shouted, "Lee!" I noted that the voice was not angry but I was still scared as I went to her. To my utter surprise my teacher apologised to me; she had found her pen that morning. My mother did not apologise but fussed over me, straightening my uniform and rubbing my cheeks as though creaming my face. My nightmare was over. My teacher gave the class a lecture about the dangers of lying. Despite the way it ended, the pain of that experience has lived with me. I did not get at the boy who had lied, but I decided then that I would fight back the next time someone told a lie on me.

Revenge Is Not Sweet

The summer I was nine years old, my brother Alvin and I went with Gangan to visit our family in Kingston. A guava tree from next door had a few branches hanging over the roof of Aunt Wrightie's kitchen. My cousin Joe and I decided to climb onto the roof to get at the nice yellow guavas begging to be eaten. We were surprised when Gangan appeared as if from nowhere and warned us not to go on the roof again as it was dangerous.

A few days later she came upon my brother and me eating guavas. She immediately accused me of disobedience. I said I had not climbed the tree and that Joe had given me the guavas. She said that she was going to report our disobedience to Uncle Tom. Now, Uncle Tom, as head of the family, was a stern no-nonsense man; even his grown-up sisters were a little in awe of him. (As children, you got to know these things by the way grown-ups talked and behaved.) I felt so strongly about being blamed for something I had not done, that I did the unthinkable. I shouted, "Don't tell any lie on me!" Completely taken aback, Gangan 'hissed' her teeth, said I needed to be taught a lesson and walked off.

As my uncle's jeep drew up to the gate, my heart began to pound in my ears. When he summoned me belligerence, like bile, rose up in the pit of my stomach. Grown-ups had too much power; it was unfair. I wanted to tell my side of the story. But as I walked into his drawing room I knew it would never be heard. "I can't understand you. You gone mad?" I was convinced grown-ups were confusing. I almost felt that he wanted me to say something, but past experience had taught me, and no doubt many children in Jamaica then, that the moment I tried to speak I would be told to shut up for being "too big for your boot". Mentally I prepared myself for the inevitable.

"I'm going to teach you a lesson." His tone had changed to a menacing one, just above a whisper. My eyes followed his hands as he undid his belt and slowly drew it from the loops at the waist of his trousers, each loop vibrating as the belt came away from it. "Hold out your hand," he ordered. I did. I saw the belt rising up in the air and descending. I felt the sting as leather touched skin. I flinched. I held out my other hand and saw the same motion repeated, first one hand, then the next. My palms grew red. I was not going to cry. But the pain was excruciating.

"You apologise now!" I heard as if from a distance. Dry-eyed, I turned to face my grandmother and apologised grudgingly.

I no longer wanted to stay in town. I was not enjoying the holiday. Anger burnt strongly in me and I was overwhelmed with self-pity. That night I made up my mind to go home. I did not have enough money for the bus fare but I intended to tell the conductor that my parents would pay when I got home, as I was sure that the bus people knew our shop.

The next morning I slipped out of the house and stood by the front garden gate for a while to make sure no-one was around to stop me. When the coast was clear I walked to the end of the street where I caught the *chi-chi* bus. This time I did not listen for the onomatopoeic 'chi-chi' sound as the doors of the Kingston omnibus opened. At Parade where country buses set out for their various destinations I found the bus that passed Daybart but the driver and conductor would not let me on. They were suspicious because there was no adult with me and I did not have enough money for the fare. Furious and determined not to be thwarted, I decided to walk for a while until I got to the country road where I would hitch lifts along the way.

I began my journey. When the sun was too hot for walking, I bought a patty and a soda, found a quiet nook and had my lunch. After a snooze, I began walking again. The only vehicles passing by were buses and trucks and I dared not ask their drivers for a lift. With the descending night, my courage wavered. I was very scared of the dark. I argued with myself as to which of two options to take. I could wait for a bus or truck going towards town and tell them the truth or I could try to get to someone's house and ask for help. But the houses had disappeared for some time, and only cane fields stretched ahead. Panic rose within me; my mouth went dry and my throat felt parched and painful. I began to run but soon was out of breath and slowed to a brisk walk before running again. I could hear myself whimpering. Something touched my shoulder. I screamed and was about to run off when a voice arrested my feet.

"*Chile, you los*?" The voice was soft and filled with concern. I spun around and met the kind eyes of an older woman. Around her head a lot of material wound upwards into a pyramid. I thought she must be a spiritualist.

"Where are you going?" she asked.

"Milk River."

"Where's that?"

"Clarendon."

"Oh! Where you coming from?"

"Kingston."

She talked with me for a few more minutes before suggesting that she take me back to Kingston as my family would be very worried. I agreed, feeling very guilty. The kind lady took my hand and rubbed it in a comforting manner. She stopped the first bus going towards Kingston and we rode to Parade. I slept from exhaustion. From Parade we took a *chi-chi* bus home. I was so tense, anticipating the telling-off in store for me, that I deliberately kept my eyes closed.

When we arrived at the house, only Gangan and Alvin were there.

"Lee, where have you been?" Gangan demanded as she hugged me to her. "Thank you, Massa Jesus!" she said looking heavenward. I heard the lady telling her that as she was about to sit down to her dinner, she had a vision of a child running away and needing help. She was directed to where I was and saw me just as I had appeared in her vision. My grandmother thanked her profusely. I was told to go and have a shower. After that I was tucked into bed where I had my dinner. The others out searching for me soon returned. As I ate my meal I could hear them talking quietly in the next room. What happened had so frightened them all, that the worry in their voices was clear as they discussed what I had done. They thought that only children who were abused ran away from their families and they could not accept that I thought I was being abused.

Aunt Lucille stayed in the bedroom with me. She fiddled about for a while, then, unable to contain her anxiety anymore, she sat on the bed and took one of my hands in hers.

"Lee, you frightened the hell out of us, man."

"Sorry." I was penitent.

"What we would tell Nez, eh?" Exhausted, I fell asleep.

The next day Gangan would not let me out of her sight. At lunch she tried to get me to tell her why I had run away.

"I miss Mama and Papa." It was not the whole truth but I could not hurt Gangan any further. I never mentioned the incidents to my parents. I had learnt that grown-ups make serious mistakes, but my grandmother's adage, "Two wrongs don't make a right" made sense to me.

Hurricane Charlie

The annals of Jamaica record the devastation wreaked by Hurricane Charlie in the summer of 1951. It was the school holiday and my cousin, Sonia, was visiting. She was ten and lived in Spanish Town. She had gone to Gangan's for her holiday and they had come to see us for a couple of weeks. We were having lots of fun wandering about the district, playing hopscotch and chatting, chatting, chatting.

The day of the hurricane was like any other until a so-called *madman* came into the square. In those days men who wore their hair in locks were thought to be mad and dirty, outcasts in our society. This man started preaching that Babylon was going to be destroyed by flood and fire. A few men came into our shop and remarked that the man had smoked too much weed, referring to marijuana. All this was exciting to us. Sonia and I inched our way to the front of the shop and then to the roadside to hear him better. He warned that Jah was going to teach

Babylon a lesson. Babylon was Jamaica ruled by the greedy British, who caused suffering to innocent black people. We soon got bored, not understanding what he was saying, and wandered back home for lunch.

Marie, our helper, who had gone to May Pen to do some shopping came back all excited and told my mother that a hurricane was on its way. Some people came into the shop seeking confirmation that a hurricane was coming. The radio confirmed Marie's news and soon the shop was inundated with people buying kerosene oil and storm rations. We ran out of kerosene oil before we closed the shop to go and make our own home safe. Will, our handyman, was very busy battening down windows, making sure we had enough water and wood and tethering the cow near the kitchen. My cousin and I made ourselves useful rounding up the chickens and putting them into their coop. We made a lot of noise echoing the squawking of the chickens. Meanwhile my mother was everywhere, sorting and supervising the operation. My father had not returned from May Pen.

We children were sent early to bed. Sonia and I, sharing a bed, were too excited to sleep. My brother and sister went off to sleep while we chatted and giggled, waiting for the hurricane. It had begun to rain and to grow dark, but that was all. We could hear the grown-ups talking in subdued voices and, in the background, the noisy squawking of chickens as they flew about, demented. We eventually fell asleep.

During the night Sonia shook me awake. The wind was howling, a noise my mother described as "howling like a banshee". We huddled together, frightened, as the wind rose to a crescendo, paused, then started all over again. Raindrops pelted the zinc roof of the house. My mother and Gangan pulled the dressing table, wardrobe and dining table from their places and put each in front of one of the three doors leading outside. As I listened to the howling of the wind and the creaking of the acacia tree in the yard, I felt sure that our roof was going to be blown off. Gangan was in my mother's room and I could hear her praying for our safety and for the safekeeping of her disabled son, Uncle Papa, and her home back in Manchester. The lamps were left on, probably to give Gangan and Mama the courage to get through the hurricane.

Inside the house grew quiet. I nudged Sonia and suggested that we get up and look out. We crept to the door and took turns peeping through a chink. Outside all was pitch black and eerie; the only sounds were those of the shrieking gusts of wind. Frightened, we crawled back to bed and I went off to sleep trying to block out the noises that seemed so close and so very threatening.

By morning, Hurricane Charlie had wreaked havoc and left our shores. People had been killed by flying debris, many were homeless, a lot of roofs had been blown away and crops destroyed.

Gangan woke us up and outside we were greeted by a weak sun trying to shine through a louring sky. We were lucky that our property had not suffered any major damage. The acacia tree near the kitchen had blown down and Gangan thanked God that it had not damaged the kitchen as it fell. The pond had overflowed and flooded the path to the shop. The guinep tree near the shop had several broken branches laden with fruit, on which, when the grown-ups were busy, Sonia, Alvin and I feasted. Under its green skin, the fruit has a succulent yellowish flesh covering a large seed. A guinep grows sweeter as it progresses through the ripening stages. Children were always being warned not to eat guineps until they were ripe, and my mother shouted dire warnings at us that we would have our hides skinned if we ate them green because no-one had any time to cope with our being sick.

After a late breakfast we kicked off our sandals and played in the clear pools of rainwater that formed a patchwork quilt on the land. The marl main road glistened in the pale sunlight and everything was washed clean; the gutters had become gurgling, gushing streams in which we raced paper boats. We followed their progress from the bank and watched them bob up and down, capsize and sink. For us it was a fun-filled day and the fact of a national disaster did not really touch our consciousness.

A New Monarch

Queen Elizabeth II acceded to the throne in 1952. The occasion was celebrated in Jamaica as it was in Britain and the rest of the empire. Preparation for her coronation and the coronation itself were reported in the *Daily Gleaner*, our national newspaper. Our school took an avid interest in this to ensure we were aware of its historic relevance.

Our headteacher's zeal led to singing practice of not only the British national anthem, which the whole school knew, but also songs such as *"I vow to thee my country"* and *"Rule Britannia"* that now stick in my throat. There we were, children of a subject people whose forebears had been enslaved by the British, being taught to sing:

> *Rule Britannia, Britannia rules the waves.*
> *Britons never, never, never shall be slaves.*

In 2002 watching the BBC Prom held at Buckingham Palace to celebrate the Queen's golden jubilee I saw the evening brought to a close with the song *"Land of hope and glory"*. As the audience's voices soared I recalled how I, too, had sung this with gusto and childhood innocence in the 1950s. I did not realise then, and I wonder how many singing that evening in 2002 realised, that the sentiment in that song is in support of empire building.

In 1952, we children sang with passion, oblivious of imperialism and racism.

On Coronation Day a bus took us from our school to the Coronation Rally in the small town of Race Course. Children from all the schools in Vere sang and listened to speeches. It was a jolly occasion and we were given mementoes that we clutched like precious jewels all the way back to our homes. I remember getting a pencil graced with the Queen's head.

Jamaica did not have long to wait to meet its new ruler and the island welcomed the Queen, accompanied by the Duke of Edinburgh, on her state visit to the British West Indies. Our school organised a trip to Kingston where children from all over the island gathered to greet the royal couple. Everyone on the trip was madly excited; we were going to see the Queen and the Duke whereas our parents were not so lucky because the Royal couple would not travel through our part of the island.

At Sabina Park we found a sea of children. It was the first time I had seen so many children in one place. We were shepherded to our designated spot cordoned off with a rope. There was a general buzz of expectancy. At last the open-topped car cruised into sight and wave after wave of cheers echoed along the route as the royal couple, stood in their car and waved at the crowd. The Queen was smiling. I was quite surprised at how small in stature she was. In newspaper photographs she had appeared at least five foot six and very regal. That day she looked quite ordinary. Some of the older children remarked that she looked no different really from the white women they saw in magazines. Some of us had expected a fairy tale queen with her crown and regalia because, after all, she was the great Queen of England and the British Empire.

Memorable Year

The innocence of my childhood began to evaporate when I was ten; several incidents occurred that year, most of them sad or disturbing. The happy memory is the birth of my youngest sister, Annie. As my mother's little helper, I was sent to fetch the midwife who lived in Rest.

I got on my bike and rode quickly to the midwife's home because I could see that my mother was in pain. The midwife was very quick and we soon set off. With her black bag attached to the rack behind the saddle of her lady's bicycle, she rode much slower than I did and soon it became boring riding alongside her.

To make the three-mile journey more exciting, I would every now and then race ahead, free-wheel down a hill and wait for her to catch up. I was quite a good rider and could ride 'no hands', often challenging the boys to a race.

When the midwife and I arrived at my house, my mother told me to go and help Marie in the shop. She depended a lot on Marie, who was now like a member of our extended family. Years later I understood their relationship when my mother told me that Marie was the only person she trusted as she never felt a part of my father's family with the exception of his sister, Aunt Beryl. They remained friends for over fifty years until Aunt Beryl's death. My mother rarely visited my father's relatives who lived close by and was very aloof when they visited us.

Gangan, however, visited us regularly and she was staying with us at the time because it was customary for a family expecting a new baby or with someone ill and in need of nursing care, to have a female relative come to stay and give additional support. Gangan took charge of the younger children and was the one who called us into my parents' bedroom to meet our baby sister.

'The Lord giveth and the Lord taketh away . . .'

My sister was born a day after my father lost his father. There had always been a strong bond between the two men and my poor father must have felt that saying applied to him.

A few days after my grandfather's funeral, my parents were placed under even more stress by my stupidity. Marie and my father managed the shop and when I came home from school I took over, usually from Marie, from 4:30 until we closed the shop between 6:00 and 6:30 as it began to grow dark. I was the only person other than my parents to have the combination numbers for the padlock. That evening Will stayed with me until I locked up and then he left. Marie helped Gangan to get the other children ready for bed. I took the tin oven with the patties into the kitchen a few feet from the shop. I placed the kerosene lamp that I had brought with me from the shop, on the kitchen table. I was hungry and decided to eat a patty. As I put the patty to my mouth I heard the crunching sound of footsteps outside. It was a pitch-black night. I peered out, calling, "Who's there?" Nothing but stillness. I picked up the lamp to make my way quickly to our new house next to the shop and, as I did so, I again heard footsteps, this time near the kitchen door. As I looked in that direction I truly believed that I saw my grandfather passing by. In a culture in which stories of ghosts, *duppies* as we call them, abound, I thought that my grandfather was coming to take me away. I was petrified! I screamed, tripped over a chair and dropped the lamp. The next thing I knew my light cotton dress was on fire. Afire, I became hysterical and dashed into my mother's bedroom. She was in bed nursing the baby but I took no notice of this fact as I leapt onto the bed. I needed my mother. "Oh my God!" she screamed. As if by magic, Gangan appeared. She pushed me onto the floor where she rolled me over to put out the flames.

I was in agony, badly burnt around the middle. My mother hugged me tenderly and tried to console me. I fell asleep in Gangan's arms, too burnt to lie in bed. When my father came home he rubbed my head and talked soothingly to me, trying to stop my whimpering by diverting my mind from the stinging sensation I was suffering. I cried long into that night.

Early next morning, my father took me to the nearest hospital in Lionel Town where I was admitted. The hospital was scary; it smelt strongly of disinfectant. Doctors and nurses buzzed about among the beds. Everything seemed to be white: the walls, the bed sheets, the doctors' gowns and the starched uniforms of the nurses.

I sat up in bed until a doctor and a nurse came to examine me. Portable screens were quickly placed around me. The doctor pricked the skin of all the bubbles encircling my midriff and the water flowed out. They dressed the burns with something cool and soothing. The burnt area stopped about an inch on either side of my navel. When I returned home, my parents said I was very lucky not to have been more badly burnt and they were thankful God had been so good to us.

Hospital was not a horrible experience but I wanted to go home. I read a lot during my confinement and hated having to miss school. My only visitor was my father because of the distance and the family situation. I was very happy when my father came to take me home. Marie, telling the story of that awful night, embellished it somewhat, claiming that I had frightened them out of their wits when I ran into the house like a *rolling calf*, this fabled animal supposedly a *duppy*.

I was to learn the almost unbelievable truth, that history was repeating itself that day. My mother had also got burnt in the kitchen as a child, an experience so painful that for years she refused to talk about it. To hide the ugly burn mark encircling her upper arm, she wore dresses with sleeves until she was over sixty-five.

She was seventy when I finally heard her story and even then her eyes clouded with the pain from sixty years earlier.

Her father was a stonemason and, like all families with land in their district, he also did small farming to provide for the family and sell the excess to augment his earnings. Tragedy struck when my mother was ten. He became ill with a fever and a week later began to deteriorate rapidly. The fact that the doctor had to make a house call meant that he was seriously ill as the surgery was a few miles away. The day he died the doctor had told Gangan there was no hope, pneumonia had won. My mother, her two sisters and her brother were fetched from school. Her father hugged each of them in farewell and then they were kept out of the house. Later that day, a cousin broke the news to them, "Your father died."

My mother's oldest brother, Uncle Tom, had emigrated to Panama where he was clerk/assistant to the pharmacist in a drugstore and her oldest sister, Aunt Wrightie, was in Grand Cayman working as a nanny. They could not come home for the funeral. Jim, my mother's baby brother, was only three months old. Family members and village elders came to comfort Gangan and to temporarily take over the management of the home.

Her father's body stayed in the bedroom overnight but the children were not allowed in. Two old ladies from the village washed and dressed his body in readiness for burial. The local carpenter made the coffin from one of the cedar trees cut from the family land. My mother spoke of the sadness she had felt at the funeral. The memory was poignant. The coffin was placed on two chairs on the barbecue for people to pay their respects. As people gathered someone shouted, "Lift her over him!" They lifted my mother and passed her from one side of the coffin to the next. This was meant to ensure that her father's spirit would protect and guide her. At a given time six men lifted her father's coffin onto their shoulders and the funeral procession walked the quarter-mile to Frankfield Church. After the *churching* of the body, the burial service, the procession returned to the home where the body was interred in the family's *burial ground*. My mother remembered Gangan being inconsolable for days.

In the Jamaican tradition of family support, Gangan's family in Spanish Town suggested that my mother should live with them, leaving one older girl to help Gangan with the three younger children. My mother joined the family, sharing a bedroom with their daughter. Though by no means ill-treated, she resented the fact that the two boys in that family lived the life of Riley with the girls and the helper always at their beck and call. It was a big comfortable six-bedroom house and there were three teachers lodging with the family. My mother's morning chore was to wash up after breakfast. She always felt pressured because she and the family attended early morning mass before breakfast after which she had to do the washing-up very quickly and run all the way to school to avoid being late. The caning they earned for late arrival was intended to teach punctuality and discipline. One morning, in her hurry to get her chore done, she tripped on a wet patch in the kitchen and fell against the kitchen range; a flailing arm overturned a pot and she was burnt and scarred for life.

The saddest memories of my tenth year were the incidents that made me aware that my parents' marriage was unhappy; small cracks grew into gaping holes. The occasional spats turned into full blown rows, ugly to witness.

The day after one such row my mother went off to Gangan's. For days we all wore long faces until my mother returned. But things were never the same again.

No longer did she laugh with the customers. Her liveliness had evaporated, to be replaced by a lingering, pensive air.

Not long after this she taught me about *pardner* money. She was the banker for a group of men who saved a fixed amount each week from their pay. There were ten men so the *pardner* was 'thrown' over a period of ten weeks and each week one of them got the full ten weeks' savings. This he would either send to his family or leave with the banker to collect at *crop-over* when he would go home. As a thank-you gesture, the banker received a small sum when each man got his draw. My mother showed me the book in which she kept a record of names, the amounts each person saved and was paid. She also showed me where she kept the money, in a tin, locked and hidden for safekeeping.

Without telling me in so many words, my mother thus conveyed to me how much she trusted me, at the same time indicating that she had lost all trust in my father. The new responsibility did not overwhelm my childish mind as I did not comprehend our family's dire situation. Nonetheless, it was a turning point in my life; I became very protective of my mother and began to lose trust in my father.

Sex Education

In 1953 I met 15 year-old Lydia, dark, skinny and suffering from acne, the only child of the couple who had rented our old house. She became my confidante.

Lydia had a beautiful voice and if I close my eyes and think of her I can hear it tinkling like a bell on a cold winter's morning singing "*A Spanish Cavalier*" She also taught me the contralto accompaniment to "*My Name is Solomon Levy*", so that we sang it as a duet. We had such fun singing 'country and western' songs and hymns.

As I approached puberty, it was she who taught me about the female body. One day I rushed up to her and grabbed her from behind playfully. She snapped at me and I was offended. It was then that she explained the menstrual cycle and that she was that day suffering such discomfort that she could not bear to have anyone touch her.

"Don't let any boy touch you!" That was my mother's version of sex education

"Why?" I countered. "Everybody touches at school."

"Where you're covered is private." This was followed by a dead stare that meant "Don't even say another word!" At such times I hunched my shoulders and walked away in disgust at grown-ups.

I was enlightened on the subject of sexual molestation by Lydia and the 'big girls'. At the time I was in 'Fifth Class' and felt privileged to be an honorary member of the big girls' group which I earned because it was what Lydia wanted.

She was popular and I was her little friend. These older girls aged between fifteen and sixteen in 'Sixth Class' would soon be leaving school and acted almost as grown women. They were the source of all knowledge of things that adults did not want us to know.

One day as we were lying in the tall grass bordering the hard area of the school-yard where skipping, hopscotch and ball games were played, I mulled over my mother's warning. I wanted to hear what the big girls had to say on the subject.

"Why shouldn't boys touch us?" I asked. They all looked at me as if I had gone insane. "Well?" I persisted timidly. They tittered, shared knowing looks and then gave me a lecture on sexual molestation. They had been given the identical warning by their mothers. I would later find out that it was not the boys our parents should have been warning us about but men, some of them our relatives or others who claimed to be family friends.

The pranks played by the boys were innocent. I learnt that when boys pushed each other onto a girl, it was to touch her breasts; some cheeky boys would go even further to win a dare by pinching a girl's nipple. Another popular prank was to covertly put down a mirror on a step and as the unsuspecting girl stepped over the mirror, the boys would catch a glimpse of her underwear. Once aware of these pranks, I became more wary and was very pleased when a boy was caught out and was pummelled by a group of girls.

The more serious issue, however, was that of girls being abused and the ease with which men set sexual traps. They seemed almost immune from sanction, as the general practice was for parents to blame their daughters when girls complained or an act of abuse came to light. This to me seemed outrageously unfair. As the big girls talked, I listened, becoming painfully aware that many of us had all been sexually touched by men. Men who tickled girls when their parents were not present and, in so doing, succeeded in touching developing breasts and thighs; men who, in a friendly manner, pulled girls down to sit on laps, where innocent bottoms squashed against trembling, lecherous bodies. Some were daring enough to squeeze budding breasts and grab nubile buttocks. I heard how men forced girls to have sexual intercourse with them. But the worst crime they agreed was when it was a father who did it. One girl gave a long hiss of the teeth, "*Bway, dis life no fair, yuh know. Yuh own mumma don't even believe yuh.*" I wanted to ask more questions but the bell rang for the end of the recess. My mind was a buzz. The girls did not mention the words 'rape', 'sexual molestation' and 'incest'; but what came through loud and clear was that the onus was on girls not to be caught out by these men, because if it happened the men would get away with it. No-one would go to prison and the stigma would most certainly be ours.

Suddenly, I understood what had happened to poor Nora, our neighbour's granddaughter! Village gossip was rife when Nora got pregnant at sixteen. She had just left school. Before she had the baby, Nora left Daybart to live in May Pen. After the baby was born the gossip grew. It was whispered that Nora's father had got her pregnant, thus making him also her child's father. I found this difficult to work out and my mother refused to explain it to me.

"Go 'way from me, child! Take up your book and mind your own business. Don't ask anybody no more questions!" As she rolled her big eyes at me, I knew better than to persist.

Less than two years later the gossip reached a crescendo; Nora had had another baby and it was rumoured that, once more, it was her father's child! I heard that the children had six fingers on each hand, a sure sign of incest. On a couple of occasions when I went to May Pen with Marie I wheedled until she gave way and we visited Nora. Even I with my nosiness could not ask her about the paternity of her children, but that did not stop me quickly checking their hands. The older child had a small knob attached to his little finger on one hand but I saw no such protuberance on the baby's hands.

I never discussed Nora with the big girls because they would make fun of her and she had been my friend. I knew Nora's father. He owned the bicycle shop in Rest near where some of my father's family lived. How could he do such a thing to his own daughter? He did not look evil; in fact he was always nice to me. I just could not understand it and dreaded ever again meeting him at close quarters. Suddenly he was the devil incarnate.

What I carried away with me the last time I saw Nora was the change that had come over her personality. Gone was the happy schoolgirl who was like a big sister to me; in her place was a very sad young woman.

Splintered Family

Our lives changed dramatically when I was eleven years old. That summer my parents rented their home and shop and we moved to the parish capital, May Pen. As children we were not given any explanation for this upheaval.

From a property with lots of space, we were now confined to an apartment, half of a house. In the next apartment lived Joyce and Roy with their grandmother, Nanny P. Their parents were working in USA. Roy was my age and Joyce a few years older, but she acted very grown-up and never joined in any of our children's games. Within a few days Roy and his cousin, Tony, who lived next door, became our friends. They helped us to settle in.

Living in May Pen was similar to being in Kingston. The nicest thing was having piped water, indoor shower and toilet, electricity and street lights. The nights seemed less dark and far less frightening. People were on the road after nightfall and, unlike Daybart, life was not so strongly governed by daylight.

What I missed, however, were the trees at the back of Grandfather's house that had created nooks for hiding away from the grown-ups. The only tree growing in the yard was a cashew, which I had never seen before. The cashew fruit hangs like a bell with the nut downwards and I learnt very quickly from experience that the ripe fruit is sweet and succulent but unripe it burns the lips.

Our new home was near the Jamaica Fruit Company's packing factory on the outskirts of town. I was fascinated by the busy road. Trucks rumbled up and down the road, their drivers honking their horns and talking loudly to each other above the noise of their engines. I had only seen this much traffic in Kingston. I watched as trucks laden with fruit from citrus farms approached the factory to disgorge their produce while others emerged with labelled boxes of fruit for Kingston Harbour. I would think of place names in England that I had learnt in geography lessons, towns to which I imagined the fruit would eventually be transported.

My mother had overnight changed into a full-time housewife but she still had someone in to help with the washing and ironing. She seemed more preoccupied than usual and the unhappiness that had overshadowed our last couple of years in Daybart did not disappear; it further enveloped us and as the months went by it was almost suffocating. My parents no longer had rows, they simply coexisted in our shared space. Then my mother left.

Earlier that day she had confided in me that she had to go to Kingston for a while and stay with Uncle Tom. I helped her pack her suitcase with clothes for her and my baby sister, Annie. Before leaving the house my mother, who was not normally given to such displays, hugged the four of us and warned us to be good whilst she was away. We all trooped out of the house after her to await the arrival of the Kingston bus. It seemed to get there all too soon and, as our little group watched from the roadside, clutching Annie in her arms she embarked and found a seat on the left side so we could wave goodbye. My mother looked so sad as she waved and threw us kisses. And then they were gone.

I did not see her again for four and a half years.

I shepherded my brothers and sister back to the house. Nanny P had been asked to look after us until my father's return that evening. He appeared very concerned at the news that my mother had gone to Kingston. The next day Nanny P's daughter came to the house, introduced by our father as the person who would be taking care of us while our mother was away. Aunt Lin came daily. My younger brother, Bonnie, became fretful because he missed his mother. I grew anxious when one week passed and then another and my mother had not returned. By the time I received a letter from her I had already written to Gangan, worried about my education and my father's response to my future. My mother's letter made me very sad but I understood that her leaving us did not mean she did not love us. She told me that she missed us very much and that we would be together again; till then, she said, we should be good children.

Before leaving Daybart I had sat the entrance exam for Clarendon College, a boarding school that my headteacher had seen as ideal for me, Daybart being too far to go to as a day student. I had visited the college with him and was looking forward to being there, so when a letter from him arrived in May Pen, I hovered about to hear the news. My mother, who was still living with us, was away in Manchester for a few days staying with Gangan. My father read the letter then passed it to me. Teacher Reid's letter told my parents that he and his wife wished us well and said they hoped to see me before I went off to Clarendon College. My father's response to my good news was negative. I wanted to know when I could get my uniforms made and shop for books.

"I can't deal with this right now," he said stopping me in my tracks. As he walked off, I thought it best not to pursue the matter but to await my mother's return. I begged her to do something quickly. I could hear my parents arguing heatedly about it and I prayed every night for two weeks that they would agree to send me to Clarendon College. My prayers were in vain. In my anxiety I decided to broach the subject. My father then made it quite clear that I would not be going to Clarendon College. I cried bitterly.

After the holiday, Alvin, Lillian and I attended May Pen Elementary School. After my mother's departure, Bonnie stayed home with Aunt Lin. This school was massive compared to our old one. I was glad that we had made friends before our first day as they looked out for us, easing our way into the school milieu. I missed the intimacy of the big girls' group. My old headteacher's house had been like my second home with all the warmth of belonging. Here we were strangers.

Nothing particularly exciting happened in the time I spent there. The headteacher was a jolly man with a gentle smile, but seemed somewhat less in the thick of things than Teacher Reid had been at Milk River. Lessons followed the pattern I was used to and I settled in very quickly. A new subject for me was Domestic Science where we were taught cooking, baking, sewing and other domestic chores. It was for girls only, reinforcing gender role. I hated it! In sewing, I managed to cut out from patterns an apron with a heart-shaped pocket and an underskirt. I was taught to use the sewing machine for straight stitching and to do hemming and overlocking by hand. Whereas some girls were excellent at sewing, my pieces, to get to a satisfactory standard, were grubby from undoing and restitching. The only lesson I enjoyed was baking an orange sponge cake. My cake came out of the oven looking perfect and I was very proud of my achievement. In addition, everyone at home enjoyed it.

One memorable occasion at school was the visit of The Honourable Sir Alexander Bustamante, our Prime Minister who, after his death, was made a national hero. As he walked along the school-field with the headteacher and other dignitaries, he stopped to speak to me. He asked me how I was, to which I replied, "Fine, thank you, sir." He then asked me about school and how I was getting on. When I said that I was working hard he patted me on the shoulder and said, "Good, good." Then he moved on. The children in my class who were not nearby to hear our conversation were very excited that the great man had spoken to me and they badgered me to tell them exactly what he had said. I told them that he reminded me of a genial uncle. They were amazed that I should take it all so calmly.

May Pen was a different world from Daybart. It was a busy little town with a square where the clock stood as a landmark. There were four main exits out of May Pen. Several named streets radiated from the square and from the main roads. The square was, from morning to evening, a hive of activity. The market in the square overflowed with people buying and selling, handcarts pushing their way through the bustle and hawkers carrying their wares on their heads or protectively in front of them, as they tried to persuade people to buy. Sometimes I sauntered through the market captivated by the colourful scene as the different smells tickled my nose. If a hawker's eyes caught mine he would try to trap me with, "Buy something nuh, darlin'".

The school was on the quiet street next to the market and the post office was almost opposite the school. Back in the square the main thoroughfare was lined with stores, wholesale shops, restaurants and an ice cream parlour. My pocket money was often spent on ice cream and a patty on a Friday. A group of us, feeling quite grown-up, would meet and walk into the square for our treat, then stroll along the road leading out to Old Harbour. We would stop by the bridge over the Rio Minho; to us this marked the boundary of May Pen. Up at the Alms House, perched on a steep hill nearby, we would see the destitute of the parish moving about like ghosts. To my child's eye, the building and its inhabitants seemed remote from the rest of the town, not at all a part of it.

Some girls at school encouraged me to join the Girl Guides. It was something to do outside of school and it expanded my circle of acquaintances. The highlight that term was a trip to Bull Head Mountain for guides and scouts. I managed to wheedle the money for the trip out of my father.

That morning the bus left May Pen very early with about forty of us, excited and chattering like monkeys. As we left May Pen and climbed into the hills the countryside grew greener. At the foot of the mountain we got out of the bus and trekked to the top, walking in small groups of friends, with the scout master leading the way up the track and the guide mistress bringing up the rear. The leaders suggested a steady pace uphill but being energetic young people we found the pace far too slow and were determined to make it to the top in record time, so we quickened our steps. At first the climb was gentle and I enjoyed the freshness of the countryside. Houses were dotted along the track; the dew still hung on the leaves of trees and bushes, glistening jewels in the early morning sunlight. I recognised a profusion of Spanish needles and began to recite Claude McKay's poignant poem, composed as he shivered in the cold of New York, U.S.A., homesick and lonely:

> *Lovely dainty Spanish needle*
> *With your yellow flower and white*
> *Dew bedecked and softly sleeping*
> *Do you think of me tonight?*

The group remained silent for a while, the poem touching our young hearts.

In an hour or so the climb became harder and the slope steeper and steeper. Our pace slowed dramatically and, by now, most of us had aching legs and shoulders. We were typical town kids, not used to walking the long distances our relatives in the rural areas did daily. The hut squatting atop the mountain was a welcome sight. We quickly unloaded the rucksacks and bags with our food that we had lugged up the mountainside and tethered the goat that would be cooked for our lunch. We welcomed refreshments and some time to flop down and relax.

After our rest we were divided into work gangs. A few of the boys were in charge of slaughtering the goat. The other tasks were gathering brushwood for the fire, fetching water from the river close by, preparing the meal and washing up. Most of us had free time while the meal was being prepared. I wandered off to a quiet spot to drink in the panoramic view. The hills, like crumpled paper against the skyline, fell away gradually as the plains took over, leading to the sea. The view was spectacular!

For lunch we had our feast of curried goat and rice in the open air fanned by a balmy breeze. Someone started singing as the meal ended:

> *Evening time, work is over now it's evening time*
> *We going to run and jump, dance and play ring ding*
> *On the mountain top . . .*

Everyone joined in. Folk songs were sung one after the other. Next came the storytellers with their ghost stories and the popular tales of 'Anancy', the wily spider. As the washing-up team chatted and laughed to lighten their labour, the rest of us frolicked in the river and the mountainside echoed our merriment. We then had organised games finishing with a tug-of-war. The trudge downhill was painless and no-one complained about the quick pace as we sang and cracked jokes all the way. When we arrived back in May Pen, most of us had fallen asleep having enjoyed the trip immensely.

Denbigh Agricultural Show was, and still is, a big all-island event in August. There were exhibitions and prizes for all sorts of home produce. The 4H Clubs' booths were very interesting with their displays of young people's work, such goodies as guava halves in syrup, mango chutney and mango jam and from coconut fronds or sisal, hats, bags, slippers and table mats. I was interested neither in the foodstuff nor the animals but followed our group, Roy, Joyce and Tony, as they wandered around because there was very little else to do on that bank holiday weekend and, as a group, we had fun.

I had grown quieter over the months since we moved to May Pen. I missed my mother and deep within me blamed my father both for her leaving and for not allowing me to go to Clarendon College. Added to these feelings was the realisation that Aunt Lin was taking my mother's place.

Years later, my father and Aunt Lin got married. She was a very good wife to him and we grew very fond of each other.

Life With My Grandmother

But to return to that sad time, quite unexpectedly one day, Gangan paid us a visit. I was overjoyed to see her. She and my father had long talks and the next day my father called us together and Gangan told us that our mother had gone to England. Lillian and I would be going back with her for the time being while the boys would go to Harmons to stay with my father's mother. I welcomed this arrangement, as did Lillian. The only sad note was that our brothers would not be with us but I knew it was useless to beg the grown-ups to change their minds about this.

A couple of months after moving to Frankfield with Gangan, Bonnie joined us. He was unhappy living with his paternal grandmother. He cried a lot because he wanted to be with Lillian and me. Bonnie was our pet and when Gangan asked if I wanted to go with her to Harmons to fetch him, I readily agreed.

Harmons was not far by car but we were going by donkey and foot through the mountains. Gangan saddled Queenie, her faithful donkey, and we set off. Gangan walked most of the way. She said that, as I was unused to walking long distances, I should ride. On the way I had to insist I would walk for a while and she should ride, to which she grudgingly agreed. Gangan was then in her mid-fifties, but had tremendous energy and I cannot remember her ever being ill.

On the journey to Harmons we stopped at Green Pond to see some of Gangan's relatives and to have lunch, as well as to give Queenie a well-deserved rest.

At Harmons, Bonnie was so pleased to see us that he would not let go of my hand. The journey back went very quickly. Gangan kept us talking all the way back as she walked, never once complaining about being tired. For acts like these she holds a special place in our hearts.

I was to learn that things change and that living with Gangan would prove totally different from spending holidays there. I did not relish doing chores that I had never had to do before, but Gangan was very firm and expected obedience without *back chat*. My main chore was cleaning the house. The floor was polished and a coconut brush was used to make it shine. The coconut brush was a half of a dried coconut husk with the flat, fibrous part used for shining. My grandma showed me how to clean the wooden floor and the concrete steps. I had to scrub the latter with a handful of Spanish needles and buff dry with a cloth. This was my Saturday job; another was washing our clothes, Lillian's, Bonnie's and mine. Gangan washed hers and Uncle Papa's. Lillian and I had the daily chore of having to fetch water from our tank a little way from the house down a steep incline. This had to be done morning and afternoon for household activities such as cooking and for bathing. At the tank, attached to a rope, was a bucket that was lowered to collect the water.

We had a few chickens and some goats. Occasionally on Sundays we would have one of our chickens instead of the beef, pork or mutton bought from the local butcher. Gangan would kill the chicken on Saturday and season it. She chose the victim and we caught it. She would then put it under a big basin with its head sticking out. The poor fowl squawked and flapped about in a panic as the basin was held down firmly and it was decapitated with a sharp cutlass. I had to help to pluck the feathers after the body had been dunked in hot water to facilitate the process. Next, the plucked chicken was gutted, washed, cut up into pieces, seasoned with herbs, salt and black pepper and left to marinate overnight.

Saturday was soup day: beef soup, mutton soup, chicken soup, bean soup or gungo peas soup. The pulses were flavoured with salt pork or salted beef and coconut milk. These were mouth-watering and filling meals with yam, coco, breadfruit, cho-cho, pumpkin and sweet potato also dumplings, a favourite of most Jamaican children. Gangan was an excellent cook and I only had to cook the odd meal as part of my training. Sometimes my rice and peas got burnt but Gangan was very patient with me.

The goats were Uncle Papa's domain. In the morning he took them to graze somewhere on the property, a different spot each day. In the evening he fetched them home and tethered them just beyond the yard where they were visible from the house. He made sure they had enough water to drink and were in good health. He and Gangan decided when to sell a goat. The rams ensured that there were always kids keeping up the number in the herd. The goats also supplied us with nourishing milk but, however hard I tried, I never acquired a taste for goat's milk. Gangan was very protective of Uncle Papa. He was reserved and kept himself to himself, as Jamaicans say. My mother had told me the sad story about Uncle Papa's permanently drooping right arm and right foot that dragged behind when he walked.

There was a cane press under the breadfruit tree near the house and it was his duty to cut the sugar cane that grew on the property and extract the juice by pushing each stalk between the press' two rollers while turning the handle for them to rotate. When he was fifteen a tragedy befell him. He had extracted a pail of juice which he poured into the pan to boil to the consistency of wet sugar. As he turned away he fell. My mother and her sister, May, who were fanning the fire in the backyard thought he was messing about but when his body started convulsing they shouted for Gangan. He was taken into the house and rubbed down with rum and a spoon was placed in his mouth to stop him from biting his tongue. Gangan sent for the neighbour and some-one went to fetch the doctor. The diagnosis was already apparent. He had suffered a stroke. With Gangan's ministering and support, he gradually regained his speech but he found it difficult to formulate certain words; he spoke with a stutter that became more pronounced when he was angry. He lost some of the flexibility in his right leg. He had to use his left hand to move his right arm which remained lifeless and permanently crooked. His disability, however, did not stop him from being productive. He helped Gangan with her small farm, clearing the land, planting and reaping crops as well as looking after the goats and chickens.

Gangan had some quaint country practices. She would never cook just enough food for the family's dinner, there would always be an extra share in case someone came by. If several people came by and the food prepared was not enough to *stretch*, then dinner would not be served until the visitors had left. The visitors would be offered lemonade or ginger beer and anything else that we had, such as cake or pudding. Gangan never threw food out. Leftovers were fried as part of the next day's breakfast or given to the dog, Rover.

People who attended Frankfield Church but lived a long way off, would stop on the way to church for a drink of water which was always kept ice-cold in a Spanish jar, a huge earthenware jar with handles. In it was a small, smooth stone which people claimed was a thunderbolt with the ability to cool water. These thunderbolts were much sought after at the time, for rural areas had neither electricity nor refrigerators.

When I went to live with Gangan, her second husband and Uncle Jim were working away from home. For labour intensive jobs such as clearing and planting crops in a short time Gangan needed help which came in the form of a *field day*, a cooperative method that worked well for small farmers. The morning would begin at six o'clock when Gangan and the female relatives would prepare cups of coffee and chocolate tea and cut up hunks of bread for breakfast. The men would arrive to be served at about six-thirty. They would then go off to work, leaving the women to get down to the serious business of cooking lunch. Some of the food from the field, including green bananas and plantains would, along with dumplings, be prepared with *curry goat*. Once their work was over, the men would return more than ready for their meal which was washed down with home-made lemonade or ginger beer. A *little taste* of some over-proof Jamaican white rum would complete their meal. The atmosphere would be jolly as the men relaxed after a hard morning's work.

Harvested food such as yams and potatoes as well as gungo peas, broad beans and sweet corn was divided into two parts, one for home consumption and the other for selling to the higglers who resold it in the big markets of Mandeville, May Pen and Kingston. I loved the aroma created by the escallion, mint and thyme that grew in the herb garden by the tank and I often would pick a few leaves from one of the herbs, rub them between my fingers and enjoy the aroma.

Church became an important part of my life. I attended Sunday school and the service that followed. All of the young people in the choir also attended the school next door. I enjoyed singing in the choir. For special occasions such as Christmas and Harvest, our weekly choir practice was extended to two or three hours after which the younger members would lark about in the vestry. In my first year I won first prize in the Sunday school competition. This included a written piece and reciting Psalm 19. My reward was a Methodist Hymn Book that I still have.

Our church had a visiting minister who came monthly on communion Sunday; lay preachers, of whom my headteacher was one, conducted service on the other Sundays. The minister, Reverend Blackburn, was from England and when he brought his new wife to meet the congregation most of us had difficulty understanding her. Our ears were not attuned to her strange accent that the young people found very amusing. We also had a good laugh at her rolling gait. A clever dick opined that, having travelled from England on a ship, she had developed the rolling movement of the sea.

Sometimes we sat by the church wall to study. Our church was a stone structure on a knoll and sitting outside provided us with a view of the surrounding hills. It was here that I first became conscious of the breathtaking beauty of the Jamaican sunset. The setting sun would brighten up the late afternoon sky with shades of yellow, orange and red. It would grow into a magnificent red ball, as if suspended, then pieces seemed to break away and disappear behind the clouds as the sun moved further and further away over the hills, decreasing in size until it crested the highest peak and vanished altogether. Suddenly dusk would fall and we would hurry home.

School I enjoyed, as always. My only disappointment was Gangan's insistence on getting the village shoemaker to make our school shoes. She wanted us to have sensible shoes for everyday wear. We trooped behind her to the shoe shop in the village to be measured by the shoemaker. When the shoes were ready I found that mine were of soft brown leather with thick soles and laces. Fashionable they were not! I was thankful that my dress shoes had been bought by my Aunt Lucille in Kingston and were fashionable.

On my first day in school I was placed in the class taught by the headteacher and given a seat next to Colleen, his daughter. We became firm friends and studied together. Everyone at Frankfield Elementary School was friendly and helpful. Within a few weeks I was settled in the group studying for the Common Entrance Examination in a bid for places in high schools across the island. Another group of pupils, mainly sixteen-years-olds, was studying for the First Year Jamaica Local Examination, the first of three examinations which would provide another route to higher education and training for professions such as nursing, teaching and administrative posts. It was the popular route for pupils whose parents could not afford the expense of a secondary school or for pupils who had not won a place at one of those schools. Teacher Campbell was an excellent teacher and head who expected everyone in our group to work to his or her optimum. He introduced Algebra, Geometry and Trigonometry as well as Latin because he wanted to ensure that those of us who were thirteen or fourteen would not be disadvantaged when we were placed in classes with children who already had one to two years of secondary school education.

Colleen and I spent a lot of time together, mainly at their house, which was a stone's throw from the school, separated from it by a fence and a small garden. She had two younger brothers whose activities were different from ours. Mrs Campbell was mother hen, solicitous and always pleasant. She had the habit of slightly opening her mouth as she listened then, as if suddenly realising that her mouth was open, she quickly inhaled and shut it firmly. Teacher Campbell, at about five foot six inches, was the same height as his wife, spare with a nut brown round face and small wise eyes that seemed to look straight into your soul. He spoke softly and tended to clear his throat before speaking. In the classroom he was firm but at home he had a *wicked* sense of humour. He was always generous to me. For instance, on the day of the Common Entrance Examination he drove Colleen and me to the examination centre in Mandeville about fifteen miles away, thus saving me from a long, early-morning bus ride. After the examination, he quietly put up with our non-stop chatter all the way home. He would also invite me to join in family activities, refusing to take no for an answer.

During the summer holidays, Colleen's older sister, Merle, came home from Kingston where she was a boarder at Wolmer's High School. To me she was very sophisticated; she also played the violin. I wanted to be like her, beautiful and full of self-confidence. Teacher Campbell's younger brother, a master at Kingston College, spent a part of his summer holidays with them. He played the piano and loved playing classical music and singing. He was also a bit of a comedian and would often have us in stitches with his jokes.

Joyce and Hugh Dyer were two other fellow students I liked. Their parents ran the shop at the other end of our district, opposite to Hermitage. My grandmother and Mrs Dyer were friends and when the Dyer children reached our gate on the way to school I would join them. There was a brother with Down's syndrome who did not attend school. The family members were very protective of him. They set a wonderful example to others by not hiding him away, as was the custom then in our culture where people who were physically and mentally challenged were, and sometimes still are, often mocked, especially by other children. Hugh is one of the nicest human beings I have ever met and handsome to boot. When he went off to West Indies College and I to Excelsior High School, he gave me a photograph of himself to ensure that I would not forget him.

In 1993 I met Hugh again after thirty-four years, an older version of that schoolboy. We spent some happy hours together in New York.

The near drowning of my sister was a most frightening experience. It was lunchtime and Teacher Campbell was going over the Latin homework with us when I heard someone screaming, "Teacher Campbell! Teacher Campbell! Lillian in the tank . . .!" I dashed for the door on hearing my sister's name and as I reached the tank I saw her head bob above the water, hands flailing. Teacher Campbell and I reached over, caught her and pulled her to safety. As she coughed and spluttered, I was shaking with fright. Mrs Campbell and another female teacher took off Lillian's wet clothes and wrapped her in a warm blanket. Teacher Campbell drove us home. Gangan thanked *Massa God* and dressed Lillian. We then took her to the doctor in Pratville for a check-up. She was fine. Asked how she managed to fall in, she explained that she had grown bored and was walking by the tank - which was out of bounds - when someone coming from the opposite direction bumped into her; she tried to sidestep, but lost her balance and fell in. From that experience she developed a great fear of water. I, too, had a fear of drowning until, at 53, I was encouraged by my granddaughter to swim and it is now one of my hobbies.

In a poem by 'Miss Lou', the doyenne of the performing arts, she captures the adventurous spirit of her fellow Jamaicans who, she says, travel near and far and can be found all over the world. I met one such traveller when she was invited to our school to tell us about Belize where she had lived for a while. Jamaicans love to hear about people's experiences abroad and this lady had an attentive audience. She was a brilliant raconteur and conjured up for us, with the help of pictures, the jungle of Belize. We saw the indigenous Indians of Belize and their artefacts as well as the country's geographical features. My appetite to travel was whetted. This was far better than geography lessons that touched only briefly on the lives of people living in different parts of the world; I yearned to learn more about other people and their cultures.

The majority of Jamaicans are Christians but, unknown to most of them, their belief system also embraces the African view that the dead also share our space and are a force to be reckoned with in our everyday life. Like many children, I was afraid of ghosts, but had what many would consider a strange habit: at weekends or holidays one of my favourite spots for spending leisure time was the family cemetery. It was in no way morbid. The tomb of each adult was about two-and-a half feet high with a smooth surface where I loved to lay down to read or day dream. As a child I felt close to those departed ancestors of the Wright family, my maternal grandfather's family. I would help Gangan to clean up the place, weeding around the tombs. None of the family now lives in the old house, but when we visit, we ensure that this sacred spot is cleaned up.

There is a navel orange tree near the burial ground, whose fruit are sweet and juicy. Gangan told me that it belonged to Uncle Tom, her first-born, because his umbilical cord had been planted with the tree. My umbilical cord also was planted with a fruit tree on Gangan's land where I was born. Now out of vogue, this was a common Jamaican practice to weld a child to family land.

In the 1950s of my childhood, letters and telegrams were the communication links between people living at some distance from each other. Telegrams were delivered by the post office because they usually announced urgent information such as the death of a relative. In Kingston letters were delivered by the postman but in rural areas mail was collected from the post office. Gangan's family kept in touch by letters and one of my duties was to walk the three miles to Pratville to collect our mail, usually on Saturdays. It was a leisurely walk, with time to have refreshment with one of our Spanish Town cousins who was the postmistress, but if a letter had to be posted or collected urgently in the week, it meant a brisk walk after school in order to get back before dark. I was able to see the behind-the-scenes operation of the post office - the sorting of letters for placing into pigeon holes, the telegraphing of messages and the packaging of letters and parcels for the mail van.

One eagerly awaited piece of mail was our monthly letter from my mother in England. When I collected it I would hurry home to hear the news. Gangan would call us to her and read parts of the letter to us. Usually my mother told us how much she missed us, asked us to "be good for Gangan" and, of course, gave us an update on the weather in Nottingham where she lived. In every letter were postal orders, money to take care of us. After reading the letter, Gangan always said a prayer of thanks to *Massa Jesus*, asking him to keep my mother safe and healthy. The postal orders we sometimes changed at the post office but more often at Arthur Biggs' grocery store where we shopped.

Gangan gave us monthly pocket money from the money my mother sent. Once in a while my father visited us and when he left Gangan would confide in me telling me how much money he had left. My mother's strength, or her weakness depending on one's view, was an uncomplaining nature. She never mentioned in any of her letters that she had been seriously ill, having contracted pleurisy and had been hospitalised for several months. The letters had arrived with the accustomed regularity. Years later I learnt of this and how she had sent her sickness benefit to take care of her children. To me this was a wonderful demonstration of my mother's love.

It was the kind of self-sacrifice that left an indelible mark on my consciousness and, with the love of my mother's family, in particular Gangan's, taught me the importance of family and the love that makes self-sacrifice a joy.

I continued to indulge my passion for English Literature; I read voraciously and loved poetry. Those that moved me I read aloud as if to an audience. I wrote poems to my mother that she never saw, as they stayed in my exercise book and I would peruse them when I missed her bringing a whiff of sadness to the air. I did become brave enough to write a poem to our departing governor, Sir Hugh Foot. The *Daily Gleaner*, our local newspaper, informed the nation of the governor's imminent return to England and the role of the governor was discussed in one of our lessons. I cannot remember what in particular prompted me to write a commemorative poem about our island and his departure, after the fashion of Wordsworth's pastoral poems; childish stuff. I was completely taken by surprise when a personally signed letter arrived from Sir Hugh thanking me for my poem and kind thoughts, and praising the beauty of Jamaica which he said he would miss.

Colleen and I were excited to be offered places at Excelsior High School, in Kingston. Teacher Campbell had directed us to choose Excelsior because of its connection with the Methodist church. In 1957 it was revolutionary that a school should be co-educational, all the older established ones then being single-sexed. I had hoped for this opportunity for so long and now, at last, had come the chance to further my education. I loved learning, to me it meant self-development and possibilities for the future.

Short-lived Dream

My family were all happy for me. In August, Gangan took Lillian, Bonnie and me to Kingston to oversee the preparations for the beginning of my school year in September. Miss Elvy, our dressmaker and family friend, made my uniforms. My other school gear and books were purchased. Uncle Tom, as head of the extended family, was my guardian. He took his role seriously, establishing rules on expectations both academically and behaviourally. I lived with Aunt Wrightie, next door to Uncle Tom.

Joe and I sometimes went to visit our grand-uncle, Gangan's only brother. His pet name was *Massa*, the Jamaicanised version of Mister, so we called him Uncle Massa. Why such a name? All countries have strange customs, puzzling at times and Jamaica's colonial past has left some customs that have thankfully now been eradicated. For instance, a lighter skin colour no longer automatically puts one on a pedestal. In my childhood, this custom prevailed and was even more so when my grandmother was a child. Her features showed her mixed parentage as African and European; her brother's features were even more European, what some of our countrymen would call *Jamaican white* and this was the genesis of their childhood names of Miss Doll and Massa in the village. Uncle Massa was tall and erect. Although we knew he had fought in the war, he never spoke of his experiences with the children of my generation. He had no children himself, which I thought very sad because he was jolly and fun to be with. When we visited him at home, his wife was prim and proper and we had tea served in china cups and saucers. This was much less fun than when we visited him Downtown in his office at the Banana Board. Joe and I would always get a treat and be fussed over. We would also get treats when Uncle Massa who was very fond of Uncle Tom visited him regularly. He was always immaculately dressed and quite dashing in his khaki shorts. He encouraged me to work hard in school and to aim at becoming a doctor or a lawyer, which he saw as highly prestigious professions.

Friendship patterns change with age and circumstances. By the end of my first term at Excelsior, Colleen and I only saw each other at school and at church. We attended Coke Methodist church Downtown, were in the young people's choir and attended weekly choir practice as well as Sunday school and church service. We joined the confirmation class and were confirmed by Reverend Hugh Sherlock who was to become an important public figure in Jamaican society. He is especially remembered as the author of our national anthem. In the mid 1990s I met his wife and, as we talked, was awed by his contribution, not just to the Methodist church, but also to Jamaica.

Two new friends entered my life. Hazel lived on the same street and her family were acquaintances of my uncle; Norma lived nearby and attended

Excelsior. Norma and I travelled together to and from school. We spent time at each other's home doing homework and indulging in girl-talk. What did we talk about? - Clothes, boys, pop music, what we wanted to do when we grew up and gossip about people at school. Hazel and I saw each other at weekends and during the holidays. We listened to WINZ, an American music station and sometimes I spent time with her instead of going to the cinema with my cousin, Joe.

When my uncle agreed I could have piano lessons I was over the moon; but my euphoria was short-lived. The piano teacher recommended to him was horrid. She had the cruel habit of rapping my knuckles with a ruler whenever I made a mistake. I wanted to play and play well but I gradually grew to dislike her and to hate the piano. My uncle was dismissive when, to his question about how I was getting along, I expressed my unhappiness with the teacher. His response was that if I did as I ought to then the teacher would not have to rap my knuckles, the onus was on me. Although I did not have the power to change things then, I objected to being taught by bullying tactics.

Uncle Tom drove me to school on my first day. I was awed by the size of the campus, housing numerous form rooms, a gymnasium, the music room, science laboratories and the refectory. There were so many students milling around on that orientation day. There were rules to remember, textbooks and exercise books for each subject. Having subject teachers was a novelty. My form had about twenty-five thirteen- to fourteen-year-olds, all new entrants. Our form tutor was Mr Reid, a Barbadian. He pronounced my name, Lawson, ending the 'son' on a higher note which sounded quite foreign to my ear. He was also the Latin master. I jumped at the opportunity to earn extra pocket money for helping a couple of lads in our form who found the subject difficult. Teacher Campbell's special tuition was paying dividends.

I was introduced to another foreign accent, two of our teachers hailed from Yorkshire in England but their accent was quite different from that of Mrs Blackburn, the minister's wife in Manchester. Mr Bradley, the science teacher, had bright fiery-red hair which made him visible from a distance; he was freckled, tall and wiry with quick movements and a tinny voice. When not teaching his dry wit came to the fore and he loved to regale us with sayings in the Yorkshire dialect. One day during a chemistry lesson the Bunsen burner flared up and the class broke into an uproar, but only for a few minutes before Mr Bradley had us all in our seats and back to work. The other Yorkshire man was Mr Senior, the geography teacher. He reminded me of a country farmer, rather laid back, rotund and slow of speech as well as movement.

Years later, in the mid-1980s in England, I was invited to lunch by the Rivers who lived in the next village. I was introduced to another of the lunch guests whom I was told had taught in Jamaica. Something seemed familiar. Was it just the Yorkshire accent?

"I had a geography teacher at Excelsior named Senior."

"Good Lord!" Madge Rivers exclaimed "What a small world!"

It was indeed the Mr Senior. John and Madge had met him and his wife in Jamaica. Both men had taught in Jamaica for a while and married Jamaican wives. Mr Senior was back in Yorkshire and still teaching.

My school day was now different from elementary school hours of nine to four. At Excelsior the day began at eight in the morning and finished for academic work at one-thirty, after which students were expected to participate in extracurricular activities such as house sports and drama. Many students also did prep, to get their homework and general studies done before going home. The whole school had assembly each morning and as we filed from our form rooms to the auditorium, the sharp eyes of teachers checked that we were properly attired. Boys wore khaki trousers and shirts with epaulettes of the school colours. Girls wore cream short-sleeved shirts, pleated skirts, green ties and straw hats called 'jipi japa'. White socks and black shoes were standard footwear. Off campus, a girl in uniform without her jipi japa hat and tie, if caught by a prefect, would suffer the consequences of having broken a school rule, a warning for a first offence and a detention for a further breach. I have noticed that today Excelsior girls no longer wear jipi japa hats.

I had a tendency to delay leaving home and some mornings as I rounded the corner near the bus stop, I would see the bus pulling away and I was left waiting for the next one that would get me to school late. In my first term I had several warnings from my form tutor and was sent to see the principal, Mr Wesley A Powell whom we called 'Wap', his initials. I was warned in a soft but deadly serious voice to be punctual. By the time he was through with me, I was sweating profusely and determined to leave home earlier.

My uncle and I spent quality time together on Sundays. Sometimes we went for a drive or a visit. One Sunday we were relaxing on his veranda when he said, "I've got to see your principal tomorrow." Curious, I waited for the reason. I was enjoying my school life and was surprised when my uncle dropped a bombshell. After what seemed an eternity, he continued, "Your mother has sent for you." I could not believe my ears. I dearly loved my mother but I had not had an inkling of this plan. Over the last months I had worked out that I wanted to go on to university to study languages then teach in a high school and write novels. Norma, Hazel and I expected we would get married and have children, but that would be much later. I wanted to visit several countries but live in Jamaica. I was jolted back to the present; a child had no say in such weighty matters. It was a fait accompli.

A few days later Wap summoned me to his office. As I had not accomplished any outstanding deed, I worried all the way there. He invited me to have a seat. His manner was pleasant and as he praised my school work I relaxed a little. When he asked me about my home situation, the penny dropped. What would I prefer, he wanted to know, to stay in Jamaica or to join my mother in England? I told him I wanted to stay at Excelsior until I took the School Certificate Examination. He said in his opinion it would be advantageous for me to stay in Jamaica until I took the Higher School Examination as I had the ability to do well and it would give me the entrance qualification for a university in Britain. He reminded me, however, that the decision rested not with him or me, but with my guardian. With hindsight I realise that he knew how difficult it would be at my age to adjust to a new school at such a critical period in my education. Hindsight also tells me that my mother thought she was doing her best as a parent. She had decided not to return to Jamaica and wanted her children with her. She also thought that there were opportunities in the *motherland* for me to have the best education possible.

And so, later that year a Miss Wood from the Social Services Department visited Jamaica to investigate the situation of children whose parents had applied for their dependants to come to England. Her report stated that Excelsior was an excellent school providing a comparable education to that of grammar schools in England and agreed with my principal that I should stay in Jamaica until the end of my secondary education. My mother strongly disagreed with Miss Wood; I left Excelsior and began the wait to go to England.

The family highlight of 1958 was my youngest aunt's wedding. There were months of preparation and, as a bridesmaid I had to have several fitting sessions at the dressmaker's. Aunt Lucille made a beautiful June bride in her white wedding dress with tiered skirt. She had four bridesmaids, a maid of honour and my brother Bonnie was the page boy. The wedding reception was a lively affair with speeches preceding the refreshments and the dancing. Some of the speeches, intended to be humorous, were a turn-off for us teenagers. A group of us sat together and made our own jokes *sotto voce*. We did not join in the dancing of old-time music and had fun watching some of the older folk waltzing on each other's toes and big-bellied men trying to get close to their partners. After several failed attempts by the grown-ups to get us to join in their fun we were finally left to do our own thing, standing or sitting around talking and laughing until the party ended at midnight.

My heart was heavy with the thought of my impending departure, but I looked forward to seeing my family and friends in Manchester when I went to spend the summer holidays at Gangan's. It was an uneventful summer. I read a lot. My world had shrunk. When September came and went Gangan was as worried as I about my education. Bless her, she decided to act. She went to see Teacher Campbell and asked for his help. He suggested I join the students who had passed their First Year Jamaica Local Examination and were studying for the Second Year Examination. The syllabus was different from Excelsior's and did not include Latin and Spanish but Teacher Campbell kindly offered to tutor me in these. One had to learn to cope with what one could not change. I spent a lot of time on the knoll where the church stood, my back against the stone wall of the church, angry at the situation. I watched many sunsets and sometimes forgot my studies, blanking out everything around me.

Then one day after crying my eyes dry, consumed with self-pity, I kicked the grass and gravel as I walked from the knoll down to the church gate. Glancing to my left, I caught sight of the graveyard as if for the first time. My spirit immediately lifted as I grasped a simple fact - I was alive and healthy; there was hope. I decided then and there to put my dreams on hold, never to give up but to be creative within my limitations. I remembered how I had felt when I could not go to Clarendon College. I knew within myself that I would get the education I wanted, although it might not be along the route I wished and it might be a long journey. That summer I took the Second Year Jamaica Local and passed. This gave me a renewed sense of achievement.

Finally, Gangan received a letter from Uncle Tom with instructions for me to return to Kingston to get a passport. After nearly a year's wait, things began to move quickly. We went to Chin Yee's Travel Service to book my fare for which we paid seventy pounds. I was due to go on a BOAC (British Airways) flight on the last day of July. Our dressmaker made me a very chic outfit, a dusty pink 'A-line' linen dress. My accessories were a pink pillbox hat, and white shoes, gloves and handbag. I went back to Frankfield for a few days to say goodbye to my family. My aunts and Gangan came with Uncle Tom to see me off at the airport, then called 'Palisadoes', now renamed 'Norman Manley'. It was a sad occasion. I had not yet left but was already missing my family.

As I gave my final wave before entering the aeroplane, I wondered what it would be like, this new life I would embrace within a day.

ENGLAND

New Life

After stops in Nova Scotia and Ireland, the plane finally landed at Heathrow Airport. I was put on a train to London Victoria by an airline attendant. As we pulled into the station I saw my mother's anxious face scanning the carriage. As she saw me alight, her face broke into a radiant smile. She hugged me and then we had to hurry to get the train to Nottingham all the while talking about the folks back home. So tired was I, that I fell asleep soon after leaving London and was roused as the train came into Nottingham. It was night. Leaving the train we started towards the taxi rank when a well-spoken gentleman offered us a lift home in his chauffeur-driven car. He had assumed that I was here for finishing school or further education and that my mother was my chaperone! We talked about Jamaica and when we were dropped off he gave me his card. My mother, who had not joined in the conversation found the whole thing quite amusing.

On reaching my new home my mother introduced me to her partner and my brother who was nearly two years old. I had known nothing about my mother's partner or about this brother. I was flabbergasted and upset, but suppressed my feeling of unease. My brother's childminder lived next door and it became my job to take Seymour to Mrs Drew in the mornings and collect him in the afternoon.

My mother's new relationship was not working out. Her partner had recently moved out but was very supportive and a good father. I was totally insensitive to her unhappiness. My relationship with her became difficult; I grew rebellious and she dictatorial. I wanted to go back to Jamaica.

My new home was a rented flat on the first floor of a three-storeyed house on Robin Hood Chase in St Anns. In 1959 the owners, the Singh family, occupied the ground floor. In former times the house had obviously been a beautiful three-storeyed, semi-detached Victorian residence with front and back garden on a tree-lined, enclosed avenue free of vehicular access. Its high, decorated ceiling and large front windows gave the house a feel of spaciousness and a hint of its former elegance. The stairs were wide and the first floor had a large landing that had been partially converted to a kitchenette that we shared with Alvin, a single man from our district in Milk River. The other tenant was Reg, Olga's future partner. He was then in the Royal Air Force and rarely home. The four-burner gas cooker had to be fed coins in the slot box at its side. Groceries were stored in a blue cabinet with white doors. Our work surface was a small table. The shared bathroom which was also on that floor was a huge room and the hot water geyser had a coin meter. The bathroom and the floors of the entrance hall were tiled - blue and white in the bathroom, brown and white in the hallway. The tiles were the redeeming feature of an otherwise drab interior.

Our living area consisted of two rooms, the bigger one was a bedsit, a bedroom and sitting-cum-dining area. I remember that the double bed was never without a chenille bedspread, a much-favoured item then of Jamaicans in England. The dressing table always had a white or pink three-piece crocheted set, made by my mother; in the centre one stood a crystal jewellery box and a candle holder on either side. The wardrobe and rugs on either side of the bed completed the bedroom furnishings. In the sitting-dining area were a small dining table and four chairs, a small sofa, which doubled as my brother's bed and a 'Blue-Spot' radiogram on which were the black and white television along with the family photographs. The dining table brightened this area with its cheerful gingham or embroidered cloth on which sat a bowl of artificial fruit. A small, colourful rug was at the front of the sofa. My bedroom was pleasant and comfortable with a double bed, wardrobe, dressing table and an armchair in which to curl up. The linoleum covering the floors in the rooms, the corridors and the stairs gleamed, proof of its weekly cleaning, one of my chores.

I came to realise that, as black immigrants in Britain, racism made it nigh impossible for us to find accommodation and to buy homes. Only a few black people in Nottingham owned their own homes then and these were usually small terrace houses in the poorer areas.

Two Jamaican families living close by had daughters of my age. Soon after my arrival the girls came and introduced themselves and we became life-long friends. Nettie and Doris Buchanan and Dorothy Binns were already working. When we visited each other our main recreation was listening to pop music, Johnnie Matthis, the Everley Brothers and Elvis Presley. Our parents, on the other hand, enjoyed music from artistes such as Fats Domino, Sarah Vaughan, Nat King Cole and Ray Charles. We girls occasionally went to a matinee at the cinema. I spent a lot of time with John Wray, the son of one of my mother's friends, who was at the Further Education College that I attended and whom my mother saw as my protector. We sometimes studied together and more often went for walks in the Arboretum and on the Forest then stopped by his friend, Taylor, who was like a big brother to us. Taylor's brother and his girlfriend who were student nurses were sometimes there and we had lively political debates. Sometimes we all took the country bus to Newstead Abbey, home of Lord Byron, for an afternoon outing.

The day after my arrival my mother took me to see Mr Irons. He was the Liaison Officer available to immigrant families to help them to deal with government bodies such as the Education Department and local firms that employed them. Mr Irons had been in the Royal Air Force during the Second World War and was employed by the City Council as someone from the Caribbean who had acquired an understanding of English culture and the ability to assist both immigrants and native officials. Racism in the 1950s and 1960s was blatant, many black people found government employees racist and unhelpful and they, in turn, sometimes found it difficult to get us to accept their policies. After many years of building bridges between the new settlers and the indigenous people of Nottingham, Eric Irons deservedly received the OBE for service to the community.

Mr Irons' office was in the Council House in the city centre. He welcomed us with a warm Caribbean smile crinkling his black face. We talked briefly about Jamaica and then about my aspirations. It was agreed that at sixteen I should enrol at People's College of Further Education as a full-time student to take five subjects at GCE 'O' level (General Certificate of Education Ordinary Level). I also would drop Spanish which was not available and do Latin at an evening class as it was not part of the daytime curriculum. In England GCE 'O'level had superseded the School Certificate which was still in operation in Jamaica, but the subject matter was the same so I had no difficulty fitting in.

College was the best part of my life. Students were treated as young adults and I met a lot of friendly young people, two of whom became friends. We were the same age group. They had recently left school and were re-taking some 'O' level subjects along with GCE 'A' Level subjects for university entrance. My English, History and Religious Education teachers expected me to do very well in their subjects but I was still struggling with Mathematics. In the first term I was very pleased to win the first prize for my English essay based on my memory of the trip to Bull Head Mountain in Jamaica. This was published in the college magazine. I played hockey for the college team and my Saturday mornings in the winter were taken up with practice and matches. I enjoyed the opportunity to be away from home and chores.

I saw very little of John Wray at college and spent a lot of time with my two English friends, Elaine and Jane. I liked Elaine very much, she was gregarious and funny. She invited me several times to spend the weekend at her home in Bilsthorpe, a mining village a few miles out of the city. When my mother finally allowed me to go, I enjoyed the time spent away from the city. Elaine lived in a comfortable three-bedroom semi-detached house and her parents were nice people. Although I was not fond of English food, by then I was getting used to it. I have a happy memory of riding several miles one Saturday to Elaine's aunt's tea-shop in the cathedral town of Southwell. On the way we chewed Aero mint bars, sweet and tangy, and were honked and wolf-whistled at by lorry drivers. I was too embarrassed about where I lived to invite them to my home and when I left college I severed all communication with the world I had left behind.

In the early autumn I enjoyed attending evening classes for Latin, but as winter approached and evenings grew dark earlier and earlier and the streets off the main roads were dark, I began to hate going. Classes were held in an annexe of an old, poorly heated building on a street some distance from the main road. Sometimes I could not get warm in that draughty room and did not bother to take off my coat. It was a five-minute walk from home to the bus stop and the same again from the other end to the classroom but I felt very uncomfortable walking alone. Winter was cold and inhospitable to me as a newcomer. I gave up evening classes.

I had arrived in the summer and the weather was glorious. Then autumn came and I saw the changing of the seasons for the first time. I was experiencing John Keats' "Ode to Autumn". It was a new experience for me to see trees laden with English fruit; to see the trees shed their leaves en masse and gradually become ghostly in the early evening fog as I walked briskly to keep the cold damp air from chilling my bones.

One night I went to bed under a flannelette sheet, two blankets and a bedspread. The cold was crippling! I woke next morning to a soft patter on the window. Snow! I had seen it in films and on Christmas cards but the image had up to then been abstract and unreal. Now at last, I was seeing *real* snow! It transformed the drab neighbourhood into a fairyland with a beauty all its own. That day I washed my face with it; I ate it to taste its delicious coldness. At college I joined in snowball fights, throwing big ones and watching them disintegrate on impact with someone's body. I also rolled in the snow just to see how that felt. Too soon, I discovered the dangers and hazards of frozen snow on roads, the slipping and sliding and difficulty in controlling one's feet.

Years later, the village where I lived was cut off until the snow plough could clear the roads and I experienced the feeling of being trapped, unable to get anywhere except on foot. Despite all this, I still love the softness that new snow brings in the midst of winter's biting cold and dreary days. I love walking across snowy fields with the keen wind against my face and then to the warm comfort of home and a mug of hot chocolate.

That winter I was introduced to the paraffin heater. It was like an outsized lamp, a cylindrical, black enamelled body with a plastic see-through window, to show that the flame was the correct shade of blue. A perforated top let out fumes as well as heat. A bowl of water was placed near the heater to keep the air in the room from drying out too much. In some Jamaican homes the smell of paraffin fumes was overpowering and people's clothes reeked of it. This was because coming from the tropics the cold weather affected us keenly and people tended to use the heater to warm areas without coal fires.

In the early evening a heater was placed in our sitting room area where we ate and watched television. In my room I used my heater to boil the kettle for tea, Milo really. I drank it curled up in my armchair, lost in the world of the book I was reading or simply daydreaming. At such times I felt insulated against the world. I would often dream of sunshine and of trees heavy with fruit, the air redolent with their tropical aroma.

With my spirit at a low ebb, I began to feel sorry for myself and neglected my studies, showing all the classic signs of the rebellious adolescent. I resented having to rush home to cook dinner and collect my brother before my mother got in a little before 6.00p.m because this got in the way of my participation in extra-curricular activities. I desperately wanted to attend the Drama club. Since I was only allowed out with John and I wanted to have my own way, I devised a means of spending time with some other Jamaican working girls I had met. I would tell my mother I was going to study with John at his house, go there briefly and then John would tell his mother he was walking me home but we would each go our own way and meet again after a couple of hours when he would take me home. My mother's fear, that of all the families we knew, was that a black person walking alone in the evening was an easy target for the Teddy Boys. These racist hooligans, like dogs in a pack, had been attacking black people in the 1950s but when the black men began to retaliate the attacks gradually stopped. So, I was careful not to be out alone in the dark.

I would go to the home of one or other of two friends whose families were easy-going. The three of us, like most teenage girls then and now, went into the bedroom and talked about clothes and boys as we listened to pop music. I was a fan of Cliff Richards and the Shadows. Without my mother knowing, I managed to see them after a concert. I was standing with other teenagers outside the theatre waiting for a closer glimpse of Cliff and was rewarded with a smile and a hello from him on his way to a waiting car.

It was through John that I met his friend, Stanley Jnr, whom everyone called Junior. He was in the Royal Air Force and looked very handsome in his uniform. He was charming, well-spoken and had laughing eyes. He had a voice like Nat King Cole's and played the piano as he sang. I fell in love and he became my secret love, known only to John.

Grasping The Nettle

Junior was not pushy and made me laugh and I really enjoyed being with him. This was in contrast to the way I felt at home. Things had got so bad that I decided to leave home as soon as exams were over. I did very badly, passing only three subjects.

After another row with my mother I moved out and asked Ann, a Welsh woman with whom I had become friendly, to let me stay at her house. She agreed because I was so distraught, but only on condition that I told my mother where I was. When I went to see my mother she was so angry at my leaving that she refused to speak to me. I left her Ann's address. Ann lived with her little boy; her absent husband was Jamaican. I had my own room, was very comfortable and was looking forward to getting a job while continuing my studies at evening classes.

I applied for a job in the main office of Boot's Pharmaceutical and was invited for an interview. This went well and I was offered the job subject to passing the medical. I think I would have been the first black person to work in their office although they employed black people in the factory. At the end of the medical the doctor looked very grave. He cleared his throat and dropped the bombshell. "I'm afraid you are pregnant." I could not believe what I had heard.

"No. No," I said. "That's impossible!"

"You most certainly are," he responded firmly. "You need to tell your parents and see your doctor." At this stage in a Victorian novel I would have fainted. Instead, I sat stock still in shock. I'm not sure how long I was in that comatose stage before I heard as from afar, ". . . Miss Lawson! Miss Lawson . . ."

I stood up suddenly, blurted out, "Thank you," and ran out of the office. My world was in tatters. What was I going to do? I'm not sure how I got home that afternoon. Ann saw me in tears and I blurted out, "I'm pregnant!"

"Oh, no!" she exclaimed horrified, then in a matter of fact voice added, "Well, it's not the end of the world. You're not dying of cancer."

For a while I was numb with fright and foreboding; I did not hear a word of what Ann was saying. I went to bed quite unable to think straight and fell asleep fully dressed.

The next morning I woke up a different person. I had made up my mind to face the music. I accepted that I had no options; what was done was done and I had to live with the consequences. In the 1960s being an unmarried mother carried a social stigma. Many of the white girls who got pregnant gave up their children for adoption. In my culture being an unmarried mother was also frowned upon but the family usually relented and absorbed the child into the extended family; sometimes the child was brought up as a sibling or as the child of an older family member.

I dreaded having to face my mother and told Junior first. He was in a state of shock and became quite flustered. He said that he did not have any money for us to get married and kept asking what we were going to do. I lost my temper with his indecisiveness. I felt badly let down. I became very angry at his dithering, but I also knew it was not that he wanted to walk away from his responsibility.

My mother, after the tears of disappointment, was surprisingly supportive. She arranged for me to go and stay with her close friend who was a midwife living in the Meadows. The houses in the Meadows at that time were mainly Victorian terraces. The house was without a bathroom and the toilet adjoined the coal shed at the bottom of the backyard. We had to heat water on the cooker for our daily wash. People living in these houses had to go to the Baths in the area for a proper bath. A group of three of us black teenagers went each week, carrying Dettol disinfectant to ensure that we had a clean bath. Each person paid for an allotted time and it was sheer luxury to soak in the bath for a few minutes. It was common talk among Caribbean people that the majority of English people did not have a very high standard of personal hygiene and that many of the girls were pretty and well-dressed but did not have a daily wash as was evident when they climbed the steps to the top deck of the trolley bus and a frowsy smell emanated from their flaring crinoline skirts.

My son was born in City Hospital at 11.45p.m. December 14, 1960. He weighed 6lbs. 15ozs. It was an awesome experience. When the nurse put this bundle in my arms and I saw my son for the first time, I became a mother.

During my pregnancy, Junior and I had had a reconciliation. We got married but neither of my parents attended the wedding. I was a disappointment to them. The wedding was a modest affair with twenty guests. I wanted a church wedding because I wanted my marriage to be blessed although I had stopped attending the local Methodist church since leaving home - I had found the congregation cold and felt very much an outsider. There were no other black people in attendance and I would hurry home as soon as the service was over. It was a world away from the warmth of the Methodist churches I had attended in Jamaica.

We moved to a comfortable flat in Forest Fields and I focussed on becoming a good wife and mother. Our first five years were relatively happy and we worked as a team. When Stanley was six months old I went to work. I hated leaving my baby in a nursery but I also knew that this was the only way I could help to build a future for us as a family. I got a job in the Civil Service as a clerical assistant after passing the entrance examination, and was the only black member of staff at the Telephone Manager's Office. I joined the younger set and thoroughly enjoyed working there. The office in which I worked was a huge room with several rows of three large tables grouped together to form a unit. My table had three people, a senior clerical assistant and I worked with a clerical officer ensuring the dispatch of telephone bills to a specific geographical area, chasing up outstanding payments and dealing with queries. An executive officer who sat at a separate desk was the line manager. Our busy period was two weeks each month, so we had time to read or study for exams within the Civil Service that could lead to promotion. I became good friends with my clerical officer, who was the same age as me. We kept in touch when her parents sent her off to Lucy Clayton's in London to be groomed and 'finished'. The news of her life in London until she left after marrying a barrister was often amusing and far removed from mine that was gradually becoming a nightmare.

A memory I have of this time is the awful smog. In the 1960s before coal for home fuel was banned, Nottingham suffered regularly from smog in the late autumn and winter months. Sometimes it was as thick as pea-soup and when this happened the buses stopped running. I often was exhausted by the time I completed the two-mile walk home, avoiding pedestrians, lamp posts and other obstacles on the pavements. Smog created health problems even if one was not asthmatic. It clung to everything. It got into my beret. It got into my eyes and made them weep. It got into my nose and throat although a scarf covered my face except for my eyes. The night also seemed interminable as there was no daylight until the smog lifted and the sky was again visible.

Junior and I decided to have another child to complete our family before Stanley was three so that there would not be a great difference in their ages. Shortly after Charmaine's birth in 1963, Junior left the Air Force. He eventually had his wish to be self-employed when he and his friend, Fred, began a small garage business that repaired and sprayed cars.

In 1964, we bought our end terrace house on Manor Street in Sneinton. It had a living room, dining room, two bedrooms, an attic and a kitchen with a bath in one corner. Within a couple months of moving in we had a bathroom built above the kitchen. I tiled the bathroom floor as well as painted the walls. Our neighbours, an elderly couple on one side and a young couple with children of almost the same ages as ours on the other side, were helpful and friendly. We also discovered that Blossom, whom we knew from when I lived in the Meadows, and her family now lived around the corner. Blossom worked nights at one of the hospitals; this ensured that one parent was nearly always at home. Sometimes when there was an overlap of shifts with her husband, I would babysit for them and they also babysat for me. Their children were of the same age as ours and we became close friends. We also acted as counsellors for each other.

I knew that Junior hated making decisions and I took on the role of the family planner. For a while we worked to our plan and we were very happy. When Charmaine was nearly two years old and Stanley had started at infant school, we agreed that I would work part-time in order to have more funds for the family. There wasn't a nursery nearby and Charmaine stayed with a childminder who also collected Stanley from school. Meg was white, married to Eric, a Jamaican and they lived nearby. Our families had become friends and their children, who were older than ours, often took Stanley to the park. I felt comfortable with Meg as my childminder.

I applied for a job advertised in the Evening Post and was invited for an interview. When I arrived the receptionist rang the manager to tell him I was there. His face was a picture of surprise when he saw me through the glass partition; obviously, my voice was not discernibly 'black' over the telephone. The receptionist gave the game away when she asked for the letter inviting me for an interview. It is sometimes difficult to express what exactly in a person's body language or tone makes one aware that the person is racially prejudiced but victims of any kind of prejudice will tell of that imperceptible something that they, nevertheless, discern. The middle-aged manager tried to cover up his feelings as he interviewed me but I knew I was wasting my time. The expected letter arrived in due course.

In the mid-1960s there was no recourse for situations such as this. The Race Relations Board had been instituted recently to resolve disputes but up to the mid-1970s, employers were still discriminating on the grounds of race without much fear that legal action would be taken against them. As late as 1988 a BBC programme showed that racial discrimination was still widespread in the job market. Two undercover reporters went job hunting in Bristol and the white interviewee was offered the job over and over again, never the equally well-qualified black one. The usefulness of such a programme was that it provided evidence, validating the complaints we had been making over the years that were often rebutted by the white majority.

I was furious with myself for not tackling that manager but I vowed I would never again allow anyone to think that I was not aware of this prejudice. In arranging over the telephone the time for the next interview for an accounts clerk post I said to the man, "I am Jamaican. Please tell me now if you have a problem with that?" He assured me that he did not, adding that his secretary was also from Jamaica. At the interview he commented that I was "sassy". The small office at Brown Brothers was above the parts distribution shop and had twelve staff. It was a pleasant working environment. I worked there for a few months until I decided to work full-time and took up a post in the accounts department of John Player and Sons, a big tobacco company.

It was here that I experienced first-hand the English class system in the workplace. In Nottingham, firms such as Players operated a system whereby children of their workers on leaving school were employed. As a result, there were in the offices several young girls whose parents worked in the factory; however, these parents could not have lunch in the staff canteen with their children! People in the factory were 'workers' whereas we in the office were 'staff'. Office staff also had privileges. A worker had to clock in and if a few minutes late would have fifteen minutes deducted from his/her wages whereas a staff had only to sign in and could get away with being late every now and then. I found this hierarchical system indicative of a vestigial class-ridden society.

By working, I was able to assist my mother with Lillian's and Bonnie's airfares to come to England. My father, who had also migrated to Birmingham, sent for Alvin at the same time. My parents agreed that the boys would live with him. As well as a new wife, my father now had a son. The two branches of the family visited each other on a fairly regular basis and although we did not appear to be divided, we certainly were.

I did not feel fulfilled working in an office and wanted to go back to college to get the entry requirement to get into teacher training college or to train as a journalist, my second choice. I wanted a job that would give me not just a salary but also job satisfaction. I discussed how I felt with Junior and suggested that I could take the People's College of Further Education full-time course specially designed to encourage mothers with school-age children back into education. We agreed that he would have to help a little more with the children and that I would find evening work during the holidays to help financially.

In September 1965, I left Players and went on to the two-year access course. In April 1966, I became pregnant and left college at the end of that academic year, deferring the second year of the course.

Michelle was a beautiful baby. She was a whopper weighing 9lbs12ozs and looked at birth like a three-month old! This pregnancy was not planned and although family life was still pleasant I had to learn quickly how to cope. I had Michelle in January and started back at college that September. In the morning I took Michelle to the childminder on the way to Charmaine's nursery school and Stanley's infant school before catching the bus to college. Junior did the afternoon picking up. It was hard work for us both and everything had to be tightly scheduled in order to run smoothly from Monday to Friday. I also had to learn to economise. We ate less steak and I used cheaper cuts of meat to make delicious meals. I baked bread and knitted jumpers for the children. My mother, as a trained dressmaker, made most of my children's clothes. Weekends were blissful as I could have more than five hours sleep and relax with my children. Oh, the sheer joy of a walk in the park with them!

Junior's business partner left for Canada where, like many Jamaicans we knew, he felt that there were more opportunities. The garage was thriving, including a deal with the owner of a second-hand car salesroom; however, it was not long before I discovered that Junior was gambling. Without his partner, and lacking in self-discipline, he had turned to gambling as a way of making quick money. He found all kinds of excuses for not going to work. We were on a slippery slope with very little money to take care of the home. Junior's closest childhood friend knew what was happening and one Sunday he came to see me when Junior was out. I had not had any housekeeping money for several weeks and Leonard kindly offered me a loan until Junior sorted things out. I was so embarrassed. I lied and said we were okay. He discreetly left the money.

When I tried to discuss our dire situation with Junior, he exploded and started shouting. As these outbursts continued, they were frightening for me and, more so, for the children. But I refused to be bullied into silence. He refused to talk to me about what he thought the problem was, refused to accept that his gambling was ruining our lives and refused to work to properly support his family. For a while I tried to get our close friends to talk with him but his promise to settle down to work would last a week each time before the gambling continued.

Shortly after restarting my course I discovered that I was pregnant. Once more, the contraceptive had failed. I had to give up attending college but, determined not to give up on my dream, I decided to study at home. It was at this time that Blossom and I were introduced to the West Indian Students' Association meetings held monthly on a Sunday. This was a refreshing break from the weekly chores. The topics discussed interested me because they addressed some of the issues affecting us, black people, living in a then blatantly racist society. I became co-editor for the magazine.

Meanwhile, my home-life was very unhappy. Desperate to keep my children safe and my marriage intact, I sought professional help but that too failed when Junior refused to attend the appointments with the marriage guidance counsellor. After the birth of Amanda, I was struck dumb by his refusal to sign the agreement for my tubal ligation. We had discussed the side effects I had suffered from various contraceptives and we had agreed that we could not afford any more children. Birth control was a nightmare. At the Family Planning Clinic *the coil* was suggested. I recoiled. I thought it was easier to become celibate. I was taught how to insert *the cap* with the help of a lubricant but that had failed. To me the operation was the only answer to end this nightmare. I could not believe the consultant's, "So sorry, but we can't operate without your husband's signature." At that moment something died inside me.

According to the law in 1968, I had no control over my own body! I was like a child whose life decisions had to be made by a man whom I could not trust even to support his children. Sitting in my hospital bed I cried for my lost freedom. Far from being a partnership, my marriage was a prison sentence. When he visited me, I first asked for an explanation. None was forthcoming, just an inane smirk. I then demanded the operation, then cajoled and finally exploded in anger. But all to no avail; he refused to budge. He had the power and was using it.

Revulsion at such tyranny awoke in me an iron will to find a way to support my children and myself and to not be subjected to Junior's cavalier manner. Getting a career took on another dimension; it became my road to independence. When Mandy was three months old, I took a temporary part-time job in an office within walking distance of home. Fortunately, in our small Caribbean community, people would lend a helping hand to each other and my friend's mother looked after my girls. This did not make it any easier leaving the children while I went to my morning job. After paying for childminding I had barely enough to feed us and for a while my mother subsidised us with weekly food parcels. When the utility bills began to mount up and Junior did not seem to care, I had to find the money to pay these. For a while, I took on a temporary additional part-time evening job at the soap factory nearby. I hated the work on the assembly line putting tablets of soap into gift boxes. I sneezed a lot and my head ached. By the end of my three-hour shift I was nearing exhaustion.

Looking back, I have to admit that it was only my single-mindedness that kept me going at that hectic pace. I would be up by 6:00 a.m., get ready for work, have the children dressed and give them breakfast, take Stanley to my neighbour's to go to school with her children, walk briskly, and sometimes run, to the childminder's half a mile away, settle the children and make another quick dash to the office about quarter of a mile back the way I had come. When the school holiday came Stanley joined the girls at the childminder's. With all that I was doing, whenever Junior was in a mood he would not get out of bed. I often had to plead with him to be home by 5.30p.m., so that I could get to my evening job. But I often had to take the children to stay with my friends, Paul and Blossom, on the next street. Housework had to be fitted into my weekly timetable too.

My marriage became a living hell. I thought that my trying so hard to provide for our children's needs would spur Junior into facing up to his responsibility. It did not. The marriage deteriorated to yet another level. He refused to help in any way and a complaint from me was greeted with loud verbal abuse before he stormed out. Charmaine and Michelle became 'clingy' and nervous at the sound of a raised voice. This became the perfect mechanism to shut me up.

One Sunday after another row, Junior stormed out, slamming the door hard. I stood in the kitchen totally unable to accept what was happening to my family. Hopelessness, like a dark shroud, covered me and I felt altogether alone and useless. I lost my sense of responsibility. I wanted out. I closed the window and doors and turned on the gas. Just then Charmaine shouted, "Mummy! Mummy!" and I could hear her running down the stairs. The younger ones were upstairs in their bedroom and Stanley was playing outside. My moment of madness passed and I was strengthened by my children's presence. I had had enough of this relationship.

I went to see Paul and Blossom and told them of my decision. They sympathised with me and later they talked Junior into promising that he would work regularly and pull his weight in the house. Junior's sister also berated him for his behaviour and for not looking after his children. Junior and I agreed to put the bad times behind us and begin to work together. He began to work steadily and I was able to give up work. Things improved for a while.

One morning is forever etched in my memory. Charmaine, messing about on the stairs, tripped and cut her lip. I asked Junior who was supposed to be looking after the children that day to take her to the doctor to make sure she was alright as I was preparing to leave home early for an exam. "I'm not going to be here, you know," he said and turned over in bed. I had a few minutes to get to the bus stop. I could not leave my children. I sat on the stairs and dissolved into tears, hugging poor Charmaine who was still crying. Blossom, on her way home from work came in just then. She often stopped by for a quick cup of tea. On hearing what had happened, she took control. She said she would take the children home with her and would take Charmaine to see the doctor as soon as the surgery opened. She pushed me through the door as I hesitated. I continued to cry on and off until I reached the examination centre. On my return home at lunch-time, the children were fine and my lunch was waiting for me. It was this kind of support from my mother, my sister and my friends that sustained me through the hard years.

I try not to think back on those cruel years and to keep bitterness at bay. Junior was now drinking as well as gambling. I was not sure whether he had gone mad or was just showing me that he could do as he pleased. Yet, he would be mortified the minute his outburst was spent and for several weeks after an outburst he would be an attentive father and his laughter, like sunshine, lightened the gloom that had enwrapped us. Regrettably, this did not last long, as gambling and drinking, like all addictions, are insidious and take control.

The local polytechnic had offered me a place on the Teacher Training course beginning September 1969 subject to meeting the entry requirement. I studied at home and that summer obtained the required 'A' and 'O' Levels. I was over the moon. My studying had been done mainly between 3.00a.m. and 7.00a.m. I had learned to survive on five hours sleep and it had paid off. I realised the enormity of the task ahead of me for at least four years, then I would be finally qualified, have job satisfaction and be able to support my children. I started at Trent Polytechnic in high spirits.

In that first term I was quite shocked by the behaviour of a student teacher in my son's junior school. It frightened me to such an extent that I began to treat more seriously what the children said about some teachers' inappropriate behaviour. One afternoon Stanley came home with a bruised face. He and another lad had been having a fight and when the student teacher on duty came to separate them, he had slapped my son so hard that he had left an imprint on his cheek. Junior and I took Stanley back to the school to report the incident and to confront the man. The headteacher, though disturbed by the incident, would not allow us to confront the teacher. I threatened legal action and exposure of child abuse by his staff and realising I was serious, he promised to file a report to the college and have the student withdrawn immediately. The student did not return to the school and I was told that he had been reprimanded.

When I had started the teacher training course in September 1969, Junior was supportive and everything was going well. Then, as was the pattern in our relationship, he started drinking again and stopped pulling his weight. A few days before Christmas, Junior did not come home for two days. I was making a pot of tea when he entered the kitchen. I tackled him about his disrespect for his family and told him that I could not take any more of his rubbish. The verbal abuse began. Then he threatened what he would do if I left. Shocked into disbelief I closed the kitchen door and took the tray up to the children who were awaiting their Sunday morning family tea and toast in bed. I subsumed my fear with light-hearted chatter until I heard him leave.

I took the children to see a friend. I made the decision as I left the house that I had nothing more to give to the marriage and my children deserved better. I had forgiven his unfaithfulness and a lot of his abuse but it was obvious that things were not going to get better. I concluded that Junior was one of those people who could not cope with responsibility and his behaviour was a reaction to this. He had to face up to whatever his problem was and seek help.

Lone Parent

I was homeless and penniless with four young children. My children and I stayed with Vena, a Jamaican college friend, until after Christmas, and then we went to stay with my mother in her flat until I found a place of our own. For a week I felt emotionally paralysed, unable to think straight, frightened and alone. Then I roused, as from slumber and forced myself to become focussed and single-minded; there was no time for self-pity. We needed a place to live and I needed a job.

Junior, realising that we had left home, finally sought professional help. I was asked to see his psychiatrist. Junior had told the psychiatrist that he wanted us back home to work things out and that I was to blame for his outbursts because I was "too pushy". I told the psychiatrist that I was not jeopardising five lives, that Junior needed to support his children and without me pushing him he had the opportunity to stop gambling and drinking. A few weeks later, I heard that Junior had stopped seeing the psychiatrist. He changed tack and sent me a message that I would not receive a penny from him if I did not come home. I ignored his threat. He was not bluffing. His modus operandi had not changed but my response had!

Blossom accompanied me to the Social Security Office, the one and only time I sought such assistance until I could find a job. It was one of the most humiliating experiences of my life. After a long wait, the woman who interviewed me made me feel like a parasite. Then she redirected me to another office and, after another interminable wait, I was told that, as a married woman I was not entitled to benefit; I was my husband's responsibility. We had spent nearly a whole working day there and for nothing! A few weeks later, one of their officers came to make a home visit and soon after I received a benefit book. *It gave me great pleasure to return it untouched.*

I went to see Mr Irons, the liaison officer in the Education Department, hoping that he could help me to get council accommodation which was much cheaper than private renting. Naturally, he wanted to know the situation and since he did not want me to give up my college course, within a day he arranged for me to see a housing officer and someone dealing with student grants in the Education Department. My grant was changed from a married woman's allowance covering books and bus fares to that of a head of household. This meant that I could study without the worry of financial problems as long as I was prudent.

It took a little while for the Housing Department to offer me a house. For three months I stayed with my mother in Basford. My sister who lived close by looked after my youngest child and each day I had to take the three older children on two buses across town to school and nursery school before getting my bus to college. In the afternoon I had to pick them up from Blossom's and we would make the return journey home. I was not happy with these arrangements and worried about the effect such instability was having on their young lives but I saw it as the only viable way forward.

I was overjoyed when I was offered a house on Costock Avenue in Sherwood. It was an old house but in one of the better areas of Nottingham with a mix of council homes and owner-occupied and had a reputable primary school close by. The house was small, with only two bedrooms and one room downstairs which we used as a living room; we ate in the kitchen. The house was a tip when I got it and I spent most of that Easter holiday cleaning and painting in order to create a warm home environment for us. The toilet, although attached to the house, could only be reached by going out the back door. It was like going back in time for me and it took the children a while to adjust as well.

Stanley and Charmaine began at the school nearby, Michelle continued at the nursery school in Sneinton but I could not get three-year-old Mandy a full-time nursery place, as these were at a premium. I wanted her to have a stimulating environment when I was at college so I opted for an excellent private nursery school within walking distance of the polytechnic. It was a sacrifice worth making. There was a black family a few doors from us in one of the private homes who had children at the school my two attended and the mother very kindly collected my children from school. Managing was like keeping balls in the air. The morning schedule was tight; I still had to take two buses across town, dropping off Michelle, next stop Mandy, then a brisk walk to college, but we were happier without the awful tension under which we had lived for far too long. I had no easy option; I went for short-term pain for long-term gain.

Michelle had showed signs of being affected by what had been happening in the home. Before we left her hair had begun falling out and the doctor and I had agreed that this was a sign of unhappiness. She used to hang on to my legs when her father shouted and I knew it was affecting her. I had cried at what was happening to my child and my heart had hardened against Junior. I ensured that she got a lot of attention but, nonetheless, I worried about how the tension at home was affecting her psychologically. She began nursery a couple of weeks after we left our home and I was shocked when the nursery staff expressed their concern at her behaviour. She was throwing things around the Wendy house as she had seen her father do in her own home. We kept a close watch to see if she would need help but, thankfully, she settled down.

During my four years at college, we always had Sunday dinner at my mother's. We dressed in our Sunday best, because my mother loved everyone to look smart, and we walked the mile to her home. We played "I spy" and sang to lighten the journey. My mother was an excellent cook and we ate heartily. After dinner I caught up on my sleep while the children watched television or played outside. My mother also looked after the children so that I could have a break some weekends. It was years later, when they had a choice of visiting her or staying at home, that I discovered that the two younger ones found her old-fashioned regimen too restrictive and did not enjoy staying with her. I was surprised that they never complained; I think they were being thoughtful knowing how tired I was.

Soon after moving to Sherwood, I bought a second-hand piano and Stanley and Charmaine began to have lessons from a teacher who came to the house. Stanley was not doing too well at school and I was introduced to the deputy head of Alderman Derbyshire Comprehensive School who gave him extra lessons for a very modest fee. Affording these extras for my children meant careful management of my finances. I enrolled Michelle and Amanda in Saturday morning dance class at the community centre. They attended for a while and I remember how pleased I was at seeing Michelle in her blue outfit and Amanda in her red ballerina dress taking part in the end-of-year performance and enjoying it. Despite my heavy workload, my children's welfare always took priority. I told them how much I loved them. I read with them and saw to it that homework was done properly.

Amanda was very bright and on the way home from nursery she would give me an account of her day. One day she regaled me with the story of the little green men; she used different voices for her characters and did sound effects too. As she performed, she captured the attention of some of the passengers sitting around us; their applause took her quite by surprise and, blushing, she buried her head in my lap. When she was five years old at the Jamaican Children's Christmas Concert organised by Blossom and me, she gave a flawless rendition of a Christmas carol on the recorder. She was a natural performer with quite an equable personality.

Paul, Blossom's husband, gave us a kitten, our first pet. I suggested the name Charamstamich for our beautiful, fluffy, black kitten. I had created the name by combining the start of each child's name: Char, Am, Sta, Mich. The funny thing was that people, on hearing the name, always assumed that it was Russian. One day our three-year-old cat did not come home. We searched in vain for him. I have always thought that our horrible neighbour killed our cat in one of his drunken bouts. Charamstamich would run away from him in fear. He was indeed a very cruel man who had once kicked his wife down the stairs, seriously injuring her. She and the children were pleasant enough but his shouting when he attacked his wife and her screams were upsetting to us. They tended to coincide with pay day when he came home as drunk as a skunk, his face flushed, his red hair flaming. I was determined to move as soon as I could afford a home of my own.

I obtained my Teaching Certificate in 1972 and did an additional year for my B.Ed. Despite the hard work, and often not having enough time to spend on assignments, I enjoyed college. There were many anxious moments. As luck would have it the court hearing for the divorce proceedings coincided with my end of course exams. I also knew I was unable to meet the extended deadline I had been given for the submission of my thesis. My tutor appeared at my front door as my friend, Nettie, was still typing the last chapter and I was getting the children off to bed. He was not amused to find it not ready. I got the thesis to him the next morning as I had promised, not quite satisfied with it but it was the best I could do under the circumstances. I imagine the hectic life of a single mother with young children was an alien world to him. I had never discussed my family situation with any member of staff as a reason for getting a further extension because in keeping with our Jamaican sub-culture in England only when in dire need would I discuss my problems with an outsider. One coped as well as one could. Only two mature students, Eleanor and Geoffrey, knew about my circumstances.

In my year group at college there were only two other black students, George Powe and Vena Wynter, both mature students. Vena gave up the course to go into youth work and is now a Director of Youth Services. George became a Nottingham City councillor. It was in one of the whole year group education lectures that I refused to accept what was being taught as reliable data. We were looking at research done in the USA that concluded that black American children were performing less well than their white counterparts; the unspoken assumption was that black children were less intelligent. As the lecture progressed I could feel my face flushed with indignation. I knew that George and Vena felt the same. At question time I made my point: If working-class children in England were not less intelligent but performed less well than middle-class children, then it was not surprising that black children under-performed, given the disadvantages, especially racial prejudice, that they faced, and yet researchers had not seen this as an important factor. As our college stressed the importance of students taking into consideration the impact of disadvantage when assessing working-class pupils in their inner city schools my point was duly noted but the course did not address the issues of racism and education for a multi-cultural Britain. *My training and that of my fellow students was completely Eurocentric.*

My college course prepared us well for teaching in inner-city schools as well as those in the suburbs. In the first year, students spent a half-day weekly at two schools of their choice. I went to inner city schools with multi-ethnic pupils. At Huntingdon Junior I gained insight into the challenges of teaching in a school where a lot of the parents were anti-school. Something I noticed then was that the children who had recently arrived from the Caribbean were much taller than their English peers but this has gradually changed over the years as the white children have grown taller. I think the earlier difference was due to the fact that Caribbean children had a healthier diet, although they came from economically poorer countries. I also spent time in St Anns Infant School. The building dated back to the nineteenth century. It was dark and drab and very smelly from unwashed bodies. My college supervisor on her visit advised me not to put my head so close to the pupils' as I might catch nits!

My teaching notes had been checked by the class teacher. I was confident standing before the class of thirty children until I had to write on the blackboard. My hands grew sweaty. Suddenly I was nervous knowing that my college supervisor was assessing me. This was my first teaching practice at Parkdale Primary, a suburban school with an excellent reputation. The teacher had told the class that someone was coming in to see me teach and that he expected everyone to behave well. The children were conscientious and well-behaved anyway and we had a good relationship, so the lesson went well. I received a pleasing report with one jarring recommendation to refrain from gesticulating! In discussing this point with my supervisor, she suggested that I put my hands behind my back.

My second teaching practice was quite different from my first and would have sorely tested even Job. I had to deal with pupils who were anti-school, among them a few boys with disciplinary problems. This was a tough inner-city school. Several students, faced with such classes, had given up the course and others had a lot of support from their supervisors. At the end of those six weeks, I was physically exhausted. My final teaching practice was also in an inner-city school but there it was a pleasure to teach.

I began my teaching career in 1973. In 1975 I bought our home, getting a hundred per cent mortgage from the local authority. We left the city for a village twelve miles out of Nottingham. My choice had been based on several factors; the house was cheaper out of the city; the comprehensive school there was better than the one my son was attending; I had two colleagues who had become my friends living in that area; the countryside, which I loved, was on the doorstep; and with my recently bought 'old banger' I was able to keep my family in touch with black activities in Nottingham.

In the last week of the school year, I took my family to see their new schools and our new home. I had only recently passed my driving test and felt less than confident on the motorway. When the rain came pelting down, I grew more and more tense as I concentrated on the road. Then water began to drip on us. We were gradually being soaked and regardless of the contortions we performed, could not avoid the drips. They were the longest twelve miles I have ever driven and the return journey without rain was a welcome relief.

My children did not always enjoy living in Selston; however, they were aware that they did not face any of the racism from teachers that many of their contemporaries experienced in some city schools. Stanley, Michelle and Amanda, unlike Charmaine, did not enjoy school. Charmaine and I enjoyed similar activities such as early morning walks across the fields and trips to the theatre. To celebrate one of her birthdays, we took the train to London and saw a matinee performance of the Dance Theatre of Harlem. It was wonderful and it absolutely made her day when we went backstage and met the dancers. Amanda became interested in gymnastics when Olga Korbett was a sensation and I had to take my turn ferrying her and her friend to Nottingham for their gymnastic sessions. The girls joined the local Girls' Brigade for something to do locally.

Stanley was always football mad and that became his hobby. His football matches usually clashed with activities of mine and I did not feel comfortable with football culture anyway. I accept that that was one of my failings where he is concerned. Another was my inability to give him male advice when he was a teenager and we talked about girls. As a teenager, Stanley missed having a father figure around.

As soon as he left school I worried about his safety when he was out. My fears were by no means unfounded. Like many young black men, he suffered from police harassment, especially at night. I had taught him to drive and he bought his first car just after his eighteenth birthday; he had a girlfriend in Nottingham and he was stopped regularly on his way home. He also found that he had to deal with racism at his workplace in Sutton-in-Ashfield. He was put upon to do more and had to make a stand. Unlike the other electrician, who was white, he was hindered from pursuing his electrical technician's course by being sent on jobs so far away it was impossible for him to attend classes regularly.

Parenting has been a mixed bag of joy and pain for me. I feel fortunate that, after some heartbreaking times, my children and I have a good relationship. When they were younger, I put up with the hardship of many a single parent facing the responsibility alone; however, my scariest time was when my two younger children finished compulsory education and were on the verge of adulthood. Stanley and Charmaine were conformists, we had discussed their post-school route which they duly followed; not so Michelle, who dropped out of her course at the Further Education College and left home and Amanda, who refused to do 'A' Levels. They hated school and hated living in a village with only a handful of black people. Their school friends slept over and my girls were always welcomed in their friends' homes, yet these friends made racist comments often prefaced by "You're different" or "Not you, but . . ." They dealt with this sometimes by remonstrating and sometimes by ignoring it. Michelle and Amanda thought Nottingham city, with lots more black people, would be a better place to live.

I took their rebellion as hard as my mother must have taken mine. All I could do in those few years of transition was to try and keep in touch and be there for them. I learnt the meaning of 'letting go'. My dream was that my children would embrace to the fullest the education available to them and become community activists, helping to improve the condition for other black people. I saw my dreams in tatters where Michelle and Amanda were concerned; in fact they appeared to be rejecting the lifestyle they had, and to be in search of an alternative. To cope with my pain, I immersed myself in my community work. They eventually grew out of this phase, went on to university and turned out to be good, caring people.

I am proud of my children. Stanley is an electrician and happily settled in family life. He is a martial arts teacher in karate and tae kwon do and has won international championships, including being a world champion. The three girls are graduates. Charmaine works for the Audit Commission as an inspector of local authorities; Michelle is a probation officer and Amanda a lecturer. The England of their childhood has changed for the better and black children can now see role models in most spheres of the society. Racism still exists, though, and too many of our children are failing to succeed in school and at the workplace. My children are not activists. Perhaps there is no longer a need for the activists of the past, but there still is a great need for activists to work with black people within their communities, in order to provide support and direction.

Parenting does not end when your children grow up. The biggest nightmare I have had as an adult was waiting to see if my first grandchild's heart operation was successful. Her parents and I walked the corridors and grounds of the hospital as the surgery was being done to replace a heart valve and patch a hole. I sang to her as she lay pale in the Intensive Care Unit in Groby Road Hospital in Leicester. Leeanne was only two years old and looked so tiny in the bed with several tubes connected to her body. When she fluttered her eyelids, my heart sang for joy. I had arrived at another stage in my life, knowing the double pain grandparents suffer for a child and the child of that child. My fright came from knowing that we had nearly lost her because the family doctor thought she was only constipated when in fact her organs were packing up!

I shudder at the thought of what could have happened had I not been assertive. Unhappy with the doctor's decision, I went back to the surgery with my daughter, Charmaine, and Leeanne. I said I would feel better if Leeanne was referred to a specialist. The doctor was not keen to do this and I threatened that if anything happened, I would hold him responsible. He grudgingly said he would arrange for her to see the heart specialist. Still unhappy about waiting, I rang Leeanne's consultant in Leicester. He was unavailable but I impressed upon his secretary the urgency of the matter and that I needed to speak with him. When he rang back and I described Leeanne's symptoms, he at once arranged for her to see a heart specialist in Nottingham, who said she had to have an operation as soon as possible.

Eleven years later we had to face what we had dreaded. Leeanne's heart had outgrown the valve and she had to have another operation. Charmaine and Leeanne were with me in Jamaica and, as a family trying to deal with the stress, we went to meditation classes. Our last weekend in Jamaica was spent in Negril, a pretty sea-side resort. Of us all, Leeanne was the least stressed and actually performed a miracle. I suffered from severe hydrophobia and for several years in the summer months I had nightmares about drowning. I attempted to overcome this by trying to learn to swim but could not. I had progressed to floating in the placid Caribbean Sea. Leeanne was a good swimmer and one day encouraged me to take off my armbands. She held me under the tummy and made me so relaxed in the water that I did not realise when she had stopped supporting me. After a few tentative tries on my own I gained confidence and am now a water baby!

We went back to England for her operation and we breathed a sigh of relief when it was successful. She now has a pace-maker as a backup and we continue to hope that her heart will not outgrow this valve.

I now have the pleasure of spending time with my grandchildren, experiencing again those moments of wonder at the miracle of a newborn baby, the feel of a soft warm body snuggling close to me, pudgy fingers pinching my cheeks and that unique baby smell. It is still amusing to hear a toddler talk, saying such things as: "I'm the goodest boy," or "I lub you, Ma Lee".

My children have had to put up with a lot from me. They had to attend Supplementary school where I taught on Saturdays. They had to attend African Liberation Day annually and other cultural events because it was part of our awareness raising. For years, until they were older and gained their independence, they had to participate in concerts and festival activities in which I was involved. But we did have marvellous family times; we had country walks, picnics and trips to the seaside. They remember with fondness the Jamaican day trips to Skegness, Yarmouth and other seaside towns organised by Miss Mack and Vee or Edna. We still share the pleasure of country walks.

One of our happy trips nearly ended in disaster. We climbed Mount Snowdon using the Pig Track. Amanda was the first to reach the summit. On the way back to our friend's home, where we were staying in a caravan, the brakes on the car failed as I tried to slow down. I was going downhill and at the base of this hill were a river and a T-junction. Petrified, I realised I had to make a quick decision to save us from an accident that could kill us all. I looked out for a soft verge and rammed the car into it. It was close to Swallow Falls and a man out walking his dog came to our rescue. He discovered that the car's brake fluid had leaked out. We managed to get it to a garage and I took the children to a nearby park while the car was being overhauled and the problem fixed.

As a single parent for most of my children's childhood, I have some regrets. I expected them to take on responsibilities. I also wished I had spent more time with them. But I do not think that, without the sacrifices, I would have been able to give them the rounded education they have had and, at the same time, maintain my sanity. My children received no financial support from their father after we left. The only thing he did sometimes was to take them to the dentist for their check-up and they spent a few days here and there with him during school holidays. In 1973 when I obtained my divorce, I was riled that the priority for the judge was visiting access for a father, not support for his children! Revisiting a failed marriage is painful. I realise that living in a home with tension and unhappiness is not good for children. Making such a decision in 1970 was difficult, but I know I made the right choice. I have never discussed the horrors of my marriage with my children until now. They have kept in touch with their father and when I see him at family gatherings, I cannot help but think how sad it is that he did not play a more significant part in their lives and that they don't really *know* him as a father. He has told them how much he regrets what he did.

My children thank me for making them aware of their heritage, giving them the confidence that, with effort, they can succeed, and instilling in them that a social conscience should direct their actions.

For my shortcomings, I beg their forgiveness.

Fulfilling A Dream

My first teaching job came through the deputy-head of Alderman Derbyshire Comprehensive School who gave extra lessons to my son. I began there in May 1973 on a temporary contract the week after I finished my degree and then did my probationary year starting in the September. I enjoyed teaching. It was less stressful than studying but many people do not appreciate how much work goes into effective teaching. When I was on holiday, I would buy things to be used as audio-visual aids. I was always surprised when people guessed I was a teacher simply from the things I purchased. When I started my training I saw the role firstly to help children develop the skills to learn, because, in so doing, they could discover knowledge; secondly, to give them the basic knowledge to enable them to pursue the employment they wanted and thirdly, to instil a sense of moral responsibility by which they would live as adults and as citizens of the world. The more politicised I became, the more conscious I was of factors other than helping to motivate children to maximise their educational potential. I accepted as equally important my role as a change agent, getting white teachers with negative attitudes towards black pupils to cultivate higher expectations of these pupils. Others saw me as a role model for black children in the community at a time when there were only ten teachers from the African-Caribbean community in Nottingham. My job, therefore, was not primarily about money although, fortunately, with hard work, I began to earn a fairly good salary after two years in the profession.

Before qualified status is awarded, in addition to a favourable report from the headteacher, a school adviser/inspector has to assess the teacher's competence during the probationary year. On the day my adviser's visit was due, I felt quite confident about my preparation, teaching and class management, but was a little concerned that I had a tendency to gesticulate to emphasise a point, not an English norm. When I did my final teaching practice, my supervisor had praised all aspects of my work and had advised me to try holding my hands behind my back! It was my good fortune that the adviser for newly qualified teachers did not see gesticulating as a problem; he thought I was charismatic!

The easiest period of my teaching career turned out to be the first two years. I taught English, Religious Education and Social Studies and was a form tutor. In my first year, I was form tutor for a first-year group and the pupils and I learnt the ropes together. They were a delightful group and I still have a few presents from them among the possessions I treasure. In my second year I was given a third form. The pupils in this year are known to be the most difficult because, by then, they are beginning to feel they know the school inside out, adolescence has kicked in and they do not yet have the threat of external exams. Many of them push the parameters to see how far they can go in bucking the system. It was a learning experience that stood me in good stead over the ensuing years.

Within the staff there was an informal bloc of young people, of whom I became a member. We worked together, sharing ideas, teaching strategies and survival skills and socialising after work. The female deputy head created a stir among the younger female staff when I told them her comment about my trousers. I had gone to see her in her office wearing a black suit, the jacket and trousers were trimmed with thin strips of green and yellow. After we had finished our discussion she said that she was not happy with female staff wearing trousers, and went on to imply that bright colours were 'garish'. I was stunned! I looked smart and her comment was upsetting but as a new member of staff I was not sure about the staff's dress code. In the staff meeting that week, several of the young women took her to task over her comments pointing out that we were not pupils and obliged to wear grey and black, which were the colours she favoured. In the end she gave way and women wearing trousers became acceptable.

The school was on the edge of the city and drew its pupils from Bulwell, an area with very few black families. As a result, there were less than a dozen black children in the school. I planned to apply for a post in a school with more black pupils after two or three years' experience but, towards the end of my second year, I was invited to the Education Office to discuss a career move. I was asked to join a small team of hand-picked teachers who were to become 'Community Teachers' in primary schools in inner- city areas where there were problems such as poor attendance and low educational achievement. The aim was to get school, parents and community to work collaboratively and, by so doing, to encourage the children to see school in a positive light. It was challenging but exciting. I wanted to be in a school with a high percentage of black children because I knew I would be able to communicate with those of Caribbean origin and help members of staff who were struggling to understand some of our cultural differences. For instance, I noticed in meetings that teachers saw many children of Jamaican parentage as uncooperative when they refused to use the school's spare swimming or games kits, whereas the children were only adhering to their cultural upbringing that outside the family circle, one did not wear other people's clothes. In a similar vein, children from South-east Asia were seen as sly because they would not look teachers in the eye, especially if there was a dispute between them and their classmates. In their case, this was a cultural form of respect shown to elders.

I became a community teacher and was placed in Sycamore Junior School. The majority of the children's parents were indigenous whites while about twenty-five per cent were English-born children of Caribbean parentage and a few recently arrived South Asian children. It was a predominantly working class area. I worked with teachers in the classroom for fifty percent of the time and, for the rest, I worked with parents and the community. It was ground-breaking work and as community teachers we found that headteachers were suspicious of our work. As parents became empowered, teachers had to become more open and willing to accept changes, which some found difficult. It soon became apparent that in these inner-city schools, teachers had to take on board the reality that some families needed help with social problems that might affect their children's ability to learn. It was not easy for teachers to embrace yet another role.

Community teachers needed training and support to undertake this innovative role and we received one year's training on a day-release basis. I got my certificate from Trent Polytechnic, now Nottingham Trent University. This one day each week was a welcome respite from the tension and pressure that were so much a part of our job and provided us with the opportunity to share ideas and experiences; so we continued to meet weekly after completing the course.

I found it encouraging when Trent Polytechnic asked me to lead one of their education sessions with students who would be shortly teaching. I focussed on the importance of a teacher's awareness of the multi-ethnic school and the need for teacher training to address this.

The headteacher at Sycamore School was a genial man nearing retirement and he gave me a free rein. However, that also meant that I had to face the music on my own if things went wrong. Summoned one morning to his office, I came face to face with an angry parent, a white man over six feet tall and very menacing. He ranted at me because his son had complained that I had punished him unfairly. I listened to him and, when he was done, I gave him examples of his son's behaviour. "I'm sure that's not how you expect your son to behave," I ended by appealing to his good-parent image. As he calmed down, I took the opportunity to persuade him to come and help build classroom shelves at our Summer School. During all this, the head sat in silence at his desk. Having convinced this unemployed father that he had much to offer us, he not only gave his time at Summer School but he also encouraged a few other fathers to do the same, at a time when fathers hardly ever darkened the doors of the school.

The changing milieu in the school was exciting and gave me a sense of accomplishment. Unfortunately, only the mothers attended the Parents' Group. I taught them how to help their children to read. These mothers then felt more inclined to make other valuable contributions to classes in which they helped on a regular basis. Teachers who had previously resisted having parents in began to ask for parental support because it was clear that it benefited the pupils. Parents collaborated in the running of the Summer School, managing the tuck shop and offering sessions teaching the children various crafts. One mother, who lacked confidence, was encouraged to go back to college and qualify as a Nursery teacher. The two local councillors that I had invited regularly to the school were so impressed by what they saw that they brought a group of Russians on a visit to Nottingham to see parental participation in action. The parents working that day with the children were delighted.

I wanted children in their last year at primary school and the parents to participate in a community activity, thereby reinforcing the need for community participation. In exploring possible activities, I found out about a group of elderly women at Mapperley Hospital who seldom had visitors. Although this was a psychiatric hospital, the women were not mentally ill, they had been put there as young women when they had illegitimate children! I was told that as these old women had been incarcerated for such a long time it was impossible for them to be rehabilitated into the community. Our group visited them for an hour each week, taking them gifts of home-made cakes and biscuits. The children conversed with the ladies, sharing amongst other things, experiences of childhood in the past and present. Some of the parents then made a wonderful gesture. Each family invited a Mapperley woman home for Sunday lunch. I was so sorry to learn that this project ended soon after I left. Another community activity was the school's participation in the first St. Anns Festival when a group performed Jamaican folk songs and dances.

I was shocked on discovering the conditions in which some of our children lived. Sometimes the house smelt so filthy on entering it made breathing difficult. Meals were often junk food. Then there was the swearing that was considered normal behaviour, not to mention the physical brutality to which some children were exposed. As a school such information made us more observant. Our heightened awareness of the children at risk also encouraged a closer working relationship with Social Services and other support agencies.

I remember a situation that highlighted the danger people were in when they felt unempowered. This mother who had had a hysterectomy was constantly in pain and finding it increasingly difficult to cope with her children. When I did a home visit, I discovered that she could not even climb the stairs and was sleeping downstairs. Her husband had taken her to the doctor several times and they had been told that there was nothing medically wrong with her. But I was convinced this woman was not fantasising. This was a black family who was not happy with their white doctor but had to accept his opinion. I suggested that she should see a private doctor and I helped them find a black doctor with whom they felt comfortable. What he discovered was quite frightening. The woman had developed an infection caused by a swab left inside her at the time of her operation!

It is amazing the memories people hold dear. Children in junior school are usually full of life and many are natural performers on stage. My colleague, Sue Jones, had a musical background and we decided to do a production of *Joseph*. The West End production was a big hit at the time. This was moving away from the nativity play at Christmas. It was hard work but we had great fun rehearsing. The night of the performance before an audience of parents, family and friends was a wonderful experience for all involved. The dancing girls, the actors, including those with only walk-on parts, and the backstage helpers all received standing ovations. The children were ecstatic and their parents proud. Even after many years, some of those who took part, now parents themselves, remember the occasion with pleasure.

June 1977. The community was abuzz with excitement. It was the Queen's Silver Jubilee. The Junior and Infant schools and neighbourhood groups organised a celebratory street party on Robin Hood Chase. It was held in the area where I had once lived but nearly all the old houses had gone by then, replaced by council maisonettes, a shopping centre and community services. On the big day the sun shone. The Chase was ablaze with bunting. The tables were laden with food. BBC Radio Nottingham came along to do their coverage of local activities and distributed commemorative jubilee bone china mugs. It was a day filled with fun and laughter. A wonderful community event!

Near the end of my second year the Education Department was pleased with the school's progress. The staff had come together as a team with shared objectives, parental participation had increased as had reading standards and attendance. I was asked to move to another school. I missed working in that community because I could see that the changes were paying dividends and it gave me a great deal of job satisfaction. I had the highest regard for the hard-working men and women of St. Ann who gave of their best to their children. There were others who saw it as their right to scrounge what they could from the Welfare State. Sadly, some children were disadvantaged because of the ingrained negative attitude of their parents to society and that was well-nigh impossible to change. I learnt that poverty of the mind is far harder to eradicate than material poverty.

My new school, Claremont Primary, was very different from Sycamore Junior; it was much bigger and included a nursery, infant and junior departments. Its population was also quite different. Claremont's school population had been changing recently and now had a high percentage of pupils from South East Asia, many without a sufficient level of English language for the school curriculum. Their at-home mothers spoke little or no English. The white pupils and the few children of African-Caribbean heritage came from a mixture of working-class and middle-class homes. The school had a good reputation for academic work and the head was well respected, both by the Education Department and by parents.

I was looking forward to this new challenge but soon realised that I would be working in a very restrictive environment that would cramp my individuality. In my first meeting with the headmistress, she talked me through the school's philosophy and how the school was managed.

"I require all my staff to give me a fortnightly work plan which I discuss in our staff meeting."

"That's good," I said and explained my modus operandi working with parents and the community, ending with: "So I will keep a record of all visits and meetings and give you a monthly report. Is that okay?"

"I like to know everything that's going on . . ."

"I will discuss things with you," I tried to assure her, "but I will not be comfortable having confidential information shared with all the staff."

She was adamant. "I like to know what's happening in my school and I must approve it so that there is no comeback." It took some time to convince her that my method was not in opposition to hers, only somewhat different. Clearly, she was suspicious of community teachers. When I discussed our meeting with another member of staff, I was told that the head liked "to have her fingers in every pie", a very apt description. Over the years her perception of community teachers changed and, as an education adviser, she became a staunch supporter of our work.

But at the time, her level of control dampened my creativity and in the two years there I spearheaded only two initiatives. The 'International Evening' was a huge success. There was a sharing of cuisine and cultural items of dance and music from the countries represented in the school. To me this was one way in which people of different cultures could learn something about others and appreciate differences as they spent time together in a shared activity. The 'Toy Library' was also successful but it was hard work and required much coaxing to get the

Asian mothers to come to the school, partly because of the language barrier, which left them self-conscious about their inability to speak English. Gradually they began to join in the activities with their children who, surprisingly, did not find it daunting to play with other children. The middle-class parents got themselves involved in school activities whereas the parents from the immigrant communities did not, and I had only minimal success at changing this.

I recognised that the children whose second language was English needed specialist help. The school had only a part-time Asian teacher to assist those children who attended the Language Centre for specialist help on a half-day basis and they had very little English to benefit from classes when they came back to school. The Education Department, aware of the situation and the pressure it placed on class teachers, organised to train teachers to offer these children a course in English as a second language. When I gained my certificate in this, I devoted about fifty per cent of my teaching time to supporting these pupils.

I enjoyed the ebullience of the primary-school children and their looks of wonder as they mastered a new piece of work or learnt a new concept, but I wanted to move back into a secondary school. I missed working with pupils who were on the verge of entering the world of work and especially missed the level of reasoning of the older ones. The opportunity came after two years at Claremont.

I was transferred to Manning Comprehensive School, the only state girls' school in the city. Manning's population was changing from being predominantly middle class when it was a grammar school to a more mixed one following the demise of grammar schools. Many Asian families were also moving into the area to ensure that their daughters got a place there. The ten years I spent at Manning were by far the most productive of my career. My job description was teaching English and supporting pupils from ethnic minorities, the latter being my area of special responsibility. Later I became head of the Language and Curriculum Development department, newly created to meet the needs of the school.

My introduction was by no means problem-free. The headmistress, not having been involved in my appointment, was obviously not comfortable with it assuming I was placed there by the Education Department because the school was having some problems meeting the challenges of its multicultural population. I felt harassed at times and we had many disagreeable meetings during which I was cross-examined about my community work. I felt I was constantly under attack. After one of these I went into the toilet and cried out of sheer frustration. I talked with Promilla, my Indian friend and colleague, who pointed out that sometimes change is difficult to accept and the head might be worried that she was not totally in control of the situation. Later that day I saw a senior colleague looking quite depressed; she told me that she too had had an unpleasant meeting with the headmistress. On talking with other senior staff I realised then that what I had thought was a personal attack on me was more likely to be an unfortunate aspect of the headmistress' management style. At the next meeting with her, I asked, "Do you think I'm disloyal to Manning?"

"No," she replied, taken quite by surprise.

"Then why do I feel I'm being harassed when all I'm doing is being conscientious in my teaching and community work?"

She appeared apologetic but ended accusingly with, "But you bombard me with words!"

That was our last disagreeable meeting and, in time, our relationship improved but many of the black girls and their white friends continued to consider her racist, an opinion which would have been reinforced if any of those students had been present at a party she gave for staff at her home. As she was discussing interior decorating she said, "I quite like the nigger brown." A hush descended as colleagues waited in a pregnant pause for my response. The head flushed beet-red with embarrassment. I, too, was shocked for a brief moment then, with a laugh devoid of rancour, I said, "What exactly is that colour?" She apologised profusely and I accepted it. I had come to realise that it does take a long time to unlearn some things one has been taught. I would like to think that she was not comfortable with what was alien to her and that what we experienced in the school was her temper often getting the better of her.

When I went to Egypt and saw that, until the later dynasties, the pharaohs were black and that the Sphinx has the facial features of a black man, I brought back artefacts to use at the Supplementary school where I taught on Saturdays. I wanted children to be aware that some of the information and pictures in their school's history books distorted facts and that many ancient Egyptians were black. I spoke of my concern with the headmistress who was responsive and took the books in question out of use, suggesting that I work with the History department towards developing multicultural history syllabi for the first, second and third years and, if necessary, tackle the Examination Boards. I laud her for this.

I was struck by the teaching style throughout the school where work was set at one level for all, regardless of the range of abilities. The school curriculum reflected only a European perspective and did not include anything positive about the ethnic minority cultures represented by a fair percentage of the school population. The appointment of Community Teachers as 'change agents' was a laudable effort by the Education Department; however, a lot needed to be changed. Without confidence in one's ability, hard work, keeping abreast of trends in education and having a few supportive colleagues change was nigh impossible in a school. This was more the case in Manning than in the other schools at which I had taught. I realised quite early in my relationship with staff that the most convincing means of bringing about change was to demonstrate the effectiveness of my method of maximising children's potential. The ability to deliver bred respect. I prepared lesson plans and taught classes while the subject teachers observed. In addition I became involved in the ongoing evaluation of teaching material, teaching style and effectiveness. Some staff members were receptive and it was a pleasure working with them. Others resisted wanting the status quo to remain and they moaned constantly about overload. By the end of each term I was physically and mentally exhausted.

Fortunately, I got on well with the deputies and, with their management support, succeeded somewhat in encouraging the staff to address the issues I raised. By my fourth year at Manning I was fully integrated into the staff and no longer considered an outsider. I was rewarded for the pioneering work I had undertaken in multicultural education by being promoted to working with the management team. I had three superb colleagues in my department, all knowledgeable, hardworking and creative. We worked as a team and also became friends. Promilla Gulati, Annette Huggins, who died recently from cancer, and Ann Ben Amer. We commiserated with each other when the going was tough, encouraged each other to find that extra something that would ensure that we did not give up and celebrated the sweet taste of success whenever it came our way. Annette and I were ideas people and liked to get our teeth into things, firing on all cylinders. We both were impatient to get things done while Promilla and Ann were endowed with subtlety and patience. A great deal of time was spent in the holidays planning and reading to broaden our own knowledge base. We spent many hours in each other's home working on multicultural material. When I look back, I see how unique our department was in the experiences we brought to our jobs. Promilla came from India, spoke Punjabi and Hindi and was knowledgeable about the cultures from which the majority of our newly-arrived students came. Annette's mother was German and Annette had experienced post-war prejudice. She had also taught for a couple of years in Jamaica and her husband was a medical doctor from the Caribbean. Ann, a linguist, was married to a Moroccan and had lived for several years in France and North Africa.

As the numbers of those of us committed to multicultural education grew, our friendship extended outside the work environment and we began to meet socially at the end of each half-term. We have gone our separate ways but some of us continue to meet socially.

In the early days, my strategy was working with like-minded staff and showing by example that we expected high standards. Others then came on board. Ann Armitage, Head of History, embraced the need for change. With a lot of support from my team, the history of the non-European ancient civilisations of Kush in Africa and Mohenjo-Daro on the Indian sub-continent was introduced. The syllabi also gave a global perspective, instead of the European view of history that was generally taught across England.

In English I introduced books that reflected the cultures of pupils from ethnic minorities and developed work to accompany them. My choice of books raised social issues. I felt strongly that the adults of tomorrow needed to be aware of the world they would live in and that they had a voice and could make a difference. Some of the popular books for the younger pupils were *A Village by the Sea* about two children living in poverty stricken circumstances in India; *Journey to Jo'burg* about a black child struggling in apartheid South Africa; the trilogy, *The Twelfth of July, Across the Barricades* and *Into Exile* illustrating the horrors of sectarianism in Northern Ireland and immigration, *Roll of Thunder, Hear My Cry* and its sequel, *Let the Circle Be Unbroken* about the struggles and survival of African-Americans living in the then racist society of the United States of America; for the older age group, *The Colour Purple* charting an African-American family's unique history post-slavery and *To Sir With Love*, a Caribbean man's story set in post-war Britain when racism was rife. Poetry from many cultures was introduced. At one Parents' Evening, a Bangladeshi father was surprised and very pleased to find that Tagore, Bangladesh's famous poet, was included in the poetry selection for the upper school. In the space of a couple of years, staff in the English and History departments revamped their syllabi and began to develop their own multicultural material until we were able to purchase texts from book fairs across the country.

When the film *Cry Freedom* came to a Nottingham cinema, the head agreed that we could take the fourth and fifth years to see it. For me, the most encouraging thing to come out of the follow-up discussions was that several of the staff felt that, although the film was informative and moving, it was seen from the point of view of a white, middle-class man; they thought it would have been even more informative if the film had also portrayed a black person's perspective as s/he was always on the receiving end!

Our next step was looking at language across the curriculum and encouraging staff to develop material that would benefit a wide range of pupils. The staff then went on to work interdepartmentally on concepts, reinforcing ideas across subject areas. In keeping with developments within the Education Authority, Manning was among the first schools to offer Urdu and Punjabi as GCSE options.

Manning operated a pastoral system on similar lines to its academic one. Its responsibility was the welfare of the pupils. Some staff, whether from a lack of knowledge or because of their racist attitude, did not support pupils from ethnic minorities and sometimes some quite ugly conflict situations developed. My department provided training and support for staff to improve the school milieu, aiming to achieve one in which all pupils could feel that they belonged. A few members of staff were exceptional and gave more than was required of them in their pastoral role. I would act as a conduit, directing girls to them and turning to them for help to rescue girls at risk of being suspended or excluded.

Ann Armitage, as Head of History, was young and assertive; she defended many black girls who some other teachers reported as difficult, usually girls who tended to be more assertive than was considered acceptable. Brenda Binks, Head of Special Needs, was small, bespectacled, fashionable and had an infectious grin; she was wonderful with younger pupils of all ethnicities. Toni Lilley, Head of Home Economics and also a trained nurse, was calm, motherly and a good listener; there was always a group of girls of all ethnicities around her at break-time. Toni was of black and white parentage and so, the pupils of mixed parentage identified strongly with her; they were sometimes on the fringes, neither feeling white nor part of an ethnic minority. Two welcome changes have come about in society; friendship groups are no longer so strongly based on ethnicity and in many schools children are being taught to respect all cultures.

One idea that I put forward, to which, surprisingly, the head and staff agreed, was that the names of two houses should reflect the multi-ethnicity of the school. This demonstrated how much more positive the staff had become in accepting the concept of multiculturalism. The names our department introduced were *Seacole* and *Rani*. *Seacole* was in memory of the nineteenth century nurse from Jamaica who sacrificed much more than Florence Nightingale ever had in caring for British soldiers, yet was not mentioned in history books. The other was *Rani*, in memory of the famous Indian warrior of Jhansi who died in 1858 fighting the British imperialists in the first war of Indian independence.

Shock, disappointment, sadness, emotions I experienced as a black female teacher in my relationship with many of the older black girls whose bad experiences with teachers in the school had resulted in a negative attitude towards the staff. To them I was part of the establishment and, therefore, unable to understand them. I had to find ways to reach out to them. I started a lunch club with external facilitators, in an attempt to create an atmosphere which allowed the girls to freely express their opinions. It encouraged them to achieve academically and take steps to realise their dreams, instead of wallowing in the morass of self-pity and of low self-esteem.

Bright black and Asian girls were often not pushed to do their best by staff. The majority of black girls did not conform to many teachers' perception of the academic type, while the Asian girls were seen as not interested in further education, as they would be married off as soon as they left school. In supporting teachers to provide black and Asian pupils with quality education, we had to work on teachers' attitudes and those colleagues who were covertly racist had to be challenged regarding their actions that were racist.

Sometimes the battle was with unsupportive parents. I had many with Pakistani fathers who did not want their daughters, very able students though they might be, to sit examinations and go on to further education. On the other hand, among other Asian and Caribbean parents who expected their children to achieve, some were over-optimistic and had to be dealt with sensitively. In both such cases my department was usually asked to step in.

Our first Vietnamese girls at Manning were a delight to teach. The older girl, at sixteen, was very bright and quickly learnt enough English to master the subjects she wanted to do. She wanted to be a doctor and has achieved her goal! The younger sister worked extremely hard but was not as able and struggled with her school work. Their story as refugees was really frightening. The family had escaped with very little from Vietnam and lived as boat people in a refugee camp for several years before being accepted by Britain.

The school, after a long struggle, accepted that racism existed and that combating racism had to be actively pursued. I spearheaded race awareness as part of the Personal and Social Development programme that was a compulsory subject. Our school was invited by the producers of the BBC Schools' programmes to take part in developing a series on anti-racist education and Brenda Bradstock, one of the deputies, asked if I was interested. I met several educators who were very involved in anti-racist programmes in their schools and working with them provided me with valuable information in this area. My main contribution was a chapter on the use of multicultural/anti-racist material for the teacher's manual that accompanied the videos.

Central Television in the early 1980s had a half-hour programme, *'Here and Now'*, covering news and views of the black and Asian communities in Britain. I was asked to participate to discuss multicultural education in my school. The headmistress agreed for me to be interviewed in my classroom with its display celebrating the cultures of the children in the school. Vera Gilbert, an African-Caribbean, was the interviewer and agreed to my suggestion to also show a white colleague teaching Religious Education from a multi-faith perspective. This was important to me as I did not want the television viewers to see multicultural education as a 'black thing'.

By the late 1980s, ready for further career development, I decided to do a Master's degree with a focus on finding strategies to improve the achievement of black pupils within the school system. I undertook research in three schools and also interviewed a cohort of graduates from Nottingham to find if there were common factors for their success. One of the schools was John Loughborough in London, a Seventh Day Adventist institution. It provided a caring, stress-free environment for the black pupils but, interestingly, the factors for its students' success were similar to those of the other groups and of white pupils also. Pupils succeeded because they wanted to achieve and the majority had parental support. The findings strongly indicated that black pupils who succeeded were not deterred by the great hurdles embedded in racism. They had devised ways of not letting the system destroy their ambitions and girls coped much better than boys in dealing with racism in schools. Parents, especially mothers, played a major role in supporting students, not so much in the manner of middle-class parents with the know-how to get the best out of the education system, but by being there for them, giving moral support and encouragement. Some of the horror stories I heard made me cringe; I learnt that schools were failing our black children and that those who succeeded were, on the whole, tough and clever at masking their pain and distress. They had paid, or were paying, a high psychological price for their success.

When I left for my year's secondment at the University of York, David, the Head of Science, delivered his *"Ode to Lee"*. It spoke of my work and charmingly depicted an idiosyncrasy of mine, always having my coffee cup at hand, sipping its content whether hot or cold! David was a highly respected member of staff, an academic, one of the 'old grammar school set' and not always liked by some of the staff who found him aloof and unapproachable. Several staff members thought I was in for a rough ride when I offered to help out in the Science Department with the intention of bringing a multicultural dimension to some areas and revising the language to make it appropriate for mixed-ability groups in the lower school. I went the extra mile and offered to teach a first-year Science class for a term since David's department was short-staffed. The pupils did very well in that term's examinations and David saw this as attesting to effective teaching. I was surprised and really touched to find a 'thank you' bottle of sherry on my table just before the Christmas holiday. He had taken the time to find out from my friends that I was partial to sherry.

I am amazed at the men and women I meet who remind me that I once taught them. A white staff nurse at the hospital greeted me one day, "Hello. You don't remember me but I remember you. Alderman Derbyshire . . ." The Greek-Cypriot owner of my favourite fish and chip shop, whose daughter I had taught but hadn't seen for years, still makes sure I always get the best fish. One memory that particularly touched me was that of a young white woman I met recently in a village pub where a friend and I had stopped for a drink. She and her friend were at the table next to ours and the friend, sitting nearer to me, asked if I had taught at Manning. When I said yes, she joined in, "Miss, I'm Estelle from your English class," and we did some catching up. "I remember you well, because you were the only person who gave me hope when I got pregnant. You sent me a teddy for the baby and a note encouraging me to continue with my education because I had the ability." She is now in charge of a special unit for children at a very big hospital. I did recall her name but not the memory she had carried over all those years.

In 1989 I wanted a career move into the Education Advisory Service as I thought I had enough experience to make a positive input at that level and could help to ensure the delivery of quality education within schools. I had, a few years earlier, thought of a deputy headship leading to a headship but realised that, from what I knew of the schools in those days, it would, for a black woman, be more than likely a steep, uphill struggle. I knew I could be more effective as a 'change agent' in the role of adviser in an education authority. I was short-listed for a post in Birmingham but it went to the local candidate. When another post was advertised for head of a Sheffield-based African-Caribbean Service whose team worked with black pupils in schools, I applied. In my letter I asked them to contact me at the University of York. I was invited for an interview but found this out only after the date had passed because the letter had been sent to my home address. Furious, I contacted the education officer responsible. He apologised profusely and said that I would be invited for an interview if the person offered the post did not take it.

I went back to Manning School in the September and that term received another invitation for an interview from Sheffield. The Sunday after I accepted the post I met Len Garrison at lunch at Madge's home. In our conversation he told me that he had turned down the job in Sheffield because he had heard from the previous post-holder that the education officer with responsibility for the unit was difficult to work with and he had taken instead the post of Director of a community-run education project in Nottingham. Interestingly, I had been encouraged by that project's Management Committee members to apply for that post but it was not what I wanted. Len and I kept in touch. He made an excellent contribution to the community, including programmes to promote African history, providing extra lessons for school pupils and operating a mentoring project. Sadly, Len died in early 2003.

My impression of Sheffield had been of a place of 'dark Satanic mills' and depressing, dingy streets – areas in the north of the city that I had passed through. I was pleasantly surprised at the beautiful countryside surrounding the city. Living on Edale Road, I had easy access to parks and walks and to the Peak District. Away from my home community for the first time in thirty years, I took stock of my lifestyle and decided that some changes were necessary. With the exception of the Management Committee of Acacia Court, I gave up all community involvement in Nottingham as it was too far to travel. While continuing to work conscientiously, I began to enjoy my leisure, eating out with friends, walking, going to the theatre and enjoying reading just for pleasure. I met Glen Clarke and Fatma Alioua through work and Angela Martin through Fatma; we became friends and have remained so over the years. Glen was like a younger brother and as he lived nearby he was generous in helping me to settle in. Fatma is Algerian and introduced me to North African cuisine and music. Angela is gentle, calm and quintessentially middle-class English, while Fatma and I possess a fiery temperament. When we three meet, our conversations usually cover a wide range of topics and are never less than stimulating. Other people I grew close to were Val Bernard, a fellow interviewee for the Sheffield job, and Hilda Taylor, the daughter of one of my oldest friends in Nottingham and who had been my bridesmaid! These two provided me with invaluable insights into community politics, especially the relationships between the different ethnic-minority groups and the host community. Doreen Edwards was my oldest daughter's age and she adopted me as her mentor. I watched her develop from a bright young woman unsure of her potential into a role model for young women suffering from the knocks life sometimes hurls at us. Later, when I joined the Advisory Service Linda Grainey, a Scotswoman, and I developed a symbiotic relationship providing moral support for each other at work and when I took a job in Jamaica she paid me a surprise visit to "check that you're not overworking and being taken advantage of because you feel so committed".

My job in Sheffield was Head of the African-Caribbean Support team and line manager for the Team Leader of the nursery support staff. We were part of Sheffield Unified Multicultural Education Services (SUMES). Within SUMES two other services provided support for Asian pupils and one for post-school ethnic minorities. My team was in a demoralised state and felt isolated and under-valued. The five staff members spoke with one voice as they complained of being treated less favourably than the Asian teams. My first task was to build team spirit and to develop viable work plans. Exclusions and pupil/teacher conflicts were rife in many schools and I spent a lot of time trying to improve home/school relationships. Dena Martin, head of services for the Asian Support Team (Schools), Fatma Alioua, college lecturer with a PhD in linguistics, and I designed a one-year access course to Hallam University for unqualified school support staff at SUMES to pursue the B.Ed. degree. Working on this was exciting as it included piloting some of the components. Most of the students on the access course were capable and did very well.

Although I regretted the thought of leaving SUMES after only nine months I decided to grasp the opportunity and I applied for the post of Multi-Cultural Adviser that was advertised. I got the job but continued with some of the work with which I was involved. Bursting with enthusiasm and ideas, I arrived early on my first day at the Education Office. It was certainly not what I had expected. The Chief Adviser took me out for coffee and we chatted about everything but my role in the Advisory Service. When I settled in my office I was stunned to find that there were no hand-over documents. I was introduced to various key personnel, which was very helpful and given a free rein to develop the multicultural aspect of my work with schools. While at SUMES I had worked with my predecessor in the Education Office, Chris Searle, a fairly well-known national political activist and writer on current political issues. Chris was moving on to be head of an inner-city secondary school.

I soon discovered that advisers and advisory teachers in the department often felt pressured by their workload and long working hours. I had two multicultural advisory teachers working with me but in addition to my main area of responsibility I was adviser for six primary and two secondary schools. I supervised newly qualified teachers, supported heads and staff within my schools and, with the advisory teachers, provided authority wide in-service courses and support for staff to review and revise the curriculum so that it had a multicultural perspective. I was also involved in the appointment of headteachers. Another role advisers and education officers were asked to undertake was that of clerk to a school's governing body. This provided governors with Local Education Authority support. I chose to clerk for one of the primary schools for which I was also adviser. Sometimes I was asked to run workshops in other authorities as part of their in-service training for teachers to better meet the needs of the multicultural school population. I found that many of those working as 'change agents' were dispirited because of the negativity they were experiencing in their schools and I tried to give them encouragement, others were so focussed and enthusiastic that I was suffused with hope, but the majority of teachers were at the introductory stage.

I enjoyed assisting with curriculum development and staff development, although at some in-service sessions a couple of the secondary heads seemed hell-bent on challenging ideas proposed to make the curriculum multicultural. I disliked having to manage poor headteacher/staff relationships where both sides needed support. Some situations were very sensitive. For instance, a staff in strictest confidence handed me a letter of four pages giving specific examples of poor management in matters of grave concern that she expected to be addressed by the Education Department. Fortunately, I was working with colleagues who provided valuable advice and support to the school. A lot of my time was spent addressing complaints from parents and staff regarding exclusion of ethnic minority children, especially boys of African-Caribbean descent. Very often it was difficult to achieve agreement between school and parent because of the prevalence of unfair exclusions and some schools needed close supervision and a lot of support to develop better disciplinary strategies. The days with an absence of stressful situations were much appreciated. It was a good feeling receiving 'thank you' notes from teachers. Sometimes the support sought was not about their present work situation but for helping with interviewing techniques for senior posts and career advice.

When my old school, Manning, asked me to be the guest speaker at a graduation ceremony I felt humbled and honoured as this invitation usually went to high profile individuals such as Members of Parliament. Many of the students that I had taught were graduating. I hoped that my speech reinforced the students' desire to succeed in whatever career path they chose and not to settle for second best.

In the ever changing world of the Education Department of the early nineties, additional roles were often thrust upon advisers in quick succession. One that I found particularly challenging was that of having to work with heads to produce their budget proposals. We were given a crash course to master the process in a few days. Another programme that came on stream was Teacher Appraisal. I had minimal input in the development of this but was very involved in the training of staff and in piloting the scheme. It seemed that life in the service was one long learning curve.

The job, however, gave me a degree of autonomy which enabled me to pursue areas of work that I found rewarding. Hallam University asked me to supervise the teaching practice of some of the access course students. I enjoyed this because I saw the great strides these students made in their development. With direction they prepared well for lessons but some of them in the first week lacked confidence in the classroom because they had been educated in India and Pakistan and did not feel au fait with the English cultural norms of the pupils. On the whole schools were supportive and the confidence of the student-teachers increased.

I attended the community meetings of various black and Asian groups and reported their concerns to the department for action to be taken. Sometimes I was frustrated by the slow pace of change, but continued to work with groups such as SADACCA, the African-Caribbean organisation and Sheffield Race Equality Council (SREC). As always it was challenging work.

In the early 1990s Sheffield City Council was one of the more proactive councils in the area of race relations. It had provided homes for Somali refugees fleeing the war in their country. There was a steady increase in the number of Somali children entering Sheffield schools; they had language needs to be met but more worrying were the racist threats the families faced in some neighbourhoods. They were spat upon and attacked in the streets, their homes were vandalised and faeces put through their letter boxes. Many lived in constant fear. It was a shameful state of affairs. The Housing and Education departments within the Council, SREC and other concerned bodies tried to address the issues and support the Somali community.

In 1992 the murder of the teenager, Stephen Lawrence, in London rocked the black community and created the kind of community anger and determination for justice against this child's racist attackers that made the institutions sit up and begin to take proper stock of the degree of institutional racism that had allowed his attackers to avoid punishment. *To date, no-one has been found guilty of this heinous crime.*

After leaving SUMES I had to learn how to deal with a most difficult colleague who was the only other senior member of staff in the department from an ethnic minority group. He was an Arab from Africa and until I joined the Inspectorate he was the person the Education Department referred to on all issues concerning ethnic minorities in Sheffield; he was also the person the communities saw as their conduit to the department. He welcomed me to Sheffield and, as my line manager at SUMES, we got on very well. We had an easy relationship; he would invite me over for meals and I did likewise. I had been warned by several people in the Caribbean community not to trust him but, being new to Sheffield, I kept an open mind. Once when we were having dinner he mentioned difficulties he had had with my predecessor and said that he hoped we would not end up enemies! I did not envisage what lay ahead.

The second time that I disagreed with him in a SUMES staff meeting, I was warned by another colleague not to do so because he hated not being totally in charge; it was suggested that I work quietly to achieve what I wanted until it was too late for him to change things. This seemed to me a rather underhanded tactic and I did not think it was how a team should work. This colleague, however, was strongly supported by him while I had to find strategies to deal with him as he frustrated my work with the communities when I was no longer at SUMES. He would not share information; he would not inform me of community meetings that he organised at which I should be present. As other colleagues became increasingly aware of the tension between us, I agonised over it for a while then concluded that our approaches were different. I saw my role as empowering people. I left him, therefore, to rule the kingdom of ethnic minority communities and concentrated on working mainly within schools and with groups who asked specifically for support. To demonstrate my lack of animosity, I invited him to my fiftieth birthday celebration lunch in my office and he came.

Sheffield in 1992 faced the difficult task of closing schools because of falling numbers and stringent Conservative government measures on local authorities' spending. I was part of the team that had to represent our Director of Education at closure meetings with staff, governors and parents. It was a most unpleasant task and sometimes the atmosphere became quite heated. It was at one of these meetings that I encountered David Blunkett, who later became Education Minister in Blair's Labour Government in the late 1990s. A question of his shocked me. Although he was well aware of the situation and knew that the Council had very little choice but to close schools, he supported the parents at the meeting in attacking the measures taken by the Council!

The National Curriculum for schools was followed in 1992 by a new system for inspection of schools. All the advisers in Sheffield were sent to the assessment sessions for inspector status. Having passed the assessment, we became Office of Standards in Education (Ofsted) Inspectors. The relationship with schools changed as the education authority envisaged two separate roles: inspectors to inspect and advisers to advise. Internal reorganisation meant that we had to choose whether to apply for a post as adviser or as inspector. Reducing staff at all levels within the authority also became necessary and an early retirement scheme was introduced; anyone over fifty could apply for an early retirement offer. All of us in the inspectorate who applied for this were surprised at the speed with which it was processed. It happened within a week of the approval of the offer and the member of staff's employment ceased allowing very little time in which to complete any outstanding work or to prepare hand-over documents. As soon as the scheme was announced I registered my interest. I saw early retirement with a pension as my opportunity to do voluntary work in Jamaica or Africa and to travel. However, I was not quite fifty and I was turned down.

Within the department, my desire to take early retirement was well known and senior colleagues were surprised when I applied for a post. I did this because I realised my pension would be only a third of my present salary and I would have to consider paid employment for a few more years. At the same time there was a level of underhandedness at work. For example, I saw a threatening letter addressed to one of our senior inspectors from a local head whose school was closing, in it he stated that he had been promised the post that I and others had applied for and had been subjected to an unnecessary interview without an appointment being made. It was also rumoured that the period of the early retirement offer might be limited to months. I applied for and accepted the early retirement deal but also registered a complaint at the manner in which the situation was handled although I could not mention the letter that a colleague had shown me.

I had come to the end of my career in education. It had been an interesting journey and I had learnt a great deal. I felt enriched having met people from different cultures and having had the opportunity to share in some of their celebrations and visit their homes – Africans north and south of the Sahara, Arabs, Greeks, Poles, Jews, Chinese, Vietnamese, Japanese, Indians, Pakistanis, Bangladeshi and Sri Lankans. Some of them have become my friends. I also know that through my interaction with colleagues across several education authorities, a difference was made in raising the awareness of some teachers to the needs of ethnic minority pupils. Many of them not only changed their teaching style from a Eurocentric to a more global one, taking into consideration the need for education within a multicultural society, but also became change agents.

The Nottingham Connection

Labour Of Love

Teaching was my career, unpaid community work my social commitment. Until 1967 my world was centred on my family and my home. Among friends we discussed the horrors of racism in the USA. On this side of the Atlantic, we heard through our community grapevine of police brutality and racist attacks in cities across the country. Enoch Powell and others of his ilk were whipping up anti-black sentiments with his 'rivers of blood' speeches which were being widely quoted in the media. As we lived with it, racism affected us like a nagging toothache. An incident I witnessed made me realise that, as black people, we could not sit back and wait for equality and justice, we had to fight for it on many fronts and help to create the change for a better society. That was how I became a community activist.

On that day, as children were on their way home from the Infant school near my home, I saw a white man chase a six-year-old black boy, catch him, hold him by his shirt front and slap him several times across the face. He then calmly took the hand of a white boy and strode off. I was horrified at that adult's behaviour. When I saw him hitting the boy, I ran towards him shouting, "Stop it! Stop it!" But by the time I reached the scene the man had walked off. I asked the crying child if he was alright, patted him and rushed on to tackle the swine. He must have heard me yelling, "You can't do that and walk off!" But he ignored me, crossed the busy main road and got into his van. I refused to let him get away with it and so jotted down his car registration number before going back to console the child. His face was bruised, his shirt was undone and buttons had been ripped off.

I took him to the police station about five minutes away and told the policeman what had happened. His response stunned me. He actually asked me what the incident had to do with me. I was incensed and told him I was reporting it as a responsible citizen. He wrote down the car registration number and said he would see what he could do, but it was clear that nothing would be done. I, therefore, walked across the square to the office where I worked, told them what had happened and asked to use the telephone to find out the owner of the car as I intended to write a letter to the editor of the local newspaper. I then took the boy home. As I spoke with the boy's father I remembered that the office of the Community Relations Council (CRC) was on Mansfield Road and that they were there to help people from ethnic minorities with complaints against the police. The father agreed to make a complaint and I promised to accompany him. We later discovered a most disturbing fact; the abusive parent was a policeman and to me this explained the manner of the officer to whom I had reported the incident. The father, on hearing this, thanked me and said he did not want to pursue the matter. He said he was afraid that the police would begin to hound him and plant marijuana in his home so that they could arrest him. He felt that pursuing the matter to get the officer reprimanded was not worth the risk to his family.

I accepted his decision but refused to drop the matter and went to the CRC to lodge a complaint in my name. A few days later a police inspector came to see me; he said I should leave it to him and he would reprimand his officers. He was very persuasive but I had my doubts. My husband thought that I had expended enough time on the matter and I agreed to leave the inspector to deal with the matter with the understanding that he had given me his solemn promise to do so.

Police brutality was becoming commonplace and we heard many stories of young men in our community being harassed. I had arrived in England a year after the 1958 race riots in the city and did not witness the horrors that many African-Caribbean people lived through. Some were still haunted by the vicious attacks by white youths, especially Teddy Boys, on our men. The then Jamaican Prime Minister had visited the city in an effort to calm fears and seek ways forward for a better relationship between the immigrants and the host community. Concerned people became activists and formed support organisations.

In 1967, I became a member of the Black People's Freedom Movement (BPFM). This movement was different from the West Indian Students' Association that had a more genteel approach to fighting racism; for instance, the latter group would invite the police hierarchy to meetings to discuss our concerns, hoping that this might lead to a better understanding between them and us. This approach helped a little but it was obvious to many of us that our voice had to be heard by the people who were leaders in the city and who had the power to effect change. The BPFM networked with groups in cities across the country in an attempt to learn strategies and ways to support each other. In Nottingham we held community meetings to raise awareness of racial abuse and to educate the people about taking action and making our voices heard in the Council. Initially, because I had a young family, my involvement was limited to helping with Supplementary school and attending meetings where I became more aware of black issues. BPFM gradually became highly politicised and we became a part of the Pan African Congress Movement (PACM).

The 'Ringrose incident' made me aware that harassment did not stop with black men. Ms Ringrose did not come home one evening and her children went to the other Jamaican family on the street, frightened that something had happened to their mother. The neighbour's husband came to seek my help and we found Ms. Ringrose in the hospital with a perforated eardrum and many bruises, the result of having been beaten and kicked by the police. Earlier that day she had gone to collect her passport photos from a shop that offered a one-day service. It had been her third trip over three days and she refused to leave without her photographs or a refund. The owner, who turned out to be an ex-policeman, rang his friend at the nearby Guildhall Police Station to come over and when she refused to be intimidated and insisted on getting the photos or her money back, the two men began dragging her towards the police car. When she resisted, they began to beat her and took her to the station where she was booked for attacking a police officer and put in a cell. She told another officer, who came to force her to confess, about her young children unprotected at home. This was ignored. Finally someone suggested that she needed medical attention and she was taken to the hospital. She was charged with assaulting police officers.

I alerted Berenge Bandele and others from PACM about the incident and we found a solicitor willing to take Ringrose's case to defend her against the charge and to make a counter-claim against the officers for assaulting her. In those days solicitors were most unwilling to take on such a case. The one we used was not local and came highly recommended for his work in fighting injustice. The local PACM supported Ringrose throughout those months and during the trial. The police tried to bargain, offering to drop the case against her if she did not pursue hers against them. Their case was thrown out of court but, at this critical juncture, Ringrose said she was too drained to carry on. We were very disappointed as we had hoped that, by publicising her case, we could help to bring about changes in the way the police dealt with black people.

Black people in Nottingham are wary of the police and with good reason. However, through my work in the community I have met some excellent policemen who have worked with us to improve the relationship between the police and the community. With more black young people joining the force and more interaction between black and white people, we hope the situation will continue to improve.

In 1984 our local PACM, as part of a national protest against companies trading with the apartheid regime of South Africa, held a demonstration outside the big branch of Barclays Bank in the city centre. A group of us spent several hours after work making banners and placards. The demonstration was to show the bank that we were against their policy, as well as to raise people's awareness, encouraging them not to bank with Barclays. I found it amusing that one of my senior colleagues from Manning School crossed the road when she saw me that day.

African Liberation Day (ALD) is an annual event in the movement's calendar, bringing together Africans from the motherland and the diaspora to share our experiences and strategies, in a bid to promote the wellbeing of our people. Preparing for ALD was a busy time. Some years I was more involved with organizing the two days, leading workshops and once chairing the conference. One year in Birmingham the attendance was very good and, as we marched through the streets of Handsworth demanding equality and justice, a helicopter hovered above us. We suspected it was the police taking photographs and wondered if the police were as interested in the activities of the National Front!

My girls and I loved attending ALD activities. I came back with a buzz, a feeling of belonging to a group of people actively involved in improving the lives of our people wherever they were. I also learnt a lot about the history and cultures of Africa and the societies of the diaspora. I wanted my children to grow into young people committed to helping their black brothers and sisters by making our motto a reality: "Forward ever! Backward never!"

My friend, Blossom, and I often reminisced about our school concerts in Jamaica and how sad it was that our children in Nottingham were missing out on these cultural activities. In order to ensure that children of Caribbean parentage learnt about that part of their cultural heritage, we decided to have an annual folk concert. We included folk songs such as *'Carry me ackee go a Linstead Market'* and *'Day Oh'* that were about the working life of some Jamaicans, folk dances and poetry by Caribbean poets. We also saw a concert as a way of sharing something with the white community. We decided to ask the children of our black families in the immediate neighbourhood to become part of a group to put on a 'Jamaican Concert'. We practised in Blossom's dining room, which was bigger than mine, and hired the hall at the Adult Education Centre on Shakespeare Street to hold our first concert in 1968. We invited people from the black community and friends from other subcultures to attend. Mr. Irons from the Education Department kindly acted as our master of ceremonies. The concert was a resounding success and we were invited to participate in the Nottingham Carnival. We continued with the carnival for a few years until most of the children were teenagers and had developed other interests.

I have always been keen for our culture to be seen as part of the new multi-cultural Britain and, therefore, did storytelling and talks in libraries and other venues around the county during the school holidays. I also introduced and encouraged other people in our African-Caribbean community to participate in local activities. At the time George Vaughan, another teacher, ran a successful steel band that was very popular and this encouraged several schools to start steel bands. It was wonderful to see how the participants' self-esteem increased as they became proficient on the drums!

In 1979 we put on a 'Caribbean Weekend' to celebrate our culture. Another friend, Louise, joined us in the preparations. I invited Marie Cooke, then Jamaican Consul, and community activists such as Cecil Gutzmore from London to address topical social issues. The *Caribbean Times* covered the event with a double spread. The event was well attended and a success but the three of us and Dorothy Benjamin who assisted were physically exhausted when it was over.

What I had to accept then was that only a few people were prepared to put an effort into community activities which offered no financial reward. Things have not changed!

In the early 1970s black communities began to become more vigilant in ensuring that their children were not being placed incorrectly in special education schools. This all came about with the publication of Bernard Coard's book, *How the West Indian Child Is Made Educationally Subnormal in the British School System* and the can of worms that it opened. One response was Supplementary schools run on Saturday mornings, giving black pupils additional academic support and providing them with a milieu that encouraged confidence and increased self-esteem. As a unit leader in the Girls' Venture Corps I enjoyed working with my group of black and white teenagers but gave it up when I recognised the more urgent need to help with a Supplementary school. In the beginning, mainstream schools were against this community response to their failure but eventually they came to accept that such schools played an important role in making children more receptive to school work and they saw that, an increase in self-esteem and race pride, did not undermine school and teachers. I continued to manage the weekly Saturday session of Ukaidi's Supplementary School until 1990 when I left Nottingham. It was like an extra school day for my girls and likewise for the children who attended. It ate into my family time but was such a worthwhile venture that I made the sacrifice. As is often the case, there were only a handful of workers but a lot of talkers on committees. When I visit black Supplementary Schools, now funded by the Education Department, and several of the tutors remind me that it was at our Supplementary School that they had been helped, I know the hardship was well worth it.

As part of our black studies programme in PACM, we learnt about Kwanza, the yam festival, and began to celebrate it. I thought Kwanza should be celebrated in Supplementary school and I wrote a short play for the children to perform for parents and friends. Seven children volunteered to be the bearers of the Kwanza gifts from the community to be received by the chief. Each child spoke a verse expressing the meaning of one of the seven principles of Kwanza, the essence of which was to celebrate a community that was building a better world by working together in a caring and creative way.

I was concerned that too many black children with whom I spoke felt that they were limited in their career choice. Today, I am so proud of those I meet who refused to give up on their dreams. One young lady's careers teacher wanted her to seek employment in a factory and refused to support her application for the much sought after hairdressing course at the local college. He convinced her mother who was neither assertive nor knowledgeable to agree with him. This youngster had a running battle with him and won. She is now a teacher with a Master of Arts degree! There is a female barrister who was channelled into being a typist and a doctor and a dentist who were directed to seek manual work. Teachers' low expectation of black youngsters was so common it was frightening.

Responding to this I designed a set of ten *'I want to be . . .'* posters to encourage youngsters to explore the range of career options available and not to feel limited. Each A3 card had a photo of someone from Nottingham or Sheffield - the communities in which I worked - who had succeeded against the odds. I gave a brief biography of the person and the final line in bold read: *'You too can achieve'*. The careers were those of five women and five men. These I updated in 2001. The women were a driving instructor with her own business, an electronics engineer, a soprano, a speech therapist and a potter. The men were a doctor working at a health centre, an education psychologist, a bank manager, an electrician with his own business and a journalist/assistant producer of BBC Sports. These were sold at cost to schools and youth organisations in Nottingham and Sheffield. Today, mainly through movies, soap operas and some excellent posters on national and international achievers, black youngsters are aware of the wide range of careers they can pursue.

Things have changed; Nottingham's black community members have become integrated into the wider culture and are competent and confident in their dealings with government organisations; they belong to Trade Unions and are active as councillors. The 1970s was a different world of struggles to fight racism at all levels. The open verdict on the 'New Cross Fire' where several young black people at a party perished, the 'Brixton Riots' that the black people of Britain refer to as 'protest' against police harassment and brutality, the increase in the number of young black men incarcerated for crimes that their white counterparts earned only non-custodial sentences, the number of prisoners being sent to psychiatric hospitals to be treated for schizophrenia, all these are evidence of how worrying times were for black people in Britain. The creation of Ukaidi was one of our community activists' responses to racism. It was a self-help project to assist local people facing problems that stemmed mainly from racism. We tried to raise our people's awareness by having education conferences and community meetings about concerns in the black communities of Britain. We invited national and international speakers who not only shared their experiences of racism but also helped with strategies to politicize community organisations across Britain. Courtney Griffiths, a young barrister, who happened to own a sports car shared his personal experience of having been harassed by the police in the middle-class area where he lived, thus exemplifying the problems faced by young black men, whoever they were and wherever they lived. Kwame Trure

(Stokely Carmichael) was a charismatic speaker who highlighted similarities of racist injustices suffered by black people in England and in the United States of America and the strategies needed to combat it. Speakers from South Africa gave moving, first-hand experience of the suffering of black people living under apartheid.

I was a founding member of Ukaidi and served as chairperson for several years until I resigned after leaving Nottingham. We did a lot of pioneering work with schools to reduce exclusions that disadvantaged African-Caribbean pupils, in particular boys, in the education system. Identified staff supported parents at exclusion meetings. Realising that exclusions were often the response to many teachers' fear of black boys and that racism lurked in many schools, we ran seminars focussing on positive strategies for parents and staff to work together.

Leroy Wallace, Director of Ukaidi until his demise in the early 1990s, also presented a Sunday music programme, *"Back a Yard"* on BBC Radio Nottingham that provided additional information to our black community. For a while I had a slot aimed at giving the less informed a sense of pride in their history. Too many of us had imbibed the history taught in schools that made of us a people with only the history of slavery. My mother was a regular listener and one afternoon while visiting her she was very excited.

"Have you seen this week's *Radio Times*?" she asked as I came through the door.

"Why? I usually have a look at yours."

"Well, look at Sunday's page." She refused to say more. Her pleasure was quite visible when I opened the magazine and saw my photo advertising *Back a Yard*.

In the 1980s, Ukaidi was recognised as the watchdog of our community. Deprived of the driving force of the original committee, it eventually closed in the late 1990s. I was saddened by the news.

In 1976, the newly formed Black and Asian Forum for BBC Radio Nottingham nominated me as chairperson with responsibility for reporting, from a listener's perspective, on the contents and style of programmes. My schools were supportive of my community work and I was allowed the time to attend these meetings.

As chair of Ukaidi I participated in ongoing dialogue with the City Council on issues of importance to the black community. I was approached on several occasions to join the Labour Party. I was told that they needed councillors with vision and drive from the black and Asian communities. I did not see myself in that role. In the 1980s Nottingham City Council began to reflect its multi-ethnic population. To date we have had two sheriffs and a Lord Mayor who came as immigrants from Jamaica.

One day I received a letter inviting me to an interview for the appointing of Justices of the Peace (JPs). I did not want to be a JP as I was perturbed by the narrow mindedness of some of those that I had met. I was cajoled by a friend at the CRC to attend. I had a suspicion that he was hoping I would change my mind when he said, "Just go and see what it's about." The interviewers understood my stance on a system that too often criminalised people unnecessarily instead of funding preventive measures and we agreed that I was more suited to working with an organisation that tried to steer youngsters away from getting into crime. When I questioned the rationale for asking my political allegiance, I was told that they had to choose equal numbers from the two main political parties!

Something I am proud to have been a part of is the creation in 1988 of **Acacia Court**, the first sheltered accommodation built specifically to meet the needs of the elderly of Caribbean origin. The idea for this project came out of Ukaidi's Management Committee. We decided to address the concerns of a growing number of our elderly who were not happy to be taken away from their community and did not feel comfortable in the Council's homes for the elderly. I was nominated chairperson and served in that position until my resignation in 1993. The other people who did the donkey work were Harry Joshua, Tyrone Brown, Mavis Bowen, Lyn Gilzene and Ferdi Fru. I felt great satisfaction when, in partnership with Anchor Housing Association, the building was erected in St. Anns and the tenants moved in. The Acacia Court complex has thirty-two self-contained flats, a two-bedroom flat for a warden and accommodation for a relief warden. In this project bedrooms are bigger and able to accommodate the double bed our elderly people prefer and there is a guest room for overnight visitors. Acacia Court accommodates people of all ethnicities but priority is given to those of Caribbean heritage. Nottingham now has a local black housing association, Tuntum, which manages Acacia Court where there is a warm and welcoming atmosphere. Our black elderly are at home in Acacia Court because it gives them such a wonderful feeling of belonging.

In 2002, the 'Windrush' celebration around Britain marked fifty years since the first group of Caribbean people came as economic migrants, and settled. Nottingham City Council and the local branch of the Council for Racial Equality presented awards to Caribbean people locally in recognition of their service to the community. I was most honoured to receive one.

JAMAICA

For Love Of Country

I jumped at the idea of getting away for two weeks in September1993 when Stanley suggested a family holiday. Michelle, Amanda, Stanley, Sally, Stanley's partner, and I went off to Italy. Charmaine could not join us because of work commitment.

Imagine my surprise when, on returning to England, I found a letter from National Children's Home (NCH) in London with an application form for a post as Director/ Deputy Director of NCH in Jamaica. This was in response to a telephone request. Puzzled, I rang Charmaine and all was revealed. I had planned to go to Jamaica to check what voluntary work I could do there and, at the same time, look for a home in preparation for my return. My children had decided that the job advertised in one of the Sunday papers was ideal for me. They talked me into it and when I was given an interview date, I prepared by spending hours in the library and visiting a couple of homes and special schools for mentally and physically challenged children. I ended up being one of two persons recommended to the Board of Trustees in Jamaica. I awaited the outcome.

That October, my Aunt Wrightie in the USA passed away. My mother and I flew to Boston for the funeral and stayed over for my cousin's wedding a fortnight later. While in New York, I received a phone call from NCH (London) that the chair of the Jamaican Board of Trustees was in Europe and wanted to meet me. It was arranged that when she stopped in New York on her way home we would meet at her son's home. The interview was relaxed and *'my spirit took to her'*. She was short, looked a mixture of African and Spanish ancestry and reminded me of a comfy Caribbean grandmother. Her smile was infectious and her laugh was like tinkling glass. Another thing I liked about Mrs McGhie was her honesty. She made no attempt to minimise the strenuous nature of the posts and did not conceal the fact that the Board's choice of director was a local candidate who would be au fait with the systems and the culture. She wanted me as the deputy and told me I would hear from the Board. That was in November.

I did not hear from NCH in Jamaica but I was contacted by NCH in London who warned me that it was likely to take a long time before I heard from Jamaica. In January I was offered a final interview with the Board and the opportunity to see NCH Jamaica. I think NCH in Jamaica was not sure that I would take on such responsibility for so little remuneration. Although housing and a car came as part of the package, the salary would be one-sixth of my last one! However, this was not a big issue for me as I did not see the job as a career opportunity but rather as a way of giving back something to my homeland.

And what a trip it was! On my first night there I was awakened by the roaring of a lion that seemed to be just outside the window. I leapt up, terrified and listened for some movement from the director, Mrs Parris. My room was down the corridor from hers and we were the only ones in the house. Nothing happened. When the roaring stopped, all was quiet again. It seemed awfully strange. Eventually I fell into a troubled sleep. At breakfast the next morning I broached the subject.

"Did you hear that lion last night?"

"Oh, that," Mrs Parris said between mouthfuls. "I forgot to tell you. It's the lion at the zoo behind us."

I laughed about the incident afterwards dubbing it 'the night of the roaring lion', but I was so frightened by it that I always remembered to warn visitors and new staff.

Later that morning I was greeted by a petite lady with a bright smile. Lena James, a visiting Jamaican lay preacher living in London, took it upon herself to convince me that working with the children was doing God's work. She prayed daily and got others to pray also. Once I was given a lift from a Peace Corps meeting organised by a friend of mine and I invited the driver, a senior government officer, for a glass of fruit juice. Lena joined us and as we talked, she suggested that we pray for guidance. I was taken aback by her approach, it was not part of my experience but, interestingly, the other lady did not bat an eyelid. I guess their prayers were answered; by the end of the week the children had captured my heart. The Board of Trustees offered me the post of Director as the candidate of their first choice was unable to live on site, which the Board saw as an absolute necessity. I accepted the post.

I took up my post in March. On the flight out from England I travelled with Tom White, the Chief Executive of NCH-Action for Children who was on his annual visit to NCH Jamaica. As we were being served dinner I thought it best to let him know that I was not a teetotaller and that I enjoyed a glass of wine at dinner. NCH Jamaica was a Methodist establishment and, although I knew that they frowned upon drinking, it had quite slipped my mind to ask the Board what their stance on this was for employees. I was relieved when he replied that he also drank alcohol. Tom stopped over in Miami for a couple of days and I went on to Jamaica. I had been informed that I would be collected by the Home so I waited and waited and waited at the airport. There was no answer from the Home when

I rang and in the end I had to find my way to my cousin's home. The next day I telephoned the director who apologised for the oversight. I spoke with the chairperson later that day and she accepted my suggestion that I stay with my cousin until I took up the post in two weeks' time. I did not want to be in Mrs Parris' way while she was busy packing.

There was no formal handover and I found myself in the farcical situation of following Mrs Parris around, asking questions and making notes. On my predecessor's last day I was in her office when, by chance, she opened a safe that I had not even noticed before. It was only when I asked her about it that I was given the combination! To add to this madness, the Home was without a deputy and the one senior staff member knew so little about its administration that she could give me no information on the Home. That evening there was a 'leaving do' in the hall for the outgoing director. I sat at the back, dumbfounded by the task that awaited me. Tom White introduced me to the ex-Deputy Director, Mrs Brown. Like someone drowning, I grabbed at the one person who could help. I appealed to her Christian sense of doing the right thing for the sake of the children and pleaded with her to come back to work for a term. She kept me in suspense for the duration of the function but Tom White and I waylaid her and she finally agreed that she felt I had been put in an invidious position. *Thus began my odyssey.*

NCH was a big establishment providing a home for children ranging from seven to eighteen years in need of care and protection and a Special Education School for mentally challenged children (special needs) in the Kingston area. In the Home, thirty-eight of the children attended local schools and lived in three units on the main block, another twelve attended the special school and also lived in a unit on the main block and thirty-six, who were severely mentally and physically challenged, lived in a special unit across the road on the same compound as the school. Unfortunately, when the youngsters in our special unit reached 18, there were not enough adult places in sheltered schemes for them and they had to stay on until such a place became available. A couple of young people over the age of 16 and attending vocational college lived in the Independent Unit where they each had a room and were given weekly groceries and pocket money. They were supervised by the store-woman who shared their unit. The school had approximately one hundred and twenty day pupils. The school's head and staff were paid by the Education Department and the Home received a grant for the school's upkeep. The headmistress and I got on very well together, she would stop by for coffee before starting her day and we had regular meetings regarding the running of the school. A majority of the school's staff, in particular those who were there when I arrived, did not like to be considered as part of the Home, they wanted to be seen as part of the Education Department. This stemmed from the perception that being a part of the latter was more prestigious. The Home received a government subvention for each child placed there by Children's Services, but it was quite insufficient to manage the project and support from NCH in England had been meeting the shortfall; however, the Jamaica project was in the process of becoming autonomous and fundraising was essential if the Home was to continue the services provided.

When I moved onto campus I was shocked to find that the Director's house was without living room and bedroom furniture. I had to contact the Chair of the Board and was given permission to purchase the necessary items and to have the house repainted. I stayed in the Deputy's house until mine was ready. Two Board members, Mrs Rattray and Mrs Muirhead, who came to welcome me, were very helpful and we went shopping for furniture. They, along with Miss Lusan and Mrs McGhie, were very actively supportive as Board members. Mrs McGhie has a very special place in my heart. She was more than a line manager, she became a friend.

She liked the changes I was making, above all she loved the increase in the children's self-esteem. She gave me moral and spiritual support; had it not been for her I would probably have resigned at the end of three years and not extended my tenure. I often told her she was "just like my mother" because she was so caring. Once when I had the 'flu and carried on working as we were short-staffed, she made an appointment for me to see her doctor.

"Now, I know you people from England don't like going to the doctor, but you need to and I have made the appointment." She hugged me, "My dear, please go."

It was not that I was a martyr but there were times, and these were too often, when I had little choice. Shortage of staff due to high staff turn-over is endemic in this area of childcare and although I got the Board to increase wages and tried to develop a sense of ownership of the project among our staff, we could not compete with the lure of the USA and private nursing. This situation created additional work and stress. A social worker friend of mine in England told me that they too were suffering from staff shortages and many of their Child Protection Services had a high percentage of agency workers, a situation that was costing them more than the salaries paid to employees! Imagine the situation in a developing country, like Jamaica, without such agencies.

The management of JNCH, the name I dubbed it, took over my life. I asked the Board to approve the name change to Jamaica National Children's Home in order to reflect our changing status. That was easy. On the other hand, finding a child care deputy was like finding gold. We wanted someone with a social work background and a commitment to help establish the kind of home where the children did not feel institutionalised. Of four deputies I had during my tenure, one was a fraud; one had a top executive husband who had a lot of social engagements and our working hours proved unsuitable; one, unknown to us, was there as a stopgap while she awaited a job that was in the pipeline; in fact, only one was ideal for the position. For the two years that Idris Stokes was the deputy, our management team which included our counsellor, Richard Henry, achieved many of our objectives. The Board allowed me a free hand since they liked many of the changes and improvements I proposed but, with the exception of the people I have mentioned, I felt quite unsupported.

For the first three months, the management of the project continued as before with Mrs Brown being the key person in charge of childcare. This gave me the time to observe and plan changes I felt were necessary for a more child-centred approach. At the first childcare staff meeting I was met with a wall of silence; the resentment could be cut with a knife. From what Mrs Brown said to them I realised that the hostility was not personal but a show of loyalty to the last director. For most of that year the recurring antipathy to change was expressed in the words, "That's not how we used to do to it."

Two incidents illustrate the resistance of staff members who in time became most reliable. Miss Tavares, the supervisor of Tegwyn, our special unit for the severely mentally and physically challenged, had managed it with minimal supervision. We had to convince her that supervision was for support and that working as a team should not be seen as interference. Not long after I took up the position, she wanted me to instantly dismiss a member of staff whom she considered lazy. When I suggested that the worker should be warned and her work structured to give her at least a month to begin to show improvement, Miss Tavares retorted, "That's not how we did it with the last director."

"Well, let's try it this way and see if she improves. Staff turnover is not good for the children."

"Miss," she said, sighing heavily, "I can't work with that woman."

"I understand your frustration, but there are procedures that we need to follow."

"Miss, you don't know how difficult it is . . ." I listened to her, hoping that she would work the annoyance out of her system and we could get on with the proper procedures. Then, to my surprise, she threw down the gauntlet. ". . . . If that woman stays, I go."

"Oh dear," I tut-tutted and paused for effect. "You know how much I appreciate and respect you but it would be wrong to sack someone without a warning. If you can't accept that then I will be sorry to see you go. Do think about it. I hope we can come to the right decision." I stood up and quickly opened the door indicating an end to the discussion.

`I was relieved that she stayed. It would have been difficult to replace her. Miss T, as we affectionately called her, was one of the most dedicated persons at

JNCH. She could not have cared more for those children if they had been her relatives. The unit was spotless, the children were clean and staff followed her lead, hugging, kissing and talking with the children, many of whom could not respond verbally but their eyes showed their appreciation. I managed to get Miss T a secondment to visit two NCH projects in England as part of her training to widen her knowledge and facilitate the changes needed to improve the quality of service we provided.

The other incident occurred when I started marketing our baked products to raise funds. Miss Francis was one of the housemothers whose work was exemplary, however, when she was asked to help to sell our baked products in the market she refused point blank. She told the deputy that she had not been employed to sell in the market but to care for the children. Selling baked products was not part of her job description, but leading from the front I had gone with two of the children and a housemother to start the ball rolling in this fundraising effort and Miss Francis had been asked by the deputy to relieve me. The situation was resolved when a black British volunteer offered her services. I later discovered that selling was seen as beneath the dignity of a housemother in the hierarchy of jobs in Jamaica! Over and over again I had to lead from the front, in order to show staff that we all had to multi-task if we were to maximise our funds and that no job was menial if done in the interest of our young and vulnerable charges.

I did not like the regimental approach that I found in operation at the Home. Wanting staff to take on a more parental role in the units on the main block, I suggested that we pilot this and that, if it did not work, we would return to the old way. The system meant that instead of having two shifts daily, the housemother spent ten days on site over a fortnight, with four days off. A relief housemother took over for those four days. Each housemother had time to herself in the hours that the children were at school. They were given more say in managing their unit and making it homely. It took ages to get the system to operate effectively and to get staff to participate fully in meetings when their children's welfare was being discussed internally or with outside agencies. In time some staff, with the training we provided, became excellent housemothers and were quite vociferous too! It was Miss Coke who invited members of the Rotary Club to visit the Home when they attended a service at Hope United Church. This led to the club becoming a friend of the Home.

I faced a mutiny when I banned corporal punishment. In my first three months I was horrified to see housemothers with straps in their pockets, ready at a moment's notice to flog the children for all kinds of misdemeanours. When I voiced my disapproval in a staff meeting, pointing out that there were other methods of punishment that we should try, I was told that "if you spare the rod, you spoil the child". In the opinion of the staff, the other options were soft and would encourage the children to run riot. The staff proved their point by being half-hearted in their approach, wanting the new system to fail. For a while the children would run to senior staff with complaints or we would hear threats hurled at the housemothers, "I going to tell say you hit me!" The children even told the teachers in school that they should not be beaten. The management team had to work hard to convince the children that in order to earn the right not to be beaten they must take responsibility for their actions and behave well. Mr Henry instituted a reward system to encourage good behaviour. Extra privileges and/or extra pocket money could be earned for good behaviour. I realised that the change was too rapid and I had to backtrack a little. Our team agreed to keep the no corporal punishment ban in place for the over-13s and permitted only the Director or Deputy Director to administer corporal punishment. It was a compromise until the children showed a more responsible attitude. I was then faced with a further dilemma, hitting a child was anathema to me and the few times I was called upon to do it, I suffered psychologically. Idris Stokes, as Deputy, suffered likewise. Not even the support of Tom White, the Chief Executive Officer of NCH Action for Children in London made it any easier and we quickly moved back to our no corporal punishment policy.

'Poor things that nobody wants' was the way the public tended to see our children. The prevailing feeling among the children was one of shame and embarrassment at living in a home. In my first year we worked hard at improving their self-image. We made sure they were beautifully dressed for school, provided them with all their text books and encouraged them to participate in activities outside the Home. They were encouraged to have their friends visit them. Gradually, they grew quite proud of their pleasant living areas when some of these friends declared that our Home was much more comfortable than theirs. We began to see a change in the children's attitude to the place they called home and that was wonderful!

It was heart-warming to see how generous some individuals and groups were. They brought gifts and sometimes organised treats for the children. As part of their social development, I encouraged the children to see such visitors as their friends, to talk with them and make them feel welcome. We often asked guests to share in our evening devotion. They were impressed when several hands would shoot up when we called on someone to thank the guests. Children who were slow learners were not excluded and it was pleasing to hear one of them deliver thanks using the format they had heard others employ. On Carl's first attempt, the staff's faces showed their anxiety. He was very small for his age but he made up for this with his big boy's hoarse voice and cocky manner. Holding his big head high, hands in pockets, he whistled as he sauntered about the campus making sure that the younger children knew he was 'big' and not one of them. But the staff's anxiety changed to beams and applause as Carl said, "On de be'alf of de staff an' children of de Jamaican National Children Home, t'ank you fi de giffs dem." Not standard English, but clearly understood by our guests.

The children at JNCH were like children anywhere: the good, the naughty, the likeable, the disagreeable and the downright difficult. Some were characters never to be forgotten. With the exception of Leaton Bennett, I have not used their real names. Carl was always on the fringe when there was trouble, always pleading his innocence, "Miss, Miss, mek me tell you the trut'! A neva me!" It took us a whole year to cure him from running to the car park to beg as soon as a car pulled in. He was infuriating but so endearing.

Don was fifteen when I arrived; he had beautiful white teeth and a radiant smile. One day as he was mending the bike we had, I greeted him, "Hello, Don. I see you're busy."

"Afternoon, Miss." Then his voice took on a begging tone, "Miss, de bike no good. We need a new one fi de children dem."

"Well, we'll have to see what can be done. Any ideas on how we can raise the money to buy one?" I expected washing cars or some such activity as an answer.

"Miss, you can send to England, beg dem two bicycle!"

"Don, we can ask for help for food and clothes but surely not for bikes. If the children want bikes then we all have to work for the money. Think about what you can do and let me know." That was not the answer he expected. His face showed utter amazement. After the shock subsided with a shrug he returned to mending the bike. Sadly, the children at JNCH also thought that whatever they needed could be got from England and it took some time to change this.

Belle was a born sportswoman; she played football and when she was 13, had been to England on a football trip. She was a Special Needs 16-year-old and her memory of the trip was vague except that she liked fish and chips and it was "col' you know Miss." The first day I moved into the Director's house I was surprised when I opened my front door to find Belle sitting on the pouffe watching television.

"Oh! Hello, Belle, what are you doing here?"

"Watching the telly, Miss."

"I see. But there's a telly in your unit. Why aren't you watching it there?"

"But, Miss, I always watch the telly here." I had to explain to her that this was my special place to rest after work and that I sometimes did not want to have the television on. I then gave her a little sweet treat before turning off the television and sending her back to her unit. Mrs Brown confirmed that Belle had indeed been given this special privilege, so to stop her coming to my house I gave her the role of telly monitor on her unit. Her duty was to help the housemother by supervising the younger children when it was television time.

Dealing with Mary was a nightmare. Her story was particularly disturbing. Ten-year-old Mary had been sexually abused by her father's friends and so badly beaten by her father that neighbours reported him to the police and she was put into care. Our counsellor began working with her as soon as he was appointed, a few months after my arrival. He referred her case to Dr Vaughan, a child specialist at the university, and we tried to give Mary the support she needed with our limited resources. One day I was with the store-woman when I heard a child screaming.

"Rape! Rape! *Dem a rape me* . . . Lawd God help me! Lawd! Lawd! Whoaeee!" Frightened, we both ran out and saw Mary running around the yard pursued by her housemother who was desperately trying to catch her and was pleading, "Mary, please! Mary! Mary!" But to no avail.

"Mary, Stop that now!" I called out sternly. She stopped. I walked over to her. "What's the matter?" I asked gently, as she was obviously upset. I got no reply. As the children around began to troop into the yard, gaping, I shooed them away and, taking her hand, led her upstairs to the Deputy's office. She held my hand tightly and would not let go. I finally coaxed her to talk to the Deputy who was an experienced counsellor and had worked in the area of child protection in England.

About half-an-hour later, the secretary rang me to tell me that a policeman was in the office wanting to see me. I was puzzled when she whispered that he said it was about a serious matter. She ushered him in to my office a few minutes later.

"Good afternoon, Officer. How can I help you?"

"Good day to you, Madam. It has been reported to us that a girl was heard screaming for rape," he said in his most officious voice.

"Oh dear, yes. We have a very disturbed little girl here. She was screaming earlier on."

"Are you saying this child was not being mo-lest-ed."

"Yes, of course, I am."

"Can I see her? . . ." Seeing my look of disapproval he ended sheepishly," For the record, you understand?"

Mary would not let go of me when she came into the room and saw the police officer. I assured her that everything was alright and that she should answer the questions. The officer, satisfied that she was not at risk, left. Later that evening I overheard the houseparents voicing their concern that Mary's behaviour had frightened them and it would certainly give the Home a bad name.

But even worse was in store. Such scenes were repeated; Mary would scream that she was being raped, howl obscenities at staff and run around like a banshee. After a while she began to throw bricks, smashing glass panes in doors and windows and putting the other children and staff at risk. It became so bad that we had to ask Children's Services to find an alternative accommodation for her. It was one of the hardest decisions I had to make but my colleagues and I felt there was no other choice although we were aware that her future would probably be bleaker elsewhere.

In the first year after her transfer, she ran away three times and each time, picked up by the police, she would tell them that she lived at JNCH. When they brought her to us she was as quiet as a lamb sitting in the police car, staring at me with her big, black eyes. When I hugged her and told her to stop running away, she begged, "Miss, I wa' come back." It was like a dagger piercing my heart; I felt I had let down this helpless child. It is impossible for me to remember Mary without pain and a sense of failure.

We did have our successes that made us proud. June who is deaf and dumb and was abandoned by her family is now a hairdresser and, with her business acumen, I am sure will be most successful at what she does. She created the most beautiful plaited hair designs and was our hairdresser for plaiting. We were so pleased with the way she did our hair that we all recommended her to other people from the churches we attended. Her clientele grew and included students from the two universities nearby who did community placements with us. We were impressed that, encouraged by us to save, she had a tidy sum in her bank account before she left us!

In September 2001, at Idris Stokes' fiftieth birthday party, I met one of our old boys, Leaton Bennett. He introduced me to his girlfriend, a young English woman teaching in Jamaica. Leaton was then a tall, handsome young man with a bright future before him. We danced and before I left he promised to give me flying lessons on my return to Jamaica the following year.

Leaton had been a bright boy who was attending one of the prestigious high schools when his fostering with a doctor's family broke down and he came to us. We were surprised at how quickly he adjusted to life in the Home. Before his fostering he had spent several years in another children's home after the death of his father who was a policeman and this may have been the reason for his easy assimilation into JNCH. He was one of the older, more responsible children who helped in the office, answering the telephone and doing other basic tasks. He was very articulate and sensitive. Once, when he was fifteen, I asked him to participate in the official welcome at one of our benefit concerts at the Little Theatre. I spoke very briefly and then introduced him. He held my hand because he was a little nervous at first but his address was eloquent. His speech about the Home and what we provided, brought thunderous applause. I was very proud of him.

Leaton had wanted to be a doctor like his foster father but when he did not get the grades required, instead of repeating his examinations, he decided on a career change. Fact is stranger than fiction and help came from an unexpected source. A Jamaican woman living in New York walked into the Kingston office of Children's Services and offered a sum of money to help with the education of a bright but indigent child. The Children's Officer suggested Leaton and he left us to train as a private pilot. In 2000 he became a training instructor. Imagine the shock I had in December 2001 when I received news that he had died in a terrible accident when a student had crash-landed and Leaton had been trapped in the ensuing blaze. Both Idris and I were in England and could not attend his funeral but his girlfriend and I have kept in touch.

I am afraid I cannot be philosophical about the condition of the children and young people at Tegwyn, our unit for the severely mentally and physically challenged. I think life has dealt them a very cruel blow. And yet there were some characters there that showed a spirited tenacity for life and hold a special place in my heart. When I remember Tegwyn, Pearl comes to mind. She is severely physically challenged and is also mute but her eyes sparkle when she is happy. Whenever she saw me she would make gurgling noises and jerk about in anticipated pleasure until I hugged her and chatted with her a while. As part of the improved services at Tegwyn, Pearl was taught to use her feet as hands and she grew quite skilled at it. Her vivacity led to her photo being used to introduce a television community programme. I did a deal with the station when they suggested using her; I asked them to attach the JNCH logo to her photograph in order to promote awareness of the Home's existence. This publicity has made JNCH known nationwide.

We were devastated by Queenie's death. She was a joy to have around. Her Children's Officer had asked us to accommodate her in our 'independent unit' for young people preparing to leave care because of her recent heart operation and our proximity to the hospital that she had to attend regularly. She was seventeen and in the year with us had finished her machinist course and worked in a dress shop in the plaza nearby. She and my granddaughter, Leeanne, had had similar heart valve replacement operations and had become friends.

Queenie was with a group from the home on their way to church when she had a massive heart attack. One of the housemothers rang the Home and Mrs Stokes drove Queenie to the University of the West Indies hospital. Mrs Stokes rang me quite concerned that, although Queenie was having convulsions, she had not been seen by a doctor. I got on the telephone to the chairperson who, through her contact with the hospital, was able to get a doctor to attend to Queenie. After a day the doctors told us that she needed a scan for them to identify the best treatment for her. In this large teaching hospital there was not a single working machine! I made the decision to get the scan done at a private hospital even if I had to pay for it myself. When the arrangements were made with the private hospital I was told that a public ambulance was not available and I had to arrange for a private one. On arrival at the private hospital I heard that the scans could not be done until the money was paid. I had contacted Children's Services for financial assistance to cover the cost but the director was still awaiting a reply from the government department that dealt with such cases. With time against us, I appealed to Mrs McGhie who was very understanding, and we signed the cheque to pay for the scan, not even knowing if the appropriate government ministry would refund the amount. Eleanor, my English college friend, whom I had encouraged to do a stint of voluntary work with us, was a tower of strength at the time. She accompanied me and calmed me down as I lost patience with the doctors and as I rushed between the home and hospitals to sort out things.

Back at the private hospital, this girl's emergency case could not be started in the scanning room until the cheque was cleared by the bank! Queenie died as the scans were being done. Eleanor and I knew something was wrong when we saw several staff members rushing about and a nurse approaching us. She showed me into a doctor's office and he gently broke the news. He claimed that she could not have been saved. Gulping back my tears, I told him what I thought of their heartless system in which money was more important than saving the life of a child. He defended their stance, pointing out that the service could not be maintained without money. As we were leaving, a telephone call came through for me from the ministry saying the government would meet the cost; all too late. The private hospital returned our cheque. The next day I had a visit from one of the local hospital doctors. He commiserated with me, repeated that nothing could have saved Queenie, then went on to say how fortunate she had been to have people like us who would find the money for private treatment whereas many equally needy cases were not so lucky. *Was this meant to make me feel better or to stop me from publicising the inhumane system at work?*

On reflection I expected staff to work with the zeal that drove me and this was unfair as, after all, to most of them it was merely a way of earning a living. I sought help for JNCH from all quarters. I cajoled my daughter, Amanda, to do her B.A. placement at JNCH, reorganising and computerising the office. Miss Coke, a housemother, would complain that I was working my daughter too hard, "Lawd, Miss, it's not fair. That poor chile still in the office and is 9.00 o'clock! Everybody else gone home from 6 o'clock."

One year, I found out that the accounts officer was lending money to staff without permission and he left before I could tackle him about the discrepancies in the accounts. I had to work an 18-hour day over a couple of weeks in order to prepare the accounts for the auditor. Mrs Stokes took pity on me and volunteered to help. The volunteers from England, Eleanor Gunn, a primary school teacher, and Rosie Powell, one of the first black British volunteers and a social worker, worked longer hours than the paid staff because of their commitment to the project. The local teacher volunteer, Mrs Rudder, not only taught supplementary sessions but also organised outside activities for the children. Miss Thompson, the part-time supervisor, undertook many extra duties. These people along with Mr Henry, Miss T, Miss Francis and Miss Coke gave unstintingly to the home and helped to ensure the success of some of the projects we undertook. Volunteers, such as the white wife and husband from the USA, who came for a month each year as part of their Christian outreach work, heartened me with their commitment.

I was grateful to our many donors who were always pleased to receive a letter from me giving them an update on the Home, so I began a quarterly newsletter that I called *Home News*. Its aim was to increase the feeling of partnership/ownership of JNCH. It proved to be popular both in Jamaica and in England.

Convinced that improvements could be made, I undertook to effect changes in raising the educational standard of the children and creating viable and sustainable cash projects. Some of them are still in operation, while others were short-lived after I left. The fund-raising to get them in place is, in itself, another story.

Concerned at the inadequate educational level of the majority of the children, I decided to introduce a similar system of supplementary education to that in which I had been involved in England. I combined the supplementary classes with homework sessions in which every child had to participate. This project went through a lot of teething problems because of a lack of staff and volunteers with the appropriate knowledge and skills to ensure continuity. Unable to maintain the level of my initial input, I asked the Board to appoint a teacher to head this project and I recruited student volunteers from the two universities close by to ensure adequate support for the children. Some of our children were very bright and we were able to get donors, among them local and overseas sponsors, to assist with school expenses. This is how we developed a relationship with a women's peace group in Japan and a group of Methodist ministers' wives in England.

I obtained a grant from the Jamaican Social Investment Fund, money owed by the Jamaican government to the government of the USA, which the latter in turn donate to community projects. The grant allowed us to refurbish the home, add four classrooms to the school and create a snoezlem, a special playroom, for Tegwyn. I wanted the residents at Tegwyn to get as much stimulation as possible and a group of University of the West Indies students in the Faculty of Education paid for the construction of a small pool for basic hydrotherapy while the Rotary Club built an additional covered play area for wheelchair-bound children to begin to enjoy some stimulating activities.

We put several schemes in place to train our older able-bodied children to live more independently and for our younger ones to earn their pocket money.

The creation of the Bakery Project, the Garden Project and the Chicken Project provided the home with food and also sold goods to the public to augment our funds. Rearranging the Independent Unit allowed for spare rooms in a self-contained block to be rented to university students, thereby providing us with a regular income.

Our bakery made hard-dough bread, Danish pastry, sugar buns, rock cakes and bulla cake. When I took up my post, the bakery provided only for the home and the baker had a lot of free time. I pointed out to him the bakery's potential to earn money for the Home and sweetened his labour by supporting his application to the Board for a loan for a course to improve his skills. At the same time, thanks to general fund-raising and gifts from the British High Commission and the students of the University of the West Indies the Home was able to buy the necessary equipment for a small commercial operation. As soon as the baker finished his course he wanted the kind of pay rise we could not afford. Then I discovered that he was fiddling. He left, knowing he was leaving us in the lurch and with an unpaid loan! Of course, the success of the bakery project depended on our having a competent baker and when one could not be found, it affected our production and income but we continued to make a fairly good profit from it.

With a small grant from the USA through Food for the Poor I started our Chicken Project consisting of layers and broilers. One of the duties of the younger children was to collect the eggs each morning. Every three weeks the older ones had to help with getting the broilers ready for sale. Work started at daybreak, around 6:00a.m., in order to be done before the midday heat. Some children gathered wood for the fire which kept a big pot of water heated. The gardener and one staff member killed the chickens and immersed them in the hot water before passing them to the team of children and staff for plucking. After this, another group of children with one staff member cleaned and bagged the chickens that were then ferried to the storeroom for weighing and freezing. The children worked in small groups supervised by their house-parents and a shift system ensured that no child worked longer than a couple of hours. To show our appreciation each child received an extra big breakfast and an ice cream at lunch time.

This work did not interfere with schoolwork, but a few teenagers, like teenagers the world over, sometimes did not want to help and one complained to her Children's Officer. It was frustrating dealing with this Children's Officer/Social Worker whose opinion was that the children should not be asked to help with the selling of baked goods and preparing chicken for sale. I saw this as getting the children to help as part of a family. The system in operation was that house-mothers and their children organised their roster to help with these jobs.

I took the matter to the Director of Children's Services who, as a country boy had helped his family with chores. He agreed with me that we were a developing country with limited resources and, as his service could not adequately meet the expenses for the children we had, it was not unreasonable to expect the children to help.

One day, it was brought to my attention that the gardener was often drunk and after lunch slept until 3:00p.m., when he finished his workday! It was a joke among the older children who often teased him in a sly manner. In a meeting where I impressed on staff our changing situation, I got the driver to agree to do the bulk of his work in the mornings and help the gardener at least three afternoons in order to increase the production of our cash crops - calalloo, pakchoy and runner beans. The Rural Agricultural Development Agency (RADA) provided advice and support, but the gardener returned to his long after-lunch slumber on the days the driver was not around. This remained a well-kept secret for many months as one or other of the housemothers would wake him, berate him and get him back to work. He was a quiet, mouse-like man and they felt sorry for him and did not want him to be dismissed. Then one day I wanted to speak with him and a couple of boys led me to him, sleeping blissfully and filling the air about him with his snores and the smell of rum. Sadly, the formal warnings did not have the desired effect; he had to go.

May is designated Child Month in Jamaica and one of the annual events sponsored by the Child Month organisation honours children and celebrates their talents. It is a voluntary organisation working to raise awareness of issues affecting children. I became involved in 'Child Month' as a representative of JNCH. I was horrified at the abusive and frightening situations in which some children lived. I was also humbled by the quiet courage and determination of many of them to succeed educationally, even as they dodged bullets in warring communities to get to school. One issue of grave concern to the committee was that violence perpetuated by adults was impacting on the young who copied their elders. In an effort to arrest this, Child Month focussed on conflict resolution over a period of two years. We held workshops at which the youngsters were given a conflict situation and asked to resolve it through role play. In discussing the issues, participants identified key points in resolving conflict. A video of the workshops was made and I wrote an accompanying booklet, both of which were made available to schools and youth organisations.

At JNCH, there were many challenges but one in particular made me so angry that my response to it upset a couple of Board members. The chair backed me and the result vindicated the action I took. One afternoon I was asked to see a couple from the Water Board. They were ushered into my office and, after introductions, the young woman said they were doing some checks and needed to turn off the water. I agreed and when they returned I thought they were about to tell me something needed replacing. The young woman cockily produced a bill from her briefcase and placed it on the table asking why it had not been paid.

"We don't pay water bills," I informed her, quite nonplussed. She looked at me in disbelief.

"You owe for one year's water. How are you going to pay us?"

"Sorry. You must have the wrong information. I have been here for two years and I have never received a water bill."

"Our records show that you have not paid the water bills sent to you over the last year. How do you intend to pay them?"

"Look," I said trying to be reasonable, "there is obviously some misunderstanding here. I have not received any bills. Where did you send them?"

She consulted her paper. "To Hope Gardens."

"That's it!" It was clear what had happened. "We have never seen the bills. I will contact their office and find out what has happened. I have no idea what the arrangements are about the water and will get on to it straight away to clear this up."

"That's not good enough." She replied in a steely voice. "We're not turning on the water until the bills are paid."

"Listen, I understand from what you have said that there is a payment outstanding and I will get things sorted so that you can be paid, but surely you would not lock off the water from a home looking after children, some of whom have severe disabilities?" I expected understanding.

"Why can't you pay a part of the bill now?"

"How can I?" I reasoned. "We have a budget and there is no money for water so I have to contact Hope Gardens on the matter. If we are responsible, I assure you the Board of Trustees will organise payment."

"Sorry, that's not good enough. The water is off until a payment is made." She was quite uncompromising and nothing I could say shifted her from that position.

"Well, if that's your attitude, I have nothing else to say except to remind you that we have eighty-six children living here and one hundred and thirty at the school. Are you really saying you will deprive them of water?"

"That's your concern. Mine is that you pay for the water you've used."

"In that case, good afternoon," I showed them out, incensed at her attitude. I telephoned the Water Board but no-one was available at a high enough level to have the water turned on. I left a message at the University for my chairperson and contacted the Hope Gardens office, but no-one there was available to answer my query. My next call was to the Director of Children's Services who informed me that the government was not responsible for the utility bills of private homes such as JNCH.

I called a staff meeting. Miss Coke was outraged, "So, Miss, how they expect the children to manage? Them out of order, man! Just 'cause we're a home, that's why they're treating us so." I did not agree with our taking on second-class citizen status but I certainly saw her point. As we arranged for the children to collect water from our tank at Tegwyn and for water to be boiled for drinking, an idea came to me. I shared it with the staff and, after some hesitation, we decided to take action against the Water Board. We were going to protest.

That evening we had early devotion and I told the children what had happened and that it was unjustified, so some of us were going to protest outside the Water Board's office until they turned on our water. Those children not at school were invited to join. That evening, staff and older children made banners from flipchart sheets mounted on slender branches collected from our garden.

The next morning our minibus did two trips transporting the protesters to the Water Board's office in the heart of the commercial district of New Kingston. There were thirty of us walking two abreast on the pavement, up and down in front of their building. My Deputy and I led the march; immediately behind us were six children in wheelchairs and the other children and staff brought up the rear. Our banners read, "Give Us Back Our Water!" and "Jamaica National Children's Home". We chanted in unison, "Give us back our water. Now! Now! Now!" We started at 8:00a.m. when people were on their way to work. Our aim was to garner maximum public support. As passers-by began to gather, a man's voice came from across the road, "*Gi' de pickney dem back dem water*!"

Up rolled the CVM television car and out jumped a reporter. I had contacted the TV's newsroom the night before and the reporter had rightly said he needed to talk first with the Water Board to hear their side before coming to the home to cover the story. At that point I had told him we were going to take action the next day. As the reporter was asking me the reason for our demonstration, the employees of the Water Board were filtering in. I spoke of our grievance and the high-handed manner of the Water Board representative. Just then a senior staff member of the Water Board came up and invited me in to discuss the matter with the General Manager, adding that he would like us, in the meantime, to call off the protest. I told him that the group would stand quietly outside and await the outcome. My deputy and I were ushered into the office and offered coffee. I was glad the meeting was brief as I was conscious of the children waiting outside. The two senior managers from the Water Board understood our predicament and agreed that the water would be turned on immediately.

What transpired was that Hope Garden's management had decided to stop paying the water bills for the School for the Deaf and for us, but had not informed us of this. The Water Board accepted that we would pay the outstanding amount in instalments beginning as soon as the Board was apprised of the matter in an emergency meeting. We went home to water.

At that evening's devotion I said what we had done was a lesson to all, we must stand up for our rights. In the days that followed we received many calls from well-wishers applauding our action.

I certainly found myself on a steep learning curve in those first years of my return to Jamaica. I was unaware of some of the road hazards that others accepted as commonplace and I was totally fazed by one in particular. Rosie Powell, one of our volunteers, had arranged a trip for the older able-bodied children to visit her father's farm in Christiana. She drove there and we had a wonderful day gathering the produce we used for our lunch and tea, then some of us swam in the river while others explored the woodland. As I was driving back to Kingston, we were caught in a traffic hold-up caused by an accident. A cow crossing the road ahead of us was hit by a car coming from the opposite direction. The poor cow was dazed and, stumbling down the centre of the road, fell against our minibus that was stationary. It was not something we could have avoided, it was just our bad luck. Grabbing hold of the cow's rope, I dragged it into the little shopping square and tried to find out who the owner was from the gathering crowd. No-one seemed to own the cow! A man surreptitiously whispered that no-one was going to own up because it would mean paying for the damage to the minibus. I tried to bluff, *"Well, as de cow no belong to nobady, I gwine take it and butcher it fo' me van."* I glared at the blank staring faces but there was not a flicker that would give a clue to the owner. Frustrated, I let go of the rope and stalked off in disgust. I drove to the nearest police station and lodged a report. When I had to report the matter to the Board, I thought it would be an unusual incident. But no! I was told it was a common occurrence and that we were fortunate the accident had not been more serious.

In the midst of our hectic life some moments evoked a smile. The Association of Friends raised funds for the Home and their biggest fund-raising event was a tea party held on the lawns of the home in May. Mrs Rattray, the wife of a retired Chief Justice, was one of the chief organisers and several local dignitaries attended, among them the wife of the Governor General. The deputy and I were usually rushed off our feet to ensure that everything was in place and then I had to sit at the head table smiling and welcoming guests even as I kept a sharp eye on the children who were helping to serve. One year I did not have a deputy. It was very hectic and, having responded to a mini-crisis in the kitchen, I quickly returned to the guests. I was amused by the whispered remark of the Governor General's wife, "I can tell you've lived in London; you move so quickly." That is how Jamaicans at home see us - always rushing around like mad people. Some tease that for us to return to normality our heads need defrosting! We, as returned residents, make the opposite comment; we feel that the locals move too slowly and are far too laid back, except when making money for themselves, of course!

In the tropics the day starts early. For the staff, the day at JNCH started at about 5:30a.m. because the children on the morning shift at school had to leave by 7:00a.m. It is customary for entire households to be up by then. I enjoyed an hour's brisk walk in the tranquillity and coolness of Hope Gardens at that time in the morning and sometimes one of the volunteers or a tenant would join me.

After a busy day, if we were free from duties, Eleanor, Idris and I would walk up the dirt track to the Papine main road and repair to the restaurant/pub, 'On Top'. One evening as Eleanor and I set out from the Home, the three dogs began to follow us. Sheba, a part German shepherd, had adopted me as soon as I arrived at JNCH and followed me around, but she knew she should not come beyond the front gate and the other dogs followed her example. So, when I shut the gate we thought the dogs had stayed in. Imagine our surprise when, on emerging from the pub, we found the dogs there barking their welcome. We tried to quieten them but to no avail, so we set off with three barking dogs walking in single file behind us. In typical Jamaican fashion, people pointed and laughed as we went by. We couldn't help laughing too although the situation was a bit embarrassing. We walked briskly to get off the main road and away from the stares but our dog chorus accompanied us all the way home.

My respite from work was usually a trip to the beautiful north coast on weekends, often to stay with Dolly Beecher, my friend from Nottingham. Travelling through the mountain to Dolly's was a nail-biting experience; I am convinced some Jamaican drivers think they can see around blind bends. However, as I crested the hill into St Ann's Bay or Chalky Hill, my spirit lifted and the tension melted as my eyes drank in the blue and turquoise water of the Caribbean Sea below. If it was late afternoon, I would stop at Priory and have a swim followed by a rum and coke at the beach bar before starting the final ten miles to Runaway Bay. If all I could afford was a day or an afternoon off, I would head for the home of my friend, Olga, in nearby St Thomas. My wonderful friends, knowing how hard I worked, spoiled me when I was off duty. Along with my cousin, Joe, and his wife they were my support network.

Time Up

In 1997 I lost my father. He was in hospital and very poorly. Instead of going immediately to be with my father, I allowed work to dictate my life. It so happened that a youth brass band that supported NCH in England had arranged to come to Jamaica and do three benefit concerts for us after their USA tour. Our contribution was to provide them with accommodation and meals. We had recently appointed a second deputy but she had been ill and looked under the weather even on her return to work. I, therefore, thought it unreasonable to ask her to accompany the band across the island for their first concert. I was also very much aware that the two deputies would have to take on a lot of my workload in day-to-day management as we had been unable to find an acting-director. So, before flying to England I helped to settle our guests with their host families and accompanied them on their first concert in Montego Bay.

I lost three precious days and when I finally arrived at the hospital in Birmingham directly from the airport, my father recognised me for only a few brief moments. It was as if he was waiting for me to say goodbye. As he whispered my name I held his hand and he slipped into a drug-induced sleep. I sat with him for a while until a nurse, seeing how tired I was, suggested that I should go home and come back later when he would be awake. When I returned in the evening with Lillian, and our stepmother he was no longer speaking but managed to squeeze our hands as we held his. We left when he went off to sleep again.

The telephone rang early the next morning with the news we were all dreading. Whatever issues I had with my father, I had resolved over the years. He had not been a good father to his children from his first marriage but, as he grew older, he had changed into a more responsible person, becoming a good husband to his second wife and a doting father to my half-brother, Andrew. He had also embraced Christianity and was an active church member. Lillian was very close to him and she took his death very hard. What surprised me was how long I grieved.

At the funeral I had contribution envelopes for people to support JNCH because, even in my moment of grief, I did not stop thinking about the project. After the funeral I decided to stay in England for a rest from the stress and strain of JNCH. I took my annual leave.

I returned to Jamaica as the New Year came in. I had resolved to work for another fifteen months, giving the Board time to find a new director for March 1999. The usual tardiness of the Board left me no other option but to undertake most of the work to find a director myself. I was able to effect a handover in July, leaving the JNCH in a healthier financial state than I had found it. The investment fund had quadrupled through careful housekeeping, as we had maximised on gifts in kind, never buying when we could get a donation and always fund-raising. In the process I earned the name 'Professional Beggar'. Miss Coke and Miss T were also excellent fund-raisers.

The staff, children and Board gave me a memorable send off. At the farewell party organised by the staff and children, the most touching moment was when June and Dave ended with, "We love you because you love and care for us" in sign language, for they are both deaf and June is also mute. Mrs Rudder organised a farewell African drumming session and the Board held a farewell function at the Terra Nova Hotel. I was a little embarrassed with my successor in the gathering when the Chair said in her conclusion, "She'll be a hard act to follow." I was amazed that the same staff members who had given me a hard time at the beginning of my tenure, paid me such wonderful compliments. Was this a Jamaican thing, I wondered?

What is important is that they know how much I appreciated their efforts. They are the unsung heroines of Jamaica.

Losing A Part Of My Soul

My mother was a matriarch who wielded a lot of emotional power over her family but was quite troubled about her youngest son whom she rarely saw and whose lifestyle she did not like. I am sure all this eventually affected her mental health. Although her children were not close as a family, she did her best to keep us together and we often met at her home.

My relationship with my mother grew into one of companionship as she neared retirement. When she died I lost a part of my anchor. We had shared some bad and some good times. She had always been there for me through the rough patches when I became a single parent. When she retired in 1983 I made it my duty to stop by nearly every day on my way home from school to be sure she was alright. A meal would be waiting for me and I would be pampered. It was clear that my mother was lonely and I encouraged her to come with me to community meetings. She attended the annual African Liberation Day celebrations and even marched with two of my school colleagues and me in the big London event celebrating Nelson Mandela's seventieth birthday and demanding his release from prison. She welcomed not only my friends but strangers from all over the world that I took to her home for meals or to stay over, as my own home was out of town. We grew closer when the children left home and whenever acquaintances and friends saw me, they expected to see my mother too.

My mother was very fashionable. One could see the gleam of satisfaction in her eyes when she was complimented about her appearance. I think I was the cause of her giving up on hairdressers. I treated her to a perm when she was in her mid-sixties and she never forgave me for taking her to that *"damn fool woman who bun up me head"*. The product was obviously wrong for my mother's hair and it fell out in chunks! The hairdresser offered her free treatment, but after one session my mother refused to go back. She changed her hairstyle to a low cut natural, a boy's look that she kept for the rest of her life.

Before she retired she came with the girls and me on her first continental holiday. It was the summer of 1980 and we went on a three-week trip to Europe. I asked her to come along as my son was doing his apprenticeship and unable to get time off. It was a driving holiday. We travelled from Nottingham to Folkestone, took the ferry to Le Havre, continued through France, down to La Linea in Spain and back up through Andorra to France only to find that we had to go into Belgium to get home, because of a strike at the French port. In Spain we wanted to go across to Gibraltar for a day but Britain and Spain were squabbling over Gibraltar and the Spanish authorities would not allow British passport holders across. We were disgruntled. As we returned to Malaga, a kind of drama began in the car. My mother was singing the chorus of a song popular in her youth:

Solid as a rock
Solid as the rock of Gibraltar

But instead of saying Gibraltar she Jamaicanised it to Giberalta. One of the girls piped up, "Grandma, it's Gibraltar."

"So, is what I said?" she asked, and answered herself, "Giberalta."

"No, Grandma," the voice from behind insisted, "it's Gi-bral-tar."

My mother hissed her teeth in annoyance. "See my trial, Lord!" she invoked the Almighty and then with a venomous hiss, "Giberalta! Giberalta!"

Giggles erupted from the back and I had to intercede, "Okay, everyone, we need to find out where we are."

It was that very day that we stopped off at the beach in Torremelinos, an English tourist haven. Our quiet stroll was interrupted by a broad Northern accent exclaiming, *"A didna knoaw that darkies cum heer."* My mother bristled and said loudly, *"What a dyam facety brute!"* I could not let the speaker get away with it and added, "Some people are so ignorant. Here they are in a country once ruled by the 'darky' Moors when many English were no more than barbarians. Some people are really stupid!" Then we walked on.

The holiday was full of adventure; I remember hearing my mother whispering the Lord's Prayer as we crawled along the cliff road in search of a garage, our car having developed a serious mechanical problem with the axle.

My mother had her first stroke a few months after she retired. I was in the garden with my friend, Dorita, when the telephone rang. My mother had been at the local Jamaican Nurses' Association function when her friend, sitting next to her, had become aware that something was wrong. My mother was rushed to Queen's Medical Centre where Dorita and I saw her on a stretcher about to be transferred to City Hospital nearer her home. I held her limp hand and whispered soothing words of encouragement to her as we waited for the ambulance. I told her that she would be alright, that we loved her, that her family and friends were there for her and she should not be afraid because we knew she would be up and about in no time. But even as I spoke those words, I was beseeching divine help, "Oh God, help us! Do not forsake us."

At City Hospital, Dorita and I stayed with her until the nurse sent us home telling us that there would be no change for a while. We went to my sister, Lillian, to tell her the news and she informed all our other siblings. It was a long night without much sleep.

My mother's recovery was slow at first and we greeted every sign of improvement with thankfulness: the eyes opening; the hand clutching mine; the gurgling sounds and attempts to speak. Her pleading eyes reminded me of a helpless, wounded puppy. As she grew stronger she showed a lot of spunk, forcing her body to its limits as she pushed and crawled to the bathroom, sometimes banging her head, but never giving up. She began to learn to write with her left hand when the right side appeared lifeless and later forced her right hand to work as movement slowly returned to that side. The doctors were amazed at the speed of her recovery which they said was due mainly to her will-power. She was held up as an example to other stroke patients. After a while the only sign of my mother's stroke was a slight dragging of her right foot and a stammer when she became excited. Her triumph over her illness was for me a powerful lesson in survival.

When I moved to Sheffield in 1990 I asked her to come and share my home as we were now two women on our own. She did but never really left Nottingham, visiting weekly and shunning activities for retirees in Sheffield. When I moved to Jamaica in 1994 she did not want to come and returned to Nottingham which she considered her home. She visited me in Jamaica and complained that I was working too hard. She enjoyed her stay, visited friends of hers who had retired in Jamaica, and had some fun travelling around the island and enjoying the sea baths.

In 1999 I returned to England after retiring from JNCH. I noticed that my mother had, at 76, become a recluse, refusing even to go to the Caribbean Lunch Club although a pick-up service was provided. Lillian was concerned that our mother had grown very grumpy in old age. She had begun to accuse people of stealing and had once hit Lillian with her cane. Although she appeared to be functioning normally I soon realised that all was not well. My mother cooked me a welcome home meal; a delicious Jamaican dinner, with rice and peas we know we will never taste again and we fell back into our easy relationship when I visited daily, stayed over sometimes and took her on trips to see friends.

Then I began to notice some disturbing things. Within hours of tidying the flat it would be in disarray. Clothes would be flung on the floor or heaped on the bed as if she was searching for a lost object. Everyday she tearfully claimed that her money was missing. My search would reveal the money tucked away under the seat of the settee or in a bathroom cupboard or some such place. I needed no further evidence that something was seriously wrong when my mother got into a frenzy over missing money. At a family meeting we tried to get our mother to accept that she could no longer live on her own and that she should think about either going to Jamaica to live with me or moving into a sheltered scheme where someone would always be around. But no! She wanted to remain in her flat and would brook no interference in her business. Her anger exploded and she screamed that she was going to kill herself. Terrified, I rang the doctor, got her some sedatives and stayed with her that night, convinced that things were spinning out of control.

A social worker friend gave me the telephone number of a black psycho-geriatric consultant colleague to get some advice. He was most helpful and reassuring, outlining the procedure; the first step was to contact the family doctor for a referral so that my mother could be assessed. But, I found out a week later when I contacted the psycho-geriatric consultant at Queen's Medical Centre, that the doctor was tardy in processing the referral. I contacted the doctor who apologised and I asked him to fax the referral to save time. I felt sneaky seeking advice about my mother without her consent but I knew that telling her this would require the most careful handling. I made coffee for both of us and got into her bed sitting next to her.

"Mom."

"Mmm?"

"Mom, I was talking to someone who told me that now you're getting on, it is vitally important for you to have further checks because of your stroke . . ."

"But wasn't it you who went with me to the doctor the other day?" she interrupted. I knew what was coming next, a lecture that I was not a doctor.

"Yes. I know your doctor said your health was fine but he's not a stroke specialist. I rang the hospital and have got you an appointment. Dr Sheila Gibson will come to see you." I waited for the rebuke but none came. I had a sneaky suspicion that my mother knew that something was wrong but was too scared to talk about it. That day she gave me her long-service medal from Chilwell Ordinance Depot where she had worked for twenty-seven years mainly as a storewoman. When I asked her why she was doing this she said she wanted me to take care of it!

My mother asked to have the assessment done at Lillian's. Lillian and I huddled together in the kitchen, ears to the wall, trying to make out what was being said until the consultant called us in for the family discussion. For the first time I saw my mother as an old woman, frail, sitting with hands clasped tightly in her lap as the doctor explained to us that our mother was having mini-strokes and they would most likely continue, that they had affected the brain and that she was suffering from dementia for which there was no cure and no-one could forecast the rate of deterioration. She suggested that our mother attend the nearby day centre and move into a warden-aided scheme where she would still retain some measure of independence.

"Yes," our mother agreed, "I understand."

All over the world it is accepted that women look after the vulnerable in the family - the young, the old, the disabled and the sick. Annie, my youngest sister, was in France and Lillian and I became the caregivers. We moved our mother into a warden-aided flat, making it a very comfortable home.

I had to go back to Jamaica for three months and, on my return, relieved Lillian who was physically worn out. In the space of a few months our mother could no longer cook a meal or go out unsupervised. She was by no means easy to care for and bullied poor Lillian. I began to experience what it was like living with someone suffering from dementia. The bedroom, less than an hour after it had been tidied, looked as if it had been hit by a tornado. I found shoes in the oven and the kettle in the wardrobe. On a typical day my mother would refuse to dress herself and then when the doorbell rang to tell us the minibus had arrived to take her to the day centre, she would put on two pairs of trousers, a jacket without a blouse, a shoe and a boot. It was a constant struggle to get her dressed. She would also hide any key she got hold of and I had to keep the house keys on my person.

My mother's deterioration had accelerated alarmingly over a short time and her metamorphosis was complete. I hardly recognised this new person who occupied my mother's body. The consultant agreed with me that my mother could no longer cope in a warden-aided scheme and she would be better off coming with me to Jamaica for six months as I had to sort out some business there. We asked my mother if she would like a holiday in Jamaica. She agreed, which made things easier to organise. The time had come for our family to agree where my mother should live, with me in Jamaica or in a residential home in England. Those were the options.

In Jamaica I arranged home help for two days weekly to give me a break. During my mother's brief, lucid spells she was happy and I would hug her as we laughed about family incidents; but when she was testy she became uncommunicative, uncooperative and sometimes violent. Once she attacked me in the kitchen, leaving me scared and uncertain what she might do next. She had just finished breakfast when she went towards the cooker. I intercepted her as the soup for lunch was simmering. She gave me a mighty shove and was about to grab the lid of the soup pot.

"Mom, please don't!"

Her hand hovered above the pot. "Me hungry."

"Okay, I'll get you something." I stood in front of the cooker. This was a red rag to a bull. She was so quick she caught me off guard. She grabbed me by the collar and yanked me away from the cooker. I held her hand, trying to release it from my collar but she seemed to acquire extraordinary strength as she grappled with me. She rained blows on my head. "Stop! Stop it now!" I pleaded but she ignored my pleas. I had a hard time getting away from her; she rushed after me and finally slumped into a chair on the veranda. I ran to the neighbours, who were friends, for help. The husband went over to sit with my mother while his wife offered me coffee and comfort. When I returned half an hour later she was calm, holding her head slightly sideways as she listened to Winston. Her mode of communicating at such times was to nod her head or say, "Yes. I see."

I understood the reason she aimed her outbursts always at Lillian and me, never at outsiders. At the Carers' Group in England that I had attended for a couple of sessions, we were told that this was the norm, over and over again carers remarked at the anger vented on them by the dementia sufferer. Sometimes it was as though my mother was well aware of what she was doing. Once when she wanted to shower fully dressed, she struck out at the helper who was usually very good at cajoling her into doing things.

"Mom, it's Veta. "Why are you doing this to me?" The attack stopped and my mother reverted to being the sweet old lady.

"Sorry, darling, I thought you were Lee. Where is she?"

To lighten my fear, my friends and I sometimes laughed at the things that happened; my support network was my lifeline. Friends visited and brought my mom some happiness because she enjoyed their company and never slipped into that violent other world with visitors.

My last happy memory of my mother was Christmas 2000. My son, Stanley, his wife, Sally, and Baby Masai came to spend their holiday with us. They took her on their jaunts and she played happily with the baby. The Sunday before Christmas my family and two of my friends, Olga and Doris, had a long and leisurely lunch at Joe James' 'Lobster Pot'. Olga regaled us with jokes as we sat by the sapphire blue Caribbean Sea. I went to the gallery adjoining the restaurant and, as I emerged, I saw Olga dancing with my mother to one of the 'oldies' from the sixties. My mother's face was alight with joy as the music transported her to her happiness zone and she tossed away her walking stick.

"Go there, Miss Inez!" Olga said encouragingly. "Music sweet, man!"

My mother laughed uproariously and when the record ended, the staff cheered. After a leisurely drive through the countryside we went to Doris' for dinner where her cook made a fuss of my mother, "Respec', Mam, I have to look after you. Yeah man." After dinner Doris tucked her in on the settee to watch a movie and she was asleep within minutes.

My son left and my daughter, Charmaine, arrived with her husband and family on New Year's Eve. My mother was very pleased to see them. A few days later, on Friday January 5, we were catapulted into a living nightmare. Just after 5:00 a.m. I heard a noise and, rushing into the bedroom, found my mother in a heap at the foot of her bed. I raised the alarm and sought help from one of my neighbours who is a nurse. She said it seemed that my mother had suffered a stroke. Accompanied by Charmaine, I drove her to the St. Ann's Bay Hospital fifteen miles away. The admission process was so slow I wanted to scream. Three and a half hours later she was wheeled into a female ward; it was modern with a big television set at one end. There were more patients than would be found on an English hospital ward but this was a developing country, after all. There was no change in my mother by lunch-time, and the doctors advised that we go home and that the hospital would contact me when she regained consciousness. It was déjà vu as the memory of her first stroke came rushing back.

At this hospital we had to provide bed linen and we were advised to get a private assistant-nurse to help to take care of our mother. I arranged this but stayed with her until she regained consciousness. She had lost her speech and could only communicate with head movements. Seeing the fear in her eyes as she gripped my hand, I soothed her until she fell asleep. I realised that this stroke could be one of the big ones that I dreaded. I was filled with guilt that I had snapped at her the night before, when after reading a letter from her youngest son, she had started wailing, "I want to go home. Why are you keeping me a prisoner? I want to go home now!"

"You can go as soon as I can get a ticket," I had snapped when she would not be comforted. Charmaine had taken over then and the wailing had given way to a low moaning that went on until she fell asleep. Looking at her unmoving body in the hospital bed, I wished that I had not snapped.

I insisted that my daughter and her family continue with the trip they had planned to visit friends as there was very little any of us could do. Three days later my mother was released from hospital to recuperate. Veta came everyday as my mother was now totally helpless and incontinent. I sat with her while she was awake. Veta cooked nourishing soups for her. We massaged her unresponsive limbs. She appeared to be improving, mumbling, 'Yes', 'No' and 'Ta'. Then at the end of the third day she appeared to refuse to eat and no amount of cajoling helped. What we later found out was that swallowing was very difficult, the effect of further mini-strokes. When the doctor saw her the following day she organised a return to the hospital.

Friends warned that this could be the beginning of the end. Our travel insurance company was tremendously helpful. I was assigned a contact person who spoke to me regularly as we waited for the consultant to give consent for my mother to return to England. The consultant wanted brain scans to identify whether the strokes had caused an embolism, a clot which would be easier to treat or an aneurism, which meant bleeding in the brain. The hospital did not have the equipment and I had to pay for an ambulance to take my mother the eighty miles across country through the mountains to Kingston to have the scans done privately. Only the nurse was allowed to travel with her as the ambulance was not insured for other passengers. I drove to Kingston accompanied by my mother's friend, Vee, who had come to help, and Olga who was already with me. After the scans the ambulance had to either take her back to our local hospital or to the Kingston Public Hospital (KPH). I was told that a direct move to a private hospital was not allowed; I needed a consultant's authorisation. I had seen a documentary on KPH. It was clearly a hell hole with patients waiting for ages to be seen and soldiers patrolling the grounds to stop gunmen from entering the premises to continue the eradication of their human targets. I had no intention of letting my mother stay even one night there. I did not know that since that documentary the hospital had been revamped and had the most up-to-date equipment on the island.

Soldiers were there when we arrived ahead of the ambulance and security was rigid. Olga and I had to queue for a security check before we were given a card to hand to the security guard at the main entrance to the wards. I was not happy and tried to contact a friend of mine who was a doctor and who would be able to point me in the right direction to get my mother transferred to a private hospital, but he was off duty. I had to wait for the ambulance and register my mother who was then handed over to a KPH nurse.

We accompanied them to the ward and I was quite surprised by what I found. It was cheerful and the sister on duty, who had been trained in England, was pleasant and professional. The ward was efficiently run and I did not even need to employ nurse's aides. When I spoke with the hospital consultant I was advised not to move her until she left for England. I visited morning and afternoon, staying for the permitted time. Again my mother rallied and my hopes rose as her limbs trembled and she responded to being spoon-fed. Then disappointment followed as, towards the end of the second week, the nurses had to feed her through a tube inserted into her nose. My mother stayed there for two weeks until we were given the all-clear for her return to England. Her condition did not improve.

I was allowed to dress her for the flight home. I put on her powder blue dress, her pearl necklace and gold watch, all her favourite things. I combed her hair and the final touch was a spray of perfume. Olga and I kept up a running commentary about her seeing her children and my return in the next couple of weeks after the hearing of my court case. The ambulance set off for the airport at 5:30p.m. We followed. At the airport, as we sat with her in the ambulance, she held my hand. When the two nurses employed by the travel insurance company to accompany her on the flight introduced themselves to her, she made no response and her face remained forlorn. I felt torn and wanted to go with her but took the advice of friends to stay behind. After my last hug and kiss, I stumbled blindly from the ambulance. The tears held in check for so long spilled as we waited in the car for the plane to take off. Olga and I then went to Devon House and I assuaged my sorrow in a couple of cocktails laced with Jamaican overproof rum.

My sister kept in touch. One week later she told me that the doctors had given my mother forty-eight hours to live, as the aneurism had caused severe bleeding from the brain stem; they could operate to save her but she would be left a vegetable because of the amount of brain damage she had suffered. I had less than three hours to get a seat on Air Jamaica. Having managed to do that, I was taken by Doris' driver to the airport in Montego Bay. The journey that normally takes an hour and a half was beset with traffic jams and road works and by the time we got there, the plane was taking off. There was nothing for me to do but to return home and start out again the next day in good time to get a flight from the airport in Kingston on the other side of the island.

I was met by my daughters, Michelle and Amanda, at Heathrow Airport. Poor Amanda, who was ill with a throat infection, had discharged herself from hospital that morning, against the doctor's advice, in order to see her grandmother. We drove straight to Queen's Medical Centre in Nottingham. My vigil had begun.

My mother survived the forty-eight hours and we were told that her condition had stabilised. The consultant met my mother's children and our family friend, Nettie, in a small meeting room off the ward. He asked us to make the decision whether to operate or not. He did not try to sway us one way or the other, sympathising with us in our dilemma. Our decision was based on what we thought our mother would want. We agreed that she would rather die with dignity than live as a vegetable. I do not ever wish to have to make such a decision again. I think as well as having a will, people should also have a 'living will' so that their families know what to do when faced with such decisions.

We watched our mother fade away over a period of six weeks. Waiting for death was a heavy burden to bear. There were so many visitors. The ministers from two churches came and prayed for her and her family. Lillian and I felt as if we were in a suspended capsule. Family and friends had access to her room throughout the day and Lillian and I usually stayed with her until 9.00p.m. We combed her hair, creamed her skin, massaged her legs, all the while talking to her. The nurses understood that we needed to do these small acts of daughterly love and never interfered. Her room was bedecked with flowers and cards. We read the names of the senders of the cards to her but not the cheerful messages, because we knew she would not leave the hospital alive.

A week after her admission, my mother's body refused the glucose and saline drips. I found it hard to see her parched lips and her body dehydrated and shrinking from starvation. At first we could see by the fluttering of her eyelids and opening of her mouth that she was hearing us, but soon even those movements stopped. In answer to my concern, the doctors assured me she was not in pain. Lillian and I continued to moisten her parched lips with damp cotton buds. Anxiety got the better of me one evening after I left the hospital and I rang the nurse in charge.

"I'm Ms Wright's daughter. I know you are all doing your best for her, but I'm concerned that she is not having a drip. She's becoming so emaciated."

"I understand how difficult this is for you but a drip will not help in your mother's case, it will only result in further discomfort." He went on to explain the distress that an accumulation of fluid under the skin would cause.

"I'm still not comfortable with the situation. I accept she's dying but this seems torturous. Would you try the drip again, please?"

"You do realise that you're simply prolonging your mother's death." He retorted, annoyed.

All I could think was, 'How insensitive!'

"I would like you to put my mother back on a drip," I insisted icily. "I would also like to discuss the matter with the consultant. Please arrange for me to see him tomorrow. I'll be there from 9.00a.m."

"I don't know when he'll be able to see you."

"I'll be there all day if necessary. Thank you." I cut him off and then I wept. She was put back on the drip but as the nurse had warned, it did not help.

One day I was on my own and decided to massage my mother's legs. The skin hung from the bone and as I moved upwards the sight of the hip bone poking out, shattered my ability to remain calm and something inside me snapped. I pulled up the sheet to cover her emaciated body and fled from the room. Weeping, I prayed for death to release her. An arm hugged my shoulder and the comforting voice of Reverend Neil murmured, "I know. You're finding it hard, Lovey." I nodded. "I'll go in and pray," he said giving my shoulder a couple of sympathetic pats.

"Thank you," I responded as the awful moment passed.

There were a few times when I was alone with my mother while I waited for Lillian to come after collecting her grandson from school. On one such occasion as I gazed at my mother, I pondered on human existence and recorded my thoughts.

Looking At Your Face

There you lie – completely still,
Somewhere betwixt this reality and the unknown.
And what do I see in the face I kiss?
A fierce determination,
A mother's love for those she bore
Forgiveness for all the hurts they've thrown.

Intermittently, the breath is forced loudly from your body
Like the deep, deep sigh of a dreamer.
Are you dreaming too?

I think of life
And that final breath that will separate us,
Separate your spirit/soul from your body.
And what will I remember of this moment then?

My vigil?
My perplexity?
My desire to fathom the unfathomable?

I stare at your face
And see the marks you're leaving us,
The high cheekbones, the pouting lips,
That determination for which you are known,
Genetic heritage transmitted down the ages
To be observed in generations yet to come.

So, as night's curtain gently falls to end this day,
Death's shadow hovers o'er this earthly life.
And the mystery of our being
Is but part of that mystery of the universe.

Amen.
So let it be!

The end came on a beautiful spring morning, the Ides of March. When the phone call came, I knew. The ward sister asked me to come to the hospital.

"Has she gone?"

"Yes."

"When?"

"Between 6:45 after the night nurse's check and just past 7:00 when the day staff took over."

"Thank you. I'm on my way."

Charmaine and I hugged each other for comfort.

"I'll come with you, Mom. Just let me take the children to nursery."

I appreciated this, for suddenly it was as if I had gone numb as the reality of my mother's death kicked in. At the hospital we were joined by my brothers and Lillian. As I looked at my mother's still form, not different really from her stillness of the day before, I felt cheated. I wanted to have been there at the final moments, to hold her hand as she left us. Dying alone seemed so terrible. I felt cheated that I had not spent as much quality time with her as I had intended. I felt that life had cheated her of time with her family, tending her garden and dying in her own bed with her family around.

The doctors said she was the longest surviving patient without food and water that they had seen. The hospital staff were wonderfully supportive. They laid her in the Chapel of Rest and left us to grieve. The week that followed was filled with funeral preparations: getting the death certificate; choosing the coffin and burial spot; arranging the church service; organising the funeral lunch and food for the nine nights following my mother's death. A typical Jamaican *'nine-night'* was held at Lillian's with our family friend, Nettie, in charge of the kitchen. People from the community dropped in, bringing alcoholic and soft drinks and staying to talk and share the meals we prepared - fish, curried mutton, chicken, rice, bread, bun and cheese.

As is customary in Jamaica, I wanted to help to dress my mother for her funeral and so did Charmaine, heavily pregnant though she was. I did not want her to see the emaciated body of her grandmother, I thought it would be far too upsetting for her, so until Nettie and the mortician had covered my mother's body, I surreptitiously shielded Charmaine as she sat waiting. Annie had bought a lovely evening gown, simple and elegant but without sleeves. I could not leave her arms exposed. My mother always covered them to hide what she called her "ugly burn mark". It was the day before the funeral so I rang my cousin, Sonia, and asked her to make a bolero. I combed my mother's hair for the very last time. I looked at her face and saw that she was without lipstick. The mortician said she had difficulty finding suitable lipstick for black people and that the lipstick she used tended not to blend in. I was amazed at this and suggested that she visits Boots Chemists next time. I had a tube of my mother's lipstick in my handbag and I handed it to the mortician. With that final touch, my mother looked beautiful, just as if she was resting in her pale pink casket.

I thought that if she could have told me, she would have said she was pleased with her send-off. My mother's only living sister and her son flew in from Florida for the funeral. There were over three hundred and fifty people in the church on Robin Hood Chase in St Anns where she spent most of her adult life, some I had not seen in years, others I had never met. My friend, Dorita, sang 'Amazing Grace' and as her voice lifted up to the heavens, so beautifully moving and filled with pathos, the congregation applauded spontaneously. I am agnostic now and the sadness of not knowing where her spirit had gone, the thought that I might never see her again, prevented me from wholly sharing in the redeeming features of the song. For a few moments my body convulsed with the sorrow of it all. The grandchildren's tributes spoke of the time they had spent with their grandmother and the encouragement she had given them to achieve goals. Laughter rippled through the church as some of the events were related. I did the eulogy that told of the hardships she had surmounted and her love of life until she was struck down with dementia. The service was one of thanksgiving for her life. Left to say their final farewell, family members kissed our mother's stone-cold cheek. We held on to each other as the lid of the coffin descended noiselessly and her earthly body was with us no more, erased from earth forever.

We laid her to rest at Redhill Cemetery. Her final wish was executed, a "good spread for people to eat" at ACNA, the African-Caribbean centre. The contribution collected at the church was shared between it and the Kingston hospital where my mother was a patient. The hospital received a donation of bed linen for the ward.

I lost a part of my soul when my mother metamorphosed into someone I could not reach. When she was no longer physically with us it was as if there had been two deaths. The road she travelled in the last two years of her life was a difficult one for all of us. When I visit her grave and put fresh flowers in the urn, I talk to her; I tell her about the family, our joys and our troubles. Wherever she is now, I hope she has found everlasting peace.

No Problem

My experience of buying a home in Jamaica has left me believing in kismet. Whatever plans I made did not materialise and I can only accept that I was being taught a lesson in endurance.

When I went to Jamaica, I had planned to spend some time looking for a home where I intended to spend the rest of my days. In 1997, I was introduced to a building contractor by his neighbour. I chose a plot that he was selling. It met my dream of a sea view and easy access to a beach. It was agreed that I would buy the land and he would build the house I wanted. I was to pay him an initial 33,000 pounds, then the same amount when the ceiling of the ground floor was in place and the final 34,000 pounds when he handed me the keys to my completed home.

I made a serious mistake in not having a lawyer check the details of the contract which appeared straightforward. I retained a lawyer only for the completion. There were a couple of clauses in the original contract that I queried. One that held me responsible for certain bills while work was in progress was removed and I was asked to ignore the one stating that after the deposit, the remaining sum was to be put in escrow. I was told that this had been included because Jamaican buyers often defaulted on their agreement and it did not apply to people from England. At the time I saw no reason to doubt the honesty of the contractor who had built the houses of two of my acquaintances from Nottingham.

Too late, I realised that I should have heeded the warning sign that came when the starting date for building was postponed, not once but several times. Building should have started in April, yet nothing was happening as late as the last week in July when I visited the site. All I got from the contractor was another apology for the delay, which he claimed was due to unforeseen problems with equipment. The building should have been near the second stage and still I could not get a starting date. Annoyed, I reinvested the second payment for three months, the time scale given in the contract from start-up date to second stage. A week later I had a call from the firm's financial comptroller, reminding me that the second payment would be due shortly and I was assured that the building would be at the stage stated in the agreement. Not convinced that so much work could be achieved in two weeks, I arranged a visit, accompanied by an engineer friend whose opinion I sought on the quality of the work. He commented that from a cursory check the quality appeared rough, pointing out a couple of flaws in the workmanship and we were assured that these would be addressed. I obviously did not have the second payment ready and, taking into consideration the delay in starting, the vendor and I arrived at an agreement by which I would pay 9,000 pounds, the rest to follow in October, when my investment matured.

In October I duly paid the outstanding sum and was assured that my house would be ready in January when I returned from England. My father died that October and I left for England. On the return leg of my trip, I stopped in Florida and shopped for the new home that I was eagerly looking forward to moving into. The goods arrived in January but I had no home for them. On a visit to the site, it appeared that work had stopped as soon as I had left the island. I was hopping mad. Fortunately, I had storage space in my house at JNCH and my furniture and household goods remained there for two years until I left that job. (My goods were damaged later on when I paid for them to be stored. What could I do? I already had the contractor in court and there seems to be a tendency amongst Jamaican attorneys to be extremely expensive and tardy.)

Getting in touch with the contractor proved well-nigh impossible and I went to see my attorney, who got nothing from the contractor's attorney but promises that never materialised. By the summer of 1998 I was still without a home. After a chance meeting with the national chairman of the Returned Residents Association, I attended one of their meetings where I learnt that my situation was not unusual; that, in fact, many Jamaicans from England had been robbed in this way by contractors and lawyers. They were finding it difficult to get redress as the legal system was slow and the lawyers expensive and often unreliable. I was advised to get a thorough engineer's inspection as there were serious flaws. We contacted Gentech, a top engineering specialist firm whose detailed report recorded major faults in the construction that would need to be remedied if the house was to be habitable and acceptable by the building standards of the country. In essence I was told that buying would be ill-advised. I instructed my attorney to demand that my money be returned. There was no response for ages to that comunication.

I felt that the attorney was not being sufficiently forceful in pursuing the vendor, so I changed my attorney and invested in one from a high-profile law firm. She also had trouble getting any action at first, then the contractor's attorney responded claiming that I had not fulfilled the contract as the amount outstanding to complete the purchase was not put in escrow. They refused to accept the verbal agreement that had been made. My attorney advised that I put the money in escrow to demolish their only point as to the reason for non-completion of the house, after which I should pursue the case on the grounds that the house was not habitable. I acquiesced against my better judgment. Nothing further happened for a while and letters from my attorney continued to be unanswered.

She was about to hand my case over to one of her colleagues as she was leaving the firm, when an article appeared in the Sunday papers of a similar case that had been taken to court and which the buyer had won. I contacted the buyer's attorney and retained him in March 1999. He was pleased to see the file I had kept documenting all that had taken place and told us it made the case preparation easier than the one that had been reported in the papers. I paid the retainer, expecting him to put into action what he had outlined. Up to one month later, and after several unanswered telephone messages, I asked for my money to be returned. I was leading a workshop when he called, apologising profusely and saying that he had prepared the papers and I should collect the summons for the bailiff to serve. The document was not ready on the date he had given. When I finally received it, I had to travel over fifty miles to the parish of St Mary to ensure that it was safely delivered to the bailiff. The legal saga had entered yet another phase.

Winning the case was but part of the battle and it has taken a lot of tenacity to get my money back with only a fraction of the interest I was owed. A friend of mine who is a judge told me she did not hold out much hope, citing a case in which, although the plaintiff won his case, the time spent, together with legal fees and other expenditure, took such a toll on his health and finances that he gave up in the end. Other people warned me about attorneys "eating out every penny you have", but I could not afford to lose the hard-earned money which I had set aside for my retirement home. I drew strength from my fountain of courage and my firm belief in fighting for justice.

I began to understand how people who were not assertive had their cases pending for years while lawyers collected fees. My attorney, a London-trained barrister, was urbane, a little arrogant, very tardy and also not very good at communicating with women. He was without a doubt a skilled lawyer but nothing was ever done in the time he allocated. I had to keep telephoning to get him to do the work for which he was being handsomely paid. Whenever I was off the island, very little got done regarding my case. I had to undertake tasks to facilitate the preparation of my case for court hearing; for instance, I had to go to two parishes to check property lists to find out what the property developer owned. He also sent me on a fifty miles wild-goose chase to a property tax office in another parish. He had been told by one of the tax officers the day and time that officer would be in to process the information required and negligently, or deliberately, sent me on the wrong day. It was fortunate for me that the officer came back to the office while I was there trying to get someone to attend to me. My attorney would also address my male cousin when he accompanied me for a conference and I had to remind him that I was the client.

In 2002 when I enquired about the exorbitant sum he had withdrawn for his fees from the money being repaid through him, he retorted that no-one could tell him how much to charge for his services because he was a barrister! I was not impressed and told him so. Frustrated with him I decided to change attorneys but no-one wanted to take up the case because he was well known and highly respected. I was advised over and over again to talk things through with him because he had already done most of the work towards winning the case. To get him to continue with my case I had to resort to seeking the help of the barrister who had been his mentor when he started out and who has a high profile in the judicial system. The response was instant. I had a telephone call from the attorney requesting a meeting. He said that he had been under a lot of pressure and had not been able to give the amount of time necessary to my case. We agreed to start again and shook hands on it but there was no change in the way he operated.

In May 2000 my case came up for hearing. The attorney for the defendant asked for a postponement as she had not been given enough time to prepare - a popular tactic, I was told. My attorney challenged this, listing the number of letters he had sent asking for a response. The matter was referred to Judge in Chamber to decide if there was a case to be heard and I had to wait a month for this to take place. I wanted to go to England to help take care of my mother but it seemed sensible to await the outcome of the judge's hearing. I made myself useful by going to help my aunt in Florida who had suffered a mild stroke and heart attack. She was on the mend and we spent some quality time together.

My attorney invited me to the hearing in the Judge's Chamber which dragged on for two days. It was obvious that the defendant's lawyer knew the truth, but being an advocate is not necessarily about justice! The case was referred for hearing and I returned to England to find my poor mother's mental health problem worsening. In January 2001 when my mother was flown back to England having suffered several strokes, I made the difficult decision to stay behind for the hearing which was set for February 12; however, a week before the hearing I had to fly to England, the doctors having given my mother forty-eight hours to live. I left a letter for my attorney and the court giving the reason for my inability to attend. I was barely coping with my mother's impending death when a telephone call informed me that the case could not be heard without my evidence. Another painful decision had to be made. Postponement of my case would mean another year's wait, given the backlog of cases in court.

I flew to Jamaica that Saturday, had a meeting with my attorney on the Sunday afternoon and was in court on the Monday morning. My nerves were in a jangle; I could not believe it when the case was called and my attorney was nowhere in sight. The judge was annoyed and said that she would move on to the next case. Ignorant of court etiquette, but desperate for my case to be heard and not put aside, I raised my hand.

"Yes?" said the judge.

"Your honour, he will be here any minute now. I've come all the way from England . . ."

"I am not prepared to wait for attorneys. Court starts at 9:30."

"Your honour, he is on his way. I saw him parking his car." This from one of the defendant's lawyers sitting directly behind me. She patted me on the shoulder. My panic was visible. I am usually very good at coping, even when I am shaking inside, but that morning I lost control. My attorney arrived a few minutes later.

At lunch-time the excuse he gave me was that judges normally started at 10.00a.m. and he diverted the blame to the new female judge who 'did not know how things operated!' The next morning he was late again. She took him to task and in her admonishment said she hoped he would not be late again. At the end of the second day, he surpassed himself by asking for a later start the following day as he urgently needed to go to the dentist and 9:00a.m was the only appointment he could get. She gave him a half an hour's grace. No sooner was he out the door than he asked me for his three days' court appearance fee. Not only had he waffled a lot to waste time, for which the judge had pulled him up several times, but it now became obvious that his asking for time was to ensure I could get to the bank. When I said this to him, as expected, he denied it.

On the third day, the judge made it clear that she did not want the hearing dragged out by attorneys reiterating points. My attorney's complaint was that the contractor had not met his contractual obligation to build me a house that was habitable in the time agreed. The technical expert from Gentech testified to the poor standard of construction of the house that would, in essence, need to be rebuilt. The defendant's attorney claimed that I had reneged on the agreement by not putting the last instalment into escrow and that was the reason for the delay in the completion of the building. My attorney's response was that, even if the court accepted that I had reneged, which I had not, the money had been put in escrow on the advice of my previous attorney, but a habitable house had still not been built. The judge noticed my distress as the war of words dragged on and on and was very sympathetic to my situation of wanting to get back to my dying mother.

The defendant's attorneys asked for some time to discuss an offer with my attorney and me. They conceded the case and agreed to repay me. I was not in for a killing and asked only for the interest that the bank was giving as this would make up for the loss from inflation. They haggled over court costs but I was so pleased with the outcome that I accepted a half of what we had asked for. I foresaw a pyrrhic victory; I would win the case but the defendant would appeal and the saga would continue for another year or two. I chose to cut my losses. The judge was satisfied with the decision. I did not feel victorious, merely relieved and thankful that I could catch the plane back to England to be with my mother.

It took the contractor nearly a year to pay me the 66,000 pounds and the court costs. To date some of the interest is still outstanding but I have put closure on the matter.

In 2002 I fell in love with a house overlooking the bay in sleepy Boscobel, which had been on the market for some time. The offer was accepted by the person acting on behalf of the owner. Two weeks later the agent was shocked when the owner decided not to sell. I lost some money because I had changed my pound sterling to Jamaican dollars to purchase the property and within days the dollar had devalued.

By this time, having lost money, having had many anxious moments and having seen much of my furniture badly damaged in paid storage for four years, my beautiful Italian settee used by the landlord now covered in ink splodges and grease marks, my video stolen and several of my books missing, I accepted that these were but material things. I returned to England and the bosom of my family and celebrated my sixtieth birthday in South Africa. Accompanied by my cousin, Sonia, we spent three months travelling, visiting the southern hemisphere to return via Hawaii and California. *I had circled the earth!*

I returned to Jamaica refreshed and things suddenly got better. Encouraged to take the chance, I bought a plot with a wonderful sea view for my dream home. It was worth waiting for!

Nightmare

The year 2001 proved to be not only the year in which I lost my mother but also the one in which I experienced the kind of nightmare that had driven my father to leave Jamaica 'for good'. Like many Jamaicans, he had wanted to return to his homeland as soon as it was feasible, and did so on retiring. His home was broken into one night not long after his return. He was bludgeoned and he, his wife and their son were tied up while the burglars ransacked the house. He was convinced that the helper was involved. The police handling of the crime was a futile exercise and no-one was ever found guilty of the crime. Frightened for his and his family's lives, he decided to brave the cold of England again in exchange for peace of mind.

I returned to Jamaica in May 2001, the time the court had given the contractor to pay me. Knowing the tardiness of my lawyer, I thought it best to be there, in case the money was not paid and action had to be taken. My fears were not unfounded. So, in June I was house-sitting for my friend, Doris, while she was in the USA; the temporary gardener/watchman, Steve, was staying in the cottage across the back lawn.

Early one Sunday evening, after two hours at the beach enjoying simultaneously the coolness of the water and the warmth of the sun, I returned and was relaxing with a rum punch as I watched Hitchcock's *Dial M for Murder*. The house had taken on that evening peace of summer which easily lulls one into a dreamy drowsiness. A knock on the front door jarred me back to the present. I was concentrating on the film, watching the husband hide the key for his wife's assassin. Steve had forgotten his key in the kitchen for three consecutive nights and had knocked for me to let him in. Without bothering to check the spy-hole I said crossly, "You've forgotten your key again!" A muffled response came from the other side of the door as I opened it, expecting an apology. Instead the door was pushed sharply sending me off balance. My nightmare had begun.

I stared into the big, bulging eyes of a man of medium height and felt a knife prick the softness of my tummy. I was frightened into paralysis for a moment or two before I became aware that the intruder had kicked the door shut and the horror of the situation hit me. Anger surged up from my stomach and my heart pounded in my ears. "Act calmly," my inner voice cautioned me.

"Who do you want?" I asked, mustering some control.

"You."

"But I don't know you."

"I know you." His voice was almost a whisper.

I thought frantically how I might get away. That part of the house was open-plan with an archway leading from the lounge to the study and from there another archway to the kitchen. If I could get to the kitchen I could lock myself into the laundry room next to it. The only other escape was into one of the three bedrooms off the lounge; two of which were open, while my bedroom door was closed.

I felt the knife prodding me as I was pushed towards one of the settees. I decided that I was not going to show fear and held his gaze although my legs were like jelly. I remained standing.

"Look, this is not my house. Is it Ben you want?" Ben was Doris' factotum and was seen in the community as someone not to be crossed.

"Who?" The name seemed to mean nothing to him. "Sit down," he hissed and pushed me down. The knife was no longer touching me and he walked backwards, not taking his eyes off me, and sat on the opposite settee. His look suggested that he had not decided what to do next. He began to look around and I took my chance. I quickly rushed to the door but, before I could turn the knob, I felt the knife in my back. He nudged me with the knife back to the settee, where I sat still, hands clasped in a gesture of total acquiescence.

"Don't try that again." His tone was menacing. "Listen, I won't hurt you if you stay quiet."

"What do you want?" I asked plaintively. The response was a noiseless laugh. "Let's talk." I was hoping to get him off guard to be able to run into my bedroom. "I don't know you. Do you want money? I'll give you all the money I have . . ." I heard myself gabbling on, vying with the voices in the film.

"You no know me but I see you walk to de beach in de mawning."

"Where you see me?"

"I see you in de square and on de beach."

"So you must know that I go with my friend." Hope surged. I thought I could bluff that Doris would be in soon.

"She not around."

"But my husband . . ." I was homing in on the Jamaican man's psyche of respect for 'the man'.

"Where him is?" he interrupted.

"He'll be here soon. Look," I appealed putting out my hands pleadingly, eyes lowered, "I will give you all the . . ."

"So you husband leave you 'ere, all on you own?" Lust gleamed in his eyes.

"No, no, no! He'll be back soon."

He was staring at my bosom and I was suddenly conscious of wearing only a sarong. I decided to pretend I didn't see how he was staring at me and began to talk thirteen to the dozen as I clasped my hands under my chin like a shield.

His movement was so quick and catlike that I hardly had time to react. He was now in front of me, his free hand grabbing my hair and yanking back my head.

"Get off!" I yelled and tried to push him away. His grip was strong and I felt my scalp pulled upward as he dropped down beside me and pushed me onto the back of the settee with his body. I put my hands between us and struggled against this invasion of my person. He let go of my hair and forced my head down on the settee and tried to kiss me, as his knife scraped my side. Something inside my head exploded. I was not going to allow this man to rape me! *AIDS* flashed through my mind. I expected him to cut me and my mind accepted this as inevitable but I was not going to allow myself to be raped. I fought like a madwoman. He was unable to hold the knife and kiss me at the same time and as we ended up on the floor wrestling, I managed to get my head free.

"Okay, Okay. I have money in my bedroom. Let me get it."

He put the knife to my back and told me to get up.

"See those keys?" I pointed to a set of keys on the table near my door. "The key for the door is there. The money is in the bedroom. You want it, don't you?"

I took a chance and began moving forward, saying as I did so, "I'll get them. Right, I've got them, I just have to open the door . . . the key, the key. Ah, here it is."

With the knife touching my skin, I was so nervous I fumbled with the keys until I found the right one.

"Open it," he ordered.

"Right. Okay. Here. Here." I was speaking to get him off guard but the fumbling was genuine because I was wetting myself with fear and desperation. "Oh, Jesus, I can't get it in! Come on. Come on. Damn key. It's not this one!" While I was fumbling I held the door knob. As I shifted slightly, I felt that the knife was not pressing into my back as before and I guessed that he was watching my hands. What he did not know was that the door was not locked. I acted quickly. I turned the knob, rushed in and slammed the door on the foot he was using to try to stop me from shutting the door. I kicked his foot, pushing with all my might until the door shut and I pressed the knob to lock it. He pushed against the door but by then I was across the room at the window screaming.

"Help! Police! Get the police! A man's attacking me! Help!"

My screams would have awakened the dead. I heard footsteps running and the front gate being opened. My conscious self recognised that it must be my attacker leaving but suffering from shock as I was, I refused to open the door when I heard people talking outside.

"Is she alright?" asked a man's voice.

"Miss Lee, you alright?" came Steve's voice.

Then the police came within minutes.

"What's happening here?"

"A lady was attacked but the attacker gone 'cause the front door open."

Steve knocked on my bedroom door to tell me the police were there. I slowly opened the door. My body was convulsing and I wanted to vomit. Two policemen, guns drawn were standing in the lounge. I told them what had happened.

"We'll just check to make sure he isn't here," said one of them. They searched the house and the property. While the police were carrying out their search, I noticed two men standing on the verandah; a short man with a baseball bat and his taller companion with a rock in each hand, no doubt picked up from the flower bed on his way to the house. Steve had his cutlass in his hand.

"Miss, a glad you alright," said the taller one. "My friend and me coming from nex' door when we heard you scream. 'Rahtid,' him say, an him grab de bat from him car an' we come to help. Den we buck up on Steve wid him cutlass."

"Bwoy," his companion continued, "I cyah believe dem man. You not safe inna you house anymore." This was followed by a long drawn out Jamaican hiss of pure disgust.

"I hear Miss Lee scream and jump out of me house with me cutlass . . ." Steve picked up the thread of the discussion. I stopped listening.

The men left after sympathising with me. The police said the burglar was nowhere around and that they would return the next day to take a statement. I asked Steve to sleep in the house and I spent ages in the bathroom washing out my mouth and trying to get rid of the thought of that man touching me. I did not sleep a wink that night.

I had to tell someone of my ordeal and rang my cousins in Kingston the next day. When I went over what had happened, I concluded that my attacker was probably a drug addict and that might account for the slowness of his response which, thankfully, was what saved me. The police never found my attacker. Doris thinks that Steve had something to do with it because the dogs that barked at people passing by did not bark and she found that when I left to stay in Kingston as part of my recovery strategy, Steve or one of his friends had searched her room.

Although badly scarred emotionally, and scared, having nightly nightmares for a couple of weeks after the attack and not wanting to walk alone for fear of being followed, I would not let this push me to leave my country. I have somehow learnt to put that frightful event behind me. The nightly nightmare is now a thing of the past; however, at the glint of a pointed knife, I shiver involuntarily.

My Passion

I love travelling. When I was a child I dreamt of the day when I would fly off to the distant places I read about and meet people from different cultures. I have a male friend who cannot understand this passion although he enjoys hearing me read from my travel diaries. I tell him that when I travel it is like savouring meals from different parts of the world. My big difficulty over the years has been finding travelling companions among the people I know and I have ended up doing most of my travelling solo.

In the 1970s racism stopped many black people from going on holidays. Who wants to be humiliated unnecessarily or to feel less than comfortable on holiday? Our Caribbean community in Nottingham, creative as always, continued the 'trip' tradition from back home. In the summer months there would be a couple of trips organised by Edna or Mackie and Vee to different seaside resorts in England and Wales. My mother loved these trips. For her, they were family treats. My children enjoyed them too.

My mother did all the preparation and we had only to get ourselves to the meeting point usually at Huntingdon Street where the old market used to be. There would be one or two coaches from Barton or some other coach company. The departure time of 7:00 a.m. ensured at least half a day at the resort. After the head count to see that everyone who had paid was present, the group set off to Skegness or Weston-Super-Mare or Yarmouth or Llandudno or wherever. The coach would be a buzz with people on the trip catching up with acquaintances they had not seen for a long time and there was a lot of catching up to do. After a couple of hours, the smell of coffee, tea and snacks would fill the coach as people began to feel hungry, not having had breakfast. My mother's picnic bag held our food and enough to offer others. Out would come the corned beef sandwiches, the salmon sandwiches and cake. For later, there would be fried chicken and sometimes rice and peas in a food flask, crisps, chocolate bars and drinks, hot and cold. This did not mean that we didn't eat when we got to our destination. Before disembarking we would be given a time for departure and we would go off in small groups to enjoy ourselves.

Our first caravan holiday at Chapel St. Leonards in the summer of 1970 nearly didn't happen. The children and I went; their father did not, he was not at home. His childhood friend, Leonard, saved the day. He kindly took us there and came back for us a week later. We would not have been able to go had Leonard not come to our assistance as I had only managed to hire the caravan and sort out spending money and petrol money by careful budgeting.

By our next caravan holiday in 1976, I had my second-hand Ford Escort hatchback and we were able to do a lot of sightseeing. The caravan was parked in the garden of my friend's family home in Conwy, North Wales. What fun we had climbing Mount Snowdon going up the Pig Track. And who was the first to reach the summit? Amanda, who was then eight.

It was while returning to the caravan that I had a hair-raising experience. Coming down a steep hill before Betws-y-coed, the brake did not respond. The hill ended at a T-junction and I knew that if I did not stop soon, we would end up in the river. Not wanting to frighten the children, I told them to hold on to their seats because I had to brake hard and, searching the bank till I found a soft verge, I rammed the car into it. My heart was in my mouth. A man passing by came across and after a cursory check of the car said we needed brake fluid. He was very kind and went back home, got a friend to help and we managed to get the car to a garage. While it was being overhauled, I took the children to the park, all the while thanking my lucky stars.

By 1980 we had graduated to our first family holiday abroad. It was a memorable holiday that I have mentioned in the chapter "Losing a part of my soul". We loaded the car with holiday clothes, emergency canned and packaged food, three small canisters of gas and a camping stove. I drove to Spain through France and back through Andorra, France and Belgium. From Folkestone we took the ferry to Le Havre, stopped in Potier, then went on to tour Spain. Charmaine had just finished her French and Spanish 'A' levels and enjoyed using her language skills on the trip. It was fun looking at the map, reading the information on places and then deciding where to go. We loved the beach at San Sebastian in the north and used Malaga, at that time still a sleepy town, as a base to explore southern Spain. I was fascinated by the impact of the Moors on the architecture of southern Spain. I found the cave drawings at Altimira in the north most interesting.

In a very hot Madrid we stayed in a pension run by a postmistress and her older, war veteran husband. She had a terrible temper and would beat him as she yapped at him for not having done the chores while she was at work. We also met a young African student doing film studies who took us under his wings and showed us around Madrid. One day, coming back with us to our lodgings, he had his little dog with him and the dog messed under the bed. Knowing the landlady's temper, I dreaded telling her about it. To our amazement, she came, cleaned up the mess and made a big fuss of the dog! We laughed about this for days.

Racism, however, did rear its ugly head. We were told that a pension was full, only to learn later on from a one-armed ex-soldier whom we met at the nearby petrol station that this was untrue. He came back with us and had a heated argument with the manageress who suddenly found us a pleasant en suite family room.

I was told by a friend in England that I should be very careful with my money in pensions because stealing was common in holiday places in Spain. I took his advice and placed my money under my pillow each night. Then one afternoon having driven 80 miles into Alicante and filled up at a petrol station I realised with a dreadful, sinking feeling that I had left my purse under the pillow. Fortunately, my mother was able to pay for the petrol. We had meandered into Alicante and, as it was then afternoon, I worried that whoever cleaned the room would have found the purse. I decided to go to the police before returning to the pension as I felt that it would be easier for them to get the purse returned. This turned out to be a wise decision. At first the people at the pension denied all knowledge of having seen the purse, but when the matter was referred to the inspector at the Alicante Police Station, he got the pension staff to locate the purse and I was able to collect it that afternoon. He was a funny young man who spoke very little English and, as he was not wearing a uniform, I asked him what was his job. He said he was like Peter Sellers in the "Pink Panther". He invited me to dinner that night. What a hoot that would have been with the Spanish/English dictionary as our companion! As a family we decided not to go back to Alicante but to continue on another route.

When I remember this holiday, I recall the picnics we had in fields or by a river. We shopped each morning for our picnic buying the fresh, sun-kissed fruit, lettuce, tomatoes, roast chicken or choritsa, bread, fruit juice and wine. After our picnic, we would have our siesta, sometimes hearing the music of the cicadas rising to a crescendo then dying down before starting all over again.

1973 was a milestone in my life. The first five months were traumatic because of the divorce proceedings and then the hearing coinciding with exams. I had no choice but to grit my teeth and do my best. When it was over, I badly needed a de-stressing holiday. From my years of being Junior's helpmate, working my butt off, I received just over 280 pounds from the sale of the house after all his debts were paid off. He told the children in front of our friends that most of the money had gone into the deposit on a house in Leicester which they would inherit when they grew up. That house has since been sold and the children are yet to receive their inheritance! My princely sum was used to buy an air ticket to visit Jamaica, my first trip home in fourteen years. Two of the children stayed with my cousin in Preston and the other two in London with friends, who were like extended family members. My friend, Blossom, and I travelled to Jamaica via New York where we stayed with friends and to Nassau where we stayed at the home of Blossom's sister. I left Blossom in New York and took the Greyhound bus to Niagara Falls on a one-day trip which I enjoyed immensely, especially seeing the falls and the short tour of that part of Toronto, Canada. The holiday was like a tonic and I came back to England refreshed and ready to begin my new career as a teacher.

Israel and Egypt, 'must see' biblical lands. beckoned to me. In 1974 a girlfriend and I spent nearly three weeks in Israel visiting the places of the Holy Land. It was a fly/drive holiday and we were able to see a lot of the country. The memories that have remained are not so much of the sites as of the people. When we were in Jerusalem near the tomb of Christ there was a procession with clerics of different Christian faiths and it was amusing to see them jockeying for position; it reminded me of school children when the bell rang for lining up. At the Wailing Wall, I saw Jews praying and stuffing prayer requests into crevices of the wall, some of them banging their heads as they prayed. My recollection of the Blue Mosque is of the cheesy smell of piles of shoes removed for praying. I found the Baha'i garden and the temple in Haifa tranquil oases, with the fragrance of flowers wafting in the air.

A Yemeni student who worked at the hotel where we stayed in Tel Aviv invited us to her home to meet her family. I was immediately struck by the cultural, and racial, segregation in operation. Only Yemeni people lived in her area of the city. The hostility of the Israeli police to the two Arab men with us in the car when we were stopped was awful. I really did not feel relaxed in Israel with all those police and soldiers around. It felt like a police state.

We left the car in Israel and took a long weekend coach trip to Egypt. At the border checkpoint, the poor Arab women and children looked such a despondent lot as they waited to cross over into Egypt. I, too, got fed up of the interminable waiting and, when an Israeli checkpoint staff member approached me, my body stiffened in an unfriendly manner. I regretted having shown such body language when she, nonetheless, offered me a bunch of grapes and welcomed me to her country.

I was moved by the boat crossing of the Red Sea and can still vividly remember stepping on the soil of Africa for the first time. The streets of Cairo were dirty but the trips to the Pyramids, the Valley of the Kings and Alexandria were fantastic and moving, and seeing the masterpieces of a great empire was a marvellous experience. My one regret was not getting to Abu Simbel.

That Saturday night I went to a night club with a Palestinian man on our coach who was on holiday from Germany; I saw belly dancing there for the first time. What was interesting was the excitement one of the dancers created for a young Saudi on his first trip abroad. He could barely contain himself and stuffed money into her bodice, the touch of her flesh sending him into further paroxysms of desire, I suppose. The owner came up to us and, assuming I was an Arab, spoke to me in Arabic, then in French, neither of which I speak. On the way back to my hotel we were stopped at a check point and again addressed in Arabic. The policeman obviously thought I was pretending not to be an Arab and I was accompanied back to the hotel to show his junior officer my passport. It was a tense time in both Israel and Egypt.

I cannot imagine anyone who has read about Ancient Greece and the Roman civilizations not wanting to visit those countries. There are so many sights to see that I have spent weeks at a time discovering some of the wonders of these ancient cultures. On my first trip to Italy my friend, Dorothy, and I stayed a few days in Florence, a city I would very much like to revisit. Michelangelo's David is a beautiful work of art. Some of the masterpieces in the galleries took my breathe away, the freshness of the colours in the paintings belying their age and so many of them that can be enjoyed by people like me who are not necessarily art aficionados. I was impressed by the engineering infrastructure of Pompeii and when we went up to Mount Vesuvius I almost burnt my bottom testing how hot the rocks were. In Venice, true to form, our gondolier serenaded us as we sailed at sunset.

It is amazing how people meet and become friends. At Heathrow, awaiting my flight to Greece, I was reading my newspaper when my eye caught sight of a man pushing a woman towards me. I looked up and smiled at her and in halting English she told me that she, her husband and two children were from Athens and were on their way to Hamburg to visit her husband's German friend for the Christmas holiday. The men had met while doing their PhD in Germany. What a coincidence! I told her I was on my way to Athens. Evelyn introduced her family and we chatted until I had to leave. Her husband had obviously wanted her to practise her English while they waited for their connection.

So began a friendship that lasted ten years until I left for Jamaica and we lost touch. Evelyn had a house near the seaside in Marathonas and on a visit there the following year we were joined by Tasos' friend, wife and son from Germany. One evening I looked at a map and thought how nice it would be to visit Istanbul, a train journey away. They all thought I should not and some anti-Turkish sentiments were voiced. But, not to be deterred, I was off to Turkey for ten days. Turkey is truly the meeting of east and west. I saw the hot springs of Cappodocia, visited an ancient subterranean village and Troy, then went through the Dardanelles by boat and back to Istanbul with its mosques and colourful market with so many spices assaulting and tickling my nose. It was in Izmir that I met Yusuf, a carpet merchant, who has become a family friend.

When I was a child and read about India, the image was the same as that of Africa, the colonial perception of a backward people. When I became conscious of racism and how imperialists used indoctrination in our school system to give us their perception of the world, what was worthwhile and what we should despise, I began to be more discerning in what I read. I have been fortunate to meet interesting people from many countries and, through them, to learn a little about their cultures. In 1980 when I went to teach at Manning, I became interested in Indian and Pakistani cultures because we were having a gradual increase in the number of children from these countries but knew very little of their cultures. It was the beginning of a learning process. I wanted to visit India and my friend and colleague, Promilla, arranged for her friend and sister to look after me when I arrived in Delhi.

It was a wonderful summer holiday. I stayed in the homes of family members in Delhi, Jaipur and Bangalore. On my first day in India, I was overwhelmed by the masses of people in the streets. A young woman with a sickly-looking child in her arms grabbed my skirt, "Memsahib! Memsahib!" she pleaded and when I stopped, she put her hand to the child's mouth indicating her need for food. Although my friend had warned me not to give any money or we would be surrounded by even more beggars, I could not walk away. She was right and I had to almost run to escape the beggars.

India is full of contrasts, not only geographic but socio-economic, as dire poverty and immense wealth exist cheek by jowl. At a ladies' kitty party at the home of one of my hostesses, I was dazzled by the jewellery and by the gaiety of the afternoon. I also felt privileged to join in other family activities of my hosts.

I am a free spirit and like wandering around meeting people and using different forms of transport. I travelled by train to see the Taj Mahal and by country bus to Jaipur. The Breeze Palace was spectacular. I travelled by air to Bombay via Udiapar, where I spent a night in the palace on the lake in the company of a female Japanese teacher who was also travelling alone. On the plane to Bombay, my fellow passenger and I talked about ourselves and our children and he kindly offered me a lift to a hotel he recommended. He also allowed me the use of his car and chauffeur for the two days I was there. Such generosity! During the conversation with the hotel manager it turned out that he had been to university with one of Promilla's brothers!

I used Bangalore as a base to see the area and visit temples in Mysore and the beautiful Brindigan Gardens. Remembering Mysore evokes the smell of sandal wood in the air. I took the express train to Madras and, after a day there, took the slow train to the southern tip of India to get the ferry to Sri Lanka. I experienced the Indian way of travelling over long distances. I was lucky that in the female compartment was an excellent conversationalist for most of the journey. She gave me a lot of insight into the life of the Indian middle-class.

I never knew what would happen from one day to the next, however well I planned. Arriving by train at the Sri Lankan port to get the ferry back to India, I found that the one hotel there was being refurbished. A group of us trying to find somewhere for the night decided to share one room as there was no other available accommodation. A French woman, her five-year-old son and I shared the double bed, while her husband and a young German slept on the floor!

From Madras I flew back to Delhi and then travelled north to Amritsar to visit the Sikh's Golden Temple in all its splendour. I had a long wait in Amritsar for the next bus to Kashmir and gave in to the urge to board a train that was about to pull out for Pakistan. I only wanted to go over the border to visit the museum with relics of the ancient civilization of Harrapa. After all, we were developing teaching material about this. My travelling companions in the first class compartment were a French female psychologist, an English engineer and his girlfriend who was a teacher visiting from England. We stayed in the same hotel and met for dinner. I returned to Amritsar the next day and caught a bus to Lake Dhal in Kashmir.

The bus broke down and we had to stand around for a couple of hours. The only other foreigner on the bus was the English fiancée of a young Sikh. She and her fiancé were visiting his relatives. She was a teacher from the Midlands and, in the course of conversation, we realised that we were going to the same destination and agreed to share a houseboat as a three-some. The owner of the houseboat kindly provided us with daily packed lunches, wrapped sandwiches in newspaper! This reminded me of the early 1960s in England when fish and chips were also wrapped in newspaper. Each day I gave my lunch to the first beggar I met, knowing that they would enjoy the treat. The best part of my holiday in Kashmir was pony trekking in Gulmarg, near the border with Pakistan. The mountain was green and monkeys chattered in the trees. This was like another country, quite different from the south of India.

A few years later I passed through India again on my way to Nepal but it was only for a short visit with friends in Delhi. Promilla and her sister-in-law met me in Katmandu after I had spent a week trekking through the Anapurna Range with a Nepalese guide. People usually find it amusing when I tell the tale of being attacked by leeches. I did not find it in the least funny at the time. They must have dropped from the branches of the trees we walked under whilst traversing a field. I had taken the precaution to be well covered, wearing a long-sleeved shirt, trousers tucked into my socks and a Chinese peasant hat, but the leeches still managed to attach themselves to the uncovered parts of my lower arms. I screamed when I saw the parasites on me. We were near a village and some of the villagers appeared, no doubt thinking something dreadful had happened. The poor guide had to prise the leeches off me, a much more difficult task than one imagines. The leeches stuck to the skin as if glued to it. Having sorted me out, the guide then removed them from himself, at times burning them off with a lit match. It was a horrible experience.

The trekking took me through some of the most beautiful scenery, awesome in its splendour. Trekking was strenuous at times and once, too tired to reach the rest stop, I told my guide I was going to ask the people at a house I could see to put us up for the night. The people were very kind and gave me their best bedroom. After I showered using a bucket of water behind a makeshift cloth screen, the guide and I were given a meal. The schoolgirl daughter of the family spoke halting English and we had a family get-together on the veranda. It turned out to be much more pleasant than spending the evening at the rest stop.

One summer holiday in the late 1980s, a colleague and I island-hopped around the Caribbean. Each island was unique. The Caribbean Sea was always tranquil with its clear water and its variegated colours of blue, green and turquoise. A cruise around the Grenadines was totally relaxing. I enjoyed the calypso music, rum punch and lobster.

In 1995, I visited Norway with an ex-colleague to see the land of the midnight sun. It was a wet summer but I still experienced nights without darkness. I saw the geographic changes as we drove northwards through green landscape of conifers, the tundra region and into the arctic zone. It was a common occurrence to see reindeer crossing the road.

Africa, my roots. Africa north of the Sahara is quite easy to reach for a holiday from England. Morocco and Tunisia I visited during the Christmas vacations. In Morocco, I travelled to the edge of the Sahara and in Douz saw the splendour of their festival of horsemanship and the spectacular feats they perform. However, the Africa close to my heart is south of the Sahara and I have travelled east, west and south to savour its cultures. For most of us Jamaicans, our roots are in Nigeria and Ghana. The temperament and the use of language have been well documented and became obvious when I visited West Africa.

I travelled around Nigeria by road and by air. A friend of mine, whose uncle was a chief, took me to his village where he was representing his uncle at a function. It turned out to be quite a gathering with dignitaries in their beautiful regal costumes and headdresses. I sat at the back of the marquee to observe the dances and listen to the speeches. Imagine my surprise and consternation when I was invited to join the dignitaries at the top table! I was inadequately dressed for the occasion in jeans and T-shirt and tried, unsuccessfully, at first to be allowed to stay in my seat. It was one of those occasions when it was better to acquiesce, as all eyes turned on me.

I could not visit Nigeria and Ghana without going to the sites of the horrors of the slave trade. I was saddened to see the condition of the museum in one of the slave ports in Nigeria. It was a rundown room, almost hidden away and with little indication of the tragedies that had occurred there. This was not the case at Elmina Castle in Ghana where the guided tour brought vividly to life the age of slavery. The place was eerie, I could almost hear the voices of women weeping as I entered the female dungeon with the rope ladder leading to the quarters of the ship's crew. Down this ladder European men had descended to get African women and girls they intended to rape whenever they pleased. A group of African-American women broke into sobs which grew into bawling as they traversed the courtyard. I felt it too, the pain of those poor people, some of our ancestors, hurled into these hell-holes on the way to the unknown. My body shuddered in empathy.

I travelled by local bus into the interior of Ghana to the kingdom of the Ashanti. Here I met the western-educated grand-daughters of the Chief who arranged for me to be in a procession of people meeting the Chief. It was quite ceremonious. The Chief sat resplendent on a dais and bowed slowly to each of us as we curtsied. To remember this occasion I purchased from a carver his work of the golden stool, that famous emblem of the Ashantis.

In Cameroon I stayed for a few days with the family of my Cameroonian friend. I had my first experience of living in a polygamous household and although there was a lot of respect for the first wife, she was in emotional pain. She confided in me things she felt she could not tell her family. The thought of her husband having a younger wife was not easy to live with but she had agreed to this so that her husband could have the children he and his family wanted. She had married him in a Christian church so the second marriage had to be a traditional one. The family practised the two religions simultaneously. In the weeks I spent in Africa I saw cultural norms that I had only read about, some admirable, others, like this one, heart-rending.

On my next trip to Africa in 1988, I spent nine weeks visiting Kenya, Tanzania, Zambia and Zimbabwe. In Nairobi I got talking with a couple of young women at the hotel and, after three days, agreed to visit them at home. I met and socialised with some of their families and friends. Having read Jomo Kenyatta's book, "Facing Mount Kenya", I wanted to go up that mountain but it was not the season for such trips and I decided, rashly, to visit Tanzania and climb to the summit of Mount Kilimanjaro.

On the bus from Mombassa in Kenya I met an Italian teenager and his mother, a wardrobe mistress who worked for a film company. We decided to team up for the trip to Kilimanjaro. At base camp we hired a guide and his team. The guide was the father of the others. Our cook carried the cooking utensils and stores and the other three men carried our luggage which included sleeping gear. This made it easier for us to travel but I felt uncomfortable seeing them so laden. They told me they travelled up and down the mountainside regularly and did not find their work difficult. We stopped at Kibo Hut on the third night up. It was early to bed as the last leg of the journey would begin in the wee hours of the next morning. My memory of that night at Kibo Hut remains vivid. I have never seen the sky look so beautiful as it did from that mountain. It was a velvety blackness with stars suspended just beyond reach - indeed a mystical experience.

The next morning we set out with another group of Italians. Then diarrhoea struck. I am not sure if this was a result of altitude sickness. The men were less affected whereas all the women could not finish the climb. I was devastated. Three days climbing up; seeing the changing landscape and anticipating being on that snow-capped peak. On the two days trekking down the weather reflected our dampened spirits as the skies opened and drenched to the bones we had to trudge through sludge to base camp.

Zambia gave me a taste of what it must be like living in a police state. Unaware that I was being watched by the Secret Police, I asked a student to take a photo of me standing in front of the statue of a man breaking the chains of oppression, outside the president's official residence. I admired the symbol and, as I thanked the kind student, a vicious looking little man with what seemed a necklace of barbed wire scars approached us. He berated us for taking pictures in front of the palace and we were both hauled off to the police station to be questioned. My camera was confiscated and the film checked to verify that we were not spies. Even the senior police officer was intimidated by the little arrogant brute who threw orders at him. Later that day when I returned for my camera the police officer apologised for the loss of the film and went on to offer to buy my camera!

I understood the country's need for strict security measures with the constant threat of violence from the then apartheid South Africa, but not the accompanying reign of fear that seemed to prevail. I had been warned by Zambian friends not to ask political questions and not to take pictures of government buildings as spies were everywhere. I counterbalance that nasty experience with the memory of my Zambian friends who were so warm-hearted and easy-going. I enjoyed the time I spent with this gentle couple who were living in a difficult situation with a lot of shortages of commodities we in England took for granted. As well as full-time jobs, they were farming to feed themselves; they were educated abroad and had returned to Zambia to serve their country

I wanted to leave Zambia immediately but could not get a flight. The airline desk clerk persuaded me to hitch a lift with Zimbabweans who were leaving a big trade fair to return home. I asked around the trade fair and eventually got a lift with two men and a woman going to Harare. I was glad to move on to Zimbabwe. It was the one country I had visited that vied with Jamaica as the place I would like to live. I greatly enjoyed visiting areas such as Mutare with its lush vegetation, the thunder of Victoria Falls and the amazing structure of the Great Walls of Zimbabwe. Going on Safari was a memorable occasion – seeing graceful giraffes munching leaves from branches way up high, hearing the rumbling approach of elephants, watching a herd of zebras running off across the savannah and espying hippos as we cruised down the Zambesi river. Again, I was fortunate to stay with a Zimbabwean/Jamaican family in Harare and did some of the travelling around the country with a couple of their male relatives from England. The sightseeing and meeting interesting people all contributed to making this a wonderful three weeks.

In March, 2003 I celebrated my sixtieth birthday. My cousin, Sonia, and I visited South Africa, Australia, New Zealand, Fiji, Hawaii and the USA. In South Africa, I was amazed at the hospitality of the white people we met and at the forgiveness demonstrated by the black people, anxious to leave the hatred of the past behind and work towards making their country prosperous. Robben Island and the Apartheid Museum in Johannesburg are ghastly reminders of that country's terrible history of state racism. Entering Nelson Mandela's cell on Robben Island and having a guided tour by one of his fellow prisoners was like entering into living history. Visiting those places as well as townships such as Soweto brought to life all that I had read and heard from victims of that barbarous system. It was also wonderful to meet Brother Drake Koka and Barney, once refugees in England, now settled, productive members of their country.

We travelled by train from Cape Town to Johannesburg and by car with friends to outlying areas to savour the beauty of this country and to experience briefly city and rural living. What a dizzying sensation I had standing on the cliff at the southern-most tip of Africa looking out at the ocean below!

We saw little of the continent of Australia but I realised my dream to visit the Sydney Opera House, snorkel on the Great Barrier Reef and meet Aborigines to hear from them a little about their culture. New Zealand I loved. Much of the landscape reminded me of England. We spent a month doing backpacking tours and travelling around the North and South Islands; we experienced a Maori evening of feasting and cultural presentation and visited for a weekend with my ex-colleagues from Nottingham, who have settled in New Zealand. I was very pleased to have spent a month in New Zealand and to be able to see so many of its attractions, some truly magical. The trip to Milford Sound was memorable. It was at Lake Wanaka that I did my tandem skydive, a celebration of my sixtieth year. My cousin refused to come to the airfield thinking I was too foolhardy; my children were shocked too. But it was fantastic!

Our original plan to visit Thailand and China was scuppered, owing to the SARS outbreak that was still affecting China. We, therefore, rerouted to Fiji, Hawaii and San Francisco in the USA. Fiji was interesting. The Fijians thought we were also Fijians until we spoke. They were most hospitable and my cousin enjoyed kava, the national drink. I didn't like it because it numbed my tongue. While cruising around a few of the islands we spent a half-day in a school on one of the small islets and had an interesting cultural exchange with the pupils. After the morning session we found that the sandbank that we had walked across from the bigger island where we were staying to get to the school, had disappeared and we had to yell and wave to attract the attention of a woman on the opposite beach. She sent a boat to ferry us across. At the hotel in Nadi where we stayed in a chalet, the cabaret artistes living in the next chalet gave us a special farewell performance on the beach which they used as their stage. It was a lovely end to our visit. Hawaii and San Francisco were popular holiday places and a pleasant end to the trip.

I look forward to travelling to Central and South America and fulfilling that dream I have of visiting China and walking along the Great Wall. There are so many places I have yet to visit; in the meantime, when in Jamaica I will continue to do some voluntary work in a local school and help with a food programme for some indigent elderly people in the community that I now call home.

It is also time for me to concentrate on my spiritual growth.

GLOSSARY OF WORDS AND PHRASES

A wa dis a gal a look in a mi mawning	why is this girl staring into my mouth
bligh	give an unfair advantage
bush tea	herbal tea
cho man	you don't say (dismissive)
come long	not a local
cut eye	a dirty look
cyah	can't
daughta	daughter
dressing (the corpse)	washing and dressing the corpse
kiss teeth	hiss
Ku here!	Look here!
Lawd a massie!	Lord of mercy! (in surprise)
Mi is a Jamaican ooman an nuttin frighten we	I am a Jamaican woman and nothing frightens us
nine nights	wake held for nine nights after death
ooman	woman
oono	all of you
pickney	child

run joke	making fun of / having a laugh
throwing words	responding boast to a slight
tink	stink
well before day	long before daybreak
wicked	excellent

*****

(Lee Arbouin 2003)

ABOUT THE AUTHOR

Lee Arbouin is a retired teacher. She sees herself as a citizen of England and Jamaica and has been a voluntary community worker for over forty years.

Her hobbies include travelling to places off the tourist trail and writing poetry. She belongs to a writing group whose members give free community performances of their work.

Lightning Source UK Ltd.
Milton Keynes UK
UKOW040603181112

202349UK00002B/5/P